THE SHAPE OF CATHOLIC THEOLOGY

An Introduction to Its
Sources, Principles, and History

Aidan Nichols, O.P.

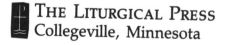

THE LITURGICAL PRESS
Collegeville, Minnesota

ISBN 13: 978-0-8146-1909-4
ISBN 10: 0-8146-1909-6

Library of Congress Cataloging-in-Publication Data

Nichols, Aidan.
    The shape of Catholic theology : an introduction to its sources,
principles, and history / Aidan Nichols.
        p.   cm.
    Includes bibliographical references and index.
    ISBN 0-8146-1909-6
    1. Catholic Church—Doctrines—History.   2. Theology, Doctrinal.
    I. Title.
BX1747.N48   1991
230'.2'01—dc20

91-7116
CIP

To
Robert Ombres, of the Order of Preachers

Quam suavis et quam jucundum est,
fratres habitantes in unum.

Nor is there singing school
But studying monuments of its own magnificence

W. B. Yeats, Sailing to Byzantium

Cover design by Don Bruno

Cover illustration:

The Triumph of St. Thomas: attributed to Francesco Traini (active c. 1320–1364), Church of St. Catherine, Pisa.

St. Thomas holds an open volume bearing a quotation from *Proverbs* with which his *Summa contra Gentiles* begins. Rays of light, symbolizing illuminating grace, descend from the incarnate Word in glory (top), as from the biblical authors: Paul (with a sword), Moses, and the four evangelists, each with his identifying symbol. The radiance of Christ falls upon these, but not on the two pagan philosophers lower down—from whom, none the less, the theologian receives understanding: Plato, holding up his *Timaeus,* with its account of the world's making, and Aristotle, carrying his *Ethics,* with its exposition of the good, and the virtues. Light, now symbolizing the synthesis of Uncreated and created wisdom, passes on from Thomas to the groups of smaller figures representing the Church on earth. At the bottom, the Arab philosopher Averroes, standing here for error, falls to the ground, his book facing downwards. Although the present study is not an exposition of Thomist theology, it exemplifies the *structure* of theology as here set forth in images by an unknown master, probably of the Sienese school.

Contents

Preface

This study is entitled *The Shape of Catholic Theology* because it is not an introduction to the material content of that theology, its subject matter, its themes and topics, but to the form in which that content is contained: its basic patterns, its constituent elements, the way or ways in which the assertions of Catholic theology are arrived at. So the reader who expects to find here a set of mini-treatises on the great compartments of Catholic theology—the Trinity, Christology, ecclesiology, and the sacraments; Mariology and the communion of saints; the last things —will necessarily be disappointed. He or she must look elsewhere. As the subtitle indicates, this is an introduction to the "sources, principles, and history" of theology in the Catholic tradition.

Although little or no technical knowledge of Catholic doctrine is presumed, it is presupposed throughout that the reader either already finds himself or herself within the tradition of Catholic Christianity or is willing to enter that tradition imaginatively, by an effort of sympathetic understanding, with a deliberate suspension, at least, of disbelief. For this no apology is offered. It is impossible to give an account of theological rationality except from within some tradition of reflection and experience, inhering in a community and uniting its members, as they believe, to a transcendent source of what it is they reason about and the manner in which they do so.

In this book, though I have tried to be as accurate as possible, the extent of the ground covered means that there is neither the fullness of treatment nor the precision that would otherwise be desirable. The select bibliographies (and the notes) are meant to help the reader to fill in these gaps. Finally, this is, overwhelmingly, an introduction to dogmatic theology. I believe that dogmatics are the center of theology, and that any theological discipline that cuts itself off from these heartlands does so at its own peril. For it is in dogmatics that theology is in touch with the heart of revelation, and only by virtue of the quality of its contact with that revelation is thinking Christian at all.

I am grateful to my students at the Pontifical University of St. Thomas (the Angelicum) in Rome for their contribution to this text which was originally in lecture form. Their comments, questions, and criticisms have led me to modify its shape, and encouraged me to offer it to a wider audience. The result is, at times, as much prescriptive as descriptive; to some degree, this is one man's vision of what shape, structure, or form Catholic theology should possess—though it is a personal view informed by the common tradition. The overview of the history of Catholic theology offered at the end of the book will help the reader to place the author's prescriptions against his or her historical background.

Given that my own teachers have been Anglican and Orthodox as well as Catholic, I could hardly, without churlishness, restrict my citations and references to those in peace and communion with the Holy See. And in any case, from the ancient Greek philosophers to the Russian Orthodox ecclesiologist Afanas'ev, cited at the Second Vatican Council, such exclusiveness would sit ill with the historic practice of the Church in, at any rate, those luminous periods of her history where enemies without (or even within) have failed to shake her calm.

Chapters 1 and 2 consist largely of material already published in, respectively, *The Downside Review*, CV. 361 (1987) and *New Blackfriars* 60.819 (1988). Thanks are due to the editors of these journals for permitting their reprinting here. They make, I hope, a gentle introduction to a book whose demands on the reader tend to increase as it goes on. At no point, however, should it be too difficult a text for those commencing the study of theology to take in their stride.

Blackfriars,
Cambridge,
Christmas 1990.

Abbreviations

DS   H. Denzinger and A. Schönmetzer, eds., *Enchiridion symbolorum*, 33rd ed., Freiburg, 1965.

DTC   *Dictionnaire de théologie catholique*, Paris, 1903 ff.

Mansi   Mansi, J.D., *Sacrorum conciliorum nova et amplissima collectio*, Florence, 1759–98; Paris, 1901–27.

NCE   New Catholic Encyclopedia, New York, 1967.

PG   Migne, J.-P., *Patrologia Graeca*, Paris, 1857–66; 1928–36.

PL   Migne, J.-P., *Patrologia Latina*, Paris, 1841–49; 1850–55; 1862–64.

Part One
Introducing Theology

1
The Habit of Theology

In beginning to study theology, it is no bad thing to start by looking at ourselves and asking what qualities are required of us in this enterprise. What sort of person must I be in order to become a theologian? What subjective conditions are there that I have to meet? In other words, what must be true of me as a subject if I am to grow in understanding of the object of this discipline? This may at first sight appear to be a peculiarly modern question to ask, connected with the contemporary interest in the human sciences that many people would date from the so-called anthropocentric turn that European culture took in the age of the Renaissance. But in fact, concern with the subjective preconditions of theological study is quite an ancient phenomenon in the Church. In the classical theology of the Latin tradition, it has been expressed by calling theology a habit, a particular kind of disposition which fits the human mind to deal successfully and happily with some aspect of reality.[1] Père Yves Congar appeals to this tradition in saying that "theology is the highest of the habits of mind that a Christian man or woman can acquire."[2]

This theological habit of mind, like all aspects of Christian existence, is at one and the same time absolutely ordinary and natural, yet entirely extraordinary and supernatural. It is natural in that it draws

1. The conceptualization of the theological (and other) virtues is one of the greatest achievements of Christian thought, building on both sacred and secular sources: *see* O. Lottin, *Psychologie et morale aux XIIe et XIIIe siècles* (Louvain: 1942–60), especially III/2, 99–150. Although the phrase "theological virtues" first emerges with William of Auxerre (d. 1231), the classic account is that of Thomas in *Summa theologiae* Ia. IIae. 62, 3. There those virtues are described as grace-given adaptations of man to God as his supernatural end, paralleling the natural virtues rooted in his natural orientation toward human perfection. The idea that theology itself actualizes a specific virtue draws on both supernatural and natural models.

2. Y. M.-J. Congar, "Theologia est altissimus inter habitus intellectuales acquisitos hominis Christiani," *La foi et la théologie* (Paris: 1962) 192.

on the human ability to study. It is supernatural in that its root and source is divinely given faith in the self-revealing God.

In the first place, then, the theological habit requires studiousness, just as much as does any secular academic discipline. Broadly speaking, we may say that any academic discipline requires three things: first, it requires the ability to follow an argument; second, it requires the capacity to remember a certain number of facts; third, it requires a basic flair or sense for the subject that enables us to be creative in thinking up hypotheses in its regard. For instance, to be a historian we need to understand certain arguments pertaining to historical causality: why a given institution arose, why a particular social class disappeared, why one government collapsed and another took its place. We also need to retain a certain quantity of dates, names, and other historical references. Finally, we need some kind of fundamental imaginative capacity that allows us to exercise a sympathy for the past and to suggest hypotheses for reconstructing it in the way historians do. Or again, to be a physicist we must be able to follow the largely mathematical type of arguments that physicists use, to retain some facts about the results of previous physical experiments, and to have some ability to propose fresh laboratory-testable hypotheses and, indeed, wider perspectives or paradigms for interpreting the subject as a whole. We can sum all this up by saying that a habit of study, including theology, asks that we be argumentative, retentive, and imaginative.

But in the second place, such studiousness is rooted, in theology's case, in the supernatural gift of faith. An atheist, or any non-Christian, could study the Christian religion from a purely descriptive standpoint, in what may be called an empirical way, amassing facts about Christianity: its origins, history, and present diffusion. Again, he or she might study the Christian religion in what may be termed a phenomenological way, evoking what being a Christian appears to be like, so far as an outsider can tell. Such a person may be enormously erudite but could never become a theologian. He or she might achieve celebrity as a religious scientist or phenomenologist and be elected to a chair in religious studies—a nonconfessing discipline common in Europe and North America and descended from a nineteenth-century German ancestor, *Religionsgeschichte:* the study of the history of religion.[3] Yet, if the studiousness were not rooted in Christian faith, the

3. The history-of-religions school is the first great attempt at a "neutral" scholarly study of religion. *See* H. Schlier, "Religions-geschichtliche Schule," *Lexikon für Theologie und Kirche* 8 (Freiburg: 1963) cols. 1184–85.

person would lack the indispensable spiritual milieu which an authentic theological culture needs, and any attempts to write theology would be epistemologically defective.[4]

What, then, is this faith which is so imperative for the theologian? It can be thought of in two ways: either as the body of belief which the Church, the Christian community, holds to be true, or as my own personal act of faith, my very own act of believing adhesion to God in Christ by the Holy Spirit.[5] Drawing on a medieval distinction, we can speak first of the *fides quae*, the faith which the Church believes, the articles of faith which, as a member of the Church, I regard as true, since they form that objective content of truth that is Catholic Christianity. The importance of the *fides quae* to theological activity was well brought out by the quarrel between the papacy and the Swiss theologian Prof. Hans Küng.[6] At one level, the Küng affair was about Church politics, that is, the proper form which the specifically Christian and ecclesial or churchly use of power should take. Küng believes that the power of the bishop of Rome has become excessively inflated, largely through historical accident, and that it is high time this power was cut down to size. It has been abused, he asserts, in order to narrow down what should count as the Catholic tradition and so is an obstacle to the development of that tradition, both inwards and in relation to other Churches in the ecumenical movement. The Pope and the Roman curia, on the other hand, believe that while each local Church or diocese should enjoy the freedom that the documents of the Second Vatican Council accord it, the Roman See must still maintain a strong supervisory role within the communion or totality of such Churches. In a world of constant change, the continuity and integrity of Catholic faith, worship, and action require this stabilizing center.

At another level, however, the Küng affair, like other *causes célèbres* of a similar nature since, concerned the limits of Catholic theology, the boundary which you cannot pass if you wish to keep the title of a Catholic theologian. By refusing to accept in an unqualified way the affirmation of the Council of Nicaea that the being of the one who be-

---

4. Congar, "Theologia est altissimus," 193–94. Recently, some disagreement has been voiced here. The most notable Catholic writer who holds that, in principle, Christian faith is not a prerequisite of theology is the American David Tracy. *See,* e.g., his *Blessed Rage for Order: the New Pluralism in Theology* (New York: 1975) 6–8. For an evaluation of his position, one might consult A. Dulles, "Method in Fundamental Theology: Reflections on David Tracy's *Blessed Rage for Order,*" *Theological Studies* 38 (1976) 304–16.

5. Cf. E. Schillebeeckx, *Revelation and Theology* (London: 1967) 105–9.

6. *Der Fall Küng: Eine Dokumentation,* ed. N. Greimacher and H. Haag (Munich: 1980).

came man as Jesus is divine, and by refusing to accept in any way at all the ecumenicity of the First Vatican Council, which defined, *inter alia*, the primacy and infallibility (in certain circumstances) of the Roman bishop, Küng was held, not unreasonably, to have overstepped the limits which circumscribe what Catholic theology is. The Pope's reaction, therefore, was to deprive him of his canonical mission, his formal mandate to teach theology as a member of the believing community. To be a theologian, one must share the common *fides quae*, the faith of the people of God. A theologian is not an ecclesiastical *Übermensch*, but is equally bound, with all Christians, by the Church's rule of faith. He (or she) is dependent on the Church, not necessarily financially or even sociologically, but always epistemologically. A theologian may be so gifted a writer that he can support himself without the Church's monetary aid. He may interest so many people beyond the Church's membership that his lectures and books find an adequate audience outside the household of faith. Yet there are aspects of his understanding which are only available to the individual because the Church's tradition makes them so. Any scholar can study the texts of the New Testament considered simply as intriguing religious writings from the ancient Near East. But to grasp the meaning which the Christian religion has found in these texts, it is necessary to be in touch with the *fides quae*, the faith of the Church. We can borrow here a useful term from Kant's epistemology and call this the "ecclesiological *a priori*" in theology: ecclesial faith precedes, enters into, and organizes the concrete knowledge which theology possesses.[7]

Complementary to this view of faith as a body of doctrine giving true insight into God, there is also what the medievals called the *fides qua*, the faith by which I turn to God in Christ by the Spirit through my acceptance of what the Church believes. If the *fides quae* is objective faith, then the *fides qua* is the subjective faith, not in the sense of partial, individual opinions about faith, but the faith that pertains to me as an acting subject in my own right. As described by St. Thomas Aquinas in his theologian's primer, the *Summa theologiae*, subjective faith opens the mind to God's own truth, enabling objective faith to become the medium of direct contact with God himself.[8] The light

---

7. C. Ernst, *Multiple Echo: Explorations in Theology* (London: 1979) 139.

8. *Summa theologiae* IIa. IIae. 1–7. A valuable introduction, and useful notes and appendices are found in the modern English Dominican edition, *St. Thomas Aquinas, Summa theologiae*, vol. 31: *Faith* ed. T. C. O'Brien (London: 1974). Again, in his *Compendium theologiae* 1, 2, Thomas describes faith as that which "makes our future blessedness to exist in us inchoatively": his account of the eschatological character of faith turns

which the *fides qua* brings to the mind derives from God's radiant being and enables us to share here and now in the knowledge which the saints enjoy in heaven and which, more fundamentally, God has of himself. St. Thomas refers to it as the *semen gloriae*, the seed of glory, or the *inchoatio gloriae*, the first shadowy sketch of the vision of God. Infused into our minds, it gives us a sympathy or connaturality with God's revelation, orienting us in an obscure but real manner toward his truth.[9]

The importance of the *fides qua* here can be seen if we consider the persistent unwillingness of the Christian tradition to give the title "theologian" or "teacher" (Doctor) to more than a handful of people exceptional for the quality of their personal faith.[10] In the Greek tradition, for instance, one can point to the fact that only three writers bear the title *ho theologos*, "the theologian": the evangelist John, the fourth-century bishop Gregory of Nazianzus, and the eleventh-century monk Symeon of Constantinople, the so-called New Theologian.[11] Though this fact is to be explained in part by the caprices of piety and liturgical usage, nevertheless an attempt is being made to single out three individuals who shared a similar quality. By the outstanding character of their faith, they were able to enter into God's mystery in an intimate way and so communicate that inwardness of divine revelation to others. Almost any reader of the Gospels can detect that the Gospel of John is in a class of its own when compared with the other three. And if biblical scholarship be worth anything at all, the qualitative difference between the Fourth Gospel and the others derives, at least partially, from the special qualities of religious insight with which the Christian mind of St. John was liberally endowed.[12] Again, in the Western tradition, there is the practice of naming certain saints *doctores Ecclesiae*:

on the Vulgate text of Hebrews where faith is declared to be *substantia sperandarum rerum*, "the substance of things to be hoped for."

9. For an account of Thomas' reflections on discernment *propter connaturalitatem*, or *per modum inclinationis, see* T. Gilby, "The Dialectic of Love in the *Summa*" in *St. Thomas Aquinas, Summa Theologiae 1: Theology* (London: 1963) 124–32.

10. As M.-D. Chenu has said, faith is "(une) connaissance réaliste, c'est-a-dire qui touche la *chose* divine. Perception directe, impregnée de l'affectivité," "L'unité de la foi: réalisme et formalisme," *La foi dans L'intelligence* (Paris: 1964) 15–16.

11. V. Lossky, *The Mystical Theology of the Eastern Church* (English trans., London: 1957) 9.

12. The special qualities of John were early acknowledged in the Church's history: see F.-M. Braun, *Jean le théologien et son Évangile dans l'Église ancienne* (Paris: 1959); M. Wiles, *The Spiritual Gospel: The Interpretation of the Fourth Gospel in the Early Church* (Cambridge: 1960).

outstanding teachers of the Church.[13] Particular popes, acting as the Church's chief pastors, thus attempted to draw the attention of the community to some figures more deserving of the title "teacher" than others. Here studiousness and conformity to the *fides quae* are presupposed, and to the resultant qualities of erudition and orthodoxy is added the test of holiness, by which faith, the subjective response to the self-revealing God, is rooted in mind and heart. It is perhaps instructive to reflect on the implications of the difference between these liturgical and canonical titles and the professional titles of lecturers in a university theology faculty today.

Yet, though the root of the theological habit is supernatural faith, that faith takes on a particular quality when exercised theologically because of its entering into symbiosis with the natural human quality of studiousness. The specific mode in which faith lives in the theological enterprise is Christian wonder, or curiosity.[14] The studious believer who wishes to become a theologian wants to know, Why? Why do we say that God exists? Why did this God make the world? How, if the God of Christian faith exists, does evil coexist with such a God? Why did God's Word, or self-expression, become man and, more specifically, a Jew of the house of David? Why did he conduct his ministry as he did? In what way did he save the world? By what means is he still present and active through his Spirit in the Church? All of these questions and a hundred and one others deserve an answer. Probably everyone who takes his or her faith at all seriously has thought about one or more of them at some time. But there is a difference between the ordinary person who may discuss these things occasionally over a pint of beer at the local pub, or worry about them for a while before dropping off to sleep, and the person who makes a serious lifelong commitment to struggling with them and turns that commitment into a part of his or her very self-definition. For one cannot say, I've finished theology; now I'll move on to another subject. There is a sense in which one might say something similar of Akkadian grammar or the family tree of the Hapsburg dynasty, but one cannot reasonably assert it of exploration into God's revelation, which is, by definition

---

13. V. Pugliese and others, "Dottori della Chiesa," *Encicopledia Cattolica* 4 (Rome: 1950) cols. 1902–7. The first Western list, that of Bede in his *Epistola responsoria ad Accam episcopum*, depended like Lossky's modern Eastern triumvirate on received custom; but stimulated by Trent's praise of Thomas, Pope Pius V began the practice of canonically naming new Doctors in 1567. The most recent creations are the first two women Doctors, Catherine of Siena and Teresa of Avila, named by Pope Paul VI in 1970.

14. Schillebeeckx, *Revelation and Theology*, 109.

infinite in its implications for human understanding. To be a theological student in the full sense of those words cannot be a temporary state or a preamble to something else, such as the ministerial priesthood or an all-round education. Rather, it is a solemn engagement to developing over a lifetime the gift of Christian wonder or curiosity, which is the specifically theological mode of faith. As theologians, then, we commit ourselves to the lifelong study and reflection which the satisfaction of such curiosity will need. Our faith is from now on, in St. Anselm's words, *fides quaerens intellectum*, "a faith that quests for understanding."[15]

Such an engagement implies another aspect of the theological habit, the willingness to be stimulated by appropriate objects: the kind of objects which have, in point of fact, stimulated the curiosity of theologians. Such objects can be thought of as arranged in three concentric circles. The first and largest of these circles can be labelled "existence" or, more colloquially, "anything you care to mention." In principle, any existent thing could elicit theological wonder. We should not fall into the trap of thinking that only directly religious things can be cues for theological reflection. For those like myself whose work takes them to Rome, where the symbols of Catholicism lie all about them and where most of their colleagues and students and they themselves live in ecclesiastical institutions, it is tempting to narrow the theological vision to the internal life of the Church and that alone. But giving in to such a temptation would be a disaster. The work of God is as wide as the whole of creation, and the story of grace includes every human soul, whether he or she knows it or not. Two examples drawn from the history of culture may help to illustrate this.

The first is the poetry of Gerard Manley Hopkins, the Jesuit priest and writer who lived in England and Ireland from 1844 to 1899. Hopkins, looking at nature with the penetrating eye of an artist, found in it evidence of the divine creativity. Thus, Hopkins brought to life a commonplace of patristic and medieval theology, namely that nature is a book in which we read of God. In fact, a study of his visual world is entitled, significantly, *All My Eyes See*.[16] With Hopkins' help, we learn how to see the most ordinary things—a bird, a star in the night sky—

15. The subtitle of Anselm's *Proslogion*; Cf. his *Epistola de incarnatione Verbi* 1: "The one who does not believe has no experience, and the one who has no experience, does not know." For Thomas' version see *Scriptum super libros sententiarum* III. 23, 2, 2, 1 ad ii.

16. R. K. R. Thornton, *All My Eyes See: The Visual World of Gerard Manley Hopkins* (Sunderland: 1975).

in a new, theological light, as marked or, in Hopkins' word, "in-stressed" by God's creative act. We also learn how to see certain ex-traordinary and terrible things—such as shipwreck—as related not simply to the continuous act of creation but to the finer divine activity of re-creation through a travail of suffering and destruction.[17] A sec-ond example is the writings, more especially the thoughts, *Pensées*, of Blaise Pascal, the devout French scientist-philosopher who lived from 1623 to 1662. Pascal looked at the people around him in order to give us dramatic evidence of the Christian understanding of humankind. According to Christianity, people are made for God and open to God. At the same time, they are sunk in original sin, having a built-in ten-dency to what is evil. Humans are essentially a paradox, what Pascal calls "the glory and the refuse of the universe."[18] To see this as really the truth we need the assistance of men like Pascal, of novels, plays, and films as well as our own observation of the people we meet.

In these two cases, then, nature and people rather than anything specifically religious spark off theological wonder. They invite us to set out on a theological exploration. In Hopkins' case, we would be exploring the doctrine of creation, and of re-creation, through sharing in Christ's death and resurrection. In Pascal's case, we would be ex-ploring theological anthropology: the doctrine of humans, their origi-nal righteousness, fall, and need for redemption. To take a leaf out of their books, I advise my students at the Angelicum in Rome to go walking in the Alban hills, or to read some classical novels, or just to loiter in the Pincio Gardens or the Piazza di Spagna on a Sunday af-ternoon, places where all Romans go to play the favorite Roman sport, which is people watching. This is not necessarily time subtracted from theological study. In principle, theological wonder can be stimulated by any human experience, and any human experience is a proper start-ing point for theological reflection.

Coming now to the second, smaller concentric circle, I would label this "the sacred history." Although anything can spark off theologi-cal wonder, the central focus of that wonder for the Christian must lie in history.[19] Christianity is a historical religion. Its central figure lived

17. *See*, e.g., G. M. Hopkins, "The Windhover," "The Starlight Night," "The Loss of the Eurydice," "The Wreck of the Deutschland": *The Poems of Gerard Manley Hop-kins*, ed. W. H. Gardner and N. H. Mackenzie (Oxford: 1967) 69, 66, 72–76, 51–63. A theologically informed reading of the poems is presented in J. F. Cotter, *Inscape: The Christology and Poetry of Gerard Manley Hopkins* (Pittsburgh: 1972).

18. B. Pascal, *Pensées*, ed. L. Lafuma (Paris: 1962) no. 131; cf. nos. 78, 149, 430, 470, 613, 629. *See* A. Krailsheimer, *Pascal* (Oxford: 1980) 50–68.

19. O. Lewry, *The Theology of History* (Cork: 1969) 10.

two thousand years ago. And this central figure cannot himself be understood without a grasp of the religion of his people Israel, a religion whose own history dates back at least another fifteen hundred years. Similarly, the central figure of Christianity cannot be understood without a grasp of the tradition that flowed from him, the tradition of the Church. The historical nature of the Christian religion means that we cannot reinvent the Christian faith in our own age to suit our own tastes and using our own speculation. We are always in dependence on the people of the past. Certainly, our age has its own contribution to make to an understanding of the faith. Each generation is open to God, and, in fact, this century has seen a positive torrent of theological writing, unprecedented, at least in quantity, in the history of the Church. Nevertheless, we make our contribution as part of a dialogue, and in this dialogue the initiative belongs firmly with the past, since it is out of the past that Christ comes.

This basic truth about Christianity, a truth often minimized or overlooked by people looking for immediate relevance, means that our original outer circle labelled "existence" or "anything" is not a sufficient guide to the field of play of theological wonder. We need a second circle, a circle for the special history that has defined the Christian faith. Much of the time, specifically Christian theological wonder takes the form of what we can call "historical sympathy," sympathy for the people of the past. By sympathy I do not mean that we should feel sorry for them. I mean that we should deliberately try to put ourselves on their wavelength. By historical sympathy we place ourselves in the position of those in the past, insofar as that is humanly possible. We try to understand their viewpoint, their mind-set, their hopes and fears. Historical sympathy is a very special kind of charity toward our neighbor. It is a kind of love in which we reach out to the long-dead generations and make their thoughts and words live again by re-creating them in our own minds.[20] This is not an easy task, because many of these people lived in a world very different from ours, with preoccupations that are, at first, quite alien to us. It requires an enormous effort on our part to get inside the mind of the author of the Book of Lamentations, to grasp the situations and problems facing St. Paul or St. Augustine. But if we are not willing to make this effort, then there is little point in our trying to study the theology of a historical religion at all.

---

20. R. G. Collingwood, *The Idea of History* (London: 1946) remains valuable on this aspect of the historian's approach.

The third and smallest concentric circle I propose to label "the Bible." This may sound like a strangely Protestant remark in what is intended to be an essay on getting the habit of Catholic theology. After all, in the scheme I am presenting, the smallest circle is the nearest to the center of all. But it is in point of fact a sound principle of Catholic theology that all of Christian revelation is contained in Scripture in some manner.[21] The crucial phrase there is obviously the words "in some manner." Naturally, Catholics will say that certain aspects of revelation cannot be found easily in Scripture unless one reads Scripture within Tradition, but they will also say that the idea that one could read Scripture theologically outside of the tradition of the Church that produced it is crazy anyhow. (Evidently, the Church only canonized the Old Testament, though it created the New; but quite apart from the "preexistence" of the Church in Israel it is the union of Old and New Testaments which definitively constitutes Scripture.) The ecclesiological *a priori* works here just as well as everywhere else in theology, for the operation of theological wonder in a Christian presupposes the faith of the Church as well as one's own individual act of faith. It can be said that tradition is more a medium than it is an object. Though tradition has its own *loci*, it is more an environment or context or atmosphere in which we read Scripture than an object set side by side with Scripture. If we are looking for an actual object, a tangible monument to serve as the supreme concentration of stimuli to theological wonder, an object that expresses in a paramount way the historical religion which is Christianity, then that object can only be the Bible. Pondering on the Scriptures is the most important and fertile source of theological wonder that we have. For the average Catholic, such stimulus will come through the reading of the Scriptures in the liturgy and, if he or she is fortunate, the comments thereon of the Church's ministers. For the contemplative monk, one thinks in addition of the longstanding custom of *lectio divina*, the prayerful chewing over of the Bible in one's private room. For the young or the enthusiastic "groupie," there are Bible study groups meeting in presbyteries or parishioners' homes.[22]

The theological student must take further the trajectory that all of these represent. Every theological student should possess a copy of the Bible in a study edition, that is, a Bible with good critical introduc-

---

21. Y. M.-J. Congar, *Tradition and Traditions* (English trans., London: 1966) 376–424.
22. For a general orientation in the Catholic use of the Bible, *see* C. Charlier, *The Christian Approach to the Bible* (Westminster: 1958).

tions and notes. In practice, in the English-speaking world, this will mean the *New Jerusalem Bible* which is as well adapted for such study as it is ill adapted to the needs of Christian worship.[23] It is never too soon to become familiar with the layout and content of the Bible. In the recent past, few lay Catholics were capable of finding relevant passages in Scripture, but in a theological student this deficiency would be inexcusable. In the course of working with the Bible, the theologian learns to see it as a human product, like any other text from the ancient world. But if we are to study Scripture as theologians, and not simply as Semitic scholars or students of Hellenistic Greek, then we have to sustain our sense that this very human product is also a divine gift. In a saying no less true for being oft repeated, the Bible is the Word of God in the words of men.

Theological wonder may begin anywhere in any of these three circles, but the closer it is to their common center (the self-revealing God), the closer it will be to the heart of Christian truth. However, the three circles are not, of course, mutually exclusive. Their concentricity shows their interconnection. A practical example may illustrate this. Suppose that my theological wonder is aroused during the Mass of Christmas Day by hearing the words of St. John's prologue: "In the beginning was the Word, and the Word was with God, and the Word was God. The same was in the beginning with God. All things were made by him, and without him was not any thing made that was made."[24] Stimulated by this great text (starting point), I might trace back the idea of the living and creative Word of God, here identified with Jesus Christ, through the sapiential and prophetic books of the Old Testament (Bible). From there I might try to find out how faith in God as Creator arose among the people of Israel (sacred history), thus moving from the first circle to the second. Finally, I might reflect on what philosophers of science today might think of the idea of creation, perhaps themselves stimulated by research into the origins of the cosmos (existence, or anything). Having thus crossed into the third circle, I might begin the journey back to the original starting point more richly furnished with data and reflection relevant to the prologue, and use that to study further the presentation of the figure of Jesus in the Gospel of John, and so come at last to the mystery of the incarnation of the Creator within his own cosmos, which the liturgy of Christmas presents as the full meaning of the Johannine text.

23. New Jerusalem Bible (London: 1985).
24. John 1:1-3.

Cultivating theological wonder by openness to such stimuli and developing his or her natural studiousness in order to exercise it with profit, the theologian will be led to ask a very large number of questions. In order to understand the organization of contemporary theology, it is imperative to sort out these questions into various distinct types. In all, the theological habit finds itself confronted by five basic kinds of question. First, there are questions concerned with the foundation of faith. How is faith to be justified? On what is it based? This leads the theologian into what was formerly called "apologetics" and is now more usually termed "fundamental" or "foundational" theology, a less combative but somewhat bland title. Second, there are questions about the historical origin and development of the faith. What does the biblical text mean? How is later doctrine derived from it? This would take us into historical theology—if the exegetes will forgive us for including biblical studies under this more capacious term. Third, there are questions about the interconnection of the contents of the faith. How does it all hang together? How is one truth related to another? Such questions entail trying to relate in a systematic way the various elements that make up the teaching or dogma of the Christian religion. So they belong to systematic or dogmatic theology. Fourth, there are questions to do with the way faith should affect the behavior of the individual or the group. How are my ethical standards altered by becoming a Christian? How should a Christian community behave? Answering these questions would involve an exploration of the basic principles of Christianity as a life, an exploration known as "moral" or "pastoral" theology. Finally, we can group together a number of rather heterogeneous questions that deal with the implications of the Christian faith for the rest of human knowledge. What does natural science look like in the light of faith? Or social studies? How does faith modify our approach to literature or art or psychology? There is no generally agreed portmanteau for such questions, but a suitable one might be "practical" theology. Such theology would look at the consequences that faith has for our practice of a variety of human disciplines (anything from parapsychology to poetry), the manifold ways that we have of moving intelligently about the world. And certainly we could include here such disciplines as sociology, economics, and politics, thus making a connection with an increasingly widespread use of the term "practical theology" in writers influenced by the political and liberation schools of theological thought.[25] However, to re-

25. A. T. Hennelly, *Theologies in Conflict: The Challenge of Juan Luis Segundo* (Maryknoll: 1979) 9–10.

duce practical theology to the concerns of social politics or social economics would mean a grave impoverishment of its human materials.

In any case, if the theological habit is in good working order, it will not wish to deal with any one of these five types of question on its own, despite the fact that each is rich enough to occupy the energies of a lifetime. If theology is to be studiousness made supernatural, enquiring faith stimulated by various kinds of objects to ask a variety of questions but in a specifically Christian way, then it must always keep in mind the meaning and truth of Christianity as a whole. And so another vital aspect of the habit of theology emerges, and this is the urge to connect. In the Christian religion there are a great number of beliefs and practices. There are special texts, special ritual actions, special institutions, special ethical qualities, all of which are said to be distinctively Christian things. Also, within any one set of these things there is a sometimes bewildering diversity. The Bible, for instance, is not just one book, but a whole library of books of different kinds from different periods. The theologian wants to know how all of these different books are connected into a single, unitary whole. He or she wants to know how the Christian religion is a unitary belief system, and how it offers a unitary way of life. The attempt to show that Christianity is a coherent system of beliefs is another definition for systematic theology. The attempt to show how the Christian religion can be lived as a coherent way of life for an individual or a community is another definition of moral and pastoral theology. And these two types of theology are surely theology's central themes, since questions dealing with the rationale and genesis of Catholic Christianity (fundamental and historical theology) have something of the nature of a preamble, while questions dealing with the implications of theology for the practice of other human disciplines (what I have called practical theology) are by way of being a coda, though in practice—as we would say—a profoundly important one for human living.

In order to preserve this sense of the unity of God's approach to us through a medley of discrete facts and truths, the theologian must always be concerned to develop his or her own personal relationship with the Christian Absolute found in all these particulars: the God of Jesus Christ. And this brings us back in conclusion to the idea that to see the theological habit at work, we should look to its highest practitioners, the Doctors of the Church. The final aspect of that habit, which needs highlighting, is the quality of the intersubjective friendship between a theologian and the Lord. Ideally, the theologian should be a saint; at any rate, all theology should be what the Swiss theologian

Hans Urs von Balthasar called *die betende theologie* or *la théologie à genoux:* "theology on one's knees."[26]

Although the personal relationship of the theologian with God is a reality wider than prayer, since it necessarily involves the entire Christian life, nevertheless prayer is its conscious heart. The fourth-century desert Father Evagrius of Pontus had a saying, "If you pray, you are a theologian."[27] The saying has been, perhaps, a little overexposed and not a little misunderstood. The term "theologian" here carries a somewhat specialized meaning. It really means someone who contemplates God as the Trinity. But at least we can echo Evagrius and say, "If you do not pray then you are not a theologian." It is a necessary (though not a sufficient) condition for becoming a theologian (in the non-Evagrian sense) that one has some kind of prayerful quality to one's life and thought. How we should understand this is a delicate business. Clearly, it is not the case that if we flop down in a church for half an hour a day we shall emerge from the pew reborn as a latter-day Duns Scotus. But continued exposure to God and a God-centered vision of reality brings a greater quality of intuitive ability when it comes to theological judgment. In other words, if two people who differ on some aspect of theology share a comparable theological culture, but one prays and the other has stopped praying, it is the one who still prays that we should be well advised to follow.[28]

From an account of the habit of theology, we must now pass on to an investigation of its task. Having learned something of the subjective preconditions of theology, we need to enquire further into its objective content and its wider place in the Christian community, the Church.

26. H. U. von Balthasar, "Theology and Sanctity," in *Word and Redemption. Essays in Theology* 2 (English trans., New York: 1965) 49–86.

27. Evagrius, *On Prayer* 60. *See* I. Hausherr, *Les Leçons d'un contemplatif* (Paris: 1960).

28. J. Leclerq, *Theology and Prayer* (English trans., St. Meinrad, Ind.: 1963).

2

The Task of Theology

I will begin by mentioning three possible definitions of the theological task that I cannot accept, on the principle that many good definitions are arrived at by ruling out what things are not. Each of these negative definitions will be to some extent a caricature, yet all caricatures have some relation to reality. Moreover, each of the rejected definitions will prove to have incorporated an element of value. This element is capable of being disengaged and used afresh in a positive definition of the theological task, to be offered in the second part of the chapter.

Three Negative Definitions

A first account of the theological task that one might meet has it that theology is the misguided attempt to turn into a science something that is strictly mysterious: the dogmas, or as we say more precisely, the mysteries of the Christian religion. Since these mysteries by definition transcend the scope of the human mind, what is the point of trying to work them out intellectually? As Lord Dacre of Glanton has put it, theology is "sophisticated ninnery."[1] If we have accepted a revealed religion we must take the consequences. The consequences are that we cannot theorize about a revelation. We can only reform our own attitudes and feelings on the basis of it. In other words, one can have a spirituality but not a theology. One can claim that grace has changed one's heart, but it does not make sense to claim that grace has changed one's mind. This tendency to dismiss the rational claims of theology is not, of course, restricted to retired regius professors of modern history. A conviction of the superfluity of theology often ac-

1. Cited in H. A. Williams, *Some Day I'll Find You: An Auto-Biography* (London: 1982, 1984) 90.

companies periods of spiritual revival as well as of agnostic debilita-
tion: classically, in the *devotio moderna* of the Netherlandish Middle
Ages. More recently, Raïssa Maritain, despite her admiration for the
Catholic poet-prophet Charles Péguy, wrote blisteringly of his deliberate espousal of a ''discord between the soul's infused faith on the one
hand and on the other the actions and the very thoughts of a man who
has received this gift of God . . . scorning, in the name of faith, the
theological wisdom which he glories in not knowing.''[2] However, if
faith contains, as Thomas Aquinas insists, an inbuilt tendency toward
the vision of God, being the inchoate form of that vision, this first definition will not do. Though, to begin with, while faith is less perspicuous, less clear, than are other kinds of knowledge, it is in fact moving
toward a state of total clarity, intellectual union with Truth himself.[3]
If this is so, then faith must permit continuous growth in the understanding of what it believes, and the spiritual (or not so spiritual) anti-
theologism of the first definition may be set aside. *En passant,* we can
note that in claiming for theology a continuity with the vision of God
on the grounds that it is an intellectual habit rooted in the act of faith,
we are accepting that it is a science—in the special, and now archaic,
sense of the word indicated by Thomas.[4] For Thomas, theology is a
science insofar as it draws its own first principles from an utterly certain and transparent or self-evident kind of knowing, namely God's
own knowing of himself. Theology cannot be reduced to spirituality
because it is a way of knowing and understanding and not just a way
of feeling. While Christian affectivity is itself a valuable theological
theme, this does not mean that the only sensible theology would be
a description of Christian affectivity.[5]

The element of truth in the attempted transposition of theology
into spirituality derives from the fact that the fire of spirituality should
be burning in all theology. Faith, together with its necessary attendants,
hope and charity, is the foundation of all spirituality, all lived relationships with God, while at the same time, by entering into union with
studiousness, faith is also the foundation of the theologian's work. One
cannot approach theology as though one were a humanist. The theo-

2. R. Maritain, *Les Grandes Amitiés* (Paris: 1948) 272.
3. *See Summa theologiae* IIa IIae, qq. 1–7; *Compendium theologiae* 1, 2. For Thomas'
account of faith and its intellectuality, *see* St. Thomas Aquinas, *Summa theologiae,* vol.
31: Faith, ed. T. C. O'Brien (London: 1974) *passim.*
4. Ia q. 1, a. 2, *corpus.*
5. For a splendid example of such spiritual theology, fully conscious of its task and
limitations, *see* C. A. Bernard, *Théologie affective* (Paris: 1984) and notably 10.

logical student needs the basic natural *desiderata* of all students of anything, which we have summed up as argumentativeness, retentiveness, and imagination. But such qualities, taken by themselves, are insufficient equipment for a theological mind. The mind must be in some way in love with God or it will lose a certain fundamental sympathy, or tact, for Christian truth. There is indeed such a thing as theological sensibility, a kind of theological good sense which is not simply rational but which depends on our remaining within a spiritual culture.[6]

This appeal to the authority of God as providing theology, via revelation and faith, with its distinctive epistemological basis may suggest a second definition of the theological task. On this second version, the task of theology is said to be the transcribing in a more intelligible, or rationally acceptable, form whatever the divinely guided voice of Church authority may determine. Certainly, theologians have a duty to defend the defined teaching of Holy Church and to cooperate with the pope and bishops in clarifying or refining such teaching as may have an inadequately articulated form. But such duties, on this view, circumscribe the task of theology itself: they constitute the very borders of its home ground. Here the idea is that the starting point of all theology is the pronouncements of pope and bishops in both their extraordinary and ordinary magisterium, theology's job being to prove authorized ecclesiastical pronouncements by a regressive method which seeks arguments in the sources, Scripture and Tradition, as well as in reason, for their truth. The support given by Pope Pius XII to this picture of theology in his encyclical *Humani generis* of 1956 was rightly criticized by Fr. (now Cardinal) Joseph Ratzinger in his essay on the Second Vatican Council's dogmatic constitution on revelation, *Dei verbum*.[7] Theology is something wider than the direct assistance the theologian can afford the magisterium. The bishops, and especially the pope, are the guardians of the *fides quae*, doctrine, the objective content of the Christian creed. But the *fides quae* itself is the heritage of every believer who, on the basis of theological wonder, explores the riches of this shared faith by putting ever-new questions to it and about it. There is no reason to think that episcopate and papacy have ever thought of all these questions, much less of the answers to them. The

6. The value of a spiritual culture vis-à-vis theological activity is evoked in J. Leclerq, *The Love of Learning and the Desire for God: A Study of Monastic Culture* (2nd ed., English trans., New York: 1974). Needless to say, monastic culture provides a paradigm for a Christian culture here, rather than being its exclusive content.

7. In *Commentary on the Documents of Vatican II*, ed. H. Vorgrimler, III (English trans., New York: 1969) 197.

role of Church authority is to say when a given theology has detached itself from the *fides quae.* It is not to prescribe in advance what the theologian's work shall be. Let us also note here that the *fides quae* does not come to us simply from learning what the ecumenical councils or the popes when teaching *ex cathedra* have defined, nor by listening to what the bishops and pope are teaching today. It also comes to us, and in more ample fashion, from Scripture, and from Tradition—of which the past teachings of Church authority are only one element, one set of "monuments." From this point of view, we might even say that theology does not so much echo the present-day teaching of bishops and pope as make it possible—by providing the Church's pastors with an informed and circumstantial grasp of what the sources of revelation contain.

And yet there is a nugget of truth in the assertion that the task of theology is the transcription of the teachings of the magisterium. Because of theology's dependence on the Church's life of faith, it cannot ignore what the pastors of the Church are saying at any given time. By the sacrament of orders, the bishops, and preeminently the Roman bishop, are set over the Church by the Church's Lord. Through their distinctive activities of preaching the gospel to the unconverted, catechizing the faithful, explaining the mysteries celebrated in the Church's liturgy, and caring for the lives of Christians from the cradle to the grave, the bishops, and those other ministers—notably, priests— whom they co-opt to assist them, are in a good position to see the Christian faith as a lived totality. They can help the theologian to see the *fides quae* in its complete outline rather than to concentrate on some one aspect of it that may happen to be of particular interest in a given culture. Conversely, the pope and bishops may also, through their reading of what the Second Vatican Council called the "signs of the times," specifically encourage theologians on behalf of the whole Church to devote their attention to some aspect of theological research deemed likely to be especially helpful at some given time.[8] Finally, in those unresolved disputed questions, which from time to time mar the unity of the Church's life of faith, the theologian may, by and large, have confidence in the rightness of that side of a case to which pope

8. For the mutual aid which should mark the relations of episcopate and theologians, *see* the International Theological Commission's "Theses on the interrelationship between the ecclesiastical magisterium and theology," which can be consulted, with a commentary, in F. A. Sullivan, *Magisterium: Teaching Authority in the Catholic Church* (Dublin: 1983) 174–218. For the concept of the "signs of the times," *see* M.-D. Chenu, "Les signes du temps," *Nouvelle revue théologique* 90 (1965) 29–39.

and bishops lean—since the charism of truth bestowed on the apostolic ministry will naturally have its effect on the expression of that ministry, both in the local Church and in the Church universal.[9]

The appeal to the *fides quae* as a common inheritance, embedded in the rich historical data of Scripture and Tradition, might suggest, however, a third definition of the task of theologian. For some, theology consists in the acquisition of a very large number of facts about ③ the Bible and the Church. Fundamentally, on this view, theology is an exercise in the memorizing of data. Theologians are "professional rememberers." The trouble with this picture of theology is that just heaping up facts and references does not in itself give one a coherent account of the Christian faith. Christian curiosity about the revelation received and the urge to connect its various facets, something that mirrors the ultimate unity of God and the mind of man, cannot rest satisfied with this purely factual or, in the technical word, "positive" view of theology. The emergence of historical theology in the sixteenth century as a mode of theological practice created the possibility of mistaking for the theological task the registering of what others have thought of God. It may be that Anglican theology has been peculiarly subject to this temptation, as such different voices in the Church of England as Dr. E. L. Mascall and Prof. S. W. Sykes have suggested.[10] In Catholicism, similar strictures have been levelled against Cornelius Jansen (1585–1638), who roundly declared that theology was an affair of the memory and not of the reasoning faculty, and against his French disciple Antoine Arnauld (1617–94).[11]

Nevertheless, we can agree that without positive theology, without a knowledge of facts about the Bible and Church tradition, the content of systematic theology would be extemely thin gruel. In the opening question of his *Summa theologiae*, Thomas gives the impression at one point that the only materials theology has to go on are the articles of the Creed.[12] Were this true, theology would be mightily diminished. *response* In point of fact, Thomas had an impressive familiarity with Scripture, the Fathers, and the early medieval divines as well as with the teachings of councils and popes, the texts of the Roman liturgy, and the

9. Sullivan, *Magisterium* 172.

10. E. L. Mascall, *Theology and the Gospel of Christ: An Essay in Reorientation* (2nd ed., London: 1984) xvi. The difficulties such "positivism" can create for an entire ecclesial tradition are characterized in S. W. Sykes, *The Integrity of Anglicanism* (London: 1978) 79ff.

11. This must surely have had its effect in their reading of Augustine's achievement as Jansenism.

12. Ia q. 1, a. 2, ad i.

principles of canon law. The quality of his factual or positive resources concerning the *fides quae* is one major reason for the quality of his theology as a whole.[13] The same could be said of the work of more modern writers like Matthias Josef Scheeben (1835–88) or Hans Urs von Balthasar (1905–88).[14] Thus it is true that facts are important, though they are not all-important.

To sum up, then, what theology is not. It cannot be dissolved without remainder into spirituality, though it cannot do without spirituality either. Nor can it simply be a commentary on papal or episcopal utterance, though papal and episcopal utterances are vital to it, as it to them. Nor, again, can it just consist of positive theology, facts and figures, though these give it much of its concrete substance.

A Working Definition

What, then, is the task of theology? The working definition I propose to suggest is brief and unadventurous yet would suffice to sustain the rest of a theological life. The task of theology is the disciplined exploration of what is contained in revelation. Each of the main component terms of this definition, "disciplined," "exploration," "revelation," must now be unpacked.

Starting first with "revelation," it is surely plain that we would not be interested in theology without an acceptance of revelation. If we regarded Catholic Christianity as one religion among many, a belief system that happens to exist in some parts of the world just as do, say, Buddhism or Hinduism, we might be interested in studying theology from outside, as spectators, but we would not wish to study it from inside, as participators. Theology presupposes the truth of the Christian faith. It assumes from the outset that what we are involved with in the life of the Church is a divine reality and not just a figment of the corporate imagination of a group of people. Whereas in pursuing religious studies, we are not committed to the view that a given religion is true, or even partly true, in learning to be theologians we

13. Well brought out in M.-D. Chenu, *Toward Understanding Saint Thomas* (English trans., Chicago: 1964) 150–55.

14. An introduction to the work of M. J. Scheeben can be found in G. Fritz, "Scheeben, Matthias Joseph," DTC 14/i (1939) cols. 1270–74. A full study is E. Paul, *Denkweg und Denkform der Theologie von Matthias Joseph Scheeben* (Munich: 1970). A useful introduction to von Balthasar is the prefatory essay by D. MacKinnon in H. U. von Balthasar, *Elucidations* (London: 1972). A well-nigh exhaustive account is found in A. Moda, *Hans Urs von Balthasar* (Bari: 1976). *See also* A. Nichols, "Balthasar and his Christology," *New Blackfriars* 66, 781–82 (1985) 317–24.

are committed from the start to the position that at the origins of the Church, an authentic revelation of the one true God took place, and that we are put into contact with this same God revealing himself through our share in the Church's common life. Theology is, therefore, essentially concerned with revelation.[15]

Theology may be termed, indeed, a ministry carried out in the service of revelation. Theologians have a high calling, and they must acquit themselves with a profound sense of responsibility. They are servants of the divine Word, the Logos, just as much as are the bishops or the pope, though in a different mode. Theologians consecrate themselves to the meaning of revelation, and this suggests a more intimate relation with revelation than that possessed by the Church hierarchy, who are its guardians more than they are its interpreters. Unfortunately, the Holy Spirit has not been vouchsafed to theologians *qua* theologians, whereas the Spirit *has* been vouchsafed to the guardians of revelation, the Church hierarchy. The reason for this is simple. If the deposit of faith has not been successfully guarded, there will be nothing there to interpret. If the deposit of faith has not been successfully interpreted theologically, it will still be there for someone else to interpret in another age.

How can our theological efforts be said to serve revelation? The wonder, curiosity, and ever-deepening pursuit of truth implicit in the act of faith generates (as we saw in the last chapter) a variety of questions, which may be sorted into five portmanteau categories. These are fundamental, historical, systematic, moral, and practical theology. The attempt to answer these questions has applications of great utility to all actual or potential recipients of revelation. Thus, fundamental theology helps one to help other people keep the faith by removing difficulties they may have about believing. It also helps one to convert others to the faith by suggesting considerations relevant to the truth of Catholic Christianity. Historical theology helps one to discern the impression Jesus Christ made upon those who first met him (the New Testament), the situation he lived in (the Old Testament), and the way his image and teaching have been preserved and presented in the Church (the history of doctrine). In these ways, historical theology enables one to present the faith in a way that is concrete, circumstantial, and historically correct. Systematic theology helps one to show people

---

15. *See* R. Latourelle, "From Revelation to Theology," in *Theology: Science of Salvation* (New York: 1969) 3–10. This section can be regarded as a bridge to the subject of theology from his earlier study of revelation, *Theology of Revelation* (New York: 1966).

how the faith hangs together, how it all makes a satisfying design that is an inspiration to live by. Moral theology is useful in showing people how they might be growing personally in relation to God and their neighbor. Practical theology shows them the relevance of their religion to their professional work or private passions, to their general knowledge or social situation. In putting it so, I may be giving the impression that it is nearly always someone else who wants help and never, well, hardly ever, oneself. In fact, just as preaching is directed first toward (or even against) oneself, so is theology.

Theology, then, is bound up with revelation, and is a form of service by some individuals on behalf of the whole Church. From this, certain other things immediately follow. Above all, it must follow that the primary sources of theology will not be found in the world around us as with other disciplines, but in the revelation to which the Church is the witness. These primary sources, therefore, will be Scripture and Tradition. How Scripture and Tradition are related as the source of revealed understanding is a question of some moment in its own right, but the first thing to realize is that they are our primary materials. Whether they are seen as two separate but complementary sources or as two aspects of a single source is a relatively minor question compared with the basic point: Scripture and Tradition are the font of theological knowledge. This means, in turn, that in order to be theologians we must have a good knowledge of, on the one hand, the Old and New Testaments, and on the other, of the Tradition of the Church as expressed in ways other than Scripture. If one asks, What are these other ways of expressing Christian truth that bring us revelation, the only possible answer is that in effect, they are everything involved in the Church's life. They include the liturgy, the Fathers of the Church, the creeds and other doctrinal definitions, the evidence of Christian art and archaeology, the witness of ordinary believers. When we talk about the Church's Tradition we are referring to all these (and more), seen as an interconnected unity, the life of the Church.

Tradition

As we come to study these primary sources, Scripture and Tradition, we find that we have two what may be termed "aids to discernment" which will help us. In the first place, we have our own Christian experience. The gift of faith makes possible for each of us our own Christian sense of reality. Through the sensibility which faith gives, each of us can to some degree recognize what is an exaggeration in theology, what is a deviation in theology, and what, on the contrary, sounds right in theology. In the second place, we have the help, as already mentioned, of the contemporary day-to-day teaching of the pope and bishops, what is termed technically the "ordinary magisterium." In all these ways—Scripture, Tradition, Christian experience, and the teaching office of the bishops—theology is concerned with and dependent on revelation and the personal and corporate grace which accompanies and enables our response to the self-revealing God.

But I also said, in my working definition, that theology was the disciplined exploration of revelation. First of all, then, theology is an exploration. It is not simply the reassertion of something that is obvious to all believers. The statement that, for instance, God is our Creator is a straightforward statement of a truth of faith such as might be found in a catechism or a prayer book. It is not in itself a theological statement, or perhaps a better way of putting this would be to say that the ability to make this statement does not yet prove that one is a theologian. The exploratory role of theology takes many different forms. I have outlined the five great questions that theology asks, questions that lead to its primordial forms: fundamental, historical, systematic, moral, and practical theology. But in order to answer these questions, theology finds itself moving out into a whole host of subdisciplines. For example, in order to understand the context of the life of Jesus, central to historical theology (taking this to include the history of Christian origins) and vital also to fundamental theology, the theologian may want to learn more about the geographical sites involved in the ministry of Jesus. Thus arises biblical archaeology as an offshoot of theological exploration. Or again, for the same basic reasons, one may wish to know more about the way the Gospels were written so as to achieve a better insight into the reactions to Jesus of the first disciples. So a new theological subdiscipline joins the club, historical-critical exegesis. In such ways a question which has started life in historical theology pure and simple, or even in fundamental theology, cannot be answered without further exploration, which generates whole new disciplines like biblical archaeology and New Testament criticism. It should be obvious that answers to questions about what exactly happened in the ministry of Jesus, in the concrete context of his time and place, are going to be quite complex and detailed. A catechism answer would hardly suffice. So theology is not just *any* expression of revealed truth. It is different from the expression of revelation that we find in preaching or in catechizing or in devotion. It differs from these by being an exploration of what is not at first obvious, even to someone who knows and accepts the faith of the Church.

Finally, in my working definition, I said that this exploration which is theology has to be disciplined exploration. Certain elements of order and structure should be present. The question as to what these elements of order and structure ought to be is the question of theological methodology, method in theology. It seems to me that the structural or ordering element in theology is twofold. First, there is a principle of order in all theologies which derives from outside of theology. In a broad sense, this pretheological principle of order may be said to come from philosophy, assuming that we take the word "philosophy" in a sufficiently general kind of way. Many people have what are in effect philosophical convictions or philosophical questions without realizing that these are in fact philosophical. Every culture carries with it one or more basic ways of interpreting the world, of saying what is important in life, what questions are the most urgent, what values are paramount. From this pretheological or, in a broad sense, philosophical background, we come to the exploration of revelation with a certain agenda, a certain list of priorities, a certain number of already formed convictions about the nature of reality. Because of the intrinsic richness of revelation, no matter what questions we bring to it, it is able to throw light on them. So we interrogate the sources of revelation, Scripture and Tradition, using our aids to discernment, Christian experience and magisterium, and we come up with a theology, a disciplined or ordered exploration of what is contained in revelation.

The second structural element in theology derives not from outside revelation but from inside it. Once again, because of the intrinsic richness of revelation, no one theology can hope simply to reproduce revelation in some kind of complete and unconditional way. We can say of no one Christian theology, There, that is the Christian truth. Every theology takes as its central axis some facet of revelation and tries to relate everything to that. It selects one item within revelation and arranges all the others around it, like planets circling a sun. So, for instance, Augustine's theology revolves around the theme of grace; Thomas' theology revolves around the idea of the coming forth of creatures from God and their return to him; Rahner's theology, around a version of the doctrine that people are the image of God, and so on. Here we have a second ordering or structuring or disciplining principle in theology, and this time it is itself strictly theological, that is, it derives from within revelation and not from outside it.[16] So far as this theological principle of order is concerned, I want to defer con-

16. *See* for a fuller account of this idea, A. Nichols, "Unity and Plurality in Theology: Lonergan's *Method* and the Counter-claims of a Theory of Paradigms," *Angelicum* 62 (1985) 30–52. Also, ch. 20 in this book.

sideration of it until, having mastered the other elements of theology, we come to look at the history of theology in Part 6 of this book. The reason for this is that until we have some idea of the enormous variety of writings that have counted as Catholic theology in past and present, what I might have to say about the theological ordering principle would be somewhat rootless and abstract.

That suggests that I plan to take the other three elements we have identified—sources, aids to discernment, and philosophical principle of order—in that chronological sequence. But in fact I propose to deal with the role of philosophy in theology first, and only then to go on to look at the sources and the aids to discernment. The reason for this is that, really, philosophy has two roles to play in theology, and one of these two roles is logically prior to a consideration of the sources and how we might be helped to interpret them.

Apart from being a principle of order in theology, philosophy also has a vital part to play in laying the foundations for acceptance of revelation and so in providing the essential groundwork for theological activity. Philosophy is vital to what is called the "preamble of faith," in other words, to the way in which we justify our acceptance of revelation in the first place. Philosophy has to help theology to get started by showing the basic compatibility of revelation with human rationality. Obviously, if revelation were basically incompatible with human rationality, then there would be no point in doing theology as classically understood, and the "spiritual antitheologians" mentioned above would be fully justified. In the preamble of faith, theology calls on philosophy to help deal with such issues as the existence of God, the problem of evil, the possibility of revelation, and the nature of the claim that the actual revelation we have is historically well grounded. But this role of philosophy vis-à-vis theology is obviously prior to anything else in theology, because without it theology could not get off the ground at all. Consideration of the task of philosophy in the preamble of faith then leads naturally to looking at philosophy as a principle of order in theology, since many of the ideas philosophy uses in the preamble of faith—ideas about God, for instance—are still relevant when one comes to theology proper. Another way of putting this would be to say that philosophy has two contributions to make to theology: one is to fundamental theology, to an account of the foundations of the act of faith; the other is to systematic theology, to an explication of the content of faith. So this is the order we will be following: the role of philosophy, both as rational foundation of theology and as principle of order within theology; the roles of Scripture and Tradition as sources; the roles of experience and magisterium as forms of illumination of those sources; and, finally, the theological principle of order in the context of the history of Catholic theology, its plurality, and its unity.

Part Two

The Role of Philosophy in Theology

3

General Principles

There are many kinds of philosophy on the market, and some attempt must be made to adjudicate between them. It may be said at once that some kinds of philosophy have little or no relevance to theology because they define themselves too narrowly to get in touch with theology's subject matter. So, for instance, if one defines philosophy as an analysis of ordinary language or as a study of the logical status of propositions, then there will be no problem of the general standing of philosophy within Christianity.[1] Philosophy based on such definitions would have no theological point of contact worth speaking of. The kinds of philosophy that do have a point of contact with theology are all in a broad sense metaphysical. That is, they regard the task of philosophy as an attempt to throw light on human life, and on the wider realm of reality in which life is set, by looking at these within the widest possible context of interpretation. Such a definition of philosophy covers nearly all the principal schools or movements that philosophy has known, not only in the West but also in, for example, India and China—both of which have philosophical cultures as significant as our own.[2]

1. However, if one understands "ordinary language" as including the (ordinary) use of language in religious practice, one might well find a philosophical connecting point with theology: see, for instance, I. T. Ramsey, *Religious Language: An Empirical Placing of Theological Phrases* (London: 1957); S. McF. TeSelle, *Speaking in Parables: A Study in Metaphor and Theology* (London: 1973); J. M. Soskice, *Metaphor and Religious Language* (Oxford: 1985). And for an attempt by a Polish philosopher to argue that the desired connecting point *should* be found in a study of the logical status of religious propositions, see W. Lubian, "Father Innocent Bocheński, or the Intensity of Experience," *Christian Life in Poland* (1989/1) 109–19, with citation of a Bocheński lecture, "Logic and the Philosophy of Religion," delivered at Cracow on October 24, 1987.

2. For a discussion of the fundamental character of philosophy as so defined, *see* W. H. Walsh, "Metaphysics, Nature of," *Encyclopaedia of Philosophy* V (New York: 1967); E. Gilson, *Being and Some Philosophers* (2nd ed., Toronto: 1952); *The Nature of Metaphysics*, ed. D. F. Pears (London: 1957).

Roughly speaking, philosophy so defined covers three questions. First, What is man? or Who am I? This is the problem of human existence and the nature of the self: philosophical anthropology and its extension, ethics. Second, What is the world? or What is this whole interconnected reality of which I form part? This is the problem of cosmology: of nature and the extension of nature, history. Third and finally, What are the fundamental terms on which the world exists? What are its conditions of possibility? This is the problem of ontology, well summed up by the contemporary German philosopher Martin Heidegger when he asked, "Why is there something rather than nothing?"[3] If these are the basic questions that philosophy deals with, we can say that philosophy is an almost inescapable part of all human life. No one simply eats, drinks, sleeps, and makes love. Everyone at some point asks in some form these questions or something like them. No doubt a Stone Age human or a modern Eskimo would not phrase these questions exactly as I have. Nor—come to that—would a London bus conductor or a Roman ice-cream seller. But some form of them would occur to such people nevertheless. There is no culture which has not made some attempt to pose and answer such questions, not necessarily in formal philosophy or even in writing at all, but perhaps in art, in music, or even in the way people bury their dead. Philosophy is the attempt to say who we are and what kind of a world we live in, drawing on the resources of human experience as clarified by reflection.

Because philosophy tries to give a universal answer to these fundamental questions, it necessarily comes into relation with theology. Indeed, for some people, it necessarily comes into conflict with theology, since these are just the kind of questions theology itself deals with, on the basis of revelation, from the higher vantage point of Christian faith. Theology has its own answers to the questions, What is man? What is the good life for all people? What is their final destiny? (anthropology and ethics); What is reality like? What meaning does history hold? (cosmology and the philosophy of history); What is the ultimate ground of reality? What is not only the source but also the goal of the world (ontology). And if theology has answers to these questions, why not just listen to theology and forget about philosophy? If theology deals with the same questions from higher up, surely we can dispense with the more lowly science of philosophy. If you want

---

3. M. Heidegger, *An Introduction to Metaphysics* (English trans., New Haven and London: 1959) 1: "Why are there essents ("existents," "things that are") rather than nothing?"

an aerial photograph and you possess a helicopter, you will not bother to borrow a balloon as well.

In the ecclesial communities that date from the Reformation of the sixteenth century, the rejection of philosophy by theology has been a fairly frequent occurrence, though it is much sharper in Luther than in Calvin.[4] Partly, this has been based on the idea just mentioned, that philosophy is superfluous once you have revelation. But predominantly, philosophy has been rejected because it has been regarded as a dangerous competitor to theology: it is too hot to handle. If philosophers have their own concept of God and their own view of human life, is there not a danger that they will alter or suppress the concept of God and the view of life found in revelation? Theologians may say that all they want to do is to use philosophy, but perhaps they will end up by being used. The philosopher will call the tune.

This radical suspicion of philosophy has not been limited to the Lutheran and Reformed traditions, even though it is at its strongest there. From time to time, such views have been held by thinkers in the Catholic tradition also. Usually, they have not taken the form of systematic theories as to why theology should not touch philosophy with a barge pole, such as may be found in writers influenced by the great neo-orthodox Swiss Protestant theologian, Karl Barth.[5] In Catholicism, similar views have found a more low-key expression in feelings of anxiety or unease in the presence of philosophy, or whenever philosophy has had a marked influence on theology. Thus, when some of the early Fathers of the Church called Christianity "the true philosophy"—and in early Christian art Christ is often portrayed dressed as a philosopher—they meant to imply that Christianity answered the questions set by philosophy better than the philosophers themselves.[6] Thus, they felt, Christian revelation had rendered phi-

4. W. Link, *Das Ringen Luthers um die Freiheit der Theologie von der Philosophie* (2nd ed., Munich: 1955); nevertheless, it remains possible to present Luther's thought as providing an interpretation of concrete, historical existence and so of philosophical interest: *see* A. Agnoletto, "La Filosofia di Lutero," *Grande Antologia Filosofica* 8, ed. M. F. Sciaccia (Milan: 1964) 1012. Philipp Melanchthon (1497–1560) provides an interesting contrast to Luther by his much more positive estimate of philosophy: F. C. Copleston, *A History of Philosophy* 3 (London: 1967) 227–28. As for Calvin, while he can be bitter against humanists, as in his *Treatise upon Scandals*, he retained a good deal of the humanist—especially Stoic—heritage, most clear in his presentation of the themes of natural law and of Providence. *See* F. Wendel, *Calvin* (English trans., London: 1963, 1965) 2.

5. For Karl Barth's attitude to philosophy, *see* especially *Die kirchliche Dogmatik* I.2, *Die Lehre vom Wort Gottes* (Zürich: 1938) 818–25, 865–67.

6. On Christianity as the "true philosophy" *see* e.g. Lactantius, *Divinae institutiones*

losophy out of date. On occasion, this suspicion of philosophy by the Fathers or by later Catholic writers is expressed pretty strongly. For instance, the third-century African writer Tertullian once declared that Athens "had nothing to do with Jerusalem": in other words, that there is no common ground between philosophy and revelation.[7] In a similar vein, Blaise Pascal, already mentioned, drew a sharp contrast between what he called the "God of the philosophers" and the "God of Abraham, Isaac, and Jacob": by which he meant the biblical God, the God disclosed in Scripture.[8] But in fact both these men, Tertullian and Pascal, use concepts in their religious writings which we can only call philosophical—since they certainly do not stem from revelation itself. Tertullian even has arguments for the existence of God of a rather simple sort, based on the fact that even atheists when they are in trouble exclaim, "Oh God!"[9] Actually, Tertullian's argument is more sophisticated than this reference might suggest. He held that the soul was "naturally Christian" and only overlaid by a superficial carapace of ideology in the case of atheists and agnostics. So even the theologian who wants to get away from philosophy finds it hard to do so.[10] Probably the only way of doing so entirely would be to make theology consist in a repetition of the language of the Bible. But this would hardly be theology at all but rather a mere rearrangement of the biblical text.

But apart from the question of fact, Can a theologian get away altogether from philosophy? there is also a question of principle, Should he or she want to? In effect, it is the position of the Catholic Church that the theologian should *not* want to get away from the philosopher. I say this because of the teaching found in the dogmatic constitution of the First Vatican Council of 1870 on the Catholic faith, usually referred to by its opening words, *Dei Filius*.[11] A relation between theology and philosophy is implied in this text because a relation between

III.30. Cf. P. Brown, "On the sarcophagi of the age, he (Christ) is always shown as a Teacher, teaching His Wisdom to a coterie of budding philosophers," *Augustine of Hippo: A Biography* (London: 1967) 42. For an iconographic example, *see* the account of the "Brescia lipsanotheca" in A. Grabar, *Christian Iconography: A Study of Its Origins* (London: 1969) 138.

7. Tertullian, *De praescriptione* 7.

8. Blaise Pascal, *Pensées* ed. L. Lafuma, (Paris: 1962).

9. Tertullian, *De testimonio animae* 2; *Apologia* 17.

10. Thus, historians of philosophy have produced such studies as C. de L. Shortt, *The Influence of Philosophy on the Mind of Tertullian* (London: 1933), or C. C. J. Webb, *Pascal's Philosophy of Religion* (Oxford: 1929).

11. Vatican I, *Constitutio dogmatica "Dei Filius" de fide Catholica*, ch. 4: DS, 3015–20.

faith and reason is explicitly presented, and presented as based on the Church's understanding of the relation between grace and nature.

Catholicism holds that, in the first place, there is an essential difference between nature and grace—between our human nature with its own inherent powers and capabilities and what is sometimes referred to as the "second nature" or "second gift" of grace. The grace of God transforms human nature so that it is capable of behaving in ways not native to it. We can see this at its fullest in the saints. The saints are atypical human beings, but this is not simply because they are statistically unusual. More than this, some of the things they do are not derivative from ordinary human nature as such: giving one's life in continuous self-sacrifice for others, for example, or enjoying the friendship of the Blessed Trinity. Our understanding of this transformation by grace comes from revelation and when formally expressed is theology. But this still leaves open the possibility, indeed it posits the necessity, of a more limited but still valuable understanding of an independent kind: an understanding of the nature that is thus transformed by grace. This understanding derives from ordinary human experience and when formally expressed is called philosophy. So the distinction between nature and grace in Catholic teaching has a mirror effect in a distinction of two kinds of understanding, one possessed by reason and the other by faith, and crystallizing out in philosophy and theology.[12]

That this is close to the heart of the matter may be confirmed by noting that a major reason for the distrust of philosophy by classical Protestant thinkers lies in the tendency of the Reformers to see human nature as totally corrupt after the Fall.[13] If human nature is totally corrupt and grossly unreliable, then human reason, as an integral part of human nature, is unlikely to be in a much better state. And if human reason is radically corrupt, then the philosophy it produces is not likely to be of much service to the gospel. The Catholic episcopate at the Council of Trent repudiated this extreme pessimism about nature after the Fall. In its place they proposed that although human nature has been savagely wounded by the Fall, it has not been totally corrupted. Its powers, and thus its activities, have been seriously damaged by sin, but its deepest foundation is still what God made it. This will mean, then, that human reason will be fallible, and so the philosophical tra-

---

12. A. Léonard, *Pensées des hommes et foi en Jésus-Christ* (Paris: 1980) 23–31.
13. H. H. W. Kramm, *The Theology of Martin Luther* (London: 1949).

dition of *Homo sapiens* may well be full of errors. Nevertheless, in itself
reason is still capable of apprehending truth and so philosophy is too.
Although people can no longer attain God in a way that will ultimately
satisfy them by their own resources alone (if, even before the Fall, they
ever could), their resources still give them access to reality, to truth,
and so, ineluctably, in some degree to God.[14] In fact, we could go so
far as to say, building on the insights of Trent and the First *Vaticanum*,
that the Church expects and requires people to investigate the world
philosophically. Just as grace requires nature to build on, so theology
requires philosophy as a necessary infrastructure. Christ came to save
the world. This presupposes that there was already a world worth saving. In a similar way, theology is the Christianizing of human thinking, and this implies that human thinking is a worthwhile pursuit in
its own right. Just as grace would look silly without nature, so theology would look silly without philosophy. And as a matter of fact, the
history of theology shows conclusively that theologians have drawn
on now one, now another philosophy in order to state the faith of the
Church. Before going on to consider the implications of this historical
variability in the theological use of philosophy, perhaps it may be helpful to sum up what we have so far about their interrelation in a dia-
grammatic form that masquerades as a mathematical equation:

$$\frac{\text{redemption}}{\text{creation}} = \frac{\text{grace}}{\text{nature}} = \frac{\text{faith}}{\text{reason}} = \frac{\text{theology}}{\text{philosophy}}$$

So far we have agreed, then, that somebody's philosophy should
play a part in theology, but nothing has yet been said about whose
this will be. The next question we must tackle, therefore, is *Which* philosophy? To this question not only are various answers possible, but
various kinds of answer are possible. A first kind of answer would be
to say that this is not a proper question to ask in the first place. Which
philosophy one is going to adopt is for students of philosophy themselves to decide. *Nihil contra philosophiam nisi philosophia.* It is not for
theologians to dictate what Christians should think philosophically,
nor even how they are to do their philosophical thinking. This is no
more legitimate than would be an attempt by theologians to lay down
the law on what Christians should think about astronomy, or the best
techniques for cake making. There is indeed an element of truth in
this response. As we have seen, philosophy does enjoy a certain auton-

14. J. Alfaro, "Nature and Grace," *Sacramentum mundi* 4 (English trans., Bangalore:
1968) 176–81.

omy vis-à-vis theology, just as nature does in relation to grace. On the other hand, theologians can certainly report on the use their predecessors have made of different philosophies and can say whether they think the results are a success. Very importantly, a theologian has the right to say whether, in his or her view, a particular philosophy is compatible with revelation or not. Even more than this, the theologian has a duty to say so, just as, analogously, the Church's magisterium had the duty to come to a judgment about philosophical theses relevant to the truth of Christian doctrine—at least in those cases where such theses are currently commended by an intelligentsia for wide-scale adoption in the community of faith.[15]

A second type of answer would be to say that although theology needs philosophy, it can, if it is clever enough, generate its own philosophy. This is the idea, much supported in Catholic circles in the period from the First World War to the Second Vatican Council, that there can be such a thing as a purely Christian philosophy.[16] Revelation, as we know, enables us to get a grip on truth about the ultimate philosophical issues: Who am I? What is the world? Why is there something rather than just nothing? But it may be that some of the truth we get from revelation can be restated in philosophical terms.[17] Theologians have often held that some revealed truths are completely beyond reason but others are just difficult for reason to grasp with sureness. The second set of truths might be, so to speak, detached from revelation and erected into a philosophy in their own right: a Christian philosophy. For instance, it is clear from revealed religion that there is a God, that this God satisfies our deepest needs, that we as persons reflect in some way the life of this God, that there is a moral law written in our hearts. All of these ideas could be allowed to set up shop and do business under their own name. Although in fact they came from revelation (at least in a given culture this may well be so), in principle they could be defended by reason alone and so make their own way in philosophical history. Furthermore, the reflection which Christian philosophers would carry out on them would develop and enrich their content. So the Church would have its own philosophy—a genuine philosophy, not a theology—yet one that would avoid the risks that

15. C. Nicolosi, *Fede cristiana e riflessione filosofica. Il problema della filosofia cristiana. Teoria e storia di un dibattito* (Rome: 1973) 437.

16. M. Nédoncelle, *Is There a Christian Philosophy?* (English trans., New York: 1960); E. Gilson, *Christianisme et philosophie* (Paris: 1936); idem., "What Is Christian Philosophy?" in *A Gilson Reader*, ed. A. C. Pegis (New York: 1957).

17. Cf. Thomas Aquinas, *Summa theologiae* IIa. IIae., q. 2, a. 4.

people like Tertullian and Pascal identified because this philosophy would come from within revelation itself.

Historically, there can be little doubt that a great deal of the philosophy written by Christians has emerged in exactly this way. The great historian of medieval philosophy Etienne Gilson showed that the main thematic differences between Western philosophy and the philosophy of the ancient world (notably, of course, Greek philosophy) derive from the influence of Christianity during the late antique and medieval periods.[18] On the other hand, Gilson's case could easily be overstated. It would not be true to say that the entire philosophical outlook of a medieval theologian like St. Bonaventure or St. Albert was a precipitate of revelation. Some of it was indebted to a philosophical tradition that antedated the arrival of Christianity on the scene. In any case, while historians may show that philosophy has been influenced by revelation in its choice of themes and even in the way that it has dealt with them, this does not oblige us to draw the prescriptive conclusions to which the supporters of the idea of a Christian philosophy subscribe. That is, we need not necessarily conclude that what the Church allows to happen, she positively expects to happen.

In principle, it might be said—and this would be a third kind of answer to our original question, Which philosophy?—the orders of philosophy and theology are utterly distinct, with different departure points and ways of arguing. Although revelation has the right to pass judgment on a philosophical conclusion, it has no right to declare a preference for one way of reaching it rather than another. This has been the position taken up by, among others, the devotees of neo-Scholasticism over against those of the Christian philosophy school.[19] On this view, there can be no halfway house between supernatural truth and a search for natural truth based simply on evidence seen in the light of rationally defensible first principles.

Finally, a fourth answer and one which I commend would be a mediating position between the last two tendencies I have discussed. We could say that a good philosophy (from the point of view of theological fruitfulness) will consist of, formally speaking, the best purely natural reasoning available, but that materially speaking or content-wise, revelation can help to identify the areas to which natural reasoning could most profitably be directed. Thus, the form of philosophy

18. E. Gilson, *The Spirit of Mediaeval Philosophy* (New York: 1940) 1–41, 403–26. For Gilson's work, *see* L. K. Shook, *Etienne Gilson* (Toronto: 1984).

19. J. M. Quinn, *The Thomism of Etienne Gilson: A Critical Study* (Villanova: 1971) 3–4.

as practiced by Christians would have no reference to revelation, but its content would. Here revelation directs the philosopher's interests but not the methods or ideas. Whether a philosophy has thus proved theologically fruitful or not will be evaluated by asking how helpful it has been in the work of our theological predecessors—though obviously this criterion would not be of much use if some highly original philosophy were to be worked out in our lifetime. Thus, for instance, the philosophy of Emmanuel Lévinas, a philosophy of divine transcendence disclosed in the human face, though still in the process of being written, is already being utilized by theologians.[20]

From the viewpoint of the history of philosophy, then, who are the main candidates for the vacant post of *ancilla theologiae*, the handmaid (or, possibly, handmaids) that theology is looking for? Something like what I have called the "mediating position" has been actualized in different ways in different periods of theological history. We can identify at least six principal periods in this regard. To begin with, in the early Church philosophy most commonly took the form of some variety of Platonism,[21] supplemented by Stoic ethics, and peppered with pieces of the Aristotelean corpus. Platonism—in its later antique forms, in which it became a house spacious enough to accommodate elements of these other philosophical traditions—was the favored philosophy of the patristic period because of its clear doctrine of transcendence, the idea that there is a single (divine) principle on which all things depend. For the same reason, it would be revived much later by such Christian humanists of the Renaissance as Marsilio Ficino and Pico della Mirandola.

In the medieval West, philosophy took a turn toward Aristotle, because his analysis of the structure of finite beings (humans included) seemed to provide a good account of nature to complement revelation's account of grace.[22] This was the dominant position of the great Scholastics, though the Aristoteleanism of a figure like Thomas Aquinas

20. This was the view adopted by such students of Scholasticism as P. Mandonnet, S. Ramirez, and F. van Steenberghen. For the internal variety of the Thomist school on this as on other points, *see* H. J. John, *The Thomist Spectrum* (New York: 1966).

21. E. von Ivanka, *Plato Christianus: Übernahme und Umstaltung des Platonismus durch die Väter* (Einsiedeln: 1954); M. Spanneut, *Le Stoicisme des pères de l'Eglise de Clément de Rome a Clément d'Alexandrie* (Paris: 1957); for the use by the Fathers of Aristotle, *see* S. Lilla, "Aristotelismo," in *Dizionario patristico e di antichità cristiane* 1, ed. A. di Beradino, (Casale Monferrato: 1983), *sub. loc.*

22. As Simon Tugwell has written "It was largely through the Arabs that Aristotle had been brought back to the West, and their Aristotle was part of an essentially Neoplatonist package. He brought with him the pseudo-Aristotelean *Liber de causis*, de-

was also heavily indebted to the Platonic tradition. Again, philosophy as practiced by Christians in the early Modern period (the seventeenth and eighteenth centuries) moved more in the direction of a rational metaphysics attentive to the natural sciences: in the line of Descartes, through Leibniz, to Christian Wolff.[23] These writers were admired for the coherence, or close conceptual interrelatedness, of their systems. They showed the systematic intelligibility of a world which springs from the Logos, or Reason of God.

By the nineteenth century, Christians were frequently found drawing on the idealism of F. W. J. von Schelling and G. W. F. Hegel.[24] The principal attraction here was a doctrine of history. For the German idealists, history is the self-manifestation of the Absolute, or God. The nature of the historical process was a major concern of the German Catholic theology of the first half of the nineteenth century, understandably so since Catholic Christianity regards the salvific process as taking historical form.

In the middle years of the twentieth century, existentialism and personalism were the two main preferred philosophies of innovative theologians: existentialism because it raises the religiously relevant question of a meaning to life, and personalism because it takes personality to be the most important phenomenon in the world. In addition, an interest in sociological thought corrected the somewhat individualistic tendencies of much existentialist- and personalist-influenced writing and stressed the corporate nature of human life.[25] All three contributions are of great interest to those investigating Chris-

rived from the *Elements of Theology* by Proclus, one of the last great pagan Neoplatonists, and he was accompanied by the works of the Arab commentators, especially Avicenna, and, slightly later, Averroes. And in addition to this wealth of supposedly Aristotelean learning, which was often in fact more Platonist than Peripatetic, a veiled Platonism was also exercising a considerable influence through the writings of 'Dionysius the Areopagite,' which had begun to enjoy a new vogue in the twelfth century." S. Tugwell, "Albert the Great: Introduction," in *Albert and Thomas: Selected Writings*, ed. S. Tugwell (New York: 1988) 10. And compare Albert the Great's comment, "You cannot be a complete philosopher without knowing both philosophies, Aristotle's and Plato's," *Metaphysica* I. 5. 15, cited in Tugwell, *Ibid.* 31.

23. For the period from Descartes to Wolff, *see* J. D. Collins, *God in Modern Philosophy* (Chicago: 1959) 55–89. For more detailed studies, *see,* e.g., H. Gouhier, *La Pensée religieuse de Descartes* (Paris: 1924); J. Iwanicki, *Leibniz et les démonstrations mathématiques de l'existence de Dieu* (Paris: 1934); M. Campo, *Christian Wolff e il razionalismo precritico* (Milan: 1939).

24. For post-Kantian transcendental philosophy *see* F. C. Copleston, *A History of Philosophy* 7 (London: 1963) 1–31; H. Gross, *Der deutsche Idealismus und das Christentum* (Munich: 1927).

25. J. MacQuarrie, *Twentieth Century Religious Thought: The Frontiers of Philosophy and Theology 1900–1960* (New York: 1963).

tian doctrine, especially, perhaps, theological anthropology and ecclesiology, the doctrine of the person and in particular of the "ecclesial person." Concern with the manner in which Christian truth descends through time has since been enlivened by the stimulus of hermeneutical philosophy—the philosophical investigation of the process of interpretation as represented by, most notably, Paul Ricoeur and Hans-Georg Gadamer,[26] while the importance of reflection on language in their (originally) French and German writings respectively has been taken further in the English-speaking world, thanks to the achievement of Ludwig Wittgenstein.[27] These philosophies are clearly pertinent to Christian theology, since that theology can be thought of as the continuous interpretative reappropriation of a religious tradition, a tradition which sees itself as the carrier of a divine revelation, for which our primary metaphor is the Word, precisely, of God. The need to contextualize the particular realities that form the subject matter of these theological areas within the wider realm of being as a whole has also sustained interest in philosophies concerned to look with fresh eyes at the traditional ontology of Western metaphysics: here the later thought of Heidegger and such dissident disciples of Heidegger as Lévinas may be singled out for mention.[28]

Such a hasty historical rundown gives us an idea of the menu but does not tell us which dish to order. Speaking from within the tradition of the Dominican Order, I will be forgiven for saying a word more about the enduring value of the second historical epoch, that of Christianized Aristoteleanism (which included, by the way, a fairly hefty dose of Platonism also). For Thomists, the philosophy of St. Thomas perfectly expresses the mediating position mentioned above.[29] The philosophical elements in Thomas' thought are rationally cogent, and they reflect areas of concern close to the heart of the Christian faith. For the most militant Thomists, the philosophical part of Thomism constitutes a sort of eternal philosophy, *philosophia perennis,* a system of philosophical thought which cannot really be bettered except in details. What are the elements in Thomism that have called forth such

26. J. C. Weinsheimer, *Gadamer's Hermeneutics* (New Haven and London: 1985); R. C. Holmes, *Reception Theory: A Critical Introduction* (London: 1984).

27. For a wide-ranging study, *see* F. Kerr, *Theology After Wittgenstein* (Oxford: 1987).

28. *See,* for instance, B. Forthomme, *Une philosophie de transcendance: La métaphysique d'Emmanuel Lévinas* (Paris: 1979).

29. A good guide is E. Gilson, *The Christian Philosophy of St. Thomas Aquinas* (English trans., London: 1961). For Gilson's own place on the Thomist spectrum, *see* J. M. Quinn, *The Thomism of Etienne Gilson: A Critical Study* (Villanova: 1971).

extravagant claims? At least five features of Thomist philosophy render it particularly attractive to Catholic theologians. These may be rapidly enumerated. First, there is the fact that Thomism begins from sense experience. As the celebrated Thomist adage puts it, "Nothing is in the mind that was not first in the senses." This means that Thomists share common ground with the ordinary person, both *l'homme moyen sensuel* and the good pagan enquiring about the truth of the Catholic faith. Second, on the basis of reflection about what is involved in this process of knowing things through the senses, Thomism comes to describe the human mind itself and to prove—at least to its own satisfaction—that the mind is immaterial and so immortal. Third, from a consideration of certain general features of the world as perceived in ordinary experience, Thomism hopes to show that this world is dependent on an unlimited source, which "all men call God." Fourth, Thomism regards all realities save God as a unity of form and matter, that is, of a communicative intelligibility and an individuating principle of identity. This matter-and-form or hylomorphic analysis of things is highly suitable to a sacramental religion like Christianity. The Church sees the presence of God as expressed through material realities—the humanity of Jesus, the sacraments, which are his extended action, and so forth—and thus as having an incarnational structure which lends itself to hylomorphic description.[30] Finally, because of the Thomist principle that an effect must resemble in some way what caused it, Thomism has worked out a theory of analogy whereby certain qualities found in the world are ascribed to God, though in a way that quite surpasses our conceptual understanding.[31] Thomist philosophy can thus build up a picture of the divine nature by describing the perfections—goodness, unity, beauty, and so on—which belong ultimately and supremely to God but which are also found in various limited ways in this world. Thomism, in sum, claims to be able to speak to all people on the basis of shared experience, to prove to them that they have immortal souls, and that there is a God on whose existence this world depends. Furthermore, it encourages them to see material things as expressing meaning and so prepares them for the idea of the incarnation and for its corollary, the sacramental principle in the life of the Church. Finally, its God is not simply an unknown God but can to some extent be spoken of in terms of perfection.

---

30. W. A. Wallace, "Hylomorphism," NCE 7, 284–85.
31. M. T.-L. Penido, *Le rôle de l'Analogie en théologie dogmatique* (Paris: 1931); E. L. Mascall, *Existence and Analogy* (London: 1949).

In all these ways, Thomism seems manifestly a good thing. Why, then, are there so many dissenters, so many people who, especially over the last thirty years, have become discontented with the Thomist dominance of Catholic thought? The objection is not so much to any particular conclusion that Thomists may come up with but to the very idea of a *philosophia perennis*, a once-for-all philosophy that will remain forever the chosen handmaid of theology. And this objection seems to be partly correct. All philosophies take their rise from meditation on some particular aspect of experience. To the degree that Thomism is Christianized Aristoteleanism, this would be, primarily, our experience of the natural order; in other philosophies, it might be our experience of historical change, or of ourselves and each other as persons. On the basis of such a slice of human experience, a philosophy tries to come to a universal statement about reality. But the likelihood is that in this a given philosophy will be to some degree selective. Precisely because of its (necessarily) limited starting point, it will see some things better than others, be strong on some aspects of the real and weak on others. If this is true, then theologians should welcome a certain philosophical eclecticism. They should be happy to draw on more than one philosophical tradition, so long, of course, as this does not lead them into plain self-contradiction and so into nonsense. Hence the importance for theologians of acquaintance with the history of philosophy, which is a storehouse of concepts that may well be of great use to them in their work.[32] In this, theological students will need the same kind of historical sensitivity that the investigation of their strictly theological resources also asks of them, for, whereas philosophers, like theologians, are now mainly to be found in universities where they are salaried and professionally qualified, with their work proceeding in specialist books, periodicals, and conferences, operating with very limited audiences, in the past this has not been so. "In the past, philosophy has been conducted in quite different environments: in informal schools that met in corners on the Athenian market-place, or in monasteries under the auspices and intellectual authority of the Church, or as an aspect of salon-life in the eighteenth century cities.[33]"

32. Hence the usefulness to the student of such compendia as F. Copleston, *A History of Philosophy* (London: 1946–75); *The Encyclopaedia of Philosophy*, ed. P. Edwards (New York and London: 1967); J. Hirschberger, *Geschichte der Philosophie* (2nd ed., Freiburg 1954–55); *Storia della filosofia*, ed. C. Fabro (Rome: 1954).

33. J. Waldron, "The forums of the ages," commenting on D. W. Hamlyn, *A History of Western Philosophy*, in the *Times Literary Supplement* for April 10, 1987, no. 4384.

As may be imagined, these differing environments have had their effect on such tasks as making an argument, criticizing and responding to criticism, and developing a sustained view on issues that, by their very nature, strain the expressive capacities of thought and language.

And yet, although because of this historical variety with its built-in possibility that something missed in one age or milieu will be understood in another, the objection to a *philosophia perennis* turns out to be, in one sense, quite justified; in another, it is surely misplaced. We cannot be totally eclectic. We have to choose some fundamental way of reading the structure of the universe. Into this fundamental pattern we can then go on to insert extra elements drawn from alternative philosophies. We need a kind of bread-and-butter philosophy to give us our basic diet before we add the honey and jam of other philosophies to enrich and supplement the basic philosophy. And in the choice of such a skeletal structure, Thomism still has much to commend it. In fact, we can say that by disengaging the notion of "being" as the central notion, whether explicitly or implicitly, of all philosophical thinking, Thomism has provided us with the key to the unity in plurality of the philosophical history which the theologian should study. The history of philosophy is the history of the different ways in which "being" is conceived and encountered.[34] Further, the fundamental way of reading the universe which we select must have some kind of family resemblance to Thomism in that it must satisfy certain demands, implied by divine revelation and met in Thomism in an exemplary way. I have in mind such notions as, first, the transcendence of the human beings vis-à-vis the physical world; second, the correlate of this transcendence in the absolutely infinite being, God; third, the creative freedom of this transcendent universal cause of the world and thus the nondivinity of the world's own being; fourth, the independence of human beings in their moral agency, a self-determination which extends beyond death; and fifth, the unity of all human beings as a single order within the world.[35] Theologians may use philosophies whose affirmations fall short of these exigencies in limited aspects of their work; but the total infrastructure of a Catholic theology must, in its sum of elements, do justice to such requirements as these.

34. F. O'Farrell, "Is There a History of To Be?" *Gregorianum* 68. 3–4 (1987) 671–703.

35. *See* W. Kern, "Observaciones a la cuestión: Una filosofía plural (como medio de una teología plural)?" in *El pluralismo teológico* (Madrid: 1976) 219–30. The original, not accessible to me, was published as *Die Einheit des Glaubens und der theologische Pluralismus* (Einsideln: 1973).

4

The Existence and Concept of God

The Chrisitan faith presupposes certain truths of reason and of history. Without these it cannot make sense and its theology cannot become airborne. First of all, the Christian faith presupposes that there is a God. It is no use telling people that Jesus is the Son of God if they do not believe in God in the first place. Of course, the concept of God which a pagan possesses will need to be modified in the light of the account of God offered in the Church's preaching. But this is a question of, precisely, modifying, transforming in certain respects something which is already present (or at least, should be) in the mind of the person who has not yet entered the Church. The Old Testament teaches that the true God is Yahweh, God of Israel. The New Testament teaches that this same Yahweh is more fully known when we can say of him that he is the Father of Jesus Christ. But to receive either of these pieces of intelligence we must have some idea of what is meant by saying that the true God is X or Y in the first place. The word "God," after all, is not a biblical word; that is, it is not a transliteration of a personal name occurring in the Scriptures. "God" is a Germanic word for the divine realm, and its origins lie far back in the experience of our pagan ancestors. The same is true for the French *Dieu*, cognate with the Latin *Deus*, itself linked to the Greek *Theos*. All of these words are indebted to a religious sensibility which antedates Christianity by hundreds if not thousands of years. The philosopher's task in this regard is to ask whether this language about the divine realm corresponds to anything in reality: whether, in short, there is a God. So this is the first philosophical element in the preamble of faith that we must deal with.

There is no general consensus among Catholic writers as to the best way of establishing the existence of God, the supreme presupposition of our faith. The First Vatican Council, in the course of

55

the document *Dei Filius*, had occasion, however, to frame a declaration in these words: "The one and true God, our Creator and Lord, can be known through the creation by the natural light of human reason."[1] We can gloss the council's teaching by saying that images of the divine found in natural religion in all cultures can be purified so as to produce a concept of God as the Creator Lord, the source of nature and history alike. And further, this concept can be shown to have application, to be actually exemplified in reality "through the natural light of human reason." So the First Vatican Council insisted that a rational discovery of God's existence is always possible, but it refrained from saying how one should in practice set about it. It is easy to caricature the council Fathers as saying, "Of course there's a proof of God's existence; the only trouble is that nobody's found it." But the council did not mean to do theologians' work for them. As Karl Rahner once put it, definitions are much less an end than a beginning. The theologian has the right, in other words, to choose those materials from which he or she hopes to construct an approach to God's existence.

To give an idea of the possible richness of choice here I will mention six kinds of material that could give philosophically minded theologians their cue—each being both an experiential signal and a kind of argument. First of all, there is the experience of wonder at the fact that there is a world at all. All of us are familiar with wonder before certain particular things: the colors of dawn, the grace of an athlete, the intricate workings of an organ like the eye. But sometimes we generalize this sense of wonder and extend it to the fact that there is a world at all. In this case the object of wonder is not the particular world we live in, which is a sum total of the particular things that exist, but the consideration that there should be any particular world at all. After all, there is nothing logically entailed in the concept of a world which makes us say, Of course, I realize that there had to be a world. Writers as diverse as Ludwig Wittgenstein and G. K. Chesterton have regarded this sort of experience as philosophically important.[2] From it there emerges the argument that since the world is not self-explanatory, or ontologically self-sufficient, it requires us to postulate a ground for it. Such a ground would have to be transcendent vis-à-vis the world; that is, it could not be less than the world itself. But the notion of the tran-

---

1. DS, 3004.

2. N. Malcolm, *Ludwig Wittgenstein: A Memoir* (London: 1958) 70; for Chesterton, see A. Nichols, "G. K. Chesterton's Argument for the Existence of God," *The Chesterton Review* 20. 1 (1986) 63–70.

scendent ground of the world is at any rate a part of what people mean by God.

Second, a very different kind of experience relevant here is the experience of moral obligation.[3] From time to time we do things not because it is in our interest to do them but because they are intrinsically right. If we left them undone, we might say, we could not live with ourselves. The voice of conscience would not let us be. In such a case, it is not just that as a matter of rational ethics we would knowingly have done the wrong thing. Beyond this, our sense of what is involved in doing the wrong thing can be at times terrifying. It is almost as though we were in the presence of a judge of irreproachable character who saw us and was obliged by his own righteousness to condemn us. Expressed less pictorially, the values we put into our system of values (whatever these may be) do not entirely behave as things we have created. We seem to be tributary to them, rather than the other way round. Those who do not care for the implications of such experiences of moral obligation may hypothesize that they derive from the effects of parental conditioning upon us. Either our own parents or that corporate parent we call society has put a taboo on certain ways of behaving, and the taboo sticks. When we defy it we are covered with feelings of guilt, just as if we have offended a wonderfully good and sensitive person. But on the other hand, some of the most interesting examples of conscience must surely be those that occur to individuals who, having assessed facts and arguments, feel obliged to depart from some prior moral consensus and break through to a new level of moral awareness. So the experience of obligation is not so easily cut down to size, and it points toward the existence of a supremely holy one as its own ultimate explication. This was Newman's own preferred approach to transcendence.[4]

A third kind of experience relevant here is the experience of our own dissatisfaction. This may seem a strange sort of starting point for an argument in metaphysics, but dissatisfaction with any of the objects we can attain in this world must surely be the greatest single source of religious belief. Genetically, we are not programmed in such a way that we can know from the outset what objects will bring us satisfaction. Of course we have certain drives—toward physical nourishment, sexual intimacy, and so forth. But the satisfaction of these

3. See H. P. Owen, *The Moral Argument for Christian Theism* (London: 1965).
4. A. K. Boekraad, *The Argument from Conscience to the Existence of God According to J. H. Newman* (Louvain: 1961).

drives is not exactly *our* satisfaction. We may satisfy them as much as we will, and yet when we are finished we are still left with such questions as What is the meaning of life? Where will I find lasting happiness? and so on. None of these questions, it may be said, finds any full solution within the world. So the further question suggests itself, If a being exists has no goal within the world, a being whose desire to know and need to love appears to be in some sense endless, then perhaps the goal of this creature's striving lies beyond the world in what the religions of the world call God. The Greek Father Gregory of Nyssa already came near to this conative argument for God (from the Latin verb *conare*, "to strive": we are striving for something beyond this world, and it seems more reasonable to posit that something as the ground of our striving rather than to write off our striving as absurd, something strictly unintelligible.)[5]

A fourth dimension of human existence that fits in here is the experience of hope. We all have hopes for particular things. We hope for peace in our time, for nice friends, for a better book on introducing Catholic theology. But this is not the experience of hope I am thinking of. What I have in mind is that general attitude of hopefulness as a response to the future which so many people evince in quite impossible situations, and which seems almost a necessary condition for the survival of humanity in hard times. People hope against hope that tyranny will be ended; that their children's children will live to inherit this planet. But even if the worst happened, even if an evil government possessed itself of the world or a nuclear holocaust devoured the earth tomorrow, people would still go on hoping amidst the ruins. They would crawl out of the holes and burrows and start to pick up the pieces. This is natural to us because it is natural to us to hope. The question is, Does this point to anything metaphysical? It could be argued, as did French philosopher and dramatist Gabriel Marcel, that it suggests an unconscious grasp of the reality of God as the ground and guarantor of human history, of human destiny.[6]

---

5. On Gregory's crucial notion of *epektasis, see* J. Daniélou, *Platonisme et théologie mystique: Doctrine spirituelle de saint Grégoire de Nysse* (Paris: 1944, 1953) 291–307; cf. H. Mühlenberg, *Die Unendlichkeit Gottes bei Gregor von Nyssa* (Göttingen: 1966). A modern form of the same notion is found in F. C. Copleston, *Religion and Philosophy* (Dublin: 1974), who writes that the search for a metaphysical ultimate is based on "an experience of limits, coupled with a reaching out towards that which transcends and grounds all limits."

6. Cf. C. Moeller, "Gabriel Marcel et le mystère de l'espérance," in idem., *Littérature du XXe siècle et christianisme* 4, 149–57.

Another area that repays investigation in this regard is that of mystical experience. A large number of people in various cultures have
laid claim to direct experience of the divine. Some of these people may
have been mad, and some may have been bad. Their claims may have
been made through self-delusion or by the deliberate desire to obtain
power, prestige, or money. But where records are copious, in the case
of figures who most impressed, therefore, their contemporaries, the
mystics give an impression of integrity rather than its opposite. Certainly, mystics have described their experiences in terms drawn from
the religious tradition in which they were at home: Muslim mystics
encounter Allah; Jewish mystics the *Shekinah*, or "Glory of the Lord";
Christian mystics the Trinity. But this does not necessarily invalidate
their witness. We would expect that they would use concepts and images already familiar to them to interpret a reality by definition beyond
concepts and images, namely God. Whether the concepts and images
used by one mystic, for example St. Teresa of Avila, correspond more
to the nature of the true God than do the concepts and images of
another mystic, say, the Muslim al-Hallaj, would have to be decided
on other grounds. But all the mystics share the assertion that they have
encountered what we can call the eternal reality—however they pic-
tured the reality in question. Such a weight of human testimony from
so many different cultures cannot easily be dismissed. This is, in part,
the approach to God's existence favored by the English Benedictine
philosopher Illtyd Trethowan.[7]

Sixth and finally, I would draw attention to the epistemological
argument for the existence of God associated with the late Fr. Bernard
Lonergan of the Society of Jesus. Lonergan proposed that the main
cue we need to move toward an affirmation of God's existence is found
in the very knowability of the world. For some reason, the world has
a structure such that the human mind can penetrate it by means of
its own processes of thought. How can we account for this fact? It might
have been the case that human beings had intelligence but that the
world was not amenable to exploration by that intelligence. There could
have been a lack of fit between the world and the human mind. But
in point of fact, there is not; on the contrary, there is considerable harmony between them as, among other things, the fruits of scientific
knowledge in technology demonstrate. It is argued, therefore, that the
world's intelligibility requires us to posit the existence of a creative

7. I. Trethowan, *Mysticism and Philosophy* (London: 1979).

mind, analogous to but infinitely transcending the human mind, by which the cosmos was brought into being.[8]

So much for the six main kinds of approach that have historically been popular. The list is not exhaustive. It could be extended by, for example, reference to the fact that we have a language for perfection— better known as the "ontological argument." Nothing prevents our combining these approaches on the principle that the sum total of a number of individually less-than-convincing arguments may be a convincing case. This was, as it happens, John Henry Newman's strategy in his *Essay in Aid of a Grammar of Consent*, published during the First Vatican Council, in 1870. There Newman offered a new context in which to display the various argumentative strategies and the strata of experience that are relevant to belief in God. Earlier, Newman had worked out a distinction between explicit and implicit reason, pointing out that in ordinary everyday affairs we make judgments about people and events without following any strict logical progression, any mode of explicit reason. Instead, we gather together a whole series of experiential clues and pieces of argumentation. These fragments of experience and argument then act as signals that point us in the direction of a true conclusion, which is attained, therefore, by implicit reason. In the *Grammar of Assent* Newman further refined this idea in relation to the basic tenets of Christian theism, dubbing such a manner of arriving at certitude about something or someone the "illative sense." In a jigsaw, when you spread out the pieces on a table, all you seem to have is a complete jumble, an accidental collection of bits and pieces that tell you nothing. But put them together and you have a picture. So Newman's suggestion is that we can defend belief in God by putting together a number of experiential signals and lines of thought, which converge on the conclusion that there is a God.[9]

Following Newman, it may be suggested that while none of these arguments taken singly might be wholly compelling, taken cumulatively they amount to a very strong case. This case may fall short of strict demonstration. But no matter: at least it shows that it is more reasonable to believe in God's existence than not. Clearly, if we were unable to show that it is at least as reasonable to believe in God's existence as it is not to, being a believer at all would be an irrational exercise. But more than this, as Catholic Christians with a duty to the

---

8. *See* H. Meynell, *The Intelligible Universe* (London: 1982).

9. A. Nichols, "John Henry Newman and the Illative Sense: A Re-Consideration," *Scottish Journal of Theology* 38. 3 (1985) 347–68.

Church's conciliar tradition, we are expected to say that it is in fact *more* reasonable to believe in God's existence. For whatever force is given to the assertion on this topic in *Dei Filius*, it surely cannot mean less than this.

Here, however, a fresh problem surfaces. We have accepted that the existence of the Creator Lord, who is also the God of Jesus Christ, can be known by the natural light of human reason. But this cannot leave untouched the concept of God found in Christianity: the way we think about *what* God is, not simply *that* he is. Whatever arguments we feel disposed to accept in this area must influence very markedly our theological concept of God. Any way of saying *that* God is carries implications for *what* he is. For a Christian, admittedly, the concept of God should be shaped primarily by revelation. If the Bible, and in particular the teaching of Jesus and his apostles, has nothing radically new to say to us about this, then we are scarcely Christian theologians at all. Nevertheless, a certain input from philosophy into the Christian concept of God can be defended as both necessary and desirable. How so?

First, such philosophical input is necessary. The typical form of the proclamation of a revealed religion is not, You have never heard that there is a God. I am here to tell you that there is. Quite the opposite: revealed religion presupposes that people already have some notion of God. The characteristic form of a proclamation of a revealed religion is, You already know something of what God is. I am here to give you new insight into the character of the God you worship. An excellent example of this is provided by St. Paul's speech to the Athenians at the Areopagus, as recounted in the Acts of the Apostles: "Paul stood up in full view of the Areopagus and said, 'Men of Athens, wherever I look I find you scrupulously religious. Why, in examining your monuments as I passed by them, I found among others an altar which bore the inscription, ''To the unknown God.'' And it is this unknown object of your devotion that I am revealing to you.' "[10] Any reader who comes from a part of the world with a strong religious tradition other than Christianity will understand at once what Paul meant. In the post-Christian West, on the other hand, there is effectively no religious tradition other than Christianity, at least at the level of the culture in possession. But this does not mean that there is no common ground between the post-Christian and the Christian in discourse

10. Acts 17:22-23.

about God. The post-Christian has, or can have, some concept of God on the basis of his or her reflection on the world. This concept of God may not be expressed in a highly philosophical way, yet it will be capable of reexpression in a more rigorous form. And, of course, among professional philosophers the debate about God is conducted in terms of this rational concept of God, which owes comparatively little, at any rate in a direct way, to the Judeo-Christian revelation. When people at large talk about God, they do not think in the first place of the Trinity, although the Trinity is the fundamental Christian determination of God, the way we modify the concept of God on the basis of the life and work of Jesus Christ. They think rather of that concept of God held in common by philosophical theism and revealed religion alike: the one God, the Creator Lord. In order to connect, therefore, with the preconception of God which many people have, Christian missionaries and apologists are forced, willy-nilly, to draw on this prior awareness as well as amateur or professional conceptualization of what God is like. Thus a certain philosophical contribution to the Christian concept of God is in practice inescapable.

But such a contribution is also desirable. It might *prima facie* be thought better to deal with people where possible as religious virgins or innocents: to get at them before they have had time to develop a concept of God which might be at odds with the Christian one. Then the biblical data about God could be preserved in strict isolation from any other influence that might contaminate them or water them down. But this would not be a good thing for two reasons. In the first place, in the Catholic tradition we hold that there is such a thing as natural revelation. Through the fact of creation, God has given man a certain knowledge of himself, however little this may be appreciated. This knowledge may be said to exist in two forms. In theory form, it exists in the shape of the philosophical understanding of God to which reason can give us access. In practical form, it exists as certain human kinds of behavior, of which those embedded in the world's religions through the making of myths and rituals are the most central. At the same time, a significant penumbra surrounds these in the arts, as also, if one may trust the reports of the Swiss psychologist C. G. Jung, in dream archetypes. Although such knowledge of God can be, and possibly usually is, undermined to some degree by false ideas about God, it is not wholly so. God has not left himself without witnesses.

A second reason why it would not be desirable for theologians to seek to exclude all philosophical, or pretheological, elements from their account of God is that the revelation contained in Scripture and tradition is insufficient, taken purely by itself, to give us a coherent and systematic concept of God. One might object, But who wants a coherent and systematic concept of God? Doesn't the very idea of a systematic concept of God show that we haven't understood the primary feature of the notion of God, namely that God is a mystery, and more specifically following St. John, a mystery of love? You cannot systematize a mystery, especially a mystery of love. There is something to this objection, but I would respond to it by saying that a satisfactory theological concept of God will indicate where it is appropriate to invoke mystery and where to do so would be unnecessary defeatism. If we could say nothing at all in describing God, then preaching, teaching, catechetics, and theology would manifestly dry up. Yet any claim that we could fully comprehend the divine nature (such as was made by the heretic Eunomius in the patristic Church) only proves that we have not grasped the logical place of the concept of God at all. We need to know, therefore, when is a time to speak, and when a time to keep silence. Having conceded so much, however, there remains a lot we can say. The trouble is that the biblical materials for a concept of God do not organize themselves. They do not automatically arrange themselves into a satisfactory form. They achieve that form only when the human mind, seeking to understand its own faith, begins to work on them and to set them out in more intelligible ways.

To organize the biblical materials, we soon find that we need to draw on such philosophical categories as good and evil, freedom and necessity, person and nature, mind and will, essence and existence, being and knowing. Of course, the application of these notions to God is an attempt to speak of what lies beyond the world within terms drawn from this world, and so is only justified if we always add a postscript to the effect, These terms are borrowed clothes but they are the best we have. They are being pressed into service by what Thomists would call analogy. The content of ideas like those I have just listed is already known to be patient of application to different sorts of reality in different ways. Take, for instance, the uses of the idea of the good. A good action is different from a good person, and both are very different from a good breakfast. Because such concepts are so open and flexible and appear applicable in some shape or form to an enormous variety of beings, we apply their content to the source of all that is. At the same time, we admit that we do not know the precise way in which such ideas correspond to God's reality. Again, we might say, for example, that God is supremely spirit, his knowledge and love per-

fect archetypes of our own. Yet what the inner life of one whose existence is perfect knowledge and love might be like we can neither
conceive nor imagine. Yet despite their limitations, such notions are
useful for the philosophical filling out of the concept of God. Needless to say, I am not proposing that in these matters philosophy has
the last word. Immanuel Kant once remarked that if philosophy is the
handmaid of theology, that is because she goes before her mistress
carrying the lamp that enables theology to see.[11] If we accept this image
we must add that in a Christian household, without theology's instruc-
tions the maid would not know what route she was supposed to take.
A Christian concept of God is one in which the philosophical materials for the concept of God have been reworked by exposing them to
the influence of Christian revelation as found in Bible and Tradition.
The revelation of God as Father and of God as Trinity will evidently
transform any ideas of God we have thought up for ourselves.

So much by way of defending the philosopher's contribution to
the conceptualization of God. What about its concrete content? We can
think of this, I suggest, in two ways. First, the particular arguments
for God's existence we choose to follow will play a part in determining those ideas of God that we can think up for ourselves. The argument from wonder, for instance, leads to a source or ground of the
world, an underived being from which all other beings draw their existence. The argument from conscience leads to the affirmation of an
ethically perfect Spirit immediately present to our spirits. The argument from hope leads to the affirmation of a Providence that takes
thought for human destiny within the cosmos—and so on. The human
experiences on which these arguments are based are, as it were, the
faint reflections of various aspects of the divine being itself. Our exploration of the world, including the inner world of our specifically
human awareness, leads in this way to a discovery—partial, but
precious—of the divine attributes. It is because this is so that we should
be careful not to excommunicate too quickly any approach to God for
fear that with it we may have lost sight of some dimension of God
himself.

But this in itself is not enough. The structure of argument to the
existence of God which I have commended, that of Newman, makes
space for a variety of subarguments found in the tradition of Christian
theism and drawn from a corresponding variety of areas of experience

11. I. Kant, "Der Streit der Fakultäten," in *Werke* 6, ed. Weischedel, 261–93, and here
at 291.

and reflection. Each of these subarguments will provide some kind of way in to the divine mystery and so some foundation for a conceptualization of God. But if any subargument can provide a basis for conceiving God, and if there are many subarguments, the concept of God we shall end up with will necessarily be incoherent and unsystematic. This problem afflicts not only the Newmanian approach but any approach to God's existence which is not via just one argument. And after all, Thomas had "five ways" and Kant at least two, the argument from the conditions of moral action in the *Critique of Practical Reason* and the argument (Kant prefers to call it an "impression") from our experience of beauty in the *Critique of Judgment*. So we cannot base our philosophical conceptualization of God solely on our approach to God's existence.

We need to look, then, for what we can call a "root metaphysical concept" suitable to the task. And this is the second way in which we give conceptual content to the philosophical idea of God. This search for a root metaphysical concept has provided varying answers within the Christian practice of metaphysics. Thus for Bonaventure, the root metaphysical concept was that of the good; for Thomas, it was that of *ens a se:* "wholly independent being"; for the Scotists, it was the idea of radical infinity. For later Thomists, such as the seventeenth-century Spanish Dominican John of St. Thomas, it was pure knowing; for Kant it was the concept of the *ens perfectissimum*, the "most perfect being"; for Schelling, the idea of infinite freedom; for Hegel that of the true infinite: a spirit whose essence it is to render itself an object for itself in order then to remove this distinction through love.[12] In most, if not all, of these cases, the root metaphysical concept is connected with arguments for God's existence, but those arguments do not produce the root metaphysical concept directly or inevitably. A judgment has been made about how to order the picture of God which the arguments for God's existence suggest. In any given theology, this judgment will coexist in a dialectical fashion with Bible and Tradition. On the basis of Bible and Tradition we will want to modify the metaphysical judgment and to go beyond it. But at the same time, the judgment will help us to get a hold on the materials relevant to the concept of God within the sources of Christian revelation.

---

12. I am indebted for these suggestions of historic examples to Alfred Wilder, of the faculty of philosophy of the Pontifical University of St. Thomas, Rome.

5
Theodicy and the Idea of Salvation

In the last chapter we encountered philosophy in the process of aiding and abetting fundamental theology by its contribution to the preamble of faith on the topic of God's existence. At the same time, we predicted that philosophy would also assist systematic theology by making a contribution to the concept of God—giving us a valuable preunderstanding of what God is like, an inkling which can throw light on what we find in the sources of revelation. Naturally, most of us come to all this the other way round: we get to know the revealed God through Christ's Church, and only then do we enquire into the philosophical basis of the concept of God. But this only tells us something that is true about our autobiographies, not something true about the structure of the concept of God in itself. In this chapter I want to turn to another area of the preamble of faith closely connected with a discussion of the existence and concept of God, and this is theodicy— or what is often referred to as the "problem of evil." As we shall see, theodicy (from *theos* and *dikê*, "justice," hence "enquiry into the divine justice") is also doubly relevant in theology, to fundamentals and to systematics. In fundamental theology, theodicy is important because we need to show that the existence of God is compatible with the existence of evil, of what we can call the "major defects" of the world. In systematic theology, theodicy is important because our grasp of what could (logically) be remedied among these major defects will give us a preunderstanding of the idea of salvation; and the theme of salvation is well-nigh the central motif of revelation's sources, Scripture and Tradition.

To exemplify the point, we might wish to argue that adolescence, though often painful, is built into the very idea of humanity. We could not conceive of adult persons who were fully human but never had to go through the process of becoming an independent self, a process we call growing up. If this is so, then we cannot use the tribulations of adolescence, real as these are, to cast doubt on the existence of an all-good and all-powerful God—always assuming that we regard the creation of *Homo sapiens* as a boon to the cosmos. On the other hand, we might well regard the destruction of the innocent (say, of babies by leukemia) as evidence against the postulate of God. Thus, if we decide that despite such counterindications we can accept, as theodicists, the reality of God, these counterindications will pass over into another category, namely, our preunderstanding of soteriology, the idea of salvation. Putting a stop to the suffering of the innocent is the kind of thing we would expect the Creator to do if ever he began to relate to the world in a new way—not as Creator but as Redeemer. Here I am anticipating my argument, but so as to give the reader a glimpse of the importance of this area.

Theodicy is a problem which has exercised Christian minds through the ages when wrestling with the issue of the existence of God. St. Thomas, for instance, gives it as the chief intellectual obstacle to Christian theism. He formulates the objection in his customary sharp way: "It seems that God does not exist; because if one of two contraries be infinite, the other would be altogether destroyed. But the name 'God' means that he is infinite goodness. If, therefore, God existed there would be no evil discoverable; but there is evil in the world. Therefore God does not exist."[1] To understand why evil is a philosophical problem of this magnitude for the Christian, we must remind ourselves of the Church's basic confession about God. Christianity, here reflecting its own source in Judaism, ascribes to God both all-powerfulness and all-goodness. And indeed, quite apart from the fact that this is the (overall) witness of Old and New Testaments, a number of the arguments for the existence of God touched on in the last chapter also point to these qualities as characteristic of transcendence. For example, to say that God is the infinite ground of the world is to come fairly close to saying that he is almighty; and to say that he is the explanation of our sense of absolute moral obligation comes fairly close to saying that he is all-good. Given, then, that both a pretheological and a specifically Christian consensus points to God as enjoying both these characteristics (and both ancient and modern deviations therefrom have had a frosty reception by Catholic believers), the problem of evil must be confronted. Ever since the ancient Greeks it has been formulated as a dilemma; we possess a lapidary example

1. Thomas Aquinas, *Summa theologiae* Ia, q. 2, a. 3.

from the pen of the Latin Christian apologist Lactantius: "God either wishes to take away evils, and is unable; or he is able, and is unwilling; or he is neither willing nor able, or he is both willing and able. If he is willing and is unable, he is feeble—which is not in accordance with the character of God. If he is able and unwilling, he is envious, which is equally at variance with God; if he is neither willing nor able, he is both envious and feeble, and therefore not God; if he is both willing and able, which alone is suitable to God, from what source then are evils? Or why does he not remove them?"[2]

What kind of reflection has there been on this issue in the tradition of Christian thought? From time to time Christians have attempted to resolve Lactantius' dilemma while writing strictly as philosophers; thus, for instance, we find the highly original system of Gottfried Wilhelm Leibniz (1646–1716),[3] or in a Thomist idiom in our own time, the work of the late Père Ambroise Sertillanges.[4] But it has become customary, at least in the English-speaking world, to identify the two most ubiquitous "solutions" by reference to two Church Fathers and therefore to writers in whom there is as yet no clear or systematic distinction between philosophy and theology. The more influential of these two types of theodicy is that associated with St. Augustine of Hippo (354–430).[5] This Augustinian theodicy consists basically of four points. First, it is argued that evil is not a positive reality in its own right. It is not an illusion, but it is a kind of negative reality, a privation or deprivation of something that should have been there but is not. Because evil is such a *privatio boni,* an absence of the good, Augustinians argue that it cannot be an element in the ultimate reality, which is God. Second, having proposed an ontological statute for evil, we must give an account of its origin. So far as evil conceived and executed by finite minds (moral evil) is concerned, its source may be located in free will. If God has created finite spirits endowed with free will, it must be expected that this free will is going to be abused. From such sin there flows certain other aspects of human suffering, such as the physical pain inflicted by evil people, or the fear and anxiety which good people undergo when faced with the prospect of evil people. From moral evil there may also follow kinds of suffering which could be seen as divine

[margin handwritten: Augustinian theodicy]

---

2. Lactantius, *De ira Dei,* 13.

3. Leibniz' *Théodicée* of 1710 actually coined the word. For his account, *see* N. *Rescher, Leibniz: An Introduction to His Philosophy* (Oxford: 1979) 146–62.

4. A. D. Sertillanges, *Le problème du Mal* (Paris: 1948–51).

5. I follow here the account given in J. Hick, *Evil and the God of Love* (London: 1966) 43–95, *see also* G. R. Evans, *Augustine on Evil* (Cambridge: 1982).

punishment for sin (natural disasters and the like). Third, while it may be true that the essential limitedness of everything created (metaphysical evil) is responsible for many of the imperfections of this world, Augustinians affirm that it was nevertheless right that God should have made such a world as ours. To show why this is so, they appeal to what has been called a "principle of plenitude." The principle of plenitude states that the richest and most desirable universe contains every possible kind of existence: lower and higher, imperfect and (relatively) perfect, ugly and beautiful, cholera germs and humming-birds. Finally, and connected with this third point, the Augustinian type of theodicy is often said to be "aesthetic" in character. By this is not meant that its exponents express themselves rather prettily but that they see all realities and events as englobed within a universal harmony. Even sin and its punishment belongs to this harmony, just as in music a discordant note, when resolved, makes a work more satisfying. Unfortunately, this harmony is only fully audible to God.[6]

The second and less influential theodicy has been referred to as "Irenaean," after the Greek Father St. Irenaeus, who was martyred as bishop of Lyons around the year 200.[7] This alternative theodicy sees the world as essentially an environment, a difficult, sometimes agonizingly difficult environment in which the human spirit is refined by fire. The world is a "vale for soul making." Irenaeus saw moral evil not as an interior catastrophe but as a matter of weakness and immaturity. Accordingly, Irenaeans regard the natural evil present in this world not so much as a divine punishment for the abuse of free will, but rather as an aspect of a divinely appointed milieu, an ambience of mingled good and evil, which is just what we need for growth toward perfection. In this way, the Irenaean theodicy appears to place the ultimate responsibility for much of the world's evil on the shoulders of its Creator. But at the same time it seeks to show that it was for a good reason that he created a world where evil is built in. The ultimate purpose of creation is the production of fully matured persons interacting in charity and so reflecting the life of God himself. At the end of historical time, finite persons will be greater and better because of their conflict with evil than they would be otherwise. The claim that there cannot be an all-powerful and all-good God because the creation as we know it is partly hostile to human happiness is misconceived in that it implicitly defines happiness as "having a grand old time." This world

6. *Ibid.*, 175–206.
7. *Ibid.*, 207–24.

was not meant to be a paradise, a garden enclosed, but a milieu in which the most valuable potentialities of persons are drawn out by the challenges, often terrible challenges, which that milieu contains. Any other view of the character of human life, so Irenaeans maintain, would turn us from persons into pampered animals or spoiled brats.[8]

The Irenaean theodicy joins hands with its main competitor by echoing the Augustinian idea that God as Providence can draw good out of evil—itself posited philosophically, as we have seen, in Marcel's argument to God from the phenomenon of hope. Irenaeans argue that it is precisely the sort of world we have that an all-powerful and all-good God would have made, and that while we cannot at present visualize the final state of affairs that will justify the presence of evil in the world's history, we *can* see that to expect such a final satisfactory resolution of the story is not irrational.

Needless to say, not all of these arguments have met with an equally glowing reception. Before considering the main criticisms that may be launched against them, we should note that were they in themselves an adequate and total vindication of the "justice of God," it would be exceedingly hard to find room for the theological concept of redemption, a concept which, however, lies at the heart of Christian faith. Thus Christian theodicists, aiming for total victory, swing their sabers and cut off their own heads. With this caveat in mind, let us return to the two types of theodicy, beginning with the Augustinian and its four pillars of wisdom: the privative theory of evil, the free-will defense, the principle of plenitude, and the notion of cosmic harmony.

Obj. to
Augustine

The idea that evil is essentially an absence of what ought to be a presence, that, for instance, blindness is a failure in the proper action of the eye, not an extra reality added to the eye's reality, certainly succeeds in dispensing us from having to ascribe evil to the Creator. Evil is not something God has made because evil is not something. It is important to notice that this meontic "not being" account of evil is a metaphysical and not an empirical or observational affair. That is, it does not claim to tell us what evil feels like. A tidal wave, one imagines, feels like very far from nothing, and the same may be said of the personality of Adolf Hitler. However, we might wish to ask whether a theory of the ontological status of evil can depart too far from the facts of experience and still stay credible. The meontic theory is fine when

8. *See* A. Orbe, *La antropología de san Ireneo* (Madrid: 1969).

trying to explain what happens when a carton of cream turns sour, but it is less successful in coping with the individual who says ''Evil, be thou my good,'' and then seeks what is evil with extraordinary energy and determination. One may wonder whether John Milton is not closer to the truth when in *Paradise Lost* he appears to portray Satan as a mind whose powers are rendered more formidable by alliance with what is evil. Again, Augustine's account of the abuse of freedom has not convinced all the commentators. It is hard to see why spirits that were perfectly happy and good at the first moment of their existence (such as Augustine supposes all finite spirits to be) should fall victim to temptation. Any causal account one might give of how this could happen would seem to presuppose that they had fallen already; thus, if it were pride which made them fall, then they had already fallen into the sin of pride. It is noteworthy that Kant regarded original sin as both utterly mysterious and philosophically certain.

Next comes the principle of plenitude. It has been pointed out that the Creator has not in fact placed in this world the total imaginable number of different species. No matter how many varieties of humming-bird there are, we can always say that God could have made twice as many, and if this would involve the doubling in size of the Amazon basin, then so be it. But then it is not easy to defend the existence of cholera germs on the grounds that they had to be there since without them one expression of the divine creativity would be missing.

Finally, there is the notion of cosmic harmony. Even from our limited standpoint in historical time, the theme of cosmic harmony is audible from time to time. For instance, if we think of the world as a unitary design, a cosmos, the transience of nature does not seem to be an evil after all, whereas if we restrict our attention to the withering of *this* orchid, or the expiring of *that* pet rabbit, decay and death in the nonhuman world strike us as sad and regrettable. Taking a wider view, the dissolution of plants and animals into their component parts is a condition for the fashioning of fresh plants and animals. The real difficulty with the cosmic harmony theme is when we come to moral evil. An incautious statement of the aesthetic picture of evil would lead us to say that sin is necessary to the perfection of the universe, since it is beautifully counterposed by divine justice, a point of view which (presumably) few people would be keen on putting forward as a philosophical defense of Christian faith.

The Irenaean theodicy, unlike the Augustinian, rests essentially obj. to upon a single thought, the conclusion of which is, to remind you, that Iranaeus to predict a final justificatory resolution of evil in terms of matured souls is not counterrational. But many will say that it is precisely this which is at issue. The extent of evil is far greater than a challenging environment would require. Evil is more than cold showers to encourage manliness. The excessiveness or redundancy of evil discourages us from positing a final state of affairs to justify the myriad succeeding states of affairs the world has so far known.

The conclusion which emerges, therefore, is that the argumentation found in the history of theodicy goes some way toward releasing Lactantius from his dilemma, but by no means all the way. Enough has been said to convince one that evil phenomena are not an insuperable obstacle to believing in a God of the kind that philosophy and faith (as found in fundamental theology) require. On the other hand, not everything has been cleared up. But as I have remarked, if in theodicy we *could* clear up the problem of evil to our complete satisfaction, then there would be no need for salvation as presented in Christian revelation. God comes in his incarnate Son as the world's Redeemer, and by his Spirit as its Renewer, so as to repair the world's defects. But there would be no point in redemption if these defects could be shown to be either not defects at all or things built into the very idea of having a world in the first place. We can list some of the inexplicable elements in theodicy, which must be taken over, then, into a preunderstanding of what might be involved in the story of salvation. First, there is the strange potency of evil, given that evil should be regarded metaphysically as privation. Second, there is the fall of finite spirits, who came forth from an all-holy divine ground even if, in the case of *Homo sapiens*, they were culturally and psychologically immature. Third, there is the apparent escape of nature from the rational control of Providence as evidenced in say, the suffering of the innocent in natural disasters. To these three factors we may add a fourth, namely, the fact that we have not been able to solve the problem of theodicy. We can call this factor the absence of sufficient meaning, our inability to make anything like complete sense of the world.

Here, then, we have some features of the idea of salvation. If the Creator entered our world as the Redeemer, he must, it seems, do four things. He must conquer and neutralize the potency of evil in its fundamental ground. He must give finite spirits a new supernatural principle of action to replace that given them by original sin. He must provide for the harmonization of nature with human happiness. He must overcome the ambiguity, or absence of sufficient meaning, in human life as we know it. But if there is to be such a redemptive action by God, then there must be some way in which we can apprehend his involvment with the world. Divine revelation must be possible. This is the next aspect of the preamble of faith in the elucidation of which philosophy has a role to play.

6

The Possibility and Historicity of Revelation

Here we are concerned with the role of philosophy in establishing two more portions of theology's earthworks. First, is revelation possible? And second, if it is, by what criteria can we assess the claims of the alleged revelation possessed by the Church to be historically founded? It should perhaps be mentioned at the outset that for one school of thought, the first question is scarcely worth dealing with in its own right. If we can answer satisfactorily the second question, Has a divine revelation in point of historical fact taken place? then the first question at once becomes otiose. Suppose that we were to discuss the possibility of travel between planets in different solar systems. If during our discussion an actual space traveller from the planet of another star walked into the room, there would be precious little point in going on with the conversation. Analogously, it is said, if we have reason to believe that there has been an actual revelation, we can dispense with the question of its possibility. But if we take this line, which is that of much Catholic apologetic around the turn of the century,[1] we will probably end up with a rather extrinsic and shallow view of revelation. In fact, one writer has denounced such an approach—using a metaphor from science fiction—as "robotic apologetics."[2] Since the beginning of this century, and in particular with the work of Maurice Blondel (1861–1949), apologetics (or fundamental theology) has been much more concerned with the possibility of revelation and especially

1. However, concern with "motives of credibility" has a distinguished ancestry: see, for instance, Thomas' *Summa theologiae* IIa. IIae., q. 1, a. 4, ad ii; and, in general, A. Lang, *Die Entfaltung des apologetischen Problems in der Scholastik des Mittelalters* (Freiburg: 1962).

2. G. Daly, *Transcendence and Immanence: A Study in Catholic Modernism and Integralism* (Oxford: 1980) 17.

its intrinsic fittingness to the human condition, although this is not to say that concern with the historicity of the actual revelation, established through the applying of external criteria to the sources, is unimportant.[3]

There are three questions involved here. The first is, Is there reason to think that the God whom, with philosophy's help, we have found to exist could make a further revelation of himself? The second is, Are there reasons for thinking that man is incapable of receiving such a revelation were he offered it? And the third is, If none of the objections to the second question are valid, can we say why we positively think man could receive such a revelation? (Clearly, the last two questions are simply the two sides of the same coin.) First, then, we can look at the possibility of supernatural revelation from the side of God. The self-revelation of God is unthinkable unless a theology can show, in whatever conceptual terms it prefers, that God himself is transcendent, personal, and free. God must be transcendent or he could not reveal himself. Without his transcendence of the world, God has no genuine partner to whom he can show himself. And so theories about God which consider the world to be in some sense part of God, or included within God's being, cannot concede the possibility of supernatural revelation. You cannot have a conversation unless you have someone else to speak with. But as we have seen, a number of arguments for God's existence point toward a properly theistic (as distinct from pantheistic or panentheistic) concept of God. It may be that pantheists appeal less to philosophy and more to religious feeling, reminding us that we often feel nature and nature's God to be a unity. The English Romantic poets, for instance, are full of such feelings. But once we let reason come into play to test the functioning of imagination, we find that such feelings should be analyzed within a theistic, not a pantheistic, description of the world.

In the second place, a God who reveals himself must be a personal God. The basic picture behind the idea of special or supernatural revelation is that there is a someone revealed in a something. We are all familiar with persons disclosing themselves in their actions: a smile, a handshake, a characteristic gesture, a letter, a poem, a painting. All of these are ways in which personal somebodies reveal themselves in impersonal somethings. If God were not personal it would be impossible to suppose that he could step out of his silence or hiddenness

3. The best neo-Thomists were careful to integrate both approaches: e.g. J. Falcon, *La Crédibilité du dogme catholique* (Lyons-Paris: 1933).

and show himself to us. For that to happen God must be in some way like the person who has decided to make himself known and can do or say something that communicates his inward being to others. And once again, some of the arguments for God's existence point in the direction of the personality of God. More generally, we can say that if God is the source of all created things, then these things must in some sense have preexisted in that source. But the highest things we know in the universe are interpersonal knowledge and love, being subjects capable of knowing and loving other subjects. So this too, and especially this, must preexist in its divine source. And this brings us to the third factor in the possibility of revelation from the side of God. A God who reveals himself must be not only transcendent and personal but _free_. If the world emanates automatically from God, as one takes pantheists to be saying, or if, at the opposite philosophical pole, the world is a closed system over against God, as deists say, then God is unfree vis-à-vis the world and cannot show his hand. In pantheism God cannot help but reveal himself; in deism he cannot reveal himself further even should he want to. In both cases he is unfree. If supernatural revelation is to be possible, we must grant God the freedom to go beyond the order of creation if he so wills.

But now let us look at the same issue, the possibility of revelation, from the side of man: our second and third questions in this realm. Revelation is only possible from the side of man if he is open to transcendence. Various objections are brought from time to time against this basic openness of the human being to God. These objections may be said to resolve themselves into two: one is lodged in terms of humankind's autonomy and the other, which is quite incompatible with the first, in terms of their determinedness by factors beyond their control. In the first case, it is said that human autonomy, man's taking responsibility for his own life, should rule out an appeal to revelation as a shortcut to the answers of life's problems. It is unworthy of human dignity not to decide for oneself on all fundamental questions of existence. The brief reply to this is that being autonomous does not mean being liberated from all ties and obligations but rather being free to posit such ties and obligations as one's own internal norm. But among these ties and obligations, and not the least important of them, is the duty to follow the truth wherever it leads. Thus if we have reason to think that a truth from beyond this world is being shown to us, then it is no lapse into heteronomy freely to accept and interiorize supramundane truth.

In the case of the second objection to revelation's possibility from the side of humankind, namely our determinedness, we find that we are dealing here with several widespread reductionist theories, each of which claims that human ideas are so determined by causes internal to human beings themselves that they could not respond to a truth coming wholly from outside themselves even if they wished to. Most commonly, such theories are socioeconomic (as with Marxism-Leninism) or psychological (as with orthodox Freudianism) in character. Although there is space here neither to refute fully, nor even to state fairly, such theories, it may be said, in short compass, that in each case humankind's intellectual and volitional life is seen as fully preprogrammed by one or more of its basic drives or needs. In Marxism, the need to express oneself in work is at the start of a complex theory of man which ends by regarding all doctrines save Marxism itself as examples of "false consciousness," or systematic misapprehension. Thus the concept of God can be reinterpreted as the projection on to the starry heavens of the best part of ourselves, motivated by our despair of ever realizing ourselves in society as we know it. In orthodox Freudianism, the sexual drive is seen as explaining all human activities and beliefs in some way or another by regarding the entire fabric of human culture (including religion) as an endless series of adjustments between reality and the thrust toward pleasure. All such reductionisms stem, it may be suggested, from a form of intellectual self-indulgence, that is, from the desire to be in possession of a single key that will open up all reality. Through this desire, theses about limited aspects of human behavior become total explanations of an imperialistic kind. To reduce the reductionisms to size is not only necessary in order to maintain man's openness to revelation. It is also a mercy to the elements of truth in the reductionisms themselves.[4]

Finally, can we show positively why we think man can receive a revelation? At the turn of this century there arose a school of Catholic thought dubbed the "new apologetics." The principal concern of this school, of which Blondel was the ornament, was to show how it is intrinsically fitting for men and women to be in receipt of divine revelation. Considered historically, this "new" apologetics was a revival of the defense of Christianity found in Pascal. Its approach was by way of the "method of immanence," "immanence" here referring to

4. For a fuller description and criticism of these theories, in the spirit of the approach suggested here, *see* A. Léonard, *Pensées des hommes et foi en Jésus Christ. Pour un discernement intellectuel chrétien* (Paris: 1980) 64–73, 84–97.

human interiority, to needs and tendencies in the human person that point to a divine revelation as what is required to make a human life complete.[5] Blondel's position, as offered in his *chef d'oeuvre*, called *L'action*, sets out from the observation that the will is greater than any of its possible earthly objects. By metaphysical instinct, it presses beyond them in the search for a good that is commensurate with its own infinitude. The implication is that in a created universe where nothing is as it is except for a good reason, this cannot be by chance. At some point in the past, present, or future, the supreme Object of action has offered, is offering, or at any rate will offer himself to all people as the only reality that can fully satisfy them.[6] The stress here falls not on the divine truth making itself accessible to the human mind but on the divine goodness drawing to itself the human will. But a sound account of the act of faith should really include both of these components, mind and will. We recognize the truth of revelation intellectually insofar as we are capable of grasping God's self-revelation. We also respond volitionally or affectively, by the will or heart, to the goodness of God, who is drawing us through this revelation to himself. Blondel and the new apologists concentrated somewhat unilaterally on the will, chiefly in order to correct a picture of human beings as thinking machines rather than as loving and desiring subjects which—they believed—a degenerate Scholasticism and the older apologetics had alike fostered. Others since have underlined the role of the mind, and perhaps most emphatically the late Karl Rahner in his *Spirit in the World* and its sequel, *Hearers of the Word*.[7] A balanced account would integrate both.

What we have seen so far belongs to the ambit of a subjective apologia for revelation: a defense of revelation's possibility in terms of criteria touching the divine subject and human subjects. We must now investigate the objective apologia which forms the other wing of the diptych. What are the objective criteria for determining the historical reality of an alleged revelation, in this case, that of the Judeo-Christian religion? This enquiry falls into two parts, which are, first, the histori-

5. G. Daly, "Apologetics in the Modernist Period," *Chesterton Review* 15, 1–2 (February–May 1989) 79–94.

6. M. Blondel, *L'Action* (Paris: 1893). *See* H. Bouillard, *Blondel et le christianisme* (Paris: 1961); J. M. Somerville, "Maurice Blondel 1861-1949," *Thought* 36 (1961) 371–410.

7. K. Rahner, *Spirit in the World* (New York and London: 1968); Rahner, *Hearers of the Word* (New York and London: 1969); the aim of these two sequentially related works is briefly described in J. A. DiNoia, "Karl Rahner," in *The Modern Theologians*, 1, ed. D. Ford (Oxford: 1989) 190–92.

cal credibility of the biblical narrative that presents us with claims to revelation, and second, the credibility of the Bible's own theological interpretation of this narrative.

First, then, the historical credibility of the biblical narrative, which is the vehicle of putative revelation. It seems pretty clear that the Christian religion, like its Jewish parent religion,[8] is a thoroughly historical affair.[9] Admittedly, not all of the books of the Bible are historical books in the sense of being written by people who were what the ancient world could regard as historians. In that sense, the Book of Exodus is a historical book, but the Book of Wisdom is not; the Gospel of Mark is a historical book, but the Letter of James is not. Nevertheless, all the books of Scripture are historical in the sense that they presuppose and depend on a religion which regards certain historical events as central to its own claims to be true. The authors of Wisdom and the Letter of James were not writing as historians, even by Jewish or Hellenistic standards of historiography, but they were writing as men who believed as they did because they accepted an interpretation of certain historical events, which the Jewish religion had made and the Christian religion partly inherited and partly made in turn. Both Judaism and Christianity hold that the one true God, source and ground of the world, has disclosed himself through these events of religious history—from Abraham to the close of the Old Testament period in Judaism, from Abraham to the apostles of Jesus in Christianity. The Creator Lord had entered a covenant relationship, a relationship of friendship and trust with a people: Israel, the Church. And this relationship was believed to exist because of events which had really transpired within history. Thus, the ideas about God entertained by, first, Jews and, then, by the earliest Christian generation did not take root because people who thought them out liked them so much they decided to keep them. Instead, people found themselves involved in a relationship with God because of the great historical experiences through which they had passed. The ideas element in their faith was not the basis of their belief but its further distillation.

8. On Judaism here, *see* C. R. North, *The Old Testament Interpretation of History* (London: 1946).

9. Thus history is for Christianity "a process determined by the creative act of God vertically from above," C. H. Dodd, *History and the Gospel* (London: 1938) 81. Or again, for Christian faith: "the temporal is inwardly sustained, saturated, pervaded by the untemporal," J. Pieper, *The End of Time* (London: 1954) 67. For the distinctiveness of this viewpoint vis-à-vis other religious cultures, *see* C. A. Patrides, *The Grand Design of God: The Literary Form of the Christian View of History* (London: 1972) 2–3.

Two questions arise here of a philosophical or at least semi-philosophical kind. The first question is about the possibility of our knowing the past at all. All historical knowledge is built up on evidence consisting of written or nonwritten remains. Sceptics may allege that the attempt to construct a picture of the past on the basis of these remains is foredoomed to failure. We are obliged to use our imagination to fill in the gaps; our imagination is conditioned by the fact that we belong to the twentieth century after Christ and not to the first century after Christ or the twentieth century before him. What counts, therefore, as history tells us more about our own age, the age of the historian, than it does about the age such books purport to describe. But if this be true, then it will not be possible to establish the credibility of the truth-claims of the Judeo-Christian religion, for the obvious reason that if we can know nothing for certain about the events out of which Judaism and Christianity were built, we cannot *a fortiori* know whether the Jewish and Christian interpretation of these events is credible.

The second question concerns not the status of history in general but that of the biblical history in particular. Even supposing that we are successful in rebutting the sceptical account of historical studies outlined above, we still need to show that the particular segments of alleged historical material enshrined in the Bible are trustworthy. It may be the case that while many historical remains enable us to write reliable history, those included in Scripture are not among them. Here we must temporarily show the philosopher to the door and wait for the ancient historian to call instead. However, from the viewpoint of the preamble of faith, it is not equally urgent that the ancient historian should be willing to credit any and every factual claim in the biblical narrative. What we need to know theologically is whether the general outline of the biblical history can be trusted, that is, whether the events regarded as crucial and determinative by the biblical writers themselves really happened. I am thinking here of such things as the call of Abraham; the Exodus from Egypt; the Sinai experience of Moses; the establishment of the Davidic dynasty with its messianic promises; the Exile and restoration of Israel from Babylon; the conception, life, death, and resurrection of Jesus; his founding of the Church; the descent of the Holy Spirit at Pentecost. If it could be shown that these events, or sequences (and clusters) of events, never happened, or that they happened in such a form that the Jewish and Christian interpretations of them are effectively excluded, then manifestly the claims of the

Judeo-Christian religion would fall to the ground. Of less importance are such matters as whether in the book of his name Joshua made the sun stand still, or whether in the Acts of the Apostles Herod Agrippa I was smitten in Caesarea by an angel of the Lord and was eaten by worms. In the preamble of faith there is no need to concern ourselves with the question as to whether every detail of the biblical history has a factual basis. To establish the credibility of the biblical revelation, it is not necessary to establish the facticity of such matters unless there is reason to think that the biblical revelation itself proposes them as necessary to its own cohesion. In principle, it is possible that a genuine revelation could have been recorded in writings which only in part reflect that revelation and in part reflect the imperfect geography, historiography, and natural science of their day. The notions of revelation and of inerrancy are not coterminous. What we need to know is whether or not it is credible to say that the central events of the sacred history happened through the power and guidance of the God whose character and purpose is disclosed through them. To assure ourselves of this we need to know that these central events really happened, and that the biblical interpretation of them is, at worst, believable, and at best the only satisfactory explanation possible.

First of all, then, let us look at the question of the possibility of historical knowledge as such. In English-speaking countries, the philosophy of history largely consists in an attempt to show that historical knowledge is a legitimate form of human understanding, that statements about events in the past and the possible relations of cause and effect that hold between them can be justified before the bar of philosophical reason. In other words, philosophers working in this area are looking for ways of explaining how the practice of history is possible—because of course history books are in fact being written all the time, and historians do not dream of suspending their labors until philosophers have agreed on how to justify them. The philosophy of history in the Anglo-Saxon tradition is, then, a modest discipline which does not set itself very high targets. It is in striking contrast to its sister in continental Europe where, perhaps particularly in Germany, the philosophy of history consists in speculation on the universal meaning of a history composed of particular processes, an enquiry into how any given historical movement might be said to contribute to the totality of the experience of the race seen as a meaningful unity.[10] I shall

10. Cf. W. H. Walsh, *An Introduction to the Philosophy of History* (London: 1951-58) 119-20.

not be concerning myself with the subject in this latter sense, which is perhaps just as well since it is an area where talking nonsense is more than usually easy. Rather, I am concerned in what follows with the epistemology of historical statements, since this is necessary to render secure the claimed access of Christian minds to those past events on which their faith depends.

The making and comprehending of a history book may be compared to the making and comprehending of any story.[11] The understanding of stories, narratives, is a form of human understanding which unfortunately has been somewhat played down since ancient times. Even though the Hellenes were rather good storytellers and historians, their philosophers concentrated almost exclusively on the search for universal truths, truths that held irrespective of the particularities of *those* people in *that* time and space.[12] Yet surely there is a genuine, distinctive, and important kind of understanding involved in following a story with attention and insight, even though the story deals almost invariably with particularities and hardly ever with universal truths. The difference between a purely literary story and a historical narrative can be specified in terms of certain conditions which we expect a historical story to meet.[13] First and most obviously, a historical story must be set in real time and space. A story about life on the planet Nusquam in the year 3000 could scarcely claim our interest as history. Second, a historical story must be consistent with all the known evidence relevant to the events it contains. Third, it must arise out of public materials and possess a public aim, that of giving an account of some slice of the public past. The story of an individual's love affairs would not in itself be history even if it took place in the eighteenth century, though doubtless by certain deft touches it could be rendered historically significant. If a narrative meets these three conditions—set in real space and time, consistent with all the evidence, part of the public and not just private past, then it is history. There is no harm in admitting that imagination plays a considerable part in constructing such a story. By imagination writers of both fiction and history relate one event to another in ways that strike us as plausible because they have a feel cognate with that which we ourselves know from daily life. The ability to enter into the minds of other human agents and to see separate events as part of a coherent narrative is among the most vital forms

[handwritten marginal note: Criteria for a historical story]

11. R. Collingwood, *The Idea of History* (Oxford: 1946) 20-21.
12. W. B. Gallie, *Philosophy and the Historical Understanding* (London: 1964) 22-71.
13. Collingwood, *The Idea of History*, 246ff.

of imaginative understanding we have, even though by "understanding" here something very different is meant from our use of the same word in the context of, say, the scientist at work in his laboratory. Understanding—we can say—is polyvalent: the way we understand a poem is not the way we understand a philosophical argument, and neither is the way we understand our grandmother. Thus historical explanation is not a fading echo of the explanation found in the natural sciences but is *sui generis*, standing on its own two feet. In offering a historical explanation for some event or movement or personality, historians invite us to look with them at their chosen grouping of the known facts and the questions they raise. They present us with a pattern which, they believe, they have found in the evidence and invite our judgment as to whether this pattern is really there. We judge by deciding whether a historian's highlighting enables us to follow a story more easily and renders it coherent in and of itself. Yes, it all seems to fit is the response that a successfully stated historical hypothesis should elicit.

Given, then, that the construction of historical narratives is a perfectly proper human enterprise, is there reason to think that the biblical history underlying our faith exemplifies such storytelling? Remaining on the central line of the biblical story and refusing to be sidetracked onto comparative details, we must still distinguish between historical event and theological interpretation. When, for instance, we speak of the descent of the Spirit at Pentecost, we are conflating a claimed historical event and a claimed accurate theological interpretation of that event. The alleged historical event is that something very remarkable happened to the apostolic group in the upper room in Jerusalem on the Jewish feast of Weeks in the year of Jesus' death. The allegedly accurate theological interpretation is that the something in question was the definitive gift of the Spirit of Jesus Christ and his Father. Parallel distinctions can be made right down the story line. What we have in the Bible is event plus theological interpretation.

[margin note: event vs. theological interpretation]

The result of this distinction is that we have two questions to cope with. First, were there in fact historical events of the kind presupposed by the complex description of event-plus-theological-interpretation given in Scripture? Second, is the theological account of the significance of these events compatible with what is believed about them by historians? Only exact study by historians of the biblical period can be found critically any assurance on these questions, but an attempt will be made here to sketch out the rough lines of a response. For most of the episodes in the biblical history, the Bible itself is the only direct source of evidence. However, within the Bible there are often several distinct sources relevant to the same event. Within any one of these sources scholars may sometimes discern more than one authorial hand. This opens the possibility of multiple and convergent attestation of a kind that warrants confidence. Thus, for instance, the gospel stories about the resurrection appearances of Jesus occur in multiple and perhaps composite sources whose authors can be shown to have very different aims. For St. Mark, whose resurrection-appearance story is clearly indicated but missing in the "lost ending," the resurrection is principally a consolation for Christians under persecution; for St. John, very differently, it is the foundation for the sacramental life of the Church. That writers so utterly at variance in their projects should agree on the fact of the resurrection appearances is reassuring. So because the Bible is a library of books and not a single book conceived and executed in terms of a unitary authorial scheme, it can and does contain a number of convergent witnesses to certain vital events along its central line. However, this is not always so, and even when it is so it may sometimes be shown that one account has drawn so heavily on another as hardly to constitute an independent testimony at all. The sagas of the patriarchs in the Book of Genesis are examples of stories where we have no corroborating testimony from elsewhere in the Bible, for the references to, say, the life of Abraham in the Psalter, seem simply drawn from Genesis itself. Here historians are more likely to consider the extrabiblical evidence in a somewhat impressionistic sense of that word. If what is said of the patriarchs coheres with what is known from the social history of the nations around Israel in the patriarchal period, then a chastened confidence in the historicity of the biblical narrative is once more justified.

In assessing the historical character of the biblical story, it is often found that historians working within their own frames of reference are more optimistic about biblical historicity (abstracting for the moment from the dimension of the miraculous) than are theologians. This is at first sight a paradox, but it admits of two explanations. First, theologians are naturally more interested than are historians in the theological significance of the events, and for this reason they sometimes tend to count as theological interpretation what should more properly count as event. To illustrate this syndrome, we can take the episode of the meeting of Mary Magdalene with the risen Jesus by the garden tomb in the Gospel of John. According to the evangelist, Mary mistakes Christ for the gardener. Now the theologian, struck by this vignette, may want to suggest that in the mind of the author there is a deliberate double meaning. As the New Adam leading his disciples into the new paradise Christ, is indeed a gardener; he is preparing the new earth, which another writer of the Johannine school sees descending from above in his Apocalypse. Mary spoke more truly than she knew—an example of the celebrated Johannine irony. To the theologian, the theological affirmation that Christ is the New Adam seems a good deal more important than the simple historical fact involved in whether or not a Palestinian woman mistook Jesus for a gardener, a bricklayer, or a steeplejack. The historical episode thus falls into the background. Moreover, there is a sense in which the theological affirmation stands out more clearly from the pages of the Gospel if St. John simply created the story of the meeting in order to convey his own teaching. For, after all, if Mary really did mistake Jesus for the gardener, then perhaps there is nothing more to the story than the record of that mistake, and the theologian himself is reading into the text of St. John something which never crossed the author's mind. Difficulties of this sort explain the not-infrequent situation in which theologians intent on theological meaning give the appearance of a historical iconoclasm, which, to the ordinary believer, cuts off the branch on which one is sitting. A theological interpretation without an undergirding event is like the smile on the face of the Cheshire cat; yet if the theological interpretation were to be entirely swallowed by the event, all we should be left with is sheer facticity without clear indications of wider significance.

The second cause of the paradox in question is intelligible rather than excusable. Theologians in the Lutheran tradition are customarily unhappy at the idea that objective, neutral investigation of the biblical record could play a role in establishing faith. If the pure gratuity of faith is stressed sufficiently over against all forms of "fallen" reason, including historical reason, then it becomes possible actually to rejoice when the Bible is thought to be historically defective. Thus writers influenced by Lutheranism will often prefer the Bible to be less a straightforward historical narrative and more a witness of faith to a new life given by God. This dichotomy is summed up in the distinction between the German words *Historie* and *Geschichte* popularized by the theologian-exegete Rudolf Bultmann (1884–1977). The general idea is that *Historie* is merely factual history while *Geschichte* is history laden with significance for human existence. Applied to the Bible, this becomes a distinction between scientific history or objective narrative on the one hand and, on the other, the believer's story of new life made possible through faith in Christ.[14] But the distinction between *Historie* and *Geschichte* rests on a questionable division of reality into facts and values. Bultmann's dichotomy, with its foundation in a Lutheran anthropology that we have already had cause to reject, should be of interest to Catholic theology only in encouraging us to find a better account of the relation between history and faith than his.

The question of the reasonableness of the theological interpretation put upon the central story line of Scripture by Jews and Christians cannot really be answered without at least glancing at the thorny problem of the miraculous. It is plain that the biblical record cannot stand if miracles are to be outlawed. At the level of the alleged historical events themselves, even the basic datum must sometimes be classified as strictly miraculous, no matter what wider theological interpretation we may wish to adopt. Thus, irrespective of our theology of the resurrection, we are faced with a claim (textually suppressed only by wonders of exegetical contortionism) that the corpse of Jesus of Nazareth did not rot in the grave but was resuscitated and perceived by others to have returned to life. Theologically considered, the resurrection means a great deal more than this; indeed, any account of the resurrection which spoke only of the resuscitation of a corpse could scarcely be called Christian at all. Nevertheless, it is clear that at the least resurrection does mean resuscitation and that in principle the evidence for this resuscitation is something that historians (and not simply believers) can be invited to consider as part of their account of Christian origins. When we move on to the theological interpretation of the historical events, the Bible presents us with more numerous if less inescapable instances of the allegedly miraculous. Thus the crossing of the Sea of Reeds by the fleeing Israelites might have been interpreted as a providential coincidence based on the fluctuation of tides, but the Book of Exodus does not appear to present the episode in that light. Rather, it is claimed that only the hand of God can account for what happened, not simply in the sense that the Israelites took advantage of the pattern of nature established by the Creator but in the sense that the Creator himself intervened in his creation at this point in time and space for the sake of the people he had chosen.

14. L. Malevez, *The Christian Message and Myth: The Theology of Rudolf Bultmann* (English trans., London: 1958) 188; G. Greshake, *Historie wird Geschichte. Bedeutung und Sinn der Unterscheidung von Historie und Geschichte in der Theologie Rudolf Bultmanns* (Essen: 1963).

At least since the eighteenth century, philosophers in the Christian West have felt sceptical about all such claims. The Scottish empiricist David Hume (1711–76) provided the classic formulation of the case against. Hume's objection to miracles is not that they are theoretically impossible: for someone who believes in a divine Creator there can be no *a priori* exclusion, he thought, of the possibility of particular interventions of God in his own world. Hume's objection is that all of our rational activity as human beings is predicated on the assumption that the world is predictable. I do not refuse to make plans to go swimming tomorrow on the grounds that quite possibly the sun will not rise for the first time in history. I am not afraid to cut into an orange with a fruit knife on the grounds that it (the orange or the fruit knife) may inexplicably turn into a top hat. Hume's point is that our assumption of order is so pervasive that it would take a quite extraordinary amount of evidence to convince us that in some particular case this assumption does not hold. Hume then goes on to say that in practice we never find this weight of evidence for any alleged miracle. We find evidence, certainly, but according to Hume, it is always more rational to suppose that something has gone wrong with the collection or transmission of the evidence than to suspend the assumption of cosmic order.

The reply to this is that while indeed part of rationality consists in acting on the assumption of the orderliness of reality, this idea does not in itself tell us which concept of order we should have. The Christian theist believes that the order exhibited by the universe is ultimately an order founded on God's love, a love lying behind the world's making and ahead at the world's end. But if this is the basic order displayed in the creation, then the special acts of God's providence we call miracles can themselves be seen as orderly, and not as ruptures of order. Take, for instance, such a miracle as the feeding of the five thousand. Here we have a miraculous provision of food, which fits in with two things. First, it fits in with God the Creator's provision of means for our survival and nourishment, something which goes on continually through the forces of nature. And second, it fits in with the promise of God the Redeemer that one day our spiritual hunger will be satisfied in the banquet of heaven—and while the non-Christian does not by definition credit such a promise, he or she can be brought to see imaginatively the understanding of future order it represents. On such a view of the world, the miracle of the multiplication of the loaves and fishes cannot be called disorderly, since it coheres perfectly with the order of the purposes of a loving God. For the classical theist, the divine goodness is the most fundamental principle of predictability that there is.

So far we have been thinking about physical miracles. But the approach I have outlined would apply equally to that other main category of the miraculous in Judeo-Christianity, namely prophecy, or what is sometimes referred to as "intellectual miracle." The biblical concept of prophecy is a good deal richer than simply that of accurately foretelling particular contingent events, yet such foretelling, even when shorn of simplistic interpretation, remains obstinately part of the biblical narrative. Once again, such foretelling should not be thought of as a bizarre and monstrous disruption or order. The basic order of the world is not simply the order of nature, or of the inherent possibilities of finite spirit, but the order of a God who wills to guide mankind into the knowledge of his truth.

In the central figure of the biblical narrative as a whole, Jesus Christ, we find an amazing concentration of miracle. We find physical miracles: miracles in which Jesus repairs the order of creation, as with his many acts of healing the sick and crippled. We, find, too, miracles in which he transforms the order of creation and so points forward to the new life of the world to come, as with his transformation of water into wine at Cana in Galilee. We find intellectual miracles: prophecies in which Jesus foretells the future history of the Jewish people in Roman Palestine and prophecies in which he foretells the future fate of his Church. Then in his own person Jesus is the subject of miracle: as when in his own life story he fulfills the predictions of the Old Testament prophets and when at Easter he is raised from the dead. Insofar as miracle is evidence of the presence of God inside history, this extraordinary concentration of miracle is evidence of a special intensity to God's presence in the story of Jesus Christ. And this naturally raises the question of the unique status or authority of Jesus.

This special status or authority has been expressed in two main ways within a broadly philosophical conceptuality. Either it is spoken of in terms of the moral perfection of Jesus or in terms of the unsurpassable aesthetic authority of this style of life. Each of these concepts is an attempt to cast in rational terms the sense of a further dimension to Jesus, which strikes all who, through absorption in the biblical narrative, have felt the force of his fascination. In effect, we are saying, Is there not something about the figure of Jesus which suggests that this man was not like other figures in history, that he spoke and acted with an authority not ultimately rooted in this world? The more usual way in which to present this further dimension to Jesus is to speak of his moral perfection.[15] He seems to have been a moral miracle. Among a race as deeply flawed as our own, he stood out a mile because of his ethical holiness. This is not simply a matter of degrees of virtuousness but a question of the mysterious absence of the equally mysterious but ubiquitous tendency toward evil in humanity. This contrast of moral glory with our usual experience of moral squalor in all its forms (many of them counterfeit virtue) can only be explained, it is suggested, by allowing Jesus special access to the divine resources of gracious transforming power. And such special access is itself unthinkable without positing at the same time a special place for Jesus in the divine overseeing of human history, and so a special authority.

Alternatively, the unique status or authority of Jesus can be brought out by speaking of the aesthetic rather than moral authority of his life. This way of speaking is not a matter of ignoring the ethical aspect of Jesus' transcendence but of suggesting how to conceive that aspect in the wider context of humanity's search for meaning and truth. A comparison is being instituted between the authority of Jesus and the authority of a great work of art. The latter is something before which we are brought up short, and to which we submit ourselves, because we find in it a meaning that goes beyond the realm of the everyday. The splendor of a great work of art communicates the radiance which belongs to the truth of things, what the Scholastic philosophers call *pulchrum*, beauty as a determination of being as such. In a similar way, it is proposed, the glory of God shines forth in the life and person of Jesus Christ. His words and works of love express the self-communicating goodness of being, a goodness derived from being's transcendent ground or source.[16] Once again, it becomes rationally credible to speak of him as a divine legate.

In such ways we can flesh out in reasonable terms the claim that Jesus Christ represents a unique openness of human history to God. The miracles which surround him, brought to a climax in the resur-

15. S. W. Sykes, "The Theology of the Humanity of Christ," in *Christ, Faith and History*. Cambridge Studies in Christology, ed. S. W. Sykes and J. P. Clayton (Cambridge: 1972) 53–71.

16. R. Fisichella, *La rivelazione: evento e credibilità* (Bologna: 1985), presents a global view of the credibility of revelation as the self-manifestation of the Trinitarian love showing itself in its signs, first and foremost in Christ, but then, in dependence upon him, in the Church. His approach is based on his earlier investigation of Balthasar's contribution here: R. Fisichella, *Hans Urs von Balthasar. Amore e credibilità cristiana* (Rome: 1981).

rection, are the detritus left by a unique intersection of eternity with time. As presented in the biblical story, this intersection is more than an interruption of a gracious kind. It is not merely the mending of an old order but the elevation of history into a new order, even though this new order does not negate the old but preserves it in carrying it beyond itself. Thus, what I have called the remarkable concentration of miracle in the life of Jesus signals something greater than any miracle, namely a new mode of divine presence and activity in history. As *Dei verbum*, the constitution of the Second Vatican Council on divine revelation, put it, the sign par excellence of that revelation in history is Jesus Christ himself, the "whole of his presence and self-manifestation,"[17] something the text goes on to analyze in terms of his words and deeds, his signs and miracles, and, especially, his death and resurrection, along with the sending of the Spirit of truth. That Christ is thus the central sign may be confirmed by noting that the Bible as we have it, that is, as laid out in the Church's canon, or approved sequence of authorized books, is itself centered on Jesus Christ. In Scripture, everything looks forward to Jesus Christ, as in the Old Testament, or flows from him, as in the life of the New Testament community he founded.[18]

Jesus' claims as a divine legate, and those of the Church he founded, may be defended as not unreasonable. More than this philosophy cannot do for theology without destroying the freedom of the act of faith itself, since faith is not simply coerced by evidence.[19] However, we have not entirely finished with the services of the philosopher. For we still need to know how philosophy can help us organize the materials of theology, the content of the act of faith, and not simply justify rationally the possibility of theology, the making of the act of faith in the first place—even if an account of the latter already tells us something about the former.

---

17. *Dei verbum*, 4.

18. A notion well expressed in T. S. Eliot's "The Rock": "Then came, at a predetermined moment, a moment in time and out of time,/A moment not out of time, but in time, in what we call history: transecting, bisecting the world of time, a moment in time but not like a moment of time,/A moment in time but time was made through that moment: for without the meaning there is no time, and that moment of time gave the meaning . . . ." (1934) 50.

19. Although for the First Vatican Council's constitution on faith, the miracles are said to be "quite certain signs accommodated to all minds," this does not mean that grace is not required to turn natural vision into eyes of faith: *see* P. Rousselot, "Les yeux de la foi," *Recherches de science religieuse* (1910) 241–59, 444–75.

7
The Philosophical Principle of Order in Theology

The role of philosophy in theology is not confined to its part in fundamental theology, in establishing the foundations of faith. Philosophy also has a vital task in systematic theology, and more especially in the latter's conceptual organization. Admittedly, philosophy has a smaller number of lines to say when we get into systematics proper, which is concerned with the content of revelation and so with the transcription of that content in the individual mind in the form of faith. Naturally, Scripture and Tradition will come to play an increasingly ample role from this moment on. In fact, they will be playing the preponderant role as is only right and proper, since they are, after all, the sources for what is contained in revelation. But this does not mean that philosophy will fall silent completely.

The reason for this is that many of the concepts, questions, and ways of looking at things which we have found to be helpful in fundamental theology will travel with us into systematic theology. There are four principal areas in which this is so. First, there is the concept of God. Three sets of rational notions drawn from the preamble of faith will remain important in dogmatics. To begin with, there are the elements in the concept of God which reflect our arguments for God's existence. As we have seen, no argument for the existence of God can fail to suggest something about the concept of God. One cannot provide an argument for the existence of absolute transcendence which does not at the same time give some inkling of what that absolute transcendence might be. Then again, there is what I called the "root metaphysical notion," which we must choose in order to organize our materials for the concept of God, materials that follow from our arguments for God's existence. To remind you, it is not good enough just to lay side by side such divine attributes as an investigation of the

91

grounds for God's existence may suggest. We must arrange them in a way which exhibits their coherence. Otherwise, we shall have in effect half a dozen concepts of God, internally unrelated to each other, rather than a single, coherent, unified concept of God. Finally, we saw that if revelation is to be possible from the side of God, certain things about God must be the case: for instance, genuine distinction from the world, personality, and freedom. If these ideas are not already part of our concept of God, then they must be integrated and rationally justified. The sum of these three elements, then, provides us with a philosophical principle of ordering as we come to look at what the Bible and Tradition have to say about the divine Being.

② Next, we already have from philosophy some idea of what might be meant by salvation. As we saw when we looked at theodicy, those major defects in the world which cannot be rationally justified remain *eo ipso* inexplicable and insuperable elements of evil. If the Creator is to deal with the evil in the world, it will be with these elements that he must deal. We listed them as the potency of evil in its fundamental ground, the need for finite spirits to have a new inner principle of acting, provision for the harmonization of nature with human happiness, and the overcoming of the ambiguity or absence of sufficient meaning in life as we know it. Just as the philosophical principle of order furnishes us with elements of a concept of God that will help us to write a theological treatise on God as one and three, on the Trinity, so here a philosophical principle of order will help us to write a theological treatise on soteriology, on the doctrine of redemption.

③ Third, we have found some elements in philosophy to help us write a theological anthropology, an account of humanity in theological terms. When we looked at the subjective conditions of possibility of revelation from the side of humans, we saw that they must be a certain type of being if they are to receive revelation. In a word, they must be open to transcendence in such a way that the transcendent, God, is the fulfillment of the life of mind and will. Reductionist theories of humanity will have been shown to be inadequate: though each person is a sexual person and an economic person, these are not the whole truth about them. They have an inner orientation to transcendence which indicates their final destiny. So the theological doctrine of the human being at large is already partially organized in advance in terms of these philosophical categories.

④ Fourth and last, we already have a valuable preunderstanding of the formal structure of revelation. This derives from what we have seen about the objective criteria of the actual revelation, the content of the "old" apologetics. Divine truth is mediated by a history, the biblical narrative, which has to be constantly repossessed by human minds reflecting on the significance of its central events, following the story with understanding. This history is marked by a constant recurrence of miracle, evidence of a gracious divine eruption into a world itself defined as orderly in terms of the reliability of God's goodness. The biblical story is, then, a story of both human and divine agency. Its structural center is found in the life, death, and resurrection of Jesus Christ, in whom this combined divine and human action comes to its climax. From this we gather that revelation is found in the witness to a genuine history (Scripture) mediated by a continual process of representation (Tradition). This history, which is both human and divine, reaches its high point in a person in whom the divine and the human in some sense coincide. Here we have a basic framework for our investigation of the sources of the Church's faith, with which Parts 3 and 4 of this book will be concerned.

In these four areas—God, salvation, man, revelation—philosophy can do much to help us organize our materials. If it is to be fully coherent, philosophical activity must be able to unify what it says about each of these four areas in a satisfying way. It would not do for a philosophical principle of order to be itself disorderly. However, we may reasonably doubt whether this is not asking too much of any one philosophy, even a philosophy which has selected its main interests in the light of revelation (a Christian philosophy). So once again, I should remind the reader that as theological students we are not required to nail our colors to any one philosophical mast. We can afford to have a degree of eclecticism. We may well judge that one philosophy will throw light on the nature of salvation, for instance, while not noticeably illuminating the nature of revelation. Thus, for example, the sociological ideas used by liberation theology may help us to understand what God as Redeemer is likely to do in and with this world but be comparatively useless if we ask instead about people's capacity to receive revelation. Social categories can specify evils in the world, but they cannot say anything about the noetic relation of the world to God. On the other hand, to repeat an earlier caveat, we must not let our eclecticism run riot, or we shall end up with a hodgepodge of bits and pieces of philosophy from different and probably incompatible systems or approaches.

This sounds highly abstract, but a degree of abstractness is to be welcomed in an introduction to theology. An introduction to Catholic theology should, to a certain extent, abstract from the distinguishing features of particular Catholic theologies so as to present the basic features of all theologies, or at any rate those features desirable in them all. It would be useful for the student to take one theologian, Augustine, say, or Thomas, and ask what philosophical principle of ordering is involved in his theology and how that principle contributes to his achievement. Augustine would be an easier choice than Thomas, as his philosophical principle of order is derived from the Platonist tradition in a fairly straightforward way. It would not be difficult to show that Platonism has entered into the very structure of what Augustine has to say about God, humankind, revelation, and redemption. Platonism does not only help Augustine to argue for the truth of the Christian religion, although it does do that. It also helps him to organize the materials he has received from the Church's faith: to get them into perspective—one kind of perspective, not the only perspective, or we should all be Augustinians.

By way of conclusion, it will be well to draw the reader's attention to the inherent limitations of the philosophical principle of order in theology. Philosophy is reckoned quite a high card in theology: let us call it the jack, the fourth-highest card the pack possesses. This card can be trumped by three other cards. First, it can be trumped by the king, which is <u>divine revelation itself</u>. Obviously, if a philosophical principle of order is tending in some way to distort revelation or leads to our leaving out of count things that are manifestly important to the faith of the Church, then the king will trump the jack. But in between the king and the jack is the queen. Between divine revelation and the philosophical principle of order in theology there is always <u>some theological principle of order</u>. As I mentioned in the course of roughing out a definition of theology, no one theology can ever present divine revelation in its totality. It will always take up a particular standpoint, choosing one theme as its preferred point of entry and considering all · the other theological themes in relation to this (for it) central motif.

Because a theological principle of order is equally necessary to theology and yet is derived from within revelation and not (as is the case with the philosophical principle of order) from outside it, it must be regarded as more important than the philosophical principle and so have the right to depart from it if and when it so wishes. Last, then, there is the ace. If divine revelation is the king, how can there be a card which can trump divine revelation? The ace is <u>the mystery of God in himself</u>. We cannot assume that divine revelation tells us everything there is to know about God's being and purposes. It tells us enough for our needs and more than enough. Behind historic revelation there lie the unknown depths of the divine essence. Certainly, we believe that the divine essence cannot be in contradiction to anything God has made known in revelation. As Christians, we approach the mystery of that essence from the disclosure, in the self-emptying of the Son of God made man, of that self-emptying's transcendent pattern, the eternal event of the divine processions. As von Balthasar has written, "That essence is forever 'given' in the self-gift of the Father, 'rendered' in the thanksgiving of the Son, and 'represented' in its character as absolute Love by the Holy Spirit."[1] Nonetheless, there is no reason to think that in the revelation to *Homo sapiens*, to the inhabitants of this planet, the total divine mystery has been laid bare. Beyond even revelation there lies the vision of God, which is not for wayfarers but for those who have arrived in the assembly of the angels. Not for us now, even with divine revelation, is that perfectly unified, complete, and luminous intuition of God and beings, which Dante sings of in the *Paradiso:* "O abounding grace, by which I dared to fix my look on the Eternal Light so long that I spent all my sight upon it! In its depth I saw that it contained, bound by love in one volume, that which is scattered in leaves through the universe, substances and accidents and their relations, as it were fused together in such a way that what I tell of is a simple light."[2] We must have a proper reverence for the mystery of God—founded on a just sense of the limitations of the human mind and heart, as of God's excess, in his being and plan, of all our concepts and imaginings. Such reverence is not simply also necessary for theological students. It is particularly necessary in their case—since their little knowledge, as that of their teachers, may be a dangerous thing. This warning is appropriate as we turn now to study the sources of revelation: Scripture and Tradition.

1. H. V. von Balthasar, *Mysterium Paschale* (English trans., Edinburgh: 1989) "Preface to the Second Edition."

2. *Dinvia commedia*, "Paradiso," Canto XXXIII, l. 82–90; Dante, *The Divine Comedy. 3: Paradiso*, trans. J. D. Sinclair (London: 1946, 1971) 483.

Part Three

Scripture as a Source
in Theology

8

The Authority of Scripture: Canonicity

The Bible is a modest library of ancient religious texts brought together nowadays under one cover. The accident that the word "Bible" is a singular noun in English thus conceals an essential fact to which its Greek root, *ta biblia*, "the books," a plural phrase, bears witness. The simple fact of a change in methods of book production has blurred what should be our first problem in dealing with the Bible theologically.[1] Which are the books that the theologian must regard as theologically authoritative, and why? Until the early Christian period, individual books of the Bible would have been written on scrolls, with normally one scroll to one book. In this way, had we been early Christians, we should have seen clearly that the Bible is a little library. But in the patristic period, another type of book came into fashion. This was the codex, a single bound volume which might well contain, for instance, the entire New Testament. This is what we find in some of the most famous codices, important for our earliest texts of the Gospels, such as the *Codex Vaticanus* in Rome or the *Codex Sinaiticus* in the British Museum. With the coming of the codex, and even more with its successor, the modern printed Bible, people began to lose the sense that Scripture is an assembly of diverse texts. Once we realize, however, that the Bible is essentially what I have called a "library," then certain questions at once suggest themselves.

Three questions that surface directly here are of major importance to the theologian. First, why these particular books and only these? Second, what, if any, is the significance of their order? Third, should they all be treated as of equal value? In sum, we need to carry out a

1. *See* D. J. Wiseman, "Books in the Ancient Near East and in the Old Testament," and C. H. Roberts, "Books in the Graeco-Roman World and in the New Testament," in *The Cambridge History of the Bible* 1, ed. P. R. Ackroyd and C. F. Evans (Cambridge: 1970, 1975) 30–66.

bit of historical and theological reflection on canonicity, on the fact that we have such a thing as a canon, an approved list of the books of the Bible.[2] The word "canon" is a straight transliteration of the Greek *kanôn*, meaning "a rule," and the idea behind it is easy to grasp. In order to safeguard revelation, people were anxious to identify the writings that were believed to be its primary witnesses. By contrast, books that fell outside the canon could be regarded as inessential or even, if thought desirable, ditched altogether. The canon accepted in the Catholic Church is the one drawn up definitively by the Council of Trent in the sixteenth century.[3] This date may strike us as surprisingly late. So it is, but we should not draw the conclusion that for the first fifteen hundred years of Christian history there had been general confusion about which books were really Scripture. As early as the fifth century identical lists to that of Trent were in circulation. Some of these were put out by local councils, mainly in North Africa; another occurs in a letter from Pope Innocent I to the bishop of Toulouse.[4] But a local council is not a general or ecumenical council, and a private letter to a colleague is not an *ex cathedra* statement. In the ordinary teaching of the Church, the limits of the canon were already worked out in the patristic period; but there was no solemn definition of those limits until 1546.

How was the canon arrived at? As one might expect, there is a big difference here, depending on whether we are thinking of the Old or of the New Testament. As far as the Old Testament is concerned, the Catholic Church accepts forty-six books in her canon. In a modern Bible these are laid out in three main blocks. First, there are historical narratives, ranging from Genesis, which is a history book with a pre-historical prologue, to the Books of the Maccabbees, which no one could fail to see are meant to be history, dealing as they do with a war of Jewish independence in the second century before Christ. The second main block consists of didactic and poetic books, like Wisdom and the Psalter. Finally, there are the Prophets. This order is a thirteenth century rearrangement of the Jewish Bible, which had a rather different structure with four main blocks instead of three: the Law, the Former Prophets, the Latter Prophets, and then everything else, called (for want of a better word) the Writings. But more striking is the fact that the Jews have a canon of only thirty-nine books, seven fewer than our-

2. *See* J. C. Turro and R. E. Brown, "Canonicity," in R. E. Brown, J. A. Fitzmyer, and R. E. Murphy, *The Jerome Biblical Commentary* (London: 1969) 515–34.
3. *See* the Tridentine decree *De canonicis Scripturis* of April 8, 1546 (DS, 1501–5).

selves, and in this they are followed by the Churches of the Reformation. So how did the Catholic Church come by this canon, and why does it differ from that of Judaism (and Protestantism)?

The drawing up of the canon of the Old Testament was a very long-drawn-out affair, which is not startling when one considers that the composition of the Old Testament took over a thousand years. The most ancient parts of the Jewish Bible are fragments of poetry, which have gotten incorporated into books dealing with the early history of the Israelites.[5] Some of these poems may date from the twelfth century B.C. On the other hand, the last books in the Jewish (and Protestant) canon, Daniel and Esther, were composed around the year 150 B.C., and so a thousand years after the earliest writings. The last books in the Catholic canon, Second Maccabees and Wisdom, were written later still, less than a hundred years before the birth of Jesus. Quite naturally, then, the formation of the Old Testament as an explicit collection of books also took a very long time. We can distinguish four stages in the formation of the Old Testament canon. First, there emerged the minicollection known as the Pentateuch, the five books of the Torah, the "Law" or "Teaching." This seems to have happened before 400 B.C., since around that date the Pentateuch was taken by Ezra as the basis for the reconstruction of Jewish society time after the Exile.[6] Very likely, it was the concept of a charter for a religious society, basic to Ezra's activity, which gave people the idea of formulating little canons of authoritative books. The second minicollection was that of the other history books of the Jewish Bible, what the Jews themselves called the "Former Prophets." These books offer a reading of history in the light of God's will and judgments, and in this sense, therefore, they resemble the work of the prophets. Since a number of these history books were not written until just before the Exile, scholars regard this collection as put together some time after the return from Babylon.[7] Next comes the collection known in Judaism as the "Latter Prophets," or, in plain English, "the Prophets." Around 190 B.C. the author of Sirach refers to the "Twelve Prophets" of Israel, so it looks as if this minicanon had crystallized by then.[8] Finally, we

---

4. S. Zarb, *De historia canonis utriusque Testamenti* (Rome: 1934).

5. "The Song of Miriam," Exodus 15:1-18; "The Song of Deborah," Judges 5:2-31.

6. Nehemiah 8:1. However, some scholars believe that this "book of the Law of Moses" was simply the legal collection of the Priestly school, one strand in the present Pentateuch.

7. This collection is referred to by contemporary writers as the "Deuteronomic History."

8. Sirach 49:10.

come to the portmanteau category of the Writings, a lucky dip with something for everybody. It is not clear how many books were regarded as belonging to the Writings by most Jews in the biblical period. Even in the first century A.D. people were still referring in a vague sort of way to the "other works" that the ancestors had written.[9] Thus, in the time of Jesus, Judaism had not yet closed the canon. It had defined three minicanons, or subcanons, but these were themselves situated within a total canon that was still open.

However, two definite tendencies were already in evidence. In Palestine, the trend was to take a minimizing view of the total number of sacred books. In Egypt, the main center of Jewish emigration, the trend went in the opposite direction, toward maximalization, the desire to include as many candidates as possible. The decision to "fix" the canon may have been sparked by a move to close ranks against Jews who accepted Christianity. Or again, it may simply have been a political ploy in the struggle for predominance then going on between different Jewish parties. In Palestine, Jews elected a shorter canon with only a selection of the Writings. The books of this canon are usually referred to as "protocanonical," the books of the "first canon."[10] In Egypt, there was no formal decision to close the canon, such as the rabbis (probably) took in Palestine, but a larger number of the Writings were translated for the Alexandrian Greek Bible, the Septuagint, showing that Egyptian Jews did not recognize the short canon as telling the whole story. It is now considered by historians of the Bible that the longer canon was in fact drawn up not by the synagogue but by the Alexandrian Church, using the Septuagint as a guide.[11] The extra books involved are often referred to as "deuterocanonical," belonging to the "second canon." The debate about the respective merits of the shorter and the longer canons continued right up until the Council of Trent. In the patristic period, support for the shorter canon came mostly from Eastern Christians, although Jerome of Bethlehem, the translator of the Latin Bible, was favorable as well. Later on in the West, quite a wide variety of Catholic authors had doubts about the Deuterocanonical books. These include Pope Gregory the Great in the sixth century, the Augustinian canon Hugh of St. Victor in the twelfth, the Franciscan scholar Nicholas of Lyra in the fourteenth, and, in the six-

---

9. Josephus, *Against Apion* I. 8, 39–41.

10. Whether or not at the rabbinic "Council of Jamnia" of ca. 95: *see* J. P. Lewis, *Journal of Bible and Religion* 32 (1964) 125–32.

11. A. C. Sundberg, *The Old Testament of the Early Church* (Cambridge, Mass.: 1964).

teenth, right on the eve of Trent, the Dominican theologian Thomas de Vio, Cardinal Cajetan.[12] At the council itself, not enough was known about Christian origins to make a sound historical judgment about the merits of the two canons. Instead, the bishops at Trent appealed to a different principle, that of the Church's consistent use of certain books in her liturgy and preaching.[13] This decision could today, with our fuller historical knowledge, be regarded as the more coherent in terms of Christian origins also—since it is now believed that the shorter canon was not produced until after Jesus Christ lived. In Protestantism, the Reformers tended to say that the deuterocanonical books might be used for edification but not to prove Christian doctrine.[14] Slowly, however, Protestants slid off the fence in this regard, and the Deuterocanonicals disappeared altogether from printed Bibles.[15] More recently, they have returned to favor and are always printed in the "common" Bibles licensed for Protestant, Catholic, and Orthodox use.

Turning now to the canon of the New Testament: as we know, Jesus Christ did not leave behind any written documents. On one occasion, the gospels do describe him as writing, but the writing was in that least preservable of media, sand. There is no sure evidence that any disciple of Jesus ever tried to put the gospel into writing before the year 50. Perhaps the most obvious reason for this is the concentration of the earliest Church in Jerusalem. Quite possibly, most of the Twelve did not leave the ancient holy city until its destruction during the Roman-Jewish War of A.D. 66–70. There was, then, little pressure to write, because one had the living presence of the Twelve teaching by word of mouth, as in the opening chapters of the Acts of the Apostles. So what led Christians to express their faith in written form? At least four distinct causes can be identified.[16] First, the Church began to gain converts living far away from the mother Church in Jerusalem. In A.D. 49 the Church decided to accept Gentile converts directly, without first requiring them to become Jews, and with this measure of relaxation (for which Paul offered a profound theological explanation in Galatians and Romans), converts from the Greco-Roman world

12. A. C. Sundberg, "The Old Testament: A Christian Canon," *Catholic Biblical Quarterly* 30 (1968) 143–55.

13. *See* H. Jedin, *A History of the Council of Trent* (English trans., London: 1961) II. 52–98.

14. E. g. Article VI of the *Thirty-Nine Articles.* There was a comparable hesitancy in the Byzantine East: cf. J. Meyendorff, *Byzantine Theology* (London: 1974) 7.

15. Thus, for instance, the (Anglican) British and Foreign Bible Society determined in 1827 to leave out the Deuterocanonical books from its future publications.

16. *See* Turro and Brown, "Canonicity," 525.

flooded in.[17] In fact, the Pauline letters are a good example of an a-
postle trying to preserve contact with a number of far-flung daughter
Churches. A second reason for the making of the New Testament writings was the increasing distance, not so much in space as in time, from
the ministry of Jesus. Eventually the Twelve would die, and so would
those who had known the Twelve, and the finer or more circumstantial points of the oral tradition would be lost. There was a natural impulse, therefore, to write down what was remembered before it was
too late. This remains the simplest explanation of the existence of the
four Gospels. A third factor was the threat of heresy: individuals choosing, *hairein*, an interpretation of the career of Jesus that sat ill with what
the rest of the Church believed. This seems to have been what was
behind the writing of the Johannine letters. Fourth and finally, there
was the desire to encourage those facing persecution, something which
accounts for such a text as the First Letter of Peter.

What criteria were used by the Church in evaluating the Christian
texts so produced and in the end coming to accept them as "sacred"
texts, Holy Writ on a par with the Old Testament itself? Three criteria
seem to have been invoked. The most obvious was a connection with
the apostles, usually with one particular apostle. Doubts about apostolic
authorship caused problems, as with the Apocalypse and the Letter
to the Hebrews. Today we argue that the concept of apostolic authorship must be taken broadly. If an apostle may be said to "stand behind" a writing, in such a way that the essential drift of his teaching
is preserved within it, then this is regarded as adequate grounds for
maintaining its apostolicity, regardless of whether the apostle in question ever set pen to papyrus or not. A second criterion was certainly
orthodoxy, conformity to the emerging rule of faith of the Church.
Thus, around 190 a bishop of Antioch stopped people from using the
so-called Gospel of Peter on the grounds that its author did not regard
the human body of Jesus as real.[18] Third, a particular writing had to
be valued by a Church that was itself respected for its own apostolic
origin. Most of the apostolic Churches were in the East, in Asia Minor
and Greece, and it is from there that we get the largest number of New
Testament books: most of Paul, John, and Luke-Acts. But the Roman
Church was also apostolic, and along with the Letter to the Romans,
the Gospel of Mark may also have been preserved at Rome. Curiously

---

17. Acts 15.
18. For this incident, *see* Eusebius, *Church History* VI. 12, 2.

enough, the Jerusalem Church appears to have left nothing, probably because of the massive disruption caused by the Roman War.

The composition of the New Testament canon is a much less well-documented process than is the case with its Old Testament counterpart. The first minicanon to emerge was probably the Pauline corpus. It is suggested that around the year 90, when the Book of the Acts was published, people began to realize the huge importance of Paul and so gathered his extant letters into a single collection.[19] The four Gospels were brought together by about 200, possibly because sectarians were making ever more disastrous use of the others, those we now think of as the "apocryphal" Gospels.[20] However, the Church in Syria used a single gospel, a harmonization of the four, and did not accept the canon of four distinct Gospels until as late as the fifth century.[21] As to the rest of the New Testament, it is a shady area comparable to that of the Writings in the Old Testament canon. All we can say is that judging by patristic discussion, the present twenty-seven-book canon was widely accepted in the Greek- and Latin-speaking Churches by the end of the fourth century. Although I have mentioned precedents in the patristic period for the canon of Trent, there was no universally agreed-on canon of the New Testament in the early Church. Nevertheless, the Pauline collection and the Gospels are constants.

What are the theological implications of this ill-lit process of canonization, which I have tried to outline? Three questions come to mind. What is going on in canonization? Is the structure of the canon significant? Are all its constituent books of equal importance to the theologian? We can say at once that canonization is the determination of a list of books with sufficient comprehensiveness and cohesion to serve as the primary witness to biblical revelation. In the act of canonizing, the Church declares that certain books are divinely enabled testimony to a divinely given revelation. In other words, in canonizing, the Church discovers which books, among those known to her that touch her faith, are really and truly divinely inspired. As students of Catholic theology, we accept the authority of these books because the Church

19. This theory was the brainchild of E. J. Goodspeed in *The Meaning of Ephesians* (London: 1933). It is also possible that Marcion and the Gnostics' one-sided appropriation of Paul led to the putting together of a collection consisting of the original Pauline letters, other letters from Paul's disciples, and the narrative material of Acts, coming as this did, from this same Pauline "school."

20. Cf. the affirmation ascribed to Origen that there are four gospels which are "undeniably authentic in the Church of God on earth" in Eusebius, *Church History* VI. 25, 4.

21. On the *Diatessaron*, see F. C. Burkitt, *Evangelion da-Mepharreshe* (London: 1904).

as a Spirit-guided community has deemed them to be divinely inspired. To accept a biblical book on any other ground than this would be to submit the Word of God to a purely human appraisal.

However, although this is very well for us, the fact is that the Church herself must have submitted these books to some kind of appraisal in canonizing, and we are justified in asking what form that appraisal took. Unfortunately, in historical terms, we do not know (with any complete clarity or satisfactory precision) why the canon is as it is. This is a problem, an *aporia*, for which only Karl Rahner has provided a reasonable solution.[22] Rahner argued that the sheer emergence of the New Testament books as an expression of the faith life of the primitive Church was itself what enabled the Church to recognize their inspiration. The Church saw her own faith, her own being, reflected in just these books, and that corporate intuition of hers was the discovery of inspiration and so the basis of canonicity. Factors like apostolicity and orthodoxy find their place as elements within this wider picture. On this view, knowledge of the canon is, we might say, connatural to the Church—just as knowledge of a virtue is connatural to the person practicing that virtue. The Church did not determine the canon by a process of inference from facts, but took in its contents in a unique moment of perspicuous awareness of her own identity, the consequences of which stayed permanently with her. The same argument will cover the Old Testament canon too. Until the Church came along, there was no infallible authority in salvation history that could witness to the inspiration of the Old Testament. In doing so, the Church bore witness simultaneously to the essential preparation for her own existence. Rahner's solution has the additional merit, by the way, of solving a further problem which turns on one question: Even after Trent, is the canon finally closed? It might be argued that while Trent tells us that certain books are in the canon, it does not say explicitly that *only* these books have made it. The practical bearings of this can be seen as soon as we ask what we should do if some scholar rooting about in a Coptic monastery found one of the missing letters of St. Paul. If canonization works simply from inference, for instance from the fact of apostolicity, then there would be a strong *prima facie* case for adding such a letter to our Bibles. If, on the other hand, Rahner is right, and the formation of the canon was a unique act of coming-to-self-awareness on the part of the primitive Church—the act that enabled the Church to constitute herself once and for all as the Church

22. K. Rahner, *Inspiration in the Bible* (English trans., New York: 1964).

of these Scriptures, the "Church of the New Testament" as we say—then a newly discovered letter of Paul would certainly not be taken at this late stage into the canon.

Our second question concerned the structure of the canon and its possible theological implications. It is worth noting, first of all, that there is only one canon, of which Old and New Testaments are the parts. The Maker and the Savior, creation and redemption, nature and supernature belong together in an unbreakable unity. The one Logos, finally revealed in Christ, is, as Justin Martyr insisted, at work in both. Second, there is the fact that in both canons, New Testament and Old, a definite group of books comes first: in one case the Gospels, in the other the Pentateuch. In each case, primacy is being given to the original founding moment of a religious tradition, the crucial revelatory event. The rest of what follows in each canon will naturally be judged, then, in the light of the opening collection. The history, wisdom, and prophetic activity of the Jews circle around the giving of the Torah to Moses. The history and letter writing of the early Church flow from the life, death, and resurrection of Jesus Christ, the content of the Gospels. In this elementary but important way, the structure of the canon gives theologians some marching orders about what they are to regard as central or crucial in the Judeo-Christian tradition.

Our final question asked whether all the canonical books are to be regarded as of equal importance. It is manifest that some books are concerned more directly with formal religious issues than others. No one could suppose that the Letter to Philemon, a postcard about a runaway slave, is likely to be as theologically useful as the Gospel of John. But this does not imply that there are varying degrees of inspiration behind the biblical books. The Letter to Philemon for its purposes required inspiration just as much as the Gospel of John. That is, it may not have much to teach us, but, in order to teach us that much, it needs inspiration. We can allow, therefore, that not all the members of the canon have the same standing within the theological circle, so long as we allow at the same time that all have an equal right to be there in the first place. Connected with this (but less easy to dispose of) is the problem of theological divergences within the Bible. Many people argue that there are clearly different theological emphases or tendencies within the biblical corpus, and that such divergences amount at times to open contradiction. One might think of what Paul and James have to say about the relation between faith and works, for example. It is then argued that, as a matter of pure logic, we have to follow one biblical tendency rather than another—or else end up in the sheerest self-contradiction. But in order to pursue a given tendency, we have to construct what is termed "a canon within the canon," an inner canon which consists of the books we regard as truly central to the biblical revelation. All the other books would then be relegated to the periphery: not ejected from the canon altogether but nonetheless demoted to the status of second-class citizens.[23]

What are we to make of this proposal? First of all, we can ask whether the theological divergences in the Bible really amount to flagrant self-contradiction in the way suggested. To say that the positive teaching of two scriptural books is as it stands irreconcilable is surely tantamount to denying inspiration, since, after all, we can hardly ascribe a lie to Truth itself. One might agree that there is often a high degree of tension between different approaches, major differences in emphasis, but deny that this amounted to strict contradiction. Of course, just stating this would hardly cut much ice: it would be up to a sympathetic exegete to show it on the ground. But second, the concession that there are diverging theological tendencies in Scripture is an admission that we are dealing here with a real problem. However, the idea of an inner canon is a desperate solution to this problem, dictated—it may be suggested—by the absence of any concept of Tradition as the medium for reading Scripture in the Churches of the Reformation.[24] If tradition has no authority vis-à-vis Scripture then we have no guide as to the practical use of the canon. Therefore, one is obliged to decide on the basis of theological considerations external to the canon what it is that Scripture ought to regard as essential. On that basis, one then identifies an inner canon, supposed to guide one in the actual employment of Scripture in theology. Thus, among Lutherans, the doctrine of justification by faith alone is regarded as the heart of the gospel. The canon is evaluated accordingly, and what emerges is that two Pauline letters, Romans and Galatians, constitute the inner canon. So everything else must be judged in relation to them. In effect, what people are doing here is using theological postulates to judge Scripture and then approaching Scripture in such a frame of mind that it can never correct their theology. In Catholicism, on the other hand, a guide to the practical use of the canon is found in the tradition of

---

23. *See* E. Käsemann, *Essays on New Testament Themes* (English trans., London: 1964).
24. N. Appel, *Kanon und Kirche. Die Kanonkrise im heutigen Protestantismus als kontrovers-theologisches Problem* (Paderborn: 1964).

the Church, in such things as the creeds or the liturgies.[25] Their use of biblical texts gives us an idea of what is more central and what is correspondingly less; but this idea, unlike the one we have just been considering, derives from the monuments of the Church's self-awareness, a self-awareness itself intrinsically related (as we have seen) to the recognition of Scripture's authority. And in any case, once we have constructed our theology in the light of Scripture as read in the light of Tradition, it still remains possible for a person working within this framework to deploy further aspects of Scripture to correct or supplement our theology so far. To put this in another way: the choice of a theological principle of ordering will in a sense involve the individual theologian in making a canon within the canon.[26] But no harm is done by this so long as the theologian recognizes that his or her theology is not the only pebble on the beach, not the only theology possible. In fact, one important reason for encouraging a plurality of theologies within the Church is to make sure that the total wealth of the canon of Scripture is (so far as is humanly possible) theologically deployed.

25. This key to the evaluation of the literal sense may be termed the "traditional sense," i.e., the spiritual sense as mediated by the monuments of Tradition. *See* below, chs. 13 and 14 of this book.

26. Cf. D. Kelsey, *The Uses of Scripture in Recent Theology* (Philadelphia: 1975) 101-3, 159-70. Kelsey speaks, in a way cognate with the approach presented here, of a pattern or "discrimen" whereby through a "configuration of certain criteria" the theologian draws forth a message from the biblical text.

9

The Authority of Scripture: Inspiration

In discussing the canon, I said that the basis of canonicity was the Church's discovery that certain books of Scripture were inspired. I used the word "inspiration" as though its meaning were self-evident. However, this is far from being the case. The problem of inspiration lies at the heart of the problem of the Bible's authority for theology. For it is insofar as the Bible's origin is divine that it functions as an authority *in divinis*, in theological studies. The Council of Trent, in its preamble to the solemn definition of the canon, declared that "following the example of the orthodox Fathers," it "receives and venerates with the same piety and reverence all the books of both Old and New Testaments, for God is the author of both."[1] While in this statment God is said to be the *auctor*, "source," of the two covenants of the saving history, the context makes clear that his authorhood extends to the literature in which those covenants are recorded. If God, then, be the source of these writings, it is hardly surprising that they should be taken very seriously by the theologian. In fact, while it would be excessive to require of theology that it be based exclusively on Scripture (albeit read within Tradition), it would not be going too far to say that, at any rate, all theology must be biblically informed. As Pope Leo XIII put it in his encyclical letter *Providentissimus Deus*, "Most desirable it is, and most essential, that the whole teaching of theology should be pervaded and animated by the use of the divine Word of God." But what is meant by saying that God is the source of Scripture? If canonicity deals with the question of which books have divinely given

---

1. DS, 1501. Trent refers to God here as the *auctor* of the two covenants, or saving economies, expressed in the Scriptures: the First Vatican Council provides the first example of a conciliar use of *auctor* for God's relation to the books themselves. On the meaning of its statement in DS, 3006, *see* N. Weyns, "De notione inspirationis biblicae iuxta Concilium Vaticanum," *Angelicum* 30 (1953) 315–36.

authority for the theologian, then inspiration concerns the problem of how this authority is actually mediated or present in the books that the canon includes.[2]

In the Old Testament, we sometimes hear that God commanded a prophet to write something down, but nowhere is it asserted that the books of the Israelite religion as a whole are divinely inspired.[3] This claim arose later on, though a great impetus was given it by two events within the Old Testament itself. I have in mind first the adoption of the Book of Deuteronomy as a charter of national reform in 622 B.C. by the Judaean king Josiah, a development described in 2 Kings 23. Then there is also an event I have already mentioned in connection with the formation of the Pentateuch as a minicanon, namely the decision of Ezra, in his capacity as legate of the Persian government, to make the five books of Moses the basis for a reconstruction of Jewish national life after the Exile. This happened around 427 B.C. and the circumstances are set forth in Nehemiah 8. In each case, we see the Israelite religion in the process of becoming a scriptural religion, a religion based on sacred texts. Gradually, the Jewish people became a People of the Book, as they have remained until the present day. Previously, Judaism had located authority in other things. Four such other things may be mentioned. It had found its authority in oral traditions, in customary laws, in the teaching of the priesthood at the Temple or in the shrines, and in the messages of the prophets. All of these might be, and were, seen as divinely grounded or enabled. But now the Jewish religion is shifting its primary focus from these things to books instead. We can say that, in the providence of God, this was necessary for the survival of Judaism in a world of change, and also that, from a Christian perspective, the survival of Judaism was the survival of the conditions that made possible the coming of the (in the first place, Jewish) Messiah. To conserve a book is a great deal easier than conserving a whole institutional fabric and way of life. So it was that the Jews came to see the essence of their religion as summed up in certain texts, and first and foremost in the books associated with the figure of Moses, the Torah or "Teaching."

By the time of Jesus, many Jews accepted an extremely high doctrine of the origins of the Torah. They held that it had been brought

---

2. *See* R. F. Smith, "Inspiration and Inerrancy," R. E. Brown and others, *The Jerome Biblical Commentary*, 499–514.

3. Cf. Isaiah 30:8; Jeremiah 30:2; Habakkuk 2:2.

into existence by God himself before the world was.[4] Three theories circulated as to how subsequently it might have been communicated to Moses. Either, people said, this was through mental contact between God's mind and the mind of Moses, or it was by the miraculous handing over of the text of the Pentateuch, or again, it was by dictation into the ear of Moses. The other writings of the Old Testament, while not on this exalted level in the general estimation, were also thought of as written under the influence of the spirit of Yahweh. Just as God had whispered his truth to the prophets, so, in an analogous way, he had whispered that truth to the biblical authors. Thus the literary transmission of prophecy gave Judaism its main model for understanding the inspiration of the Old Testament outside the Pentateuch, and one, at least, of its main models (the last in the choice of three above) for understanding the inspiration of the Pentateuch itself.[5] God dictated and the authors listened. Some Christians found this notion helpful also, so we shall return to it in a moment. The upshot of these developments was a firm belief in the divine origin of the Jewish Scriptures. Thus, in a synagogue today the Old Testament is kept in a shrine on the wall, rather like a tabernacle in a Western Catholic church. The scrolls in the Torah shrine are never handled directly, but only by using cloths or wearing gloves. The Jewish historian Josephus, an exact contemporary of Jesus, explained the unique position of the Scriptures to his pagan readers in these words: "Although long ages have now passed, no one has dared to add, remove or change a syllable; and it is an instinct with every Jew, from the day of his birth, to regard them as the decrees of God, to abide by them, and if necessary, to die for them gladly."[6] So for the Judaism of the time of Jesus there was a widespread conviction that the Scriptures derived in some sense from God himself.

Jesus, and the New Testament authors after him, clearly regarded the Old Testament in the same light. Jesus frequently refers to the Old Testament as enjoying a sovereign authority. Certain events in his ministry had to take place because "it is written." In the discussion of divorce in Matthew's Gospel Jesus ascribes the words of an Old Testament writer to God himself: "He who made them said . . .".[7]

4. G. F. Moore, *Judaism in the First Centuries of the Christian Era* (Cambridge, Mass.: 1927, 1970) 265–68.
5. *Ibid.*, 238–39.
6. Josephus, *Against Apion* 1, 8.
7. Matthew 19:4-5, with reference to Genesis 2:24.

All in all, the New Testament uses the term "Scripture" some fifty times when speaking of the Old; on three occasions passages from the Old Testament are described as "oracles of God"; and at one point the words of a biblical author are said to express the voice of the Holy Spirit himself.[8] Two New Testament texts in particular have been vital in forming the Church's understanding of the inspiration of Scripture: these are 2 Timothy 3:15-16 and 2 Peter 1:21. In 2 Timothy Paul writes, "Every Scripture is divinely inspired and useful for instruction." The Greek word translated here as "divinely inspired," *theopneustos*, means literally, "breathed out by God": produced, then, by the breath or spirit of God. We can note the fact that there is no reference to any constructive role for the human authors of the biblical books, nor is there any explanation of how this divine "breathing" actually produces the texts themselves.[9] On the other hand, in the other classic New Testament reference, 2 Peter, the presence of a human factor in inspiration is, by contrast, clearly acknowledged: "Being propelled by the Holy Spirit they, men though they were, spoke under the agency of God." The word "propelled," *pheromenoi*, is a metaphor taken from sailing: the scriptural writers are like sailing-ships borne forward by the wind. Thus a human factor is recognized, but it is viewed as entirely dependent on the power of God. And this is not just a question of the Jewish sacred books: the author also has in mind some at least of the Christian writings, because at the close of his letter Paul's epistles are already being talked about as themselves Scripture.[10] Apart from this allusion, the only internal New Testament reference to the inspired nature of the Christian Scriptures is in the Apocalypse of St. John, a book which ascribes its own origin to God: "This is the revelation given by God to Jesus Christ. He sent his angel to make it known to his servant John, and John has written down everything he saw and swears it is the Word of God guaranteed by Jesus Christ."[11] Despite the paucity of such references, the early Church maintained with some vigor that the Christian Scriptures were every bit as inspired as the Jewish, even when there was disagreement as to which Scriptures should be

---

8. For the computation of references to *hê graphê, see* Smith, "Inspiration and Inerrancy," 501; *ta logia tou Theou* in Romans 3:2; Hebrews 5:12; 1 Peter 4:11; *to Pneuma to Hagion dia stômatos David,* Acts 1:16.

9. J. N. D. Kelly, *A Commentary on the Pastoral Epistles* (London: 1963).

10. 2 Peter 3:16.

11. Revelation 1:1-3; cf. 22:7, 10, 18-19.

recognized[12] There was a global or general sense that the Church possessed a body of inspired (Christian) writings before there was a clear
propositional account of just which writings these were. But while the
Old Testament contains neither a claim to inspiration nor (*a fortiori*)
a theory about how inspiration works, the New Testament does at least
make the claim that it is itself inspired. To paraphrase Second Peter,
the composition of Scripture is at once something human and something divine. The question of how these two, the human and divine
elements, are related (if only we can solve it) will enable us to answer
the further question: What kind of authority does Scripture possess
for the theologian?

For enlightenment as to the nature of inspiration, we have to turn
from apostolic times to the history of theology in the later Church. The
earliest theory of biblical inspiration saw the writing of the Bible as
ecstatic or even hypnotic in character. The origin of this way of looking at the subject seems to have been the Jewish philosopher Philo
of Alexandria, who was writing in about A.D. 50. Philo imagined that
the writer was possessed by God, losing ordinary consciousness and
letting his personality be taken over by the divine power. He would
write, therefore, ecstatically, or in a trance.[13] This theory entered the
Church through a second-century Greek apologist, Athenagoras, who
held that the biblical writers lost their reason and were played upon
by the Spirit as a pipe is played by the piper.[14] But this hypnotic theory
soon aroused opposition. Thus the third-century Alexandrian Father
Origen maintained that under divine inspiration the mental powers
of a biblical author would surely not be diminished so much as en-
hanced, in order to enable him to apprehend divine truth more
clearly.[15] In point of fact, while the ecstatic theory would certainly ex-

12. G. Perrella, "La nozione dell'inpirazione scritturale secondo i primitivi documenti
cristiani," *Angelicum* 20 (1943) 32–52.

13. H. Wolfson, *Philo* 2 (Cambridge, Mass.: 1947) 24–45. Behind this is surely the
Hellenic view of mantic or oracular inspiration through possession by a *daimôn* or deity
who forces one to utter words, in a frenzied state, deriving from their divine source.
See R. Gnuse, *The Authority of the Bible: Theories of Inspiration, Revelation and the Canon
of Scripture* (New York: 1985) 17.

14. Athenagoras, *Supplication for the Christians*, 9.

15. Origen, *Against Celsus* VII. 3–4. This point was still needing emphasis as late as
the nineteenth century. It was, we are told, characteristic of the Catholic Tübingen school
writers in that epoch to hold that "the sacred writer's faculties, far from being immobi-
lized during periods of divine takeover, are hypersensitized for their task, so that while
following their ordinary human operational laws, they become empowered to transmit
a deeper, divine message." *See* J. T. Burtchaell, *Catholic Theories of Biblical Inspiration Since
1810: A Review and Critique* (Cambridge: 1969) 21–22.

plain how inspiration is divine, it would leave unexplained two large chunks of biblical reality. The first of these is the marked differences in style and tone between the various biblical books. If the writers were entirely passive one would expect Scripture to be uniform. Second, when the Bible itself gives us glimpses of the biblical authors on the job, the picture rarely corresponds to what the ecstatic theory would suggest. For instance, in the Book of Sirach the author tells us how much trouble writing has been to him and asks the reader's pardon for any blemishes his work may contain.[16] Again, Luke tells us of the research he did in getting ready to write his Gospel, and so forth.[17] Many of the early Christian theologians were perfectly well aware that biblical authors had set themselves definite literary and theological aims, and had used conscious artistry to realize them.[18] But despite this, no fully fledged alternative to the ecstatic theory emerged with any clarity until the sixteenth century.

But before leaving the hypnotic theory, we should notice what would follow for theological method were that theory true. Basically, it would no longer be possible to speak about the "literal sense" of the Bible, in other words, the meaning which the human author intended. If Scripture were a form of automatic writing, no such authorial intention would exist for us to appeal to. Nor would it be possible to speak of a historically original meaning to a biblical text, that is, a meaning constituted by the writer's relationship to his own contemporaries. The writing of Scripture would not be historically conditioned. It would only be historical in the sense that the persons used by God as mediums for the transcribing of his message lived at definite points in historical time. But, if there is no literal sense and so no historically original sense, then there would be no need for the theologian to bother with the study of Scripture using the historical, and more especially, the historical-critical method. In other words, ninety-five percent of modern biblical scholarship would become irrelevant at a stroke, leaving only the five percent which is concerned with establishing the best texts from the manuscripts available. Of course, many people confronted with the detailed scholarship and the methodological mazes of the historical-critical method might regard this as a reason for embracing the hypnotic theory! But the price to be paid would be very high. We

16. Sirach, foreword, 16–35.
17. Luke 1:1-4.
18. Cf. Cyril of Alexandria, *Exposition of the Gospel of John* 1. 10, 1, 18; Augustine, *Sermons* 246, 1.

would lose one important means of working out what the meaning of a biblical text is, for if the hypnotic theory is true, then we cannot reason about the Bible by using the analogy of how literature in general works, nor even from our understanding of how the human mind operates.

The first real alternative to the hypnotic theory was the theory of verbal dictation. The remote origins of this theory lie in the patristic period; it uses concepts drawn from the Scholastics, and especially St. Thomas. Nevertheless, in its mature form it is a product of the sixteenth and seventeenth centuries. In this theory God is said to communicate the language of Scripture to the human author, giving him supernaturally those words which best suit the writer's individuality. The author's task is simply to be as consciously receptive as possible to what God is doing. This theory may be seen in illustrated form in many Renaissance and baroque paintings of the evangelists. A dove representing the Holy Spirit hovers around the head of a man seated at a writing desk, his ears attentive to the dove and with pen at the ready. The relation of the divine author to the human writer is now seen in terms of what the Scholastics termed "instrumental causality." The divine author is said to be the "principal efficient cause," the human author the "instrumental efficient cause." An instrumental efficient cause is one that truly acts, and with a power properly its own, yet only does so when moved or used by another, the principal efficient cause. The latter, by activating the potential of the former, enables it to have an effect quite beyond it when left to itself. The stock example is of a man writing with chalk. The piece of chalk I use at the blackboard in my classroom is soft and white. It is capable, then, of producing its own proper effect, namely thick white lines. Yet left to itself the chalk is inert. To produce an effect at all it must be picked up and used. When I activate the power of the chalk I give it the effect, otherwise beyond it, of producing intelligent writing, or at any rate intelligible writing. At the same time, the instrumental cause has truly acted with its own proper power, forming the thick white lines, which are a small thing, but its own. In the Middle Ages, this idea was applied not so much to the inspiration of Scripture as to the description of prophecy. (Examples of prophecy for the medievals would include not simply Isaiah, Jeremiah, and company, but the human mind of Jesus Christ himself.) In prophecy the effect produced is the word of God. The prophet, of himself, is quite incapable of uttering this word. Yet in enabling him to produce the prophetic effect,

God as principal cause has used and elevated the prophet's ordinary human faculties, just as in writing on the blackboard I use and elevate the ordinary natural properties of chalk. It seems that according to, for instance, St. Thomas, the prophet does not have to be conscious of undergoing divine influence.[19] Prophets can receive their materials in one of three ways: either from the world around them through the senses in a common way, from images supernaturally infused into the mind, or from ideas formed with divine aid. But the essence of prophetic knowledge, in Thomas' view, is the judgment the prophet makes about these materials. It is here that God acts upon the mind, enlightening and transforming it so that it becomes an inspired mind, a mind whose self-expression in language is the word of God. Thomas himself did not pay much attention to biblical inspiration.[20] He regarded it as falling within prophecy but as being, often, a rather low-grade version of prophetic activity. He points out, for example, that many things taught in Scripture do not go beyond what natural knowledge could tell us anyway, citing a snippet of the First Book of Kings: "Solomon could talk about plants from the cedar of Lebanon to the hyssop growing on the walls."[21] Such expertise in botany is described by the biblical writer as the "gift of Yahweh." And so the development of a theory of inspiration based on Thomas' account of prophetic knowledge had to await the efforts of later Thomists, especially in the sixteenth century and just after.

Fundamentally, Thomas' theory could have been developed in either a maximalizing or a minimalizing direction. Either one could stress that God really is the principal efficient cause, or one could stress that the human writer really is the instrumental efficient cause. In fact, his teaching was developed in a maximalizing direction and so was turned into the theory of verbal dictation. Here the argument is that whereas in classical or oral prophecy God gives a person, supernaturally, ideas and images which mediate divine truth, in biblical inspiration God gives not only the ideas and images but the very language in which to express them. The words are infused or, if you like, dictated. The use of the word "dictated" probably derives from a misunderstanding of the language of the Council of Trent. The Fathers of Trent, as well as solemnly defining the canon and declaring God to

---

19. For an account of Thomas' views, *see* P. Synave and P. Benoit, *Prophecy and Inspiration* (New York: 1961).

20. But cf. the lapidary statement in *Quodlibetal Questions* 7, 6, a.14, ad v.

21. 1 Kings 3:4, cited in *Summa theologiae*, IIa. IIae., q. 174, a. 3.

be the author of Scripture, also spoke about the biblical books (and certain unwritten traditions coming down from the apostles) as either "given by the mouth of Christ himself," or *a Spiritu Sancto dictatas,* "dictated by the Holy Spirit."[22] Here the verb *dictare* is not being used to explain how the Scriptures were written but simply to affirm that their origin really is the Holy Spirit himself. But the next thing we find is Domingo Bañez, the confessor of St. Teresa and an important representative of the Thomism of his day, writing: "The Holy Spirit not only inspired all that is contained in the Scriptures. He also dictated and suggested every word with which it was written. . . . To dictate means to determine the words."[23] However, Bañez was merciful to those who did not share his view. To ascribe the literary qualities of a scriptural work to human ingenuity is not, he thought, against the Catholic faith. Bañez himself ascribed the differing literary styles of the Bible to God's condescension. God accommodated himself to the thinking and style of the individual writers, so that it all came out as though they had written on their own. But Bañez and the writers of his school, which still has its defenders, could not explain the fact that some biblical authors rattle on about their own research.

What would follow for theology if the verbal dictation theory were true? To begin with, the literal sense could be reinstated. The intention of the divine author is represented (adequately if not exclusively) by the intention of the human author, because the divine author uses and elevates the capacity of an individual to be a writer of literature. Similarly, we could once again speak of a historically original meaning. Because if God accommodated himself to the styles of expression of a particular individual, he must also have accommodated himself to the styles of expression of a particular age and culture of which that individual was a part. And to understand these styles of expression we must look at the styles of expression found generally in the literature comtemporary with the biblical books. We can thus use the expertise of Orientalists and ancient historians to help us gauge as theologians what is being said in the biblical corpus.

But this is not to say that there would be no theological inconveniences if we decided to opt for the dictation theory. First, although Scripture would have a literal sense, it would have that sense in a

22. DS, 1501.

23. Domingo Bañez, *Scholastica commentaria in primam partem divi Thomae* I. q. 1, a. 8, dub. tert., i concl. For Bañez' life and works, *see* V. Beltrán de Heredia, "Bañez, Domingo" in *Lexikon für Theologie und Kirche* 1 (Freiburg: 1957) cols. 1219–20.

purely technical way. That is, the human author would not have acquired the intention to write on a certain subject in a certain way by natural means. That intention would simply be the effect of the divine intention. Thus, even though we could determine a historically original meaning coordinate with God's accommodation of the revealed message to the writer's individuality, we could not determine historically the author's intention. And to this extent the literal sense would not be securely rooted in the soil of its historical context, thus rendering theological exegesis that much more difficult. Second, the verbal dictation theory would necessarily bind the theologian to a doctrine of verbal inerrancy. Every word in the Bible would have to represent prophetic knowledge, that is, either supernatural truth or supernaturally guided natural truth. It may safely be said that if theologians are obliged to defend the verbal inerrancy of Scripture, they will have neither time nor energies left for doing anything else with their lives. This is not to say that theologians are free to deny the inerrancy of Scripture as such. But, if possible, some view of inerrancy should be adopted which takes into account the intrinsic purposes of there being a Bible in the Church in the first place. And these purposes can have little to do with advising gardeners on how to grow hyssop.

Both the hypnotic theory and the dictation theory start from the conviction that God is the author of Scripture and then try to explain how God's authorship comes to be humanly mediated. What they regard as problematic is the human side, not the divine side. This comes through clearly in references to God as the "principal author" of Scripture (St. Thomas) or as the "only author of Scripture in the strict sense" (Henry of Ghent, a slightly later Scholastic, who died in 1293).[24]

Two other theories I would like to mention start from the opposite assumption, namely that Scripture is manifestly human, and then try to work up to God from below. The first such theory to emerge was the so-called theory of subsequent approbation, first associated with the Dominican friar Sixtus of Siena (1520–69) and revived in the nineteenth century.[25] This theory holds, in effect, that inspiration is retroactive. When the Church solemnly judges a book worthy of in-

---

24. For Thomas, *see*, e.g., *De Potentia* q. 4, a. 1, c.; for Henry, *Summa quaestionum ordinariarum* a. 9, q. 2, resp.

25. Sixtus of Siena, *Bibliotheca sancta* 1. 8, haer.12, resp. ad vii. The principal nineteenth-century representative of Sixtus' approach was Daniel Bonifacius von Haneberg, later bishop of Speyer. *See* especially his *Einleitung in das alte Testament für angehende Candidaten der Theologie* (Regensburg: 1845) 297; and *Geschichte der biblischen Offenbarung* (Regensburg: 1850) 714.

clusion in the canon, then owing to the Church's infallibility, from that moment on the book can be known to be an expression of divine truth—in other words, it may henceforth be called "inspired." As one representative of this school put it: "A book is written in a purely human manner, but later is elevated, through reception into the canon, to be an expression of divine communication to men; the Spirit of God knew from the beginning that we would adopt this work, without, however, any direct intervention in the spirit of man."[26] But the idea of inspiration is not simply the idea of revealed truth. The subsequent approbation theory really reduces inspiration to canonicity, forgetting that when the Church declares a book to be part of the canon she does not render it inspired but, on the contrary, claims that God has already been operative in its making, that "merely giving one's approval to what someone else has written does not make one the author of the canon."[27] So this theory falls down by claiming for the Church something the Church has never dared to claim for herself.

The second theory which starts from the human side is the theory of negative assistance, which originated at Louvain under the influence of the Jesuit theology of grace but which in the nineteenth century was particularly associated with a German Premonstratensian canon, Johann Jahn (1750–1816).[28] According to this idea, God leaves the biblical writers alone unless he sees that they are about to commit some egregious error, in which case he intervenes negatively so as to prevent them. He gives them, in other words, negative assistance. But this theory really takes the stuffing out of inspiration by saying that unless something goes hopelessly wrong, the Scriptures are just ordinary human artifacts. Neither of these theories is now open to Catholic theologians. Both were rejected by the Catholic Church at the First Vatican Council. To cite *Dei Filius*, the Church "holds these books to

26. Cited in J. T. Burtchaell, *Catholic Theories of Biblical Inspiration Since 1810*, 54.
27. *Ibid.*, 57–58.
28. Burtchaell locates the origins of this theory in the work of Lessius (Leonhard Leys, 1554–1623), who "aware as an exegete that the biblical authors did not need God to tell them what they already knew, and convinced as a theologian that God could not have implanted information in their minds without doing violence to their human authorship, proposed the theory of 'mere assistance, preservation from error, as a sufficient minimum of divine intervention to allow of a book's being called Scripture." *Ibid.* 46. Defended by Bellarmine, and continued in not only such Jesuit works as J. Bonfrère, *Totam Scripturam Sacram praeloquia* (Antwerp: 1625), but also the Dominican Vincent Contenson's *Theologia mentis et cordis* (1681), it reached the nineteenth century in Johann Jahn's *Einleitung in die göttlichen Bücher des Alten Bundes* (Vienna: 1802), and, rather closer to the time of the First Vatican Council, the work of Jan Herman Janssens of Liège and Franz Heinrich Reusch of Bonn.

be sacred and canonical not because, having been carefully composed by mere human industry, they were afterwards approved by her authority, nor because they merely contain revelation with no admixture of error, but because, having been written by the inspiration of the Holy Spirit, they have God for their author and have been delivered as such to the Church herself."[29] However, for the sake of completeness we can note the principal implications of these theories for theology. If, *per impossibile*, these theories were true, then there would be nothing other to Scripture than the literal sense. There would be no possibility of a *sensus plenior*, a further dimension of meaning intended by the divine author but not consciously grasped by the human author yet made available to us by such factors as the interrelation of the biblical books, their relation to Christ, the Church, and the Christian life, and their being read in light of Tradition. This further dimension, which makes all the difference between a purely historical-critical reading of the Bible and a fully theological reading, would no longer exist. The Church could of course still make whatever use she wanted of the Bible in preaching the faith, but in so doing she would as often as not be using the Scriptures by abusing them—accommodating them to purposes for which they were never intended by anyone, not even by God, since he, on these theories, is not their author.

Taking the analogy of the Christological debates in the early Church, those theories which take for granted God's authorship of Scripture but find it hard to explain how there can also be human authors might be called "Monophysite" acounts of inspiration. Just as the Monophysites were clear about Christ's divinity but unsure about the status of his humanity "after the union," so supporters of the hypnotic and verbal dictation theories may be said to be clear about the divine origin of Scripture but unclear about its human beginning. Using the same analogy, the two theories I have just been describing, subsequent approbation and negative assistance, could be called "Nestorian." For here the human aspect of the divine-human reality of the Bible is clearly affirmed, but its indissoluble unity with the divine is denied. What we need to know now is whether, in the period after the First Vatican Council, it proved possible to work out an account of inspiration that was "Chalcedonian," in other words, an account of the Bible which showed how it could be at one and the same

29. Vatican Council I, *Dei Filius* 2, DS, 3006.

time both fully divine and fully human. But first a word about background.

It was not by chance that the First Vatican Council turned out to be a watershed in the theology of inspiration. The Council met at a time when biblical study was, from a doctrinal viewpoint, in crisis. From a literary or historical point of view, however, biblical studies were not in crisis but in their most exciting and creative phase, a phase which one may perhaps regard as now over. There is not much likelihood of fresh archaeological discoveries or new types of literary analysis that would radically change our understanding of the human side of Scripture. After all, the Bible is now by far the most intensively studied body of literature in the world. But be that as it may, at least one can point to the elements in late nineteenth- and early twentieth-century scholarship which made this the greatest period in the study of biblical origins since the age of Origen and Jerome, despite the problems it raised for biblical authority.

First, there was textual criticism.[30] The collation of manuscripts enabled scholars to get a much better idea of the history of transmission of the Bible, the way it has come down to us in different textual families. One result of the massive development of textual criticism was that there turned out to be far more variant readings of the Bible than had previously been thought. For instance, even though the New Testament is better preserved than any of the Greek or Latin classics, there are nevertheless some 200,000 variant readings in the manuscript tradition. Most of these variants have no theological significance, and the majority can be resolved using critical methods. Still, quite a number are left which must be regarded as incapable of definitive solution, and these will always remain a matter of debate among scholars. The development of textual criticism made the verbal inspiration theory very hard to maintain. If God had really dictated a text, then surely that text in all its verbal exactness would have been the object of a continuing divine concern. One would have expected divine Providence to have preserved such a text from corruption. But this had not happened. Divine causality had started something it could not bring to completion. Or, alternatively, something was wrong with this picture of inspiration.

---

30. *See* S. Talmon, ''The Old Testament Text,'' and J. N. Birdsall, ''The New Testament Text,'' in *The Cambridge History of the Bible* I, ed. P. R. Ackroyd and C. F. Evans (Cambridge: 1970, 1975) 159–98, 308–76.

Second, there was source criticism.[31] The development of source criticism generated the discovery that some books of the Bible are really composite works. Either they have been edited, like the Gospel of John, by a final redactor, or they have incorporated huge chunks of other people's handiwork, like the Books of Chronicles, or, again, they may have taken over oral traditions like the Christological hymns which appear in the letters of St. Paul. This discovery was bad news for supporters of the hypnotic theory and the verbal dictation theory alike. Moreover, it meant that on its human side a biblical book may have multiple authors, and this must surely be taken into account in any sound theory of inspiration.

Third, there was the study of comparative literature.[32] This kind of research made it clear that the biblical books were modelled on various types of literature already in existence in the ancient Near East. Thus, for instance, the sapiential books of the Old Testament are a subsection of the wisdom literature of the Near East as a whole. And what was true of the literary form of biblical books was also true of a good deal of their ideas and imagery. Such notions as prophecy, covenant, creation, sacred kingship, apocalyptic, had their counterparts in several of the cultures around Israel. In the light of this, it was difficult to deny that the biblical writers had authorial intentions in many respects similar to those of their non-Jewish counterparts.

Fourth and finally, there was biblical archaeology.[33] Archaeology created the possibility of confirming empirically many of the historical assertions of Scripture. But by the same token, it also created the possibility of empirically *dis*confirming them as well. This could mean excruciating difficulties for the notion of the verbal inerrancy of Scripture, itself entailed by the theory of verbal dictation.

The cumulative effect of the emergence of these four disciplines was to make Christians who wanted to be orthodox believers very jumpy. Would not people *au fait* with the new methods be so aware

31. *See* e.g. J. Steinmann, *Biblical Criticism* (New York: 1958). After the largely abortive pioneering work of Richard Simon in the seventeenth century, this field was dominated by the mid-nineteenth century by such Protestant scholars as E. Reuss, K. F. Graf, and J. Wellhausen for the Old Testament, and K. Lachmann and H. J. Holtzmann for the New.

32. The early use of history-of-religions research by biblical scholars was somewhat unilateralist in its stress on the homogeneity of the ancient Near Eastern cultural milieu. An example is Franz Julius Delitzsch's *Bible and Babel* (English trans., London: 1902).

33. R. North, "Biblical Archaeology," R. E. Brown and others, *The Jerome Biblical Commentary* (London: 1969) 653–70.

of the human authorship of Scripture that they would forget (or deny) the divine authorship altogether, thus reversing the main tendency of the first seventeen centuries of the Church's existence? Formerly, people saw nothing but God. Now they might see nothing but humans. Thus, in 1893 Leo XIII (1810–1903) promulgated the first papal encyclical on the Bible, *Providentissimus Deus*, in which he noted that unless God has in some manner influenced the minds, wills, and writing abilities of the human authors, there is precious little point in calling him the author of Scripture at all.[34] The Second Vatican Council, in its remarks about inspiration, was content to endorse this unexceptionable statement.[35] However, between the First Vatican Council and Pope Leo on the one hand, and the Second Vatican Council and ourselves on the other, a number of new theories of inspiration emerged, all sharing a good deal of common ground.

To begin with, it is accepted, following tradition, that Pope Leo's core statement must be respected. Divine inspiration must mean divine influence on the minds and wills of biblical writers, or the words are so many vibrations of the air. Second, and following this time not the truth of tradition but the truth of established scholarly fact, the biblical writers remained people of their own time and place. It may be said that the problem of biblical inspiration consists in relating these two points in the most convincing and elegant way possible. In order to do this, theologians have sought enlightenment by comparing inspiration to our understanding of how God reveals himself to humans, as that is found in Christian doctrine as a whole. To do this is to appeal to the analogy of faith, to profit from the fact that the common faith of the Church is not a set of disparate teachings, each unconnected with the rest, but is a coherent, interconnected unity in which any one part can be illuminated by looking to the rest.

Two points are relevant in a comparison of biblical inspiration with the general pattern of God's self-disclosure to us. First, God as Creator can modify directly any aspect of his creation, and in particular the human mind and will, since these are intrinsically open to his action. But, second, God does not normally modify our minds and wills, bringing them to faith, without the cooperation of other creatures in this process. My coming to faith was made up to two things: the preaching of the Church and so the cooperation of creatures on the one hand, and on the other interior divine grace, assisting me to recog-

---

34. Leo XIII, *Providentissimus Deus*, DS, 3293.
35. Vatican Council II, *Dei verbum* 11.

nize and respond to divine truth in that preaching. Using the analogy of faith, we can compare this to what goes on in biblical inspiration. To the Church's preaching would correspond the natural environment of the biblical author. This environment is providentially placed there by God, just as the pamphlets of the Catholic Truth Society have providentially awaited a convert poking about at the back of a Catholic church. To interiorize divine grace there would correspond, then, to the charism of inspiration, God assisting the biblical author to respond to the providential but natural environment in the way God wants.[36] The natural environment, or materials of the author, are all the relevant creaturely realities known to that person—nature, historical events, general human traditions, distinctively Jewish traditions, the words, actions, and sufferings of Jesus in his humanity, the common life of the early Church, and, finally, ideas about how to write a book concerned with some or all of these. The author responds in a normal authorial way to this human environment, but God so acts on the mind and will that the author's response to his or her environment is the saving message that God wants to communicate. To resume the Christological comparison, the human life of Jesus is the life of the eternal Word as projected into space and time. So much for what is, I think, common ground to all Chalcedonian theories of biblical inspiration. We must now look briefly at some significant distinctions between them.

Three major but divergent perspectives on the common ground can be noted. First, there is the theory of formal inspiration put forward by the Austrian Jesuit Johann Baptist Cardinal Franzelin (1816–86).[37] Franzelin argued that what God did in inspiring was to communicate the divine meaning of the relevant human realities. Thus inspiration is purely formal; it has no material content in terms of actual language in the way that the verbal dictation theory alleged. Somewhat confusingly, Franzelin's theory is also called "idea" or "content" inspiration, because it holds thought content to be given by God, but not linguistic expression. But the trouble with this is that it is hard to see how a meaning could be communicated independently of language.

---

36. Cf. the Tübingen divine M. von Aberle's *Einleitung in das Neue Testament* (Freiburg: 1877) 14.

37. F. J. Franzelin, *De divina Traditione et Scriptura* (Rome: 1870). For his work *see* N. Walsh, *John Baptist Franzelin, S. J.: A Sketch and a Study* (Dublin: 1895). Franzelin's theory of inspiration attained a vastly wider audience through its adoption in G. Perrone, *Praelectiones theologicae*, a work of foundational theology which went into thirty-one editions between 1835 and 1865.

A discarnate, unembodied meaning might be compared to the smile on the face of the Cheshire cat in *Alice in Wonderland*. A world where smiles remain when the faces they have wreathed have disappeared can only be labelled "wonderland." Franzelin's theory found itself criticized, therefore, as "psychological vivisection."[38] Second, there is directionalism, the idea of Eugène Lévesque (1855–1944), who was professor of exegesis at the great Parisian seminary of St. Sulpice from 1893 onwards. Lévesque suggested that the interior aspect of inspiration is an impulse to communicate one's materials in a certain way, a certain "direction."[39] This theory has much in common with the view of inspiration put forward by the late Père Pierre Benoit of the Ecole Biblique in Jerusalem. For Benoit, the biblical author's act of writing follows from a practical judgment: not a judgment which consists in starting to believe a particular thing, but a judgment which is a decision to do a particular thing, namely, to write a particular kind of book. Benoit points out that much of the Bible is not concerned with propositional truths or even with truth as such at all. A great deal of Scripture is made up of commands, exhortations, thanksgivings, acts of penitence, expressions of joy, and so forth, and these are kinds of human utterance which can only with difficulty be said to be true or false. But while speculative judgment, judgment about what to believe, is scarcely engaged in such texts, practical judgment, judgment about how to act, is. But Benoit admitted that, obviously, other parts of the Bible *are* concerned with intellectual truth, and here we must speak of God as inspiring a speculative judgment as well as the practical judgment.[40] In other words, Lévesque's directionalism is not enough by itself. Biblical inspiration always gives the author a practical direction, but sometimes there must also be an illumination of the mind as well as a direction of the will.

And this is where it is valuable to introduce a third variant, the illuminationism of Benoit's greatest predecessor at the Ecole Biblique, Marie-Joseph Lagrange, a scholar who preserved the dignity of Catholic biblical studies in the hard times that fell upon them in the wake of the Modernist movement. Lagrange argued that the directly divine part

---

38. Cited by Gnuse, *The Authority of the Bible*, 11.

39. E. Lévesque, in the *Revue biblique* for 1895.

40. P. Benoit, *Aspects of Biblical Inspiration* (English trans., Chicago: 1965) 96–101. To some extent these ideas had been anticipated by a disciple of Lévesque: C. Crets, in his *De divina Bibliorum inspiratione* (Louvain: 1886). *See also* P. Synave and P. Benoit, *Prophecy and Inspiration* (English trans., 1961).

in inspiration is simply an illumination of the mind of the biblical author, enabling the author to judge the natural materials in a way that conforms to God's will. In effect, Lagrange was returning to the texts of St. Thomas and developing the notion of prophetic judgment he found there.[41] All in all, we can say that Lévesque, Lagrange, and Benoit between them have produced a minimalizing but convincing and credible version of Thomas, in place of the maximalizing version that held sway between the Council of Trent and the First Vatican Council.

And this is, so far as it goes, a perfectly adequate position. However, there is one element still unaccounted for. As early as the nineteenth century, source criticism had shown that many biblical books have more than one author. In the twentieth century the problem identified here has mushroomed alarmingly. First, form criticism went back behind the written sources to consider the oral stage of a tradition later set down in writing.[42] Second, redaction criticism looked at the pattern superimposed on the sources by their final editor.[43] Third, tradition-historical criticism, or tradition history, considered the process that unites all three of these moments: oral stage, written stage (or stages), final redaction.[44] No doubt each of these types of criticism was present in embryo in nineteenth-century source criticism, but they have become more mature and sophisticated since. The methodological basis of their tools of trade is not always clear, nor are their methods always fully reconcilable one with another. Nevertheless, the inescapable upshot of even the most modest concession to such scholarship is that we have to take into account a multiplicity of minds and wills at work in the making of a biblical book—and not, as hitherto thought, just one. There are various ways of coping with this state of affairs. One strategy would be to argue that only the final redactor is the inspired author, everybody else's work coming under the heading of "environment" or "materials." On this view, only one person received the charism of inspiration in the case of each biblical book. While this cer-

41. For Lagrange's idea of inspiration, *see* his "L'Inspiration et les exigences de la critique," *Revue Biblique* 5 (1896), 488–518. For the life and work of this exceptional man, see F. M. Braun, *The Work of Père Lagrange* (Milwaukee: 1963); A. Paretsky, "M.-J. Lagrange's Contribution to Catholic Biblical Studies," *Angelicum* 63 (1986) 509–31.

42. For an introduction, *see* S. H. Travis, "Form Criticism," in *New Testament Interpretation: Essays on Principles and Methods*, ed. I. H. Marshall (Grand Rapids, Mich.: 1977) 153–64.

43. *See* S. S. Smalley, "Redaction Criticism," *Ibid.* 181–98.

44. *See* D. R. Catchpole, "Tradition History," *Ibid.* 165–80.

tainly has the virtue of theological economy, it is not otherwise very satisfactory. The trouble is that in many cases the work of a final editor may be minute in comparison with the work inherited. For instance, it is plausible to suggest that the final redaction of Ecclesiastes involved merely the adding of five verses to the end. An alternative approach would be to ascribe inspiration to anyone who has played a part in formulating a linguistic response to the providential environment of revelation. Most of these people will be anonymous, and many will have contributed elements in a way that is more easily thought of as corporate rather than individual. Thus for instance, since many of the psalms in the Psalter are apparently stereotyped cultic formulae of the Jewish liturgy, to say that they were the creation of a liturgical committee may be nearer the truth than to call them the spontaneous effusions of individuals. Or again, parts of Exodus and Judges are folk songs, and judging by what happens to folk songs outside the Bible, it is likely that a whole army of bards played a tiny role in the determination of their final form. In the light of such considerations as these, various North American exegetes, in the period of the 1960s, put forward the idea that inspiration has a corporate or social as well as an individual dimension. According to these writers, notably the Jesuits R. A. F. Mackenzie and J. L. Mackenzie—though Karl Rahner's *Inspiration in the Bible* provided a theological incentive for this approach—it is not just that there are a huge number of inspired individuals, some of whom did almost nothing.[45] When you reach the point where a putative individual changing a word in a line of a ballad must be termed an inspired author, there is a plain need for a shift in the general conceptuality of inspiration. So we speak about the community, either Israel or the New Testament Church as the case may be, as the ultimate bearer of the charism of inspiration. It is the community which was inspired, and the inspiration of individuals consists in greater or lesser intensities of participation in the corporate charism of inspiration. All sorts of people acted as instruments of inspiration to various degrees. Just as Benoit had argued that inspiration is analogical, that the inspiration of the practical judgment is not the same kind of thing as the inspiration of the speculative judgment, though it is not altogether different either, so this North American school proposed that inspira-

---

45. On the social theory of inspiration, *see* R. A. F. Mackenzie, "Some Problems in the Field of Inspiration," *Catholic Biblical Quarterly* 20 (1958) 1–8; J. F. Mackenzie, "The Social Character of Inspiration," *Ibid.* 24 (1962) 115–24; cf. D. McCarthy, "Personality, Society and Inspiration," *Theological Studies* 24 (1963) 553–76.

tion is participation: there are different degrees or intensities of inspiration depending on how much one shares in or draws on the corporate gift of inspiration which belonged to Israel and the apostolic Church.

If we wished, we could write, therefore, an ontology of inspiration. Just as all things that exist share in being to different degrees and in ways that are analogically related, so the inspired men and women of the Old and New Testaments shared in different degrees in the gift of inspiration in ways that are analogically related. To each of these individuals, the analysis offered by such writers as Lévesque, Lagrange, and Benoit would apply in various ways. All of these ways would coincide, however, in being ordered to the final emergence of the canon. When the canon is closed, the charism of inspiration, like the Marxist state, withers away, its task completed. At that point, the Catholic Church ceases to be inspired, although it does not cease to be infallible, that is, to be able to preserve what it understood when it *was* inspired.[46] On such a theory, certain consequences would follow for theological method. First, the literal sense, what an author intended, would be both real and also accessible to historical investigation. Second, we should have to regard an individual book of the Bible as an accumulation of literal senses, of which the principal or superordinate literal sense would be that of the book in its final form, the sense of its final editor. Third, the ordering of inspiration to the canon, to the existence of a recognizable body of literature attesting what God has revealed and sufficiently comprehensive to guide the Church for the rest of time, would imply that the revealed meaning of a book must be sought beyond the literal sense of any individual book, in the interrelated corpus of biblical books as a whole. Fourth, the fact that inspiration is ultimately the charism of a divine society, Israel-Church which eventually produced the canon, implies that the interpretation of the revealed meaning found in that canon must be made within the tradition of the Church and not without it. Fifth and finally, the cumulative and indefinitely extensible nature of this entire process may be explained, humanly speaking, by referring to hermeneutics, that is, the study of how a text offers more and more new interpretations to its readers; yet theologically considered, the same facts raise the question of a *sensus plenior*, that is, of the ecclesially experienced difference between a limited human authorial intention and the fullness of the divine intention, granted that the Scriptures are meant to guide

46. K. Rahner, *Inspiration in the Bible* (2nd ed., English trans., New York: 1964).

humanity until the parousia. No finite consciousness could have been elevated by God in such a way as to comprehend the total mystery of salvation. So we must postulate, then, a supernatural plus of meaning, which the Church unfolds until the end of time.[47]

47. Y. Congar, "Inspiration des Ecritures canoniques et apostolicité de l'Eglise," *RSPT* 45 (1961) 32–42; R. E. Brown, *The "Sensus plenior" of Sacred Scripture* (Baltimore: 1955).

10

The Authority of Scripture: Inerrancy

Granted that Scripture is inspired, having both God and humans for its authors, and granted too that we now have a fairly clear idea of how the divine and human natures of the Bible interrelate, does it follow that every word of Scripture is the truth, the whole truth, and nothing but the truth? This is the problem of biblical inerrancy, or, if you will, the problem of the limits of inspiration. Just how far does inspiration extend? Is the Bible without any falsehoods, without even errors of detail? As by now customary in this book, we will try to consider this question in and through its history.

The term "inerrancy" was not in the past applied to the Bible in any conciliar statement of Christian doctrine. The first time it shows up in any magisterial statement is in Leo XIII's letter *Providentissimus Deus*, which we have already encountered. Nevertheless, what the term denotes was commonly believed by Christians in earlier times—and indeed by Jews, for, according to rabbinic tradition, one of the blessings to be received at the return of Elijah is the explanation of the apparent discrepancies between the Book of Ezra and the Torah. So far as Christians were concerned, belief in scriptural inerrancy appears to have derived from two sources. In part, it derived from the Church's own intuition that the Scriptures were inspired and so were God's truth. In part, it came from the popularity of theories of verbal inspiration.[1] Yet theologians were never unaware of the difficulties that a concept of verbal inerrancy brought in its train. For instance, educated medieval Catholics believed as a matter of natural philosophy that the cosmos was as Aristotle described it. (One can see this by looking at, for example, the geography and astronomy of Dante's [1265–1321] *Commedia*.[2]) But the cosmology of the Bible is not, of course, Aristote-

1. B. Menahoth, 45a, cited R. F. Smith, "Inspiration and Inerrancy," 512.
2. P. Boyde, *Dante Philomythes and Philosopher: Man in the Cosmos* (Cambridge: 1981) 57–171.

lean cosmology; it is the much more primitive mythopoeic cosmology of the ancient Near East. The inevitable discrepancies were overcome in the Middle Ages by calling biblical cosmology a "science of appearances." That is, everything that the Bible said about the cosmos constitutes a perfectly true account of what the cosmos appears to be, or seems like, to a human observer. Rain appears to come from a lake above the sky; in fact, it does not, yet it is true that it appears to. This notion of a science of appearances already rendered the theory of verbal inerrancy somewhat Pickwickian: valid only in a specialized and tenuous sense. It is interesting to note that, in this principle, the seventeenth-century Inquisition was not obliged to condemn Galileo Galilei (1564–1642). By the rules of interpreting biblical inerrancy in the medieval Church he could have passed. In point of fact, however, the consultors of the Holy Office chose to follow the opinion of Cardinal Robert Bellarmine (1542–1621) in his *Letter to Foscarini*. There Bellarmine had argued not that heliocentrism was incompatible with the biblical text but that it was incompatible with the teaching of Scripture as expounded by the Fathers and theologians of the Church.[3]

But beginning with the Renaissance, there had arisen an ever-increasing opposition to the idea of total material inerrancy, people refusing to save the phenomena by such escape clauses as a science of appearances. The first person to make a dent in the consensus was the Catholic humanist Erasmus (ca. 1466–1536) of Rotterdam. Erasmus noted that the sayings of Jesus in the first three Gospels take a slightly different form in each. He suggested that in relatively unimportant matters the Holy Spirit had not bothered to correct the faulty memories of the evangelists.[4] Various writers then took up the cue Erasmus had given. The seventeenth, eighteenth, and nineteenth centuries saw a crop of attempts to cut back biblical inerrancy, usually by claiming that it did not extend beyond the truths of faith. Semifictitious legends and improbable family trees there may be a-plenty in the Bible, but these have no relevance for faith and morals. This being so, there is no reason to expect such doctrinally irrelevant sections of the Scriptures to be inerrant. The problem became especially acute in the last century

3. On Galileo and Bellarmine, *see* J. Brodrick, *Galileo: The Man, His Work and His Misfortunes* (London: 1964). However, it is disputed whether Galileo was forbidden at the "first condemnation" (1616) to defend Copernicanism as sheer fact (only) or as a hypothesis (as well). *See* J. J. Langford, *Galileo, the Church and Science* (New York: 1966); this author points out that, while most of the Fathers did think that the earth was immobile, and the sun mobile, none held that this had to be believed as a revealed truth.

4. For Erasmus, *see* B. Vawter, *Biblical Inspiration* (London: 1972) 134.

[margin note: medieval inerrancy]

with the rise of biological science and the attendant debate about evolution (still going on in certain quarters in the United States), and also with the increasing professionalism of students of ancient history, which brought with it a variety of doubts about the accuracy of the biblical narrative.

Nearly all Catholic attempts to restrict inerrancy to an aspect of the biblical text were placed on the Index of Prohibited Books. The major exception was John Henry Newman's essay ''Inspiration in its Relation to Revelation,'' written in 1884 as a reply to Ernest Renan's (1823–1892) attack on the Church's attitude toward biblical criticism.[5] Newman argued that it was unworthy of the ''divine greatness'' that God should assume the office of historian or geographer ''except as far as secular matters bear directly upon revealed truth.'' The Bible, Newman pointed out, contained many *obiter dicta*, incidental references to what the man in the street believes. Inerrancy, on this view, touches only what is material to Scripture's purposes. If a writer mentioned some alleged fact *en passant*, this was immaterial to their direct purpose and therefore fell outside the sphere of operation of inerrancy. A more radical proposal emerged some years later, when in 1893, Maurice d'Hulst, then rector of the Institut Catholique in Paris, argued that there were grave difficulties in maintaining that absolute inerrancy was a necessary effect of the inspiration of Scripture.[6] D'Hulst's most brilliant student was the young exegete Alfred Loisy (1857–1940), soon to become a leader of the Modernist movement. Loisy would go far beyond his old teacher, postulating the possibility of moral and religious error in the Bible. He considered that the Catholic Church had corrected errors relevant to faith and morals in the biblical authors by refining their teaching over time in accordance with her own religious experience. However, the Church had no desire to be thus glorified at the expense of the Bible, and Loisy found himself excommunicated.[7]

Quite as important as the mental development of Loisy was another response to Hulst's work, the encyclical *Providentissimus Deus* of Leo XIII. On the one hand, Pope Leo warned against the currently

5. J. H. Newman, ''Inspiration in Its Relation to Revelation,'' *The Nineteenth Century* (February 1884); an intemperate attack on this article by John Healy of Maynooth, later archbishop of Tuam, led Newman to write a second, privately printed essay. For these, *see On the Inspiration of Scripture, by John Henry Newman,* ed. D. Holmes and R. Murray (Washington: 1966).

6. M. d'Hulst, ''La question biblique,'' *Le correspondent,* 25. 1. 1893.

7. Interesting aperçus on Loisy's attitude to the Bible may be found in M. J. Lagrange, *M. Loisy et le Modernisme. A propos des 'Mémoires'* (Juvisy: 1932).

most favored means of restricting inerrancy current in Christian scholarship: "It would be wrong either to restrict inspiration only to certain parts of Sacred Scripture, or to concede that a sacred author himself has erred. Neither may we tolerate the argument of those who try to resolve these difficulties by venturing to assert that divine inspiration pertains to matters of faith and morals, and nothing besides, since they mistakenly believe that the question of the truth of a passage involves not so much an investigation of what God said as of why he said it."[8] On the other hand, the encyclical did not exclude Newman's idea that Scripture contains *obiter dicta* for whose accuracy a sacred writer does not vouch.[9] The Pope indeed remarked that in matters not germane to the religious purpose of the biblical authors they had no doubt fallen back on the conventional language of their day. Here he could cite Augustine, whose *Literal Commentary on Genesis* declared that God's Spirit has not spoken through men in order to teach the laws of biology or physics, since these have no relevance to the order of salvation.[10] Hence, the Pope went on: "They did not seek to penetrate the secrets of nature, but rather described and dealt with things in more or less figurative language, or in terms which were commonly used at the time, and which in many instances are in daily use at this day, even by the most eminent men of science. . . . The sacred writers . . . put down what God, speaking to men, signified in the way men could understand and were accustomed to."[11] Pope Leo then continued, in a sentence which would be at the heart of the discussion of inerrancy by his successors and others: "The principles here laid down will apply to cognate sciences, and especially to history."[12] Did the Pope mean that, analogously to a natural science based on appearances in Scripture, there could also be an appearance-based historical science? That is, might the believer recognize in the primitive history writing found in Scripture popular ways of speaking that tend to systematize or magnify some chain of events, or stylistic procedures (such as Mark's coup-

8. DS, 3291.

9. Cf. the comments of H. J. Johnson: "The teaching of Leo XIII would not seem to exclude *obiter dicta* in the Bible in the sense of statements for whose accuracy the sacred writer does not vouch." "Leo XIII, Cardinal Newman and the Inerrancy of Scripture," *Downside Review* 218 (Autumn 1951) 427. The same author goes on to remark that, since Newman appears not to admit the existence of formal error in Scripture, his views in the essay "Inspiration in Its Relation to Revelation" and the teaching of *Providentissimus Deus* seem closer than is sometimes alleged.

10. For Augustine, *see De Genesi ad litteram* I, 21, 41.

11. Leo XIII, *Providentissimus Deus*.

12. *Ibid.*

ling phrase "after this") that lack the full logical value of an affirmation or negation in the historical order? That such was the Pope's teaching was the view of the Dominican exegete Marie-Joseph Lagrange, then engaged in founding a school of biblical and archaeological studies in Jerusalem.[13] But it had to be admitted that nothing of this sort was really spelled out in the encyclical. Curiously enough, it would be under the generally more conservative successor of Leo XIII, Pope Pius X (1835–1914), that a Pontifical Biblical Commission ruling of June 23, 1905, declared that "certain narratives thought to be properly historical had only the appearance of history."[14] Excluded from this group was any case where the *sensus Ecclesiae* affirmed historicity—presumably by the liturgical celebration of such events as the transfiguration of Christ.[15] Pius X's successor, Pope Benedict XV (1854–1922), was far less sure that such concessions were legitimized by appeal to *Providentissimus Deus*, and his own encyclical of 1920, *Spiritus Paraclitus*, caused Lagrange to rethink his own theory.[16] Pope Leo's intervention at a crucial point in the development of Catholic biblical studies was, then, Janus-like. It pointed at once in two directions and was readily susceptible to both a conservative and a liberal interpretation. But at least it identified the problem—how could *all* Scripture be at every point formally inerrant if *some* Scripture were at some points materially errant?

In the course of this century, however, a good deal of progress has been achieved in resolving this particular *aporia*. Two ideas have emerged which assist us toward a solution. The first develops Pope Leo's point about the sacred writers' accommodation to their audience, by looking at the relevance for inerrancy of the genre or literary form of a biblical book: the kind of book it is. If we go into a library we find all sorts of different kinds of books: there are novels, biographies, history books, dictionaries, manuals about how to grow vegetables or practice karate. To use the library intelligently we need to know which sort of book is which. It is no use expecting to find a detailed account of modern chemistry in a novel about a love affair in a laboratory. In order to use a book as its author intended we must identify the literary form

[margin note: Bible as library analogy]

---

13. *Le Père Lagrange: au service de la Bible. Souvenirs personnels* (Paris: 1985) *sub anno* 1899.
14. DS, 3373.
15. On the intellectual and spiritual schizophrenia which can only result from (exegetically) regarding as nonhistorical what (liturgically) one celebrates with the Church as fact, *see* B. McNeil, "Meditating on the Jesus of History," *Angelicum* 62 (1985) 403–18.
16. *Le Père Lagrange*, 181–82; DS, 3653.

of the book in question. *Some* awareness of literary form there has always been in the Church. The thirteenth-century rearrangement of the Latin text of the Old Testament into historical, didactic, and prophetical literature is a good example of an older attempt to establish literary form. But during the course of this century such attempts have become ever more refined and scientific, since so much more is known about the cultural and, therefore, general literary background of Scripture, especially with regard to the Old Testament. As Pope Pius XII (1876–1958) pointed out in his encyclical of 1943, *Divino afflante Spiritu*, it is this that enables us to determine the kind of truth to be found in a given biblical book.

> What is the literal sense of a passage is not always as obvious in the speeches and writings of the ancient authors of the East as it is in the works and writers of our own time. . . . For the ancient peoples of the East in expressing their ideas did not always employ the forms or manners of speech that we use today, but rather those used by the men of their own times and countries. . . . The investigation that has been carried out on this point during the past forty or fifty years with greater care and diligence than ever before has shown more clearly what were the forms of expression used in those remote times, whether in poetic description or the formulation of the laws and rules of life, or in recording the facts and events of history. . . . Of the modes of expression which human language used among ancient peoples . . . none is excluded from the sacred books provided the way of speaking adopted in no wise contradicts the holiness and truth of God.[17]

If, for example, the Book of Jonah falls under the library heading of romance, being a sort of extended parable, its truth will be spiritual and ethical, not factual and descriptive. At a stroke, this resolves such pseudo problems as how a whale could swallow Jonah when whales are notorious for their inability to digest the smallest fish. We look, then, through the medium of the literary form of a work to the original intention of its author, and having found this intention we decide how to apply the Church's faith that Scripture is God's undeceiving truth in each particular case. Judging by the type of book written, did the author intend, for instance, to write straight history (for such pure, though doubtless not wholly innocent, history existed in the ancient world)? Or did the use of popular stories only approximate historical truth in order to convey something of a different order? On this approach, we can still speak of the absolute or unconditional inerrancy

17. DS, 3830.

of Scripture. The Bible is entirely free from error in the sense that the meaning intended by its writers is itself error free. Investigation of literary form will help one to judge what the meaning was, while the doctrinal affirmation of inerrancy informs us that such meaning will not be overthrown by growth in historical understanding.

But the growing realization of the implications of literary form is only one factor in the solving of the puzzle of inerrancy. The other is the idea that the measure of biblical truth lies in the economy of salvation as willed by God. The intention of the biblical author, located by reference to literary form, must be judged in terms of its relevance to human salvation. As the Second Vatican Council put it in its document on revelation, *Dei verbum*, "The books of Scripture teach firmly, faithfully and without error that truth which God willed to be put down in the sacred writings for the sake of our salvation."[18] The more natural interpretation of this passage is that it reflects Galileo's dictum: the Scriptures teach us how to go to heaven, not how the heavens go— itself an echo of Augustine. That a considerable struggle was waged over the inclusion of this statement in a conciliar document is clear from Fr. Alois Grillmeier's study of the making of *Dei verbum* in the commentary edited by his confrere Herbert Vorgrimler on the text of the Second Vatican Council.[19] Yet the underlying theological principle seems eminently acceptable: if the Bible is the record of revelation then it must be ordered to the same goal as revelation itself, humanity's salvation, and be evaluated in this light. The inerrant truth of Scripture is inerrant *saving* truth. This means that the absolute, unconditional inerrancy of the Bible is a formal, not a material, inerrancy; inspiration has the effect of rendering Scripture inerrant under one formal perspective only, that of relevance to human salvation. And so one historian of theories of inspiration can conclude his account of Catholic developments in the modern period by writing, "Thus the Roman Catholic Church has rejected several views in the last two centuries . . . subsequent approval . . . negative assistance . . . verbal dictation, inspiration of ideas, inspiration of faith and morals (only), and *total inerrancy.*"[20] As this quotation rightly implies, the formality

---

18. *Dei verbum*, 11.

19. A. Grillmeier, "Dogmatic Constitution on Divine Revelation, Chapter III," *Commentary on the Documents of Vatican II*, ed. H. Vorgrimler (New York and London: 1969) III, 199–215.

20. R. Gnuse, *The Authority of the Bible: Theories of Inspiration, Revelation and the Canon of Scripture* (New York: 1985) 12.

of Scripture's inerrancy does not mean that the Bible is inerrant only in matters of faith and morals, an opinion rejected by the papal teaching office from Leo XIII onwards. The basic outlines of the empirical history of Israel, the life and death of Jesus of Nazareth, and the empty tomb, together with the founding of his Church on the apostolic group, are all salvifically relevant truth—even though such factual historical description does not fall under the rubric of faith and morals.[21] However, it is by reference to the demands of doctrine as expressed in the Bible as a whole that we can determine which of Scripture's more empirical truth-claims must be defended. Whether, in the case of a particular text, we should assert its freedom from error under another formal perspective than simply that of salvation—for example, in the perspective of rational ethics or history or biology—will depend not only on *a posteriori* considerations of its consonance with what is known of reality from other sources, such as those of natural law or historical scholarship or the life sciences, but also on the *a priori* consideration of its bearing on the message of Scripture as a whole. It is to this holistic aspect of inerrancy that we must now, in conclusion, turn.

Just at the moment when the various drafts of this conciliar text were under discussion in and around St. Peter's Basilica, a German exegete, Norbert Lohfink, speaking at the Pontifical Gregorian University across the Tiber, was proposing a further nuance to our grasp of inerrancy. Lohfink's idea is that inerrancy belongs to the Bible considered (only) as a completed whole. Inerrancy is not realized on the page until the divine author has finished his last verse. In other words, the inerrant meaning of Genesis, the first book of the Bible, is only to be found after we have read the Johannine Apocalypse, the last book of the Bible.[22] Does this mean that even the moral and religious assertions of Scripture may be regarded as provisional, up to the point of including, here and there, what would properly be termed error were such passages to be considered atomically, in isolation, outside the total context of the scriptural witness as a whole? The ethical implications of the "cursing psalms" of the Old Testament, for instance, may be deemed unwarrantable; that is, no doubt, why their maledictions have been removed from the liturgical Psalter in the Liturgy of the Hours of the Roman Rite. On Lohfink's view, such errors of judgment among

21. P. Grelot, *La Bible, parole de Dieu* (Paris: 1965) 81.

22. N. Lohfink, "Über die Irrtumslosigkeit und die Einheit der Schrift," *Stimmen der Zeit* 174 (1964) 161–81; English trans., "The Inerrancy and the Unity of Scripture," in Lohfink, *The Christian Meaning of the Old Testament* (Milwaukee: 1968) 47–82.

the recipients of biblical revelation form part of a process of inspiration and can be rectified at a later stage in the making of Scripture itself. The specific intentions of the sacred writers are subordinate to the overall intention of the divine author, and this latter intention appears only in the Bible considered as a finished whole. On this view, the subject or bearer of inerrancy may be said to be the canon itself. By the standards of New Testament moral teaching, the author of, let us say, Psalm 137, had an objectively erroneous conscience. The charism of inspiration, received into such a conscience, does not, in this particular case, correct it. Inspiration takes effect by producing a text that is unconditionally inerrant under the formal perspective of relevance to salvation, though not under that of moral philosophy. Its inerrant message is the obligation zealously to oppose a paganism which has set itself against the people of God. The errant vehicle of that message is the encouragement to practice infanticide against pagan children. But identification of this dialectic of inerrancy and error by the Church depends on her—and our—grasp of the biblical corpus as a whole, through consulting the canon of the Bible in its entirety. Though not irreconcilable with the conciliar decree, this view of inerrancy has encountered very natural resistance, for there is an understandable reluctance to allow that error can ever be a *mot juste* when applied to sacred Scripture at its ethical and spiritual heart. In particular, it has been pointed out that moral imperatives or counsel can hardly be termed either true or false, though they may be good or bad.[23]

In Catholicism, it is the duty of the pastors of the Church to guard the deposit of faith, of which the Scriptures are the primary expression. It is natural that innovatory refinements in our approach to the Bible should be treated by them cautiously, and even, at first, suspiciously. The eventual acceptance of a modest but genuine place for new scholarly tools, and the inevitable adjustment of such concepts as inerrancy which follows, is all the more impressive and reassuring for being hard won. To the conservative, such concessions are the dragging of the Trojan horse within the precincts of the City of God. To the liberal, they are an irrelevance to the progress of the free and enquiring spirit. But to the theological student who wishes to live, work,

---

23. J. H. Crehan, "Inerrancy of the Bible," in *A Catholic Dictionary of Theology* 3 (London: 1971) 98; Crehan did not live to fulfill his promise to offer a criticism of the Lohfink theory as founded on a misunderstanding of typology, but refers his readers to what he terms the "interim criticism" to be seen in E. Gutwenger, "Die Inerranz der Bibel," *Zeitschrift für die katholische Theologie* 87 (1965) 196–202.

and think from the heart of the Church, the relations between biblical scholarship and the magisterium show the Church refining her grasp of the nature of her Scriptures, a treasure in earthen vessels, simultaneously human and divine. In the contingent conditions of a cultural artifact—the biblical text—the theologian finds the unconditional authority of the biblical source, the word of God, just as in the limited historical particularities of the life, death, and resurrection of Jesus Christ they find the definitive Savior, the incarnate Absolute itself.

But of course it is not enough for theologians to acknowledge the authority of the truth of Scripture. They must also investigate, on that basis, the meaning of its content. And to see how this is so, we must turn to consider biblical hermeneutics, the interpretation of the meaning of Scripture.

11
The Interpretation of Scripture: The Letter

In this chapter, I want to move from considering the nature of the Bible's truth to considering its content from the point of view of meaning and method. We need to know how to find in concrete terms the literal sense of the Bible, and how to read this in its canonical and traditional setting. This meaning, when we find it, will be the constituent meaning of an inerrant truth, a saving truth inherent in a set of books of different literary types. In other words, we have now to consider what tools are at our disposal in our interpretation of the Bible.

And first of all, I wish to look at the literal sense of Scripture, since all the rest—canonical sense, traditional sense, plenary sense—fall under the heading of what has been called for centuries the "spiritual," as distinct from literal, sense.

To speak about the literal sense, rather than just the sense (or meaning) of a text, already implies that we have some idea of a plurality of senses. The idea that the same text can carry more than one meaning goes back, in fact, to the Hellenistic period, the first centuries of the Christian era in the Greek-speaking world. Educated people in Hellenistic society held that a great text like, say, Homer's *Odyssey*, had ramifications beyond its surface meaning.[1] Moreover, the surface meaning itself might sometimes be at variance with what the same educated people had come to believe about the nature of reality—about the nature of the gods, for example, or of the soul. So some process of interpretation was needed in order to reconcile the text as it stood with what was believed to be true on other grounds. The Greek Fathers applied both kinds of consideration to the Scriptures—the idea of the

1. H. Dörries, "Zur Methodik antiker Exegese," in *Zeitschrift für neutestamentliche Wissenschaft* 65 (1974) 121–38.

ramifying quality of a great text and the notion that it stood in constant need of intellectual reappropriation. Indeed, they developed the potentialities of these reflections more systematically than had their pagan counterparts. The result was the idea of the "senses of Scripture," an idea that lies behind hermeneutic theory, the theory of how to interpret texts, even today.[2]

We must look briefly now at the story of the emergence and subsequent vicissitudes of the literal sense, together with an account of the methods at our disposal today for locating it. To begin with, the concept of the literal sense was attended by no little confusion. In early patristic exegesis, there is a tendency to define it as though it were a literal*ist* misreading of the Bible. Origen, for example, sometimes speaks of the literal sense as the construction put upon a passage by the simplest believer, by someone so simpleminded as to be a simpleton. Thus when the author of the Apocalypse refers to Christ as "the Lion of Judah," the literal sense here would be, for Origen, that Christ is an animal![3] Understandably, the concept of the literal sense in such writers has a negative force. It is the kind of category mistake one is liable to fall into when not paying sufficient attention to the imagery used by the biblical writers. However, this way of defining the literal sense as an erroneous, literalist reading of a text is not that found in the majority of medieval exegetes, nor in any modern commentator. Nowadays, as by and large in the Middle Ages, the literal sense is regarded as the sense the author intended and expressed in language. To grasp the literal sense we have to know whether the author was using imagery or literal (that is, nonmetaphorical) forms of linguistic expression, but the choice of linguistic mode or vehicle does not in itself determine whether a passage has or has not a literal sense. Every passage must have a literal sense, simply by virtue of being written at all.

In the history of exegesis, there has been something of a struggle to keep people's interest in the literal sense of the biblical text. Lots of people, anxious to get at a meatier, more religiously relevant mean-

2. On the senses of Scripture in traditional exegesis, *see* H. de Lubac, *Exegese mediévale. Les quatre sens de l'Ecriture* (Paris: 1959–64). On the relation of exegesis to hermeneutics, *see* C. Bozzetti, "Esegesi e ermeneutica" in *Dizionario teologico inter-disciplinare* II (Casale Monferrato: 1977) 110–26.

3. More usually, however, Origen speaks of a threefold sense in Scripture: the flesh of Scripture is its literal sense; the soul of Scripture is its moral sense; the spirit of Scripture, its most perfect sense, is its eschatological sense. *See* H. de Lubac, *Histoire et Esprit* (Paris: 1950).

ing in the Bible, tend to rush past the literal sense, hardly giving it a second glance. But as St. Thomas points out, the literal sense must be the primary sense of Scripture in the sense of being the necessary foundation for any other senses that Scripture may carry. Whether or not the literal sense is always the most important sense, it has to be the foundational sense. The meaning the inspired authors attached to their own words must be the starting point of our investigation, even though it is certainly not the final goal. Whatever additional sense or senses we may feel able to postulate in the Bible, everything must have some continuity with the original meaning the authors intended.

Very roughly, we can say that there have been four outstanding movements to preserve or recover the literal sense of Scripture in the history of the Church. The first, in the fifth century, is associated with Jerome of Bethlehem, whose literal exegesis, possibly inspired by that of the school of Antioch, was eventually pushed aside by the spiritual exegesis of Origen, championed as that was by no less a figure than Augustine.[4] The second movement in favor of the literal sense is associated with the canons of the abbey of St. Victor in the northern France of the twelfth century. Although the influence of the Victorine school can still be seen in St. Thomas, it evaporated in later Scholasticism, which was too concerned to get theological mileage out of Scripture to have much patience with literal exegesis.[5] Third, in the seventeenth century, the French Oratorian priest Richard Simon revived interest in the literal sense in various circles, but this soon died away.[6] Finally, in the last hundred years (or more), there has been an unprecedented explosion of interest in the literal sense, and a proliferation of new methods for reaching it.[7]

What tools are there at our disposal for discovering the literal sense of Scripture? I have already had occasion to mention a number of them, seven in all. These are biblical archaeology, textual criticism, compara-

4. For Jerome, *see* A. Penna, *Principi e carattere dell'esegesi di S. Gerolamo* (Rome: 1950); for a comparison of the schools of Antioch and Alexandria, *see* J. Guillet, "Les exégèses d'Alexandrie et d'Antioche. Conflit ou malentendu?" *Recherches de science religieuse* 34 (1947) 257–302. For Augustine, *see* M. Pontet, *L'exégèse de saint Augustin prédicateur* (Paris: 1944).

5. *See* C. Spicq, *Esquisse d'une histoire de l'exégèse latine au Moyen Age* (Paris: 1944); B. Smalley, *The Study of the Bible in the Middle Ages* (New York: 1952).

6. H. Graf Reventlow, "Richard Simon und seine Bedeutung für die kritische Erforschung der Bibel," in *Historische Kritik in der Theologie*, ed. G. Schwaiger (Göttingen: 1980) 11–36.

7. O. Kaiser and W. G. Kümmel, *Exegetical Method: A Student's Handbook* (English trans., New York: 1967).

tive literature, source criticism, form criticism, redaction criticism, and tradition-history criticism. It should, however, ever be borne in mind that the proper context for using this toolbox is the study of ancient history itself. Without a grasp, both broad and detailed, of the historical period—its culture, its politics, its economics, and, as modern practitioners of exegesis are currently reminding us, its patterns of social interaction,[8] the use of such tools can degenerate into the manipulation of data, divorced from the living culture embedded in a distinctive society, which gave them birth. With this caveat duly entered, I want to mention as well two futher instruments: structuralist criticism and canon criticism, though the latter will take us on to the canonical sense of Scripture, itself the first step away from the literal sense in the direction of the *sensus plenior*, the plenary sense in the mind of its divine author.

I propose to say nothing here about biblical archaeology and textual criticism. These methods are really ancillary disciplines presupposed by biblical interpretation. By and large, they are methodologically unproblematic. Their practitioners may disagree among themselves on particular points, but it is unlikely that their disagreements will have major theological implications. It is obvious that these auxiliary disciplines are a good thing for the student of the Bible: if there is archaeological evidence relevant to the biblical text, then let us have it; if by comparing manuscripts we can get a better text of the Bible, then give it to us. It is hard to see how anyone could disagree with either of these two propositions. However, biblical archaeology and textual criticism do remind us of two vital aspects of the Scriptures. This primary witness to revelation comes to us from a particular historical environment, now embodied in its humble material remains, which the trowel and fork of the archaeologist excavate. Also, the Bible is inseparable from the languages in which it was composed; the interplay of sense made possible by the shape and story of the biblical languages is part and parcel of the way in which the divine message is given. Hence our indebtedness to those who have devoted long years to become expert in the sacred languages, and on whose competence the rest of the Church must, in part, rely. In this sense, we can agree with Lagrange's dictum that, in the sacred sciences, the union of monument and document is the most fecund of all methods.

---

8. E.g., G. Theissen, *The First Followers of Jesus: A Sociological Analysis of the Earliest Christianity* (English trans., London: 1978).

The tool I wish to begin with, then, is comparative literature, which, as invoked here, means the study of the literary forms present within the biblical corpus.[9] In other words, it answers the question, What genre of book is, say Proverbs or the Gospel of John? What is the basic nature of the work we are dealing with here, in the light of our understanding of literary forms at large? The ability to recognize genre is the most basic skill we need in studying the Bible and is thus fittingly referred to in contemporary studies of exegetical method as "literary competence." The founders of modern linguistics spoke of "linguistic competence," meaning the ability to identify and utilize the rules and conventions that govern a particular language, say, Italian or Swahili. But subsequent writers have gone on to argue that, parallel to this, we can speak of literary competence, that is, the ability to identify and utilize the rules and conventions that govern a given type of literature. Take, for instance, the literary genre of apocalyptic. Because of our competence or feel for such a genre, we have certain well-founded expectations about an apocalyptic book such as Daniel, and we know that we can usefully put some questions to it and not others. Thus, as Dr. John Barton has amusingly remarked, it we come across the sentence, "The stars will fall from heaven, and the sun will cease its shining; the moon will be turned to blood, and fire mingled with hail from the heavens," we know at once that the text is unlikely to continue, "The rest of the country will have sunny intervals and scattered showers."[10] In such ways, our grasp of genre helps to establish the meaning of the text. Unfortunately, though, there is a certain circularity here: a preliminary decision about the meaning of the text is necessary before we can make an intelligent decision about its genre. But this thought does not entirely erode the usefulness for biblical hermeneutics of the study of comparative literature, or, to give it its title in its more modern dress, "genre recognition."

Next, we come to source criticism. The source critic's method lies in going through a text looking for signs of multiple authorship. In the modern world, because of laws against plagiarism and the convention that authors identify themselves by name, we rarely come up against this problem of composite texts. Sometimes, however, in the report of a committee, a careful eye can spot parts of some early draft, incorporated as they stand into the final version. Indeed, one can do

9. J. Barton, *Reading the Old Testament: Method in Biblical Study* (London: 1984) 8–19.
10. *Ibid.*, 17.

this sort of detective work with conciliar texts, like the documents of the Second Vatican Council. In the case of the Bible, it sometimes looks as though different sections of some book have passed through several such "committee" stages. Source criticism arose, in fact, out of the observation of discrepancies in the text of the Pentateuch. How could a work which changes style so dizzily from paragraph to paragraph, which contains two or even three versions of the same story and is made up of narrative mixed in with poems, hymns, and laws, possibly be an original literary unity? Because no answer was forthcoming to this question, people began to wonder whether the Pentateuch might not be an amalgam of works. And when they began to identify and subtract these "plays within the play" they discovered that, lo and behold, each seemed internally coherent. Yet once again, we have to admit that there is a degree of circularity in the source critics' approach, just as there is in that of the students of comparative literature. They find their hypotheses confirmed only when they begin to read more and more passages in the light of the intuition (or hypothesis) that the Pentateuch is not originally one single work. Yet in this, source-critical method is no worse off than scientific method, which also begins with an imaginative hypothesis and asks how much of the data that hypothesis can explain.[11] The theological importance of source criticism lies in the fact that if its hypotheses are justified, then we are dealing with a multiplicity of literal senses within a biblical book, just as there is a multiplicity of literal senses within the "library" which is the Bible as a whole. I have already suggested that we can think of the literal senses of a book's sources as subordinate literal senses, and the literal sense of its final editor as the superordinate literal sense. This will mean, then, that the literal sense of, say, the Pentateuch, will consist in the amalgamation of the literal senses of its sources in the light of their evaluation by the final editor, as this is manifested in the way they are put together in the book as we have it today. However, in turning from the Old Testament to the New, and to the latter's theologically most crucial books, the Gospels, we might wish to restrict the operation of source criticism for one very good reason: namely, the possibility that the sharing of formulae in, at any rate, the first three Gospels, may be explained in part not by literary interdependence but by the character of the original apostolic group as a kind of Christian

[margin note: Caveats of source criticism]

11. *Ibid.*, 20–29; *see also* N. C. Habel, *Literary Criticism of the Old Testament* (Philadelphia: 1971); D. Wenham, "Source Criticism," in *New Testament Interpretation: Essays on Principles and Methods*, ed. I. Howard Marshall (Exeter: 1977) 139–49.

rabbinate. Jesus formed his disciples into a body whose task it was to disseminate memorized versions of his teaching and summaries of his actions. This reference to the importance of the living voice brings us to the topic of form criticism.

⑤Form criticism takes its rise from a weakness in source criticism, or literary criticism, as it is sometimes called. Source criticism, as its name suggests, is a purely literary tool. Inheriting from comparative literature a concern with literary genre, it asked what literary conventions might explain the existence of the biblical books as we have them. Believing that in some cases this question could not be answered, source critics cut the Gordian knot by positing sources or underlying texts within a given book. But as more became known about the culture revealed by the biblical books and their sources, the less likely it seemed that all significant communication in biblical times had this kind of literary character. People then began to ask about the possibility that oral, rather than written, forms of communication might lie behind the sources, just as the sources lie behind the books themselves. Such oral forms would include, for instance, narrating stories, going to law, preaching the gospel, worshipping God. To avoid confusing written with oral materials, scholars speak not of literary genres but of oral forms. An oral form is a conventional pattern of speech used in a particular society in special social contexts. Certain patterns of speech in a given society at once indicate the social context to which they belong and in or from which they must be interpreted. That context is usually referred to in biblical studies by the German phrase found in the earliest form critics: *Sitz im Leben*, "setting in life."[12] So the contribution of form critics is, first, to identify patterns in a text which apparently come from an oral context and, secondly, to interpret those patterns in terms of the conventions that govern such oral speech.

Form criticism, despite its usefulness, is not without its defects. In the first place, its use alongside source criticism raises a methodological problem. The more oral patterns are identified within a biblical book, the less need there is to postulate literary sources. If, for example, the Gospel of Matthew consists of a collection of sermon material plus a liturgical text for celebrating the Lord's passion, then the source-critical analysis of Matthew into Mark, "Q" and "M" or "Special Matthew," can be regarded as superfluous. Thus form criticism turns to

---

12. K. Koch, *The Growth of the Biblical Tradition* (English trans., London: 1969) 3–16; G. M. Tucker, *Form Criticism of the Old Testament* (Philadelphia: 1971); S. H. Travis, "Form Criticism," in *New Testament Interpretation*, ed. Marshall, 153–64.

bite the hands that fed it. In practice, however, form critics and source critics compromise. The form critics do not press their conclusions so hard as to threaten the existence of the source critics who themselves first made the form critics possible.

A second and more important difficulty with form criticism is that the more weight we allow it, the more we shall have to stress anonymous and even communal authorship in the Bible. If, for instance, a psalm represents a cultic formula, then it hardly matters which member of a worshipping community produced it. We have already seen that the social theory of inspiration was worked out in order to meet this difficulty. Here we can notice as well that this community-authorship idea, if taken to extremes, becomes incredible. In the case of the Gospels, for example, it would ultimately deny the role of the apostles in the apostolic tradition and even the creativity or originality of Jesus himself: everything would turn on the interests and needs of the early Church.[13] In fact, however, it is a *non sequitur* to hold that because the form of a unit shows how it was used in the early Church, we can infer that it originated in the post-Easter community.

Third, form criticism cannot show that units were never transmitted for their own sake. Were early Christians really so uninterested in what the Jesus of history had actually said and done? The main effect of Pentecost was surely not to render the minds of the apostles into blanks! Last, and connected with this: so far as the Gospels are concerned, the application of a method originally devised by folklore specialists, whose materials have developed over hundreds of years, to texts with a prehistory of, at most, a few decades is, to say the least, a little dubious. Despite these criticisms, however, it can certainly be recognized that the preaching, liturgy, apologetics, and inner debates of the earliest communities may well have affected the way in which the apostolic preaching was passed on. A judicious use of form criticism avoids extremes. The literal sense of the "authors" of the oral forms is recorded without denying or downplaying the literal sense of the authors of the literary sources, or, more importantly still, the meanings intended by the historical originators of the entire tradition of which the oral forms are part: Jesus and his apostles.

13. For an emphasis on the concern with accurate transmission—rather than creativity—in the religious culture of Jewish Palestine in the apostolic age, *see* H. Riesenfeld, *The Gospel Tradition and Its Beginnings* (London: 1957); B. Gerhardsson, *Memory and Manuscript: Oral Tradition and Written Transmission in Rabbinic Judaism and Early Christianity* (Lund and Copenhagen: 1961); Gerhardsson, *The Origins of the Gospel Traditions* (English trans., London: 1979).

So far, then, we have asked what kind of a book a particular book may be (comparative literature), and then analyzed it into its literary sources and oral materials (source and form criticism). But no matter how far analysis may go in dividing up a book into component parts, the fact is that somebody or other must have put the book together, must have synthesized these strands or fragments. This somebody is its final editor, or, in German, *Redaktor*. Hence our next tool, redaction criticism. At first, redactors were thought of as rather dull people who just added little link passages to stitch the forms and sources together. For instance, in the Gospel of Mark, the redactor might be held simply to have added such unimaginative connecting formulae as "after this." But gradually, it came to be realized that the redactors had their own literary aims and theological concerns.

The redactor's selection of materials, and of a sequence in which to lay them out, can betray a truly masterly grasp of the theological bearings of that tradition.[14] Redaction criticism has a flaw comparable, however, to the circularity we have found in comparative literature and source criticism. This flaw has been called the "trick of the disappearing redactor."[15] If we insist that what appear to be trivial details in the book before us represent highly significant literary and theological decisions by the redactor, what happens? What happens is that we iron out the discrepancies which gave rise to source criticism and the appearances of independent oral patterns which gave rise to form criticism. The biblical text resumes that self-consistent, unitary quality, which no doubt it possesses anyway for the innocent eye. But if there is no longer any great need to speak of sources, then by the same token there is no compulsion to speak either of a redactor of those sources. We would simply return to the traditional position that a book has a single author, Isaiah, say, or King David. Thus if perfect redactors existed, their existence could never be known by us, since *ex hypothesi* they would have removed all the discrepancies which allow us to infer their existence in the first place! However, there is no need to press redaction criticism to these lengths. In practice, redaction critics make only modest claims vis-à-vis source and form criticism, so as not to saw off the branch on which they are sitting. This way of putting things may make it sound as though contemporary biblical exegesis is largely a conspiracy of scholars concerned with paying their milkmen's bills.

14. Barton, *Reading the Old Testament*, 45–60; S. B. Smalley, "Redaction Criticism," in *New Testament Interpretation*, ed. Marshall, 181–95.
15. Barton, *Reading the Old Testament*, 56–58.

But in fact knowing how far to press a given method is part of the tact which all good practitioners of any method in any discipline must acquire, and a reason why the development of the habit of theology is more important than having a refined concept of theological method. The theological importance of redaction criticism lies in the fact that the literal sense of the final editor is, as we have seen, the supreme literal sense, containing all other literal senses and at the same time going beyond them. Thus ends our quadrumvirate of methods: comparative literature, source criticism, form criticism, and redaction criticism. Were we medievals, we would no doubt say that just as there are four points of the compass and four divine evangelists, so there are four ways to find the literal sense.

Talk of redactors in the last of these four ways would naturally bring us to the overarching redacting activity which was the making of the canon where all the Bible's books are drawn into a unity. But before going on to the canonical sense of Scripture, a word should be said about two other modern critical tools relevant to the literal sense, if more faintly so than those we have just considered. These two final tools are tradition-historical and structural (or structural*ist*) criticism. Tradition history, though a well-established branch of biblical study, has little relevance to hermeneutics. It considers the total process through which a biblical meaning has passed, from oral stage through literary source to final redaction. More especially, it considers what may be called the forgotten elements in this process: the elements left in the shadows by the makers of the oral forms, the authors of the written sources, and the final editors. There is a history of tradition weaving in and out between these three but not identical with them, nor perhaps drawn on explicitly by them.[16] For instance, a tradition historian might ask about the origin of the phrase "our Lord Jesus Christ" in the Pauline letters. He might argue that this title belongs neither to such oral materials as hymns that might have found their way into the Pauline letters, nor to any written sources we could identify, nor to Paul's own explicit or original theology. Instead, he might wish to say, it derives from the language of the Hellenistic Churches Paul must have encountered in Palestine, the Churches deriving from the Grecophile Christian Jews from Jerusalem described in Acts. Tradition history does not aim to throw light on the biblical text so much as to throw light on the history which lies behind it. Insofar as the ele-

16. R. S. Barbour, *Traditio-Historical Criticism of the Gospels* (London: 1972); D. R. Catchpole, "Tradition History," in *New Testament Interpretation*, ed. Marshall, 165–80.

ments it deals with are merely influences and not true sources, it must be said to be irrelevant to the literal sense. No person standing in an authorial relationship to Scripture ever intended the meanings which tradition historians explore. On the other hand, it could be argued that the biblical authors have after all incorporated these meanings, even if unconsciously, so in a weak form they too have a connection with the literal sense.

Last, we must devote some thoughts to a recent and controversial addition to the biblical toolbox, namely structuralism.[17] Structuralism took its rise from the linguistic studies of Fernand de Saussure and the anthropological researches of Claude Lévi-Strauss. Interest in structuralism among exegetes seems to have two causes. First, there is, alas, trendiness, the fervor for the fashionable to which most flesh is heir. However, the structuralist bandwagon has itself now shuddered to a virtual standstill. Second, and much more seriously, there is disappointment with the various forms of the historical-critical method, which we have been looking at. For when all is said and done, do these methods really help us to understand the text, as distinct from tracing its history? The essential claim of structuralism in this regard is that it can help us to seize the meaning of a text, through coming to see that meaning by way of the orderly (structural) contrasts, distinctions, and oppositions with any cultural artifact. In what has become the inevitable example: we can distinguish flowers and weeds only by their mutual contrast; for a weed is a flower in the wrong place. Although what counts as a weed or a flower is humanly determined, it is not within the power of any individual person to overthrow that determination. Thus, I could not decide to honor the Princess of Wales by presenting her with a bouquet of bindweed, just as she would not become popular with Londoners by turning over the gardens of Kensington Palace for use as nettlebeds. Similarly, it is said, in language: words and sentences only have meaning in terms of the linguistic system in which they have their parts. Moreover, in establishing their place within the overall system, it is just as important to see which roles they cannot play, as which they can. Similarly again, in literature, structuralism is concerned with the constraints to which author and reader must both submit—the author because, prior to his individual selection, various meanings were imposed on him as he sat down to work; the reader because, in the text before him, these meanings have been

17. *See* D. Patte, *What Is Structural Exegesis?* (Philadelphia: 1976); R. Barthes and others, *Analyse structurale et exégèse biblique* (Neuchâtel: 1971).

combined with that other set of meanings freely selected by the author into a single "meaning effect." Thus, to draw a homely analogy, the design effect of a handwoven blanket derives from two things: the constraints the weaver worked with, namely, the possibility of the loom, the restriction in the choice of colored threads, and so forth, but also, the weaver's own creativity. Structuralist exegesis concentrates on the first of these, the formal constraints.

Perhaps the most celebrated example of structuralist exegesis is that offered by the literary critic Roland Barthes, who died in 1982. It concerns the story of Jacob wrestling with the angel in Genesis 32.[18] As Barthes presents the text, its deep structure is that of a folktale—the hero on a quest. During his particular quest Jacob has to deal with two figures, defined in a typically structuralist way as a binary set: the originator of the quest, God, and the opponent, the man at the fords of the River Jabbok who fights Jacob to stop him crossing over to the treasure on the other side—the rich land of Bethel. For Barthes, the mysterious, frightening element in the Genesis story is that the originator and the opponent turn out to be the same: the man is Yahweh's angel, a form of Yahweh himself. This piece of structuralist exegesis, then, suggests the important conclusion that it is God himself who provides the conflictual environment in which man is placed—a radically monotheistic vision, unlike the dualism of competing gods and devils in the cultures surrounding Israel.

In the light of such an illuminating example, structuralism may seem a helpful biblical tool. Sadly, in the hands of many of its practioners it insists in doctrinaire fashion on finding formal contrasts and oppositions here, there, and everywhere. The weakness of structuralism lies in its effective elimination of the individuality of the author, and in its neglect of the historical events to which the author was responding. In this, it is a deeply un-humane approach to the text, and when applied to the Bible, revives the worst features of the more radical kind of form criticism. Its strength lies in what is called its "text-immanent" approach. That is, it sees the meaning of the text as lying in the text itself and not elsewhere. For the fact is that by ordering the text in a particular way, an author may have established meanings that were not necessarily within any conscious intention. We cannot suppose that Richard Wagner could have told us everything that his *Ring* cycle might signify, and in a similar way, we cannot necessarily sup-

18. R. Barthes, "La lutte avec l'Ange: analyse textuelle de Genese 32:123-33," in *ibid.*

pose that St. John saw all the multiple meanings which have been drawn out of the Fourth Gospel. Beyond the literal sense there is something more. Thus, although structuralist exegesis may be finally unconvincing, nevertheless, by stressing so dramatically the notion of meaning as lying in a text, it helps us to move on beyond the literal sense. Just as redaction criticism invites us to confront the idea of canon criticism, or of a canonical sense, seeing the author of the canon as the definitive final redactor, so structuralist criticism also asks us to consider the biblical text as an entire system of meanings. Since structuralist exegetes have to admit, of course, that *someone* produced the text, to this extent what they have to say is relevant to the literal sense, even though they would hate the traditional definition of that literal sense in terms of the conscious intentions of a Jeremiah or a St. Matthew. Much more importantly, however, structuralism goads us into taking our problem, biblical hermeneutics, in a wider context than that of simply asking what Jeremiah or Matthew would have said about their handiwork if they were here today to answer our questions.

12

The Interpretation of Scripture: The Spirit

The idea that meaning is text immanent with which we arrived at the end of our investigation into the literal interpretation of Scripture suggests the possibility of taking as our prime text not just any single, isolated book of the Bible but the Bible as a whole. In any case, as we saw when looking at inspiration and inerrancy, this seems theologically the best approach. Inspiration is ordered to the production of the canon of Scripture; it is the entire Bible as a self-correcting whole which enables us to identify the inerrant aspect of any one text. The ultimate redactor is the Holy Spirit, who brought together this library of books and enabled the Church to recognize them, in their unity, as divine truth. Here we move on to a sense of Scripture which forms a bridge between literal and spiritual interpretation: the canonical sense. After dealing briefly with this type of interpretation, which has played a larger role, at least as an explicitly recognized mode of exegesis, in modern Protestant rather than Catholic writing, we shall spend the rest of this chapter considering the traditional interpretation of Scripture in the Church.

The canonical sense of a book or passage is the transformation of its literal sense, which results from placing that literal sense in the context of Scripture as a whole. It is interesting to note that a school of exegesis among American Protestants has fairly recently hit upon this idea, even while lacking a dogmatic understanding of the Church as creator of the canon.[1] Arguing from the notion of a literary canon, such as Shakespeare's plays or the great novels of nineteenth-century Russian literature, these canon critics, as they call themselves, propose that

---

1. Barton, *Reading the Old Testament*, 77–103; B. S. Childs, *Introduction to the Old Testament as Scripture* (Philadelphia and London: 1979); J. A. Sanders, *Torah and Canon* (Philadelphia: 1972).

exegesis must ultimately see the Bible as a unity—a unity with an internal diversity but a unity nonetheless. Canon criticism offers, therefore, this hermeneutical golden rule: interpret every text of Scripture on the understanding that it forms part of a larger whole. What is curious about the canon critics is that they stop short at the canonical sense, refusing to go beyond it into the deeper waters of the spiritual, or as I have earlier termed it, the "traditional sense." Although canon critics take as their starting point that a canon has been established (and established, it so happens, by the Christian Church), they refuse to allow that the Church's tradition is in itself a proper medium for interpreting the books within that canon. They are not prepared to say that ecclesiastical tradition can guide one in the reading of the Scriptures. But then why, one might ask, is that same tradition considered normative when it tells us what the limits of the text should be, namely, what books are in the canon? To take as one's hermeneutic vantage point what is essentially a linking sense between the letter and the spirit is to occupy an inherently unstable position. Either one must move forward in a Catholic direction toward the traditional sense, or one must move backwards toward pure text immanence of a structuralist kind, simply regarding the text as "there" and not asking any awkward questions about its status or credentials from any extratextual viewpoint.

We come now, then, to the traditional or spiritual sense: the deeper or further meanings which the Church has found in the biblical text as she has lived and prayed it through the course of twenty centuries. The classic account of the spiritual sense is that given by John Cassian, a Church Father who died in or around 435.[2] Cassian, a Westerner but one familiar with the Eastern tradition from his travels in Egypt, identified three possibilities within a spiritual exegesis: the allegorical or Christological sense; the tropological or moral sense; and the anagogical or eschatological sense. They will be dealt with here in that order, beginning then with the allegorical or Christological reading of the Bible.

Modern scholars tend to distinguish sharply between Christological allegory and Christological typology.[3] The difference is that in allegory an exegete is not looking for what we can call major correspondences in Scripture but for any reference—however slight—

2. Cassian, *Conferences* 14: 8.
3. H. de Lubac, "Typologie at allégorie," *Recherches de science religieuse* 34 (1947) 180–226.

which can be related—however obscurely—to the person and work of Christ. Thus the red girdle that the prostitute Rahab used to guide the Israelites to safety, as described in the Book of Joshua, could be interpreted in terms of Christological allegory as referring to the blood of the cross. But the scope for arbitrariness in this sort of exegesis is so endless that contemporary exponents of the spiritual sense of the Bible understandably fight shy of it. The Christological sense as typology rather than allegory is taken much more seriously, not least because its basic principles are already found within the Bible itself. Internally, within the biblical text we can find evidence of the practice of typological exegesis, and in the New Testament such typological exegesis takes on a specifically Christological character.[4] How does this work?

In the first place, within the Old Testament we can observe one author drawing on the accounts of another by reapplying them to events or expectations which the first author did not have in mind. Thus, for instance, the prophetic writer known as the Second Isaiah, working during the Exile, wrote of the Jewish return to Judea as a "second Exodus," thereby applying what the Pentateuch had to say about the escape of the Hebrews from Pharaoh to the events of his own time. Second Isaiah treated the Exodus from Egypt as a foreshadowing or type of the return from Babylon, seeing the Exodus texts as having an application beyond themselves, pointing toward a future fulfillment far beyond what their original authors envisaged.

In the period between the Old and New Testaments, this way of looking at Scripture became deeply embedded in the Jewish consciousness. For Jews of the time of Jesus, the meaning of Scripture was not restricted to what the biblical authors consciously had in mind. Because Scripture carries the word of God, its message is open to fulfillment in ways broader and deeper than such conscious intentions. We find this approach among the Jewish sects, such as the communities who wrote the Dead Sea Scrolls at Qumran. We also find it in the mainstream of Jewish orthodoxy, in the *Midrashim*, rabbinic commentaries on the Bible, and in the *Targumim*, expositions of Scripture for Jews who knew Aramaic rather than Hebrew.[5]

When we reach the New Testament, this general typological exegesis becomes specifically Christological. The Christian conviction was that, as the Word incarnate, Jesus Christ, the God-man, constituted

4. J. Danièlou, *Sacramentum futuri. Etudes sur les origines de la typologie biblique* (Paris: 1950); L. Goppelt, *Typos. Die typologische Bedeutung des Alten Testaments im Neuen* (Gütersloh: 1939; Darmstadt: 1969).

5. See G. Vermes, *Scripture and Tradition in Judaism* (2nd ed., Leiden: 1961, 1973).

the center of history.[6] As the fullest expression of God in human terms, Jesus summed up everything that Israel had known of God. As the most perfect man, the man most in the divine image, Jesus summed up everything that Israel had understood of the human relationship to God. So in principle the whole of Old Testament revelation could be reapplied in a unique way to Christ himself. The central events and images of the Jewish Scriptures were so many types or foreshadowings of the life, death, and resurrection of Christ. Such Christological typology is the most characteristic form of interpretation of the Old Testament in the New. Sometimes it is quite conscious, being introduced by a New Testament author with a phrase like "according to the Scriptures," or "as it is written," or "in order to fulfill the Scriptures."[7] On other occasions, it is unconscious or at least never made explicit, as when St. Matthew presents Jesus as a new Moses giving the new Law not on Sinai but on the Mount of the Beatitudes.[8] Its most systematic realization is to be found in the Letter to the Hebrews with its Christocentric reading of the Old Testament priesthood and cultus.[9] This is the earliest and still the most important form of spiritual interpretation of the Bible. Perhaps the best-known example of this type of exegesis, reading the Jewish Scriptures as having a reference to Jesus Christ, is the application to Jesus of the poems about a "suffering servant" in Second Isaiah. In terms of the literal sense, the subject of these poems was either the people of Israel in the sixth century before the Christian era, or part of that people, a spiritual elite centering perhaps on the prophet's own disciples; or again, some devout individual, possibly Jeremiah, or the last king of Judah, Jehoiachim. In terms of the spiritual sense, however, a variety of New Testament references present the subject of these poems as Jesus himself, in whom their language finds its fulfillment in a way that surpasses anything their makers could have grasped.[10]

The practice of typological exegesis implies that there are in Scripture discernible patterns, which we can see once we stand back and take in the Bible as a whole. Christological typology is an application of this more general typological idea. That idea presupposes two things. First, there is a providential connection between the persons and events

6. H. U. von Balthasar, *A Theology of History*, (English trans., London: 1963) 10–21.

7. C. H. Dodd, *According to the Scriptures* (London: 1952, 1965).

8. W. D. Davies, *The Sermon on the Mount* (Cambridge: 1966) 31–32—with warning about undue pressing of parallels.

9. C. Spicq, *L'Epître aux Hébreux* (Paris: 1952) I, 12–13.

10. A. T. Hanson, *Jesus Christ in the Old Testament* (London: 1965).

of biblical history.[11] Second, God is consistent in his communication with us. If we accept these two postulates of divine providence and divine consistency, then we shall find that not only can texts speak of the future, as in prophecy; events can also speak of the future. Events can possess an afterlife.[12] Such a typological approach enables us to enjoy a richer view of one event by seeing it in relation to an earlier event, which, so to say, sketched it out in advance. Moreover, each event, earlier and later, throws light on the other. Thus, the crossing of the Sea of Reeds in Exodus throws light on the crucifixion, which is also a passage from an old world sunk in sin to a new world of liberation and joy. But retrospectively, the crucifixion also illumines the Exodus by confirming that the way of God is always a way through suffering to deliverance and growth. The typological reading of Scripture has customarily been the preferred way of the liturgy and biblically based spirituality, *lectio divina*. If among writers on the Bible this century it fell somewhat out of favor, the last decades have seen a growing recognition that it is a legitimate exercise—because of its consonance with inner biblical principles, principles I have called those of "divine providence" and "divine consistency."[13] If divine providence worked self-consistently in the biblical history, then something like typology must be true. The principal events and persons of Scripture must be related by significant correspondences, and these will come to a supreme intensity in the figure who is for Christians the center of God's self-revelation, Jesus Christ.

And so we come to the tropological or moral sense of the Bible. By this is meant the implications of a biblical text for the behavior of the reader—called "tropological" from the Greek word for behavior, *tropos*. In this century the existential interpretation of the Bible sometimes referred to as the "new hermeneutics" can be regarded as a revival of the ancient idea of the tropological sense.[14] The founders of the new hermeneutics were two Lutheran exegetes, Ernst Fuchs and Gerhard Ebeling, but its influence has spread far beyond the Lutheran Churches.

11. Cf. H. de Lubac, *The Sources of Revelation* (English trans., New York: 1968) 31–40. De Lubac speaks of an inherent continuity, and ontological bond, between the events of biblical history, whose ground is the self-identity of the divine will, actively pursuing a single design in those happenings.

12. A. C. Charity, *Events and Their After-life* (Cambridge: 1966).

13. *See*, for instance, G. W. H. Lampe and K. J. Woolcombe, *Essays on Typology* (London: 1957).

14. *The New Hermeneutic*, ed. J. M. Robinson and J. B. Cobb, Jr. (New York: 1964).

The starting point of the tropological sense is the awareness that in every book of Scripture and in virtually every passage of Scripture lies some implication for human acting. Everywhere in the Bible, we are implicitly offered models for living or counsel about living, whether positive or negative. The starting point of the new hermeneutics is the philosophical postulate that people live for the future because essentially they are decision-making animals, to which is added the further thought (based this time on the later, rather than the earlier, writings of Martin Heidegger) that it is in language that the wider realm of being in which human life is set discloses itself for our response. And here, according to the new hermeneuticists, the Bible speaks to our condition. For, in the first place, the role of all speech is to summon us in some way to decision. All significant conversations in our lives, all significant books we read, are conversations or books which could in principle change us through changing our picture of the future. Because of this, these authors describe speech as an event in a strong sense of that word. It is a happening which interrupts the normal course of things: *Sprachereignis*, the "event of language," *Wortgeschehen*, the "happening of the word." The word transforms us, opening up possibilities of existence we had not dreamed of before. Applying these ideas to the Bible, if we assume the truth of inspiration, we can say that the *Sprachereignis* which is Scripture transforms us by turning us toward our ultimate future, our salvation. The word of God uses the human words, but in terms of transformative power it is infinitely more effective than any purely human language. The word of God in Scripture brings to birth a new person. In more characteristically Catholic language for the life of grace, it generates supernatural faith, hope, and love, and in this way radically alters the pattern of human existence.

Like typology, the new hermeneutics takes the biblical text very seriously. Rudolf Bultmann and his demythologizing school had used similar philosophical principles to debunk much of the Bible, arguing that human existence must stand over the biblical text, determining what within it can count as meaningful for humanity. But the new hermeneuticists stand this idea on its head. For them, the text of the Bible interprets us and tells us what in our existence is meaningful. Naturally, this inversion of Bultmannianism produces a hermeneutical pattern much more in keeping with the Church's belief in a revelation expressed in Scripture. Nevertheless, in one sense, the sceptical and iconoclastic element in Bultmann is retained, thus distinguishing this contemporary account of the moral sense from its patristic predecessor. If biblical speech is a summons, a call to a new God-given life, then it cannot be at the same time information. Thus for these writers, the Gospels must be approached not as history but as *kerygma*, a pure statement of faith trusting in nothing save the future God has promised us, just as he brought vindication and glory to Jesus. And so the new hermeneuticists are uninterested in salvation history and, *a fortiori*, in the resurrection or the miraculous at large. From a Catholic viewpoint we can say that they have erred by trying to make the tropological sense of Scripture into the total meaning of the Bible. If the meaning of Scripture were exclusively moral, in other words, purely an incentive to Christian conversion, then all of its apparent historical claims might simply be beautiful and moving but nonfactual stories. But in actuality, as we saw when looking at the rational claims of revelation, first and foremost Scripture is the inspired interpretative record of a genuine history.[15]

The third and last of the traditional spiritual senses is the anagogical or eschatological sense. Here what is being said is that any given text of Scripture may well be relevant to the overall end and purpose of Scripture—the final destiny of humanity in God. Thus the anagogical sense enables us to rise up, *anagogein*, toward the God who is the *eschaton*, the final goal of our lives. It is difficult to make sense about the anagogical sense as a subject of discourse. Fundamentally, it is a mystical interpretation of Scripture, one that sustains the Christian relationship with God in its highest form. To understand what the mystical sense of the Bible might be, we have to bear in mind that the human intellect and will are intrinsically open to God. Thus we can appreciate not only the immediate bearings of a scriptural text, the literal sense; not only its reference to Christ as the center of revelation, the Christological sense; nor only its implications for our existence, the moral sense. We can also use Scripture as a vehicle for our own entry into the mystery of God. And it is characteristic of the mystical sense to approach the Bible in just this way. To see this kind of exegesis in prac-

---

15. Cf. A. Webster's comment on this aspect of the (Lutheran) theology of Eberhard Jüngel, indebted to Fuchs and Ebeling. "Jüngel rejects any notion of language as an information-bearing sign, in favor of a 'performative' or 'sacramental' concept of language. But the effect of this rejection of the dianoetic is in fact a narrowing of the scope of the language of the New Testament. Language functions in a variety of ways in the New Testament: it is not only imperative but also informative or argumentative, for example." A. Webster, *Eberhard Jüngel: An Introduction to His Theology* (Cambridge: 1986) 15. For an account of how the *kerygma* can be both existential call to decision and a transcription of the community's faith—which includes informational elements, *see* K. Rahner, "Kerygma," *Mysterium Salutis* 1 (Einsiedeln: 1965) 623ff.

tice, we might look at hymns, or at the writings of the great contemplatives of the Church.

These three senses together make up, then, the spiritual or traditional sense of Scripture. When combined with the literal sense, they compose the classic hermeneutic scheme found in the Catholic reading of the Bible. This scheme was summed up in a medieval *aide-mémoire: "Littera gesta docet,/quid credas allegoria;/moralis quid agas,/quo tendas anagogia."* This might be translated: "The literal sense teaches you what happened; the allegorical, how to relate what happened to your faith. The moral sense shows you how you should act in the light of this; the anagogical where it is you are finally heading for." The spiritual sense entails the claim that the literal sense can point beyond itself: first to Christ, who is the center of Scripture as of faith; second, to the individual person in his or her religious existence; and finally, to humanity's ultimate destiny.[16]

Our survey of hermeneutics should at least leave us in possession of the notion that the Bible has no one meaning. It has, rather, a plurality of meanings, although this plurality is not uncontrolled or anarchic. Our hermeneutical schema should enable us to appropriate the text of the Bible in a disciplined way, not just surrendering to the idea that any text may mean anything that any pious persons wants it to mean—or for that matter anything that any impious person wants it to mean. We must not turn hermeneutics into "an instrument of such subtlety and pliability as to make Scripture mean anything—*gallus in campanili*, the 'weathercock on the church tower,' which is turned hither and thither by every wind of doctrine."[17] By reading Scripture within the Church's tradition, a tradition that is at once a Christocentric vision of salvation, a human praxis, and an entry into the mystery of God, we come to see that Scripture can provoke indefinitely—but not indifferently—new interpretations of itself. This capacity of the Bible to suggest ever deeper interpretation is sometimes referred to as its carrying a *sensus plenior*. The theological basis of such a claim lies in the fact that the Bible has to serve as our guide in the life of faith right

16. Thus Thomas can interpret the *Fiat lux!* of Genesis 1:3 literally, as the creation of light; typologically, or allegorically, as the birth of Christ in the Church; tropologically, as referring to the fact that, through Christ, we ourselves are illuminated, encouraged, and reinvigorated in our affections; and anagogically, as teaching that, by means of him, we are led to eternal glory, which is the divine fullness of light. *See* W. Kern—F. J. Niemann, *Theologische Erkenntnislehre* (Düsseldorf: 1981) ch. 3; and, in general, on Thomas' exegetical approach, M. Arias Reyer, *Thomas Aquinas als exeget* (Einsiedeln: 1971).

17. B. Jowett, *The Interpretation of Scripture, and Other Essays* (London) 29.

until the parousia. Thus we have to believe that God has placed in Scripture a fullness of meaning, which will help and satisfy people very different from ourselves in the future just as it has helped and satisfied people very different from ourselves in the past.[18]

Exegetically, the idea of the *sensus plenior* may be said to rest on the greatest of the Gospels, the Gospel of John. In his account of the Last Supper discourse of Jesus to his disciples, St. John stresses two things. First, Jesus had more to say to his disciples than what he managed to say (thanks to their limited capacity) during his ministry (16:12). With this, by the way, we can link the closing comment of the evangelist to the effect that the world could not contain the books that could be written about the work of the Word incarnate (21:25). In other words, the apostolic tradition comprises more than was written down either by John himself or by his fellow gospel writers. Second, the Paraclete—the Holy Spirit—is to come to the disciples, to teach them. This Comforter will not only remind them of all that Jesus said but also guide them into all truth (14:26; 16:13). This total truth from and about Jesus, the Word, is the truth to be found contained in the *sensus plenior*. It consists in the Church's final penetration of revelation and, as such, will not be wholly realized until the second coming of her Lord. However, the *sensus plenior* is constantly in the making. The fuller our grasp of Scripture through historical scholarship in the literal sense, and through tradition in the spiritual sense, the more we tend toward that exhaustive comprehension of Scripture which the *sensus plenior* implies. It is because the Church grows into this fuller meaning by considering Scripture in the light of tradition, her own life over time, that the logical next stage in our consideration of the structure of Catholic theology will be to look at the concept of tradition and at its concrete forms.[19]

18. R. E. Brown, *The Sensus Plenior of Sacred Scripture* (Baltimore: 1955).

19. The continued importance of Blondel's exploration of the relation between history and doctrine, in the context of exegetical method, lies in his awareness that, though members of the Church may use a multiplicity of rational instruments (and, we may add, imaginative ones as well), the *sensus fidei* of the whole Church simply utilizes these as its wills: with respect, but not by way of slavish dependence. Only the eyes of faith of the Church as a supernatural reality are epistemologically adequate for the discernment of divine revelation in its scriptural medium: see I. de la Potterie, ''Préface,'' to P. Toinet, *Pour une théologie de l'exégèse* (Paris: 1983). From this principle there also follows the capacity of the Church's teaching office to unfold, from the biblical text, her mature doctrine: on which, see H. Kümmeringer, ''Es ist Sache der Kirche 'iudicare de vero sensu et interpretatione Scripturarum sacrarum.' Zum Verständnis dieses Satzes auf dem Tridentinum und Vaticanum I,'' *Theologische Quartalschrift* 149 (1969) 282-96.

Part Four
Tradition as a Source in Theology

13
The Nature of Tradition

Our discussion of the *sensus plenior* of the Bible naturally brings us to the topic of Tradition. The Catholic Church does not regard revelation as adequately presented in Scripture alone—if the word "alone" there is taken to mean the Scriptures divorced from their setting in the life of the Church. Over against the sixteenth-century Reformers, the Council of Trent affirmed that there is something yet more primary than Scripture or Tradition, namely, the Gospel itself, portrayed at Trent as "the font of all saving truth and rules of conduct." Nevertheless, the Fathers of Trent continue, "These truths and rules are contained in the written books *and unwritten traditions* which have come down to us." And they conclude, therefore, that "all traditions concerning faith and morals . . . come from the mouth of Christ or are inspired by the Holy Spirit and have been preserved in continuous succession in the Catholic Church."[1] Their statements are certainly directed against the nascent Protestantism of the 1540s. But equally certainly, in making them, Trent saw itself not as evolving new notions to meet an emergency but as reiterating the constant conviction of the Church, something which, in the words of the fifth-century monk-theologian Vincent of Lérins, "has been believed always, everywhere, by everyone."[2] The Vincentian canon, as it is called, is notoriously hard to apply in its full rigor to any aspect of faith whatsoever: in every age of the Church, not excluding the age of the apostles, there has been difference and debate. But in fact, Trent's concept of tradition, if not quite a perfect example of the Vincentian principle at work, does have a highly respectable pedigree.

First of all, it has a Jewish pedigree. The Judaism of the time of our Lord and his apostles had its own notion of tradition, a notion

---

1. Trent, *Decretum de libris sacris et de traditionibus recipiendis*, DS, 1501.
2. Vincent of Lérins, *Commonitorium* 2.

which forms the immediate background of the idea in early Christianity.[3] The rabbis saw themselves as preserving and passing on a certain way of reading the texts of Scripture. The original revelation of God's being and plan given to Moses was not exhaustively expressed in writing. It also existed as an oral interpretation passed down by the teachers of Israel in all ages, explaining how the Scriptures should be understood. In each generation, disciples, *talmid*, formed the links of a chain of transmission going back to Moses himself. What has been called "rabbinic ordination," a ceremony of the laying on of hands, was, at least in part, a recognition by other rabbis that the new rabbi belonged to the orthodox tradition.[4] Much of the oral tradition of Judaism in the time of Jesus found its way into the great second-century Jewish sourcebook, the *Talmud*—a work whose name means "that which was learned by heart."

Second, Trent's concept of tradition also had a Christian pedigree, and first and foremost in the Gospels themselves. The massive religious fact of tradition in Judaism soon found itself Christianized with the founding of the Church. Most obviously, Christian revelation itself had an oral form until the writing of the New Testament. There is good reason to think that this corresponds to the actual intentions of Jesus himself. The formation of an inner group of disciples, described in all the Gospels, looks very much like a Jewish teacher gathering around him a group of men to whom he would communicate his doctrine in the hope that, through them, it would reach a wider audience beyond.[5] The parables and the shorter sayings of Jesus may well have been formulated as they were simply because they would be easy to memorize and retell. The culture of Jesus' Palestine was in some ways highly literate and literary because of the paramount role that the Hebrew Bible played within it, but it was also a culture where oral forms of preserving and transmitting knowledge were still very important. We are dealing with a culture not of the manuscript alone, but of memory and manuscripts.[6] Not surprisingly, then, the principle of tradition is written into the missionary charge of the risen Christ as reported at the end of Matthew's Gospel: "Go, therefore, and make disciples

Tradition in Scripture

3. N. Rotenstreich, "On the Nature of Tradition in Judaism," *Journal of Religion* (1948) 28–36.

4. M. J. Lagrange, *Le Judaisme avant Jésus-Christ* (Paris: 1931) 295ff.

5. B. Gerhardsson, *The Origins of the Gospel Traditions* (London: 1979).

6. B. Gerhardsson, *Memory and Manuscript: Oral and Written Transmission in Rabbinic Judaism and Early Christianity* (Uppsala: 1961).

of all nations . . . teaching them to observe all that I have commanded you.'"[7]

But Matthew's Gospel also portrays Jesus as quite aware of the possibility of a misuse of tradition in the hands of fallible people: some of his hardest gibes against the Pharisees concern what he saw as their perversion of tradition: "How ingeniously you get round the commandment of God to preserve your own tradition!"[8]

The coexistence of these two statements, both ascribed to Jesus in St. Matthew's Gospel, already suggests the possibility that Jesus saw the transmission work of his own disciples as guarded and guided by more-than-human means. This suspicion is confirmed as soon as we turn to the Fourth Gospel. There, the activity of the disciples in communicating Jesus' revelation of the Father is said to be underpinned by the work of the Spirit, the "Counsellor," whom Jesus promises to send from the Father once he has gone through the gateway of his own death.

> The Advocate, the Holy Spirit,
> whom the Father will send you in my name,
> will teach you everything
> and remind you of all I have said to you.[9]

Moving from the Gospels to Paul, we can see this Spirit-guided apostolic tradition at work. Paul appeals to tradition, *paradôsis*, "what is handed on," as to an authority understood and accepted by his readers.[10] Using the technical vocabulary of the Jewish concept of tradition, Paul speaks of what has been "transmitted," what has been "received," and what must be "conserved" and "held fast."[11] In writing to Corinth, for example, about the institution of the Eucharist, he speaks of this as something which he received from the Lord and passed on to the local Corinthian Church.[12] Yet it is clear that this is not at all a claim to a private revelation. What Paul means is that the account given by the Twelve, the pillars of the mother Church of Jerusalem, about what Jesus did at the Last Supper is not just any old piece of reporting. It is holy tradition, the authorized, memorized, and

7. Matthew 28:19.

8. Matthew 15:1-9.

9. John 14:26. *See* on this C. K. Barrett, "The Holy Spirit in the Fourth Gospel," *Journal of Theological Studies* 51 (1950) 1–15.

10. L. Cerfaux, "La tradition selon S. Paul," *Receuil Lucien cerfaux* II, 253–63.

11. Y. M.-J. Congar, *Tradition and Traditions: An Historical and a Theological Essay* (London: 1966) 9.

12. 1 Corinthians 11:23; cf. J. Geiselmann, *Jesus der Christus* (Stuttgart: 1951) 70ff.

solemnly handed down account of Jesus' words and actions on the night of his betrayal. For this reason, its force is the same as if it had been a direct revelation of Christ himself. Here we can observe the principle of tradition in action. Christ himself is engaged and present in the handing on and receiving of tradition. He is not simply the Word found in a book, but the Word found in oral tradition.

The picture we are beginning to acquire is reflected in the work of Luke. The earliest full-scale ecclesiology, or account of the Church's nature, that we possess is the Acts of the Apostles, written by the author of the Gospel of Luke as the second part of a unitary work, Luke-Acts. Part 1 of this work is an account of the workings of God through the historical Jesus; Part 2 considers the same workings now mediated through the community of the glorified Jesus, the Church. The Book of the Acts presents tradition as principally the handing on of the witness of the apostles.[13] The apostles are for Luke the bearers of the tradition about the things Jesus said, did, and suffered, and the Church grows through the appropriation of their witness by new believers. In the Pastoral Epistles, which, if not late Pauline are perhaps to be associated with Luke, further precisions are added. Faith is presented as a "deposit," *parathêkê*, to be handed on. It is guarded by a living teaching authority: originally the apostles, then "apostolic men" such as Timothy and Titus, at once apostolic delegates and the presiding figures of local Churches—what Luke portrays in Acts as "presbyter-bishops."[14] Finally, in the generation following the age of the New Testament, the guardians of the deposit are identified with the bishops of the Catholic episcopate. The task of such people is to secure the deposit against attempts to corrupt it; and this desire to protect orthodoxy, the integrity of the gospel, against what would later be called heresy is already there in the New Testament. But the job does not stop with the largely negative business of defending something from attack. It goes beyond this to include the duty of transmitting the tradition to one's contemporaries across space and to one's successors across time.[15]

---

13. Thus, with reference to Luke 24:44-49 and Acts 1:1-2, Congar can write that in Luke-Acts "Tradition, witness and mission are closely bound up," *Tradition and Traditions*, 13.

14. 1 Timothy 6:20; 2 Timothy 1:14.

15. *See* D. Van den Eynde, *Les Normes de l'enseignement chrétien dans la littérature des trois premiers siècles* (Gembloux: 1933), especially at 57–67. C. H. Turner in his essay "Apostolic Succession" proposed that the notion of such a succession emerged in explicit form by way of opposition to Gnostic notions of a pedagogical succession in the

The moment has come to attempt a definition of what tradition is. We have some of the necessary New Testament materials at hand. For the early Paul, tradition is revelation itself; for Luke, it is the oral witness of the apostles. For the later Paul of the Pastoral Letters (perhaps edited by Luke), tradition is both of these things at once: it is the very faith of the community, what is believed about the new relationship with God in Christ, as witnessed to by the apostles and guarded by their successors. In a word, then, the tradition is the Christian religion itself, a reality larger than that of the scriptural text. The Christian religion, if we think of it in concrete terms, is the whole life of the Church in all its essential lines. The same religion, if we think of it in abstract or conceptual terms, as a reality reflected in how people think as Christians, is the orthodox faith of that same Church. Throughout the history of the idea of tradition, we find these two elements. On the one hand, Tradition is the institutions, rites, and practices that make up the Christian religion in all its concreteness. On the other hand, Tradition is the rule of faith of a Church in continuity with the apostles.[16] Two pairs of Latin words sum up these two complementary senses of tradition. Tradition is the *institutio Christiana,* the "Christian institution," that is, the way of life and worship that is the Church. Tradition is also the *regula fidei,* the normative expression of faith by which theological language, and especially the interpretation of Scripture, are to be judged. Concretely, Tradition is the Church's life; abstractly or reflectively, it is the Church's faith.[17] And because in Catholic Christianity, as in the New Testament, the life and faith of the community of Jesus are held to be Spirit guided, the Spirit of the risen Christ being present in the Church until the end of time, so quite naturally the life and faith of the Church are seen as the proper context in which to read, study, and expound the Scriptures. Tradition as the Christian religion itself, the life and consciousness of the Church considered as a reflection of the word of God, of God's self-communication, is necessarily a reality at once larger than the Bible and inclusive of it.

transmission of esoteric doctrine, as found in, for instance, Ptolemy's *Letter to Flora: see Essays on the Early History of the Church and the Ministry,* ed. H. B. Swete (London: 1921) 95–214.

16. Cf. Congar's statement that "the essential idea is that of the transmission of a body of truths and principles of life, both normative and efficacious for salvation," *Tradition and Traditions,* 26.

17. On patristic texts concerning the *regula fidei, see* Van den Eynde, *Les Normes de l'enseignement dans la littérature chrétienne des trois premiers siècles,* 282–306; on the unwritten traditions up to Trent as overwhelmingly liturgical in character and thus pertinent to the concept of *institutio christiana, see* Congar, *Tradition and Traditions,* 51–61.

But here a problem surfaces. For this way of putting it does not seem *prima facie* to correspond to that of Trent, which, as we have seen, appears to speak of Scripture and Tradition as sharing the same status as mediations of Christian truth. Our next task must be to look more closely into the relation of Scripture and Tradition, considered as sources for theology. Following the central methodological thrust of this book, namely that the study of what theology is amounts to the study of what made possible the actual historical achievements of Catholic theology, I propose to look at this problem in a historical way. We can divide up the relevant data into four segments, concerning in turn the patristic period, the early and High Middle Ages, the later Middle Ages, and the period of the Protestant and Catholic Reformations when the text of Trent was composed.

First, then, the patristic period. In the age of the Fathers, the unity of Scripture and Tradition is largely taken for granted. The apostolic tradition is found in Scripture; conversely, what is found in Scripture is the apostolic tradition. Faced with some alternative readings of Scripture by heretics, the Fathers are likely to reply that heretics have no right to read the Bible at all. The Bible is the Church's book, and she is its only rightful interpreter. Tertullian is the most forthright representative of this point of view, applying to heretical interpretations of Scripture the Roman legal notion of *praescriptio*, ''prescription.'' If you had a dispute with someone and both of you went to court in order to settle it, you might be able to win the case right at the outset by invoking *praescriptio*. That is, you might be able to prove that for some reason your adversary was not competent to speak in court on the matter in question. So Tertullian argues that there is no need to confute heretical exegesis in detail. Heretics simply have no right to use the Bible, it is not their property.[18] Here Scripture and the Church's tradition are implicitly regarded as coterminous. There is no possibility of playing one against the other, or even of analyzing their unity into two distinct parts.[19]

18. Tertullian, *De praescriptione* 5, 40; cf. J. K. Stirnimann, *Die Praescriptio Tertullians im Lichte des römischen Rechtes und der Theologie* (Fribourg: 1949).

19. One does find occasional appeal to unwritten traditions side by side with appeal to Scripture in the patristic period: most famously, Basil the Great, *De Spiritu Sancto* 27, 66. But the translation of *ta men* . . . *ta de* here by *partim* . . . *partim* (found first in Peter Canisius, a Counter-Reformation apologist) turned into a two-source theory what is almost certainly a statement of two modes of transmission of the same apostolic deposit. *See* J. Geiselmann, ''Das Konzil von Trient über das Verhältnis der heiligen Schrift und der nicht geschriebenen Traditionen'' in *Die mündliche Überlieferung*, ed. M. Schmaus (Munich: 1957) 172.

Moving on to the early and High Middle Ages, we find that the majority report of the Fathers remains substantially intact. Sometimes this naive or innocent view of the unity of Scripture and Tradition led to statements that sound bizarre to a modern Catholic ear: "Whatever may be arrived at, or concluded from, arguments outside the Holy Scriptures . . . in no way belongs to the praise and confession of Almighty God . . . and no one can lawfully demand that a Catholic believe it."[20] Such a statement, if made in the sixteenth century, would imply Protestantism, but in the twelfth century, where it comes from the pen of the monastic theologian Rupert of Deutz, it simply implies a one-hundred-percent trust in the unconditional unanimity of the Bible and the Church. The Church is not merely the organization that passes down the Scriptures from one generation to the next. Rather, there is a mystical unity or coinherence between the Church and the Bible. As Rupert writes, "That woman, Ecclesia, drew the Scriptures from the well of truth, the well that is set in her midst and makes her the garden of the Lord."[21] So the idea that the Church could teach something not in Scripture or Scripture teach something not taught by the Church simply never arises.

However, there were two respects in which the patristic and early to high medieval periods did show some sign of recognizing our problem. In the first place, there was the issue of the status to be accorded the Fathers and Doctors of the Church vis-à-vis the Bible. Precisely because of the idea of the coinherence of Church and Scripture, the charism of biblical inspiration was sometimes regarded as spilling over in a more diluted form to the great commentators on the Bible.[22] Around 500, Pope Gelasius added to his list of the canonical books "certain other writings," which, he says, the Roman Church has received as of faith, though they are not on the same level as Scripture. He identifies these as the decrees of the first four ecumenical councils, the writings of various Church Fathers, the decretals of his predecessors, the acts of the martyrs, and lives of the saints. In the early and High Middle Ages an attempt is made to tidy up and explain theologically the existence of such lists of what we can call "subbiblical books." In the eleventh century, Hugh of St. Victor can say that the mind of the Church considers together the books of the Bible

20. Rupert of Deutz, *De Omnipotentia Dei* XXVII.
21. Rupert of Deutz, *Commentarium in Apocalypsim* VII. 12.
22. G. Tavard, *Holy Writ or Holy Church? The Crisis of the Protestant Reformation* (London: 1959) 7.

on the one hand, and, on the other, the conciliar creeds and the works of the Fathers. He explains this by saying that the conciliar and patristic texts are, after all, summaries of Scripture and commentaries upon Scripture, and so are necessary for Scripture's evaluation.[23] In the same period, other theologians are found saying that the subbiblical books are necessary for understanding the spiritual sense of the Scriptures.[24] In St. Bonaventure in the thirteenth century we find an important distinction, that between the credibile and the intelligibile, invoked to throw light on this issue. In the *Breviloquium*, his brief introduction for beginners in theology, Bonaventure writes: "Theology is one single body of knowledge. Its subject matter considered as what we should believe, the *credibile*, is the books of the canon of the Bible; but considered as how to understand what we should believe, the *intelligibile*, it is the writings of the biblical commentators (i.e. the Fathers and Doctors of the Church)."[25] In St. Thomas, the single phrase *sacra doctrina* may be translated either as "Scripture" or as "tradition" or as "theology," depending on the context. When thinking globally about the work of a theologian, Thomas does not distinguish between the Bible and the theology evolved around it by Fathers and Doctors in the tradition.[26]

The second sign of the glimmerings of a recognition of our problem foreshadows the later notion that revelation has two distinct sources. Theologians were concerned to defend certain features of the Church's liturgical cultus: either quite wide-ranging aspects of Christian worship like the making and venerating of images, or very limited, but (to contemporaries) significant matters, like the instruction in the rubrics of the Roman Rite that at the consecration the celebrant, following the example of Jesus, should raise his eyes toward heaven, a detail not found in the Gospels. Both Bonaventure and Thomas offer an apologia for the traditional pattern of Christian worship by appealing to the unwritten customs of the apostles.[27]

When we come to the late medieval period, we find that the honeymoon between the Bible and the Church is drawing to a close. People are beginning to ask whether at least in principle there could be dis-

23. Hugh of St. Victor, *Eruditio didascalia* IV. 4.
24. Tavard, *Holy Writ or Holy Church?* 19–20.
25. Bonaventure, *Breviloquium* I. 1. iv.
26. On Thomas, *see* A. Patfoort, *Thomas d'Aquin, Les Clés d'une théologie* (Paris: 1983) 27–48.
27. For Bonaventure, *see Commentarium super sententias* III. d. 9, a. 1, q. 2, ad vi; for Thomas, *Summa theologiae* IIIa. q. 25, a. 3, ad iv; q. 64, a. 2, ad i.

crepancies between what the Bible says and what the Church says. Henry of Ghent puts just this question in his commentary on the *Sentences* of Peter Lombard, the standard theological manual of the Middle Ages. Henry begins reassuringly by putting forward the customarily accepted view: "Concerning the things of faith, the Church and Holy Scripture agree in everything and testify to the same thing." But then he goes on to say, and this is new, "Yet while there can be no contradiction between Scripture and the Church, there may be a discrepancy between Scripture and a church which seems to be the Church but is the Church only according to human opinion and not in the eyes of God."[28] Henry does not mean that there might be a contradiction about Scripture and the church of the *Waldenses*: he is talking exclusively about the Catholic Church. He suggests that it is theoretically conceivable that virtually all Catholics should apostatize interiorly from the faith. In such a situation, when the Church had become a purely nominal Church, a merely sociological reality, the last remaining believer would have the duty to follow Scripture alone and not the Church. And this shows us, Henry concludes, that in principle a Christian adheres more fundamentally to the words of Scripture than to the testimony of the Church. By this thought experiment, Henry of Ghent thus anticipated the basic problematic of the Reformation.

As the fourteenth century advanced, one finds increasingly such statements as, I believe this either on the authority of Scripture or on the authority of the Church teaching. Once this dichotomy had opened up, people began to opt for one of two courses: the subordination of Scripture to the Church or of the Church to Scripture.[29] In the fourteenth century itself, such views are usually put forward for the sake of argument, to expound theoretically possible positions. Thus William of Ockham, the English Franciscan, proposes three views of the relation between Scripture and customary Church teaching, none of which views he necessarily shares but all of which are, he thinks, quite possible. First, there is *Scriptura sola:* "The only truths that are to be considered Catholic and necessary to salvation are explicitly or implicitly stated in the canon of the Bible. . . . All other truths which neither are inserted in the Bible nor can be formally and necessarily inferred from its contents, are not to be held as Catholic even if they are stated in the writings of the fathers or the definitions of the supreme pon-

---

28. Henry of Ghent, *Commentarium super sententias*, Prologus, a. 10, q. i.
29. Tavard, *Holy Writ or Holy Church?* 28–30; Congar, *Tradition and Traditions* 99–100.

tiffs, and even if they are believed by all the faithful."[30] Second, there is the idea that besides the revelation to the apostles, God could and does reveal other truths to the universal Church: that there is, in other words, an ecclesiastical revelation alongside and supplementing apostolic revelation. And third, we find in Ockham the notion of an orally transmitted apostolic revelation, parallel to the written transmission of the apostolic teaching in the Scriptures.[31] Clearly, Ockham does not subscribe to all of these views, since they are mutually exclusive. But he regarded them as possible opinions within the Catholic theological world of his time.

In the period just prior to the Reformation we find a sharpening of attitudes to the question, prompted especially by reactions to the Great Schism which divided the Latin Church in the years from 1378 to 1417. Here, apparently for the first time, people began to believe quite sincerely some of the conceptual possibilities worked out earlier. We can distinguish four groups. First, ultra-papalist canonists held a concept of the Petrine office so high that, according to Fr. George Tavard, had they been consistent they would have ascribed to the authority of Scripture "no more than a nominal value."[32] Second, there were the conciliarists who held that only ecumenical councils could interpret Scripture, consonant with their idea that such councils speak for all the faithful by representing them through their bishops. Third, there were biblicists who postulated the radical subordination of Church tradition and authority to the written word of Scripture. Finally, there were those who held that esoteric oral traditions, coming down subterraneously from the apostles, could be used to defend existing Church practice even in the face of the silence of the Bible.[33]

Not surprisingly, then, the age of the Reformation found Catholic theology in a state of considerable disarray on the topic of the relations between Scripture and Tradition. There were still a few theologians, Thomists, especially, who held sane views on the matter, but their voice was just one among many. The crisis broke with Luther's revolt in 1517. Luther created a twofold subordination of tradition. He subordinated Church tradition to the Bible, and he also subordinated the Bible to the essence of the gospel, regarded by him as the doctrine of justification by faith alone. The task of the Church is to distinguish

---

30. William of Ockham, *Dialogus contra haereticos*, II. 3.
31. *Ibid.*, II. 5.
32. Tavard, *Holy Writ or Holy Church?* 49.
33. For references, *see ibid.*, 48–66.

the word of God from the words of men, that is, to distinguish the doctrine of justification by faith alone from all theological discourse which does not flow from this central truth. In this connection the Church is defined by Luther as all those Christians who accept the pure gospel, who hold that justification by faith is the key to biblical revelation. Here the analogy of faith, the interrelationship of doctrines within revelation, has been destroyed through the elevation of one principle above all the rest. Moreover, the Church has suffered redefinition, as those who accept that this one doctrine is in fact supreme. We have travelled a long way from that earlier consensus which saw revelation as lying in Scripture as a whole read within the total life of the entire Church.

A similar revolution takes place with Calvin, the other outstanding theological mind among the Reformers. For Calvin, the Word himself speaks through what he calls the "oracles of Scripture," but only when the Holy Spirit working in the believer prompts him to find the Word in the Bible.[34] How, then, do we know which believers to follow in the interpretation of the Bible? For Calvin, we can be sure that such reliable guides exist, because some people are absolutely predestined by God's grace to enjoy the indwelling of the Holy Spirit. However, we do not always know at any given time who the elect in fact are, though there are certain signs, such as zeal for sanctification or assurance of salvation, which are usually trustworthy. The most we can say positively is that there will always be individuals in local Churches who find and teach God's word through his oracles. Thus, in Calvinist theology, there is no objective test for discovering the meaning of Scripture. In the Reformed Churches flowing from Calvin, the need for such a test was, however, soon felt. The most common solution was to describe the Bible as self-interpreting—since any part of it may be able to illuminate any other. The task of discerning that process of self-interpretation falls to Reformed and godly scholars. Discarding the infallibility of the Church, the left wing of the Reformation ended up in the Modern period with the infallibility of exegetes—a notion which sometimes appears to have seeped into contemporary Catholic liberalism also!

The Tridentine episcopate, to whom fell the unenviable duty of sorting out the above mess, foregathered in council with views as weird and wonderful as any we have seen; naturally enough, since they were

34. J. Calvin, *Institutes* I. 7, 1.

late medieval men, formed on the writings of the period, as had been the Reformers themselves. Despite all handicaps, they made a major attempt to find a position on the interrelation of Bible and tradition which would re-create their ancient unity. In the final version of what it has to say on this subject, Trent speaks of the gospel as found *both* in the Scriptures *and* in apostolic traditions, insofar as these latter (1) pertain to faith and morals, and (2) are known to be part of the continuous practice of the Church. Over against an earlier draft, revelation is not explicitly said to endure "partly" as Scripture and "partly" as traditions. Though the exact significant of the dropping of the phrase *partim . . . partim*, and its replacement by *et . . . et* is disputed by historians, we can at least say that Trent closed off certain approaches while leaving others open.[35]

Three approaches were declared, implicitly, to be cul-de-sacs. First, Trent closed off the Protestant position in its Lutheran or Calvinist form. Second, it also excluded the late medieval concept of postapostolic revelation made to the Church. Finally, it disposed of the idea of an esoteric, nonpublic apostolic tradition coming out of the closet from time to time.[36] On the other hand, Trent kept open three other possibilities. It left open the so-called two-source theory, which came to be dominant in the period between the council and the nineteenth century. On this view, there are (alongside Scripture) confessional, liturgical, and ethical traditions in the Church deriving from ancient times and testifying to revelation.[37] Next, Trent can coexist with what may be called the "classical view" of the High Middle Ages, namely, that all revelation is virtually contained in Scripture, requiring, however, the Church's interpretation, leaning on apostolic tradition, for its explication.[38] Last, Trent cannot be said to exclude what has become in the Modern period perhaps the favored view of Catholic theologians: the view that sees Tradition (now spell with a capital *T* and distinguished from traditions in the plural) as theologically prior to the Bible, and

35. E. Ortigues, "Ecritures et Traditions apostoliques au concile de Trente," *Recherches de science religieuse* 36 (1949); J. Geiselmann, "Das Konzil von Trient über dans Verhältnis der Heiligen Schrift und der nicht geschriebenen Traditionen" art. cit.

36. Congar, *Tradition and Traditions* 164–66.

37. A view found in, for instance, Peter Canisius (1521–97), and Robert Bellarmine (1542–1621).

38. For example, J. H. Newman: cf. his *Certain Difficulties Felt by Anglicans in Catholic Teaching* II. 2. ii: "(Thus) *you* do not say, what the whole revelation is in Scripture in such sense that pure unaided logic can draw it from the sacred text; nor do *we* say that it is not in Scripture, in an improper sense, in the sense that the Tradition of the Church is able to recognize and determine it there."

defines that Tradition as the life and consciousness of the Church, of which Scripture forms an essential part.[39] On this view, Scripture can still be called the supreme norm of faith, the *norma non normata*, in the sense that to appeal to Tradition to interpret Scripture aright is not to appeal away from Scripture to something other than Scripture. For as Cardinal Charles Journet of Fribourg put it, "The Church raises Scripture above itself, much as it raises up Christ at the processions of Corpus Christi."[40] On the other hand, since Tradition is not thought of as exhaustively expressed in Scripture, we can also expect to find it alive and well in the various concrete traditions that manifest the life of the Church. Tradition with a capital *T* is, therefore, revelation in its transmission. It finds two sorts of expression: in the books of the Bible and in the unwritten traditions. To judge the Bible on the basis of Tradition as expressed in traditions is not, *pace* Protestant fears, to submit the Bible to an alien authority, but rather to identify and declare what is the Bible's own deepest reality.

We must turn now to the whole variety of ways in which Tradition comes to expression. We have seen already that the principal monument of Tradition is Scripture. Now we must look at Tradition's other monuments, other ways in which the life and faith of the Church as something larger than Scripture becomes articulate.[41] The unwritten traditions mentioned at Trent are only encountered by us when they become in some way visible and tangible, whether as a sacrament, a liturgical text, an artwork from Christian antiquity, or whatever. In effect, we are dealing here with what it is that theologians must take as authoritative for their work. By way of preamble, it is worth pointing out that the word "authority" here should not be taken too narrowly. To a modern sensibility, "authority" has a mainly legal sound

39. Cf. J. A. Möhler's statement that "Tradition is the expression of that Holy Spirit who enlivens the community of believers—an expression that courses through all ages, living at every moment, but always finding embodiment. The Scriptures are the expression of the Holy Spirit, embodied at the beginning of Christianity through the special grace given to the apostles. The Scriptures are in that respect the first component of written tradition." *Die Einheit in der Kirche, oder das Princip des Katholicismus, dargestellt im Geiste der Kirchenväter der drei ersten Jahrhunderte* (Tübingen: 1825) 56. On Möhler's view of tradition, *see* J. Geiselmann, *Lebendiger Glaube aus geheiligten Überlieferung. Der Grundgedanke der Theologie J. A. Möhlers und die katholische Tübinger Schule* (Mainz: 1942).

40. C. Journet, *What Is a Dogma?* (English trans., London: 1964) 51.

41. Congar, *Tradition and Traditions* 287–88. The concept of "monuments of tradition" derives from G. Perrone, *Praelectiones theologicae* (Rome: 1835) I, 195, and was given wide currency through J. B. Franzelin, *Tractatus de divina Traditione et Scriptura* (Rome: 1970) 306. *See* W. Kasper, *Die Lehre über die Tradition in der Römischen Schule* (Freiburg: 1962) 31.

about it: we speak of a national legislature as invested with authority, or of the police's authority to question a citizen on the street. If we are too influenced by these analogies, we shall see theological authorities as simply laying down in advance what can or cannot be said in theology, ruling certain things out of court and admitting others. But the sense of authority proper to the monuments of Tradition is not mainly that of a legislature or a police force. *Auctoritas* is the characteristic quality of an *auctor*, an "author" or "source."[42] To say that something has authority in Christian theology is principally to say that it is a perennially valid source from which insight and illumination flow down to us in the life of faith. We must not take up a wooden attitude to the texts and objects in which Tradition is expressed, for then they will not be life giving. We must come to them with a certain sensitivity, which can be compared with that of the good listener: the person who not only registers what someone is saying on the surface but hears also the deeper self-communication that is going on in, with, and beneath the language they are using. There is always more in the sources of revelation than the theologian—or even the magisterium—draws out of them.

From the sixteenth century onwards, the study of such authorities or resources for theology has been known as the study of *loci theologici,* literally, "theological places," places where you can go to look for enlightenment in the work of theology.[43] Another term sometimes used for the monuments of Tradition, especially in the systematic theology of the present century, is "theological criteriology." This somewhat unlovely phrase means that the sources for theology can also be looked on as criteria for judging our theology when we have completed it.[44] If someone writes a book on the Eucharist, for example, and we are asked what we think of it, we should judge it in the light of the sources, monuments, or criteria that come to us from Tradition. So for instance we should ask, How does the book stand in relation to Scripture's witness on the Eucharist? How does its sense of the Eucharist match up to what is found in the texts and rubrics of the

42. C. T. Lewis and C. Short in *A Latin Dictionary* (Oxford: 1951) define *auctoritas* as in the first instance "a producing, production, invention, cause"; and *auctor* as "he that brings about the existence of any object, or promotes the increase and prosperity of it, whether he originates it, or by his efforts gives greater permanence or continuance to it," 198–99.

43. Melchior Cano, *De locis theologicis* (Salamanca: 1563), analyzed by A. Gardeil in "Lieux," *DTC* 9, cols. 712–47; Y. Congar, *La foi et la théologie* (Tournai: 1962) 142–45.

44. S. di Bartolo, *Nuova Espozione dei Criteri teologici* (Rome: 1904).

Church's liturgies? In her art and architecture? In the writings of the Fathers? In the teachings of the councils? All of these are expressions of the Church's life and self-understanding, and so all of them are highly pertinent to judging the Catholicity of a piece of theological writing. No new theory about, say, the Eucharistic sacrifice or the Eucharistic presence which could not incorporate all this evidence in some way could count as really acceptable. Without necessarily being able to discover a logical flaw in the author's reasoning, we could still say that there seems to be something defective in the author's sense of this particular reality of faith. Naturally, in a matter of this sort, our personal judgment is only of validity to the extent that we have immersed ourselves in the Church's Tradition, in the entire range of articulations of the life of faith that the past has bequeathed us. To the extent that the theologian is rightly defined as a "professional rememberer," no one who has read nothing between the New Testament and Pope John Paul II could possibly be called a theologian.

In speaking of the monuments of Tradition, we can usefully distinguish between what we can call the primary and secondary monuments or sources. The primary sources must surely be Scripture and the unwritten traditions, but the latter only come to us in the form of a great plethora of secondary sources: the liturgy, the writings left by the Fathers, and so forth. The primary sources are, in a terminology commended by Père Yves Congar, constitutive *loci* of Tradition: they are the sources which make Tradition what it is, the things without which the life and faith of the Church would be unthinkable. The secondary sources will then be Tradition's declarative *loci:* the places where the reality of the Church declares itself in thoroughly empirical terms.[45] These secondary sources are, as it were, the tip of the iceberg. They do not exhaust Tradition, any more than the tip of the iceberg is the iceberg itself. But without them we could not get hold of Tradition, just as before the invention of radar sailors could not locate an iceberg except by locating the tip first. Thus for instance, a value essential to the Church such as the sense of adoration before the triune God is preserved in Tradition in the form of a variety of historic liturgies. The existence of these liturgies, whether Western or Eastern, is a matter of the sheerest historical contingency. If the main missionary effort of the Church of the first century had been to India and the Far East, rather than to the Greco-Roman world and its Syriac fringe, we

---

45. Congar, *Tradition and Traditions*, 426.

should have had a very different liturgical inheritance. Nevertheless, although the concrete form of our liturgies is contingent, through them we have access to the sense of adoration of the one God—Father, Son, and Holy Spirit—without which the Church's life is unimaginable. Through the liturgies we have, even though these are not the ones we might have had, we have access to something absolutely primary and fundamental, the theological reality of Tradition itself, revelation in transmission. The secondary sources, then, declare their primary counterparts. They do so in a way which is time bound and place bound and therefore contingent. Yet there is no other way to the essential reality of Tradition, which underlies them. Though the concept of declarative *loci* has been worked out in the context of traditions, we could very well see the texts or language of Scripture as comparable declarative *loci* when compared with the meaning of Scripture. For it is the meaning of the texts of the Bible that is constitutive of Tradition; the literary and linguistic ways in which this meaning is embedded is what sets that meaning forth.

We have looked, then, at the biblical background of the idea of tradition and, armed with a definition thereof, studied the changing modalities of Tradition's relation to Scripture in Catholic perception up until Trent. Noting that, as so often, a council leaves a plurality of options open, we elected a concept of Tradition (now graced with a capital *T*) which would enable us to include Scripture and the traditions as Tradition's two primary expressions. But these expressions must declare themselves in order to be heard. In Part 3 of this book we have already considered how the language of Scripture conveys a meaning (sense) that is authority bearing for Catholic theology. And so it remains in the rest of Part 4 to review the declarative *loci* in which that other great source of Tradition—the unwritten traditions which are Scripture's ambience—makes itself known to us.

The Liturgy and Christian Art

We have seen, then, that Tradition is never accessible in itself, in its pure form, but only comes to us via some kind of concrete mediation. The texts of Scripture are the primordial instance of such mediation, a uniquely important monument of Tradition. But there are other, less important mediations to set side by side with Scripture, and it is with these subsidiary mediations of Tradition that we will be dealing in the next three chapters. And the first of these I want to look at is the liturgy. The importance of the liturgy to theology can be demonstrated by citing a widely accepted maxim: *lex orandi est lex credendi,* "the law of praying is the law of believing."[1] In other words, the best guide to what the Church believes is what the Church says when she prays—thinking here of the Church's official public prayer, not of the unstructured private prayer of individuals or small groups. But why give such a high theological status to the liturgy as a mediation of Tradition, a source for theological insight?

To answer this question, we must try to define what the liturgy is. In the first place, we could try to define it etymologically, through looking at the genesis of the word *leitourgia, liturgia.*[2] Using "liturgy" to refer to Christian worship at large is a fairly recent innovation. In the New Testament and in Christian antiquity, "liturgy" meant the service of God in the broadest sense, including, for example, practical

1. The phrase derives from the fifth-century *Indiculus de gratia Dei* where the apostolic injunction found in 1 Timothy 2:1-4 satisfied by the bishop when he prays in the liturgy that grace may be given to all *(lex orandi)* is said to entail our believing (against Pelagians and semi-Pelagians) that grace is necessary for all *(lex credendi). See* C. Vagaggini, *Theological Dimensions of the Liturgy* (English trans., Collegeville: 1976) 529–42.

2. *See* A. G. Martimort, "Preliminary Concepts," in *The Church at Prayer: Introduction to the Liturgy,* ed. A. G. Martimort (English trans., New York: 1968) 1–2, and more fully in E. Raitz von Frentz, "Der Weg des Wortes 'Liturgie' in der Geschichte," *Ephemerides liturgicae* 55 (1941) 74–80.

service of one's neighbor. In this respect, the early Christian use of the term borrowed much of its connotation from the secular usage of the pagan Greek-speaking world. In that world, one's liturgy was one's duty as a citizen to the *polis*, the common social good. But in the Greek-speaking Church, as time went on, the word became attached not so much to the Christian's duty as a whole but to the highest form of that duty, its central act and main potive power. That highest form was one's participation in the celebration of the Eucharist. Thus among Greek Christians, *hê leitourgia*, "the liturgy" became the common name for the Eucharist as celebrated of obligation, Sunday by Sunday and feast by feast. In the sixteenth century the word entered Latin-Christian usage under the influence of Byzantine texts, and by the eighteenth century it had taken on what is now its normal meaning in Catholic circles. That is, it came to stand not just for the rite of the Eucharist but for all the rites which make up the common prayer of the Church. So much, then, for the story of the word, but how can we define the reality the word stands for in a theologically helpful way?[3] The liturgical movement, designed to bring clergy and laity a deeper grasp of that reality, received its official charter in the Roman Church with the encyclical letter *Mediator Dei,* composed by Pius XII in 1947. In that letter, the Pope summed up the conclusions of inter-war theologians of the liturgy by defining it as "the Church's continuation of the priestly office of Jesus Christ."[4] A key is offered here to why the liturgy is theologically vital.

In the normal course of affairs, it may be said, God and humanity are far apart. They are separated insofar as God is the Creator and people are the creatures; they are also separated insofar as God is all-holy and people are sinners. The office or work of Jesus Christ was and is to annul this distance between God and humanity, to atone or make-at-one these two realities, which in themselves are so diverse and indeed estranged. In the incarnation, Christ conjoined God and human in his own person; and in his passion, death, and resurrection, he opened a way for the rest of humanity into the presence of the living God. Thus Jesus Christ can be called the eternal or perma-

3. J. H. Miller, "The Nature and Definition of the Liturgy," *Theological Studies* 18 (1957) 325–26.

4. Pius XII, *Mediator Dei* 3. Cf. T. Michels, "Die Liturgie im Lichte der katholischen Gemeinchaftsidee," *Jahrbuch für die Liturgiewissenschaft* 1 (1921) 109–16. The history of the liturgical movement of which this opening number of Odo Casel's journal is the herald, may be found in E. Koenker, *The Liturgical Renaissance in the Roman Catholic Church* (Chicago: 1954).

nent high priest, through whose mediation we become immediately present to God. As the Letter to the Hebrews puts it: "He lives for ever to make intercession for us,"[5] that is, to pray, effectively, that the barriers between God and ourselves may be cast down. In *Mediator Dei*, this intercessory activity of Christ before the Father is said to be "continued" in the liturgy of the Church. In the liturgy, the Church as Christ's body unites herself to Christ her head and makes the mind of Christ her own. She glorifies the Father through Christ and prays for the salvation of the world, once again through Christ: *per Christum Dominum nostrum*, as the Roman Rite ends so many of its prayers. The liturgy is, therefore, the expression of the Church's deepest point of entry into the mystery of humanity's salvation.[6]

At the Second Vatican Council, Pius XII's definition of the liturgy was taken up and extended in the document *Sacrosanctum Concilium* on Catholic worship. As that constitution put it, "Every liturgical action, inasmuch as it is a work of Christ the Priest and of his Body the Church, is pre-eminently a sacred action, the efficacy of which no other act of the Church can equal on the same basis and to the same degree."[7] It is because the liturgy is the expression of the deepest union there can be between the Church and the Church's Lord that the various rites used in the history of the Church have so high a theological authority. Here as anywhere, in this assemblage of texts and gestures, we see the Church's self-understanding (and thus Tradition) unfolding before our eyes. The liturgy permits us to overhear the Church interpreting her own faith in the best way she knows how.

When we come to look more closely at the liturgical texts which can serve as the theologian's sources, we soon find that the Roman liturgy in its present form is not the only pebble on the beach.[8] To concentrate on the contemporary Roman Rite to the exclusion of all others would be impossibly narrow if what we are concerned with is the Church's living Tradition through the ages and not just our own neck of the woods in Bombay or Medicine Hat in 1991. When we are thinking of the liturgy as theological *locus*, as an authority in the making of theology, we have to look back in time and out across space as well. Apart from the minor variations which make up other Western rites

5. Hebrews 7:25.

6. I. H. Dalmais, "The Liturgy and the Mystery of Salvation," *The Church at Prayer*, ed. A. G. Martimort 190–211.

7. Vatican II, *Sacrosanctum Concilium*, 7.

8. *See*, for instance, A. Baumstark, *Comparative Liturgy* (English trans., London: 1958).

still celebrated here and there (and these should perhaps be called
"uses" rather than full rites), there are a number of Oriental liturgies
at least as venerable as the Roman liturgy, and enacted in local
Churches in full communion with the Holy See.[9] And then again, the
Roman Rite itself has changed notably in the course of history. It has
sometimes been reformed back to more of its old self, in the mid-
sixteenth century, for instance, and again in the mid-twentieth, but
we should beware of assuming that the primitive is always the best.[10]
The liturgical prayers of every age have treasures to offer. Theological
students need to have some acquaintance, therefore, with the history
of their own rite and with the special genius of the others. Their prayers and hymns are full of doctrine, much richer doctrine often than
the formal teaching of the Churches that produced them. The liturgy
is the poetry of the Church, and just as poetry is language at its most
intensely expressive, so in the liturgy we hear the Church's voice at
its most eloquent.

We can take some examples of how theologians might be instructed
by the liturgy. To begin with, here is an example from the Malankar
liturgy of Southern India. The small Eastern Catholic Church which
uses this liturgy is traditionally ascribed, along with other South Indian Churches, to the missionary work of the Apostle Thomas. After
a confused history, the Malankar Church, along with other "Indian
Christians of St. Thomas" not in union with Rome, adopted a version
of the Antiochene, or West Syrian liturgy. Here is the dialogue that
precedes and follows the reading of the gospel at the Sunday Eucharist,
the *kurbana*.[11] First, the deacon gives this command to the people: "Let
us stand in silence, in awe and modesty, and listen to the proclamation of the living words of God from the Gospel of our Lord Jesus,
the Messiah." At this point the priest turns and blesses the congregation with the words, "Peace be with you all." They reply, "May the
Lord make us also worthy, along with you." Then the priest announces
the gospel of the day with these words: "The life-giving preaching of
the holy Gospel of our Lord Jesus, the Messiah, from the evangelist
N. who preaches life and salvation to the world." To this the congregation responds: "Blessed is he who has come and is to come in the
name of the Lord. Praise be to him who sent him for our salvation,

---

9. I. H. Dalmais, *The Eastern Liturgies* (English trans., New York: 1960).

10. J. D. Crichton, "An Historical Sketch of the Roman Liturgy," in *True Worship*,
ed. L. Sheppard (Baltimore: 1963) 45–82.

11. L. W. Brown, *The Indian Christians of St. Thomas* (Cambridge: 1956) 219.

and may his blessings be on us all." After the gospel has been read, all sing a brief hymn, itself partly a paraphrase of a parable:

> Blessed are those good servants
> who, when their Lord comes, are found
> awake and working in his vineyard.
> He will gird himself and serve them
> who worked with them from morning until evening.
> The Father will place them round the table,
> the Son will minister to them,
> and the Holy Spirit, the Comforter,
> will make crowns, alleluia,
> and put them on the head of each.

Into this piece of liturgical conversation, there is packed a great deal of doctrinal stimulus for theology. It instructs us on the relationship between Christ, the gospel, and the destiny of the Church's own members. The gospel text when read in the assembly of the baptized brings people the life and salvation which flow from God in Christ. This does not happen automatically, however, but requires from the disciple attentiveness and fidelity. But since the same Christ who once came as Jesus will come again, the faithful can rest assured that Father, Son, and Spirit, who began their salvation, will also assist it and bring it to completion.

Because this particular Indian tradition derives the bulk of its liturgical literature from Syria where Christian hymn writing had its earliest flowering, it is not surprising to find such a rich linguistic texture, at once poetic and theological. But if we turn to the Roman liturgy, a much more sober affair, we also find it to be a teaching vehicle for theological understanding. Although the primary aim of the liturgy is not to instruct us but to adore God, nevertheless, by adoring God in a certain way, using certain images and concepts, it cannot help but be theological. Take, for instance, the ceremonies of the triduum, the three days leading up to Easter in the modern Roman Rite. The climax of the liturgy of Good Friday is the veneration of the cross, whereby we advance toward the unveiled crucifix, genuflect, and then kiss the wood which symbolizes the instrument of our redemption.

> See the wood of the cross,
> upon which hung the world's salvation:
> come, let us adore!

Here we have a statement that the salvation of the world is essentially related to the cross of Jesus, and that this cross is not simply venerable but adorable. It is the cross not just of a man but of God, of a man who was personally God. One might cite here the commentary on the ceremonies of Holy Week by Dame Aemiliana Löhr, herself a pupil of Dom Odo Casel, one of the figures in the liturgical movement who most encouraged theologians to take the liturgical symbols with full seriousness: "If one is only an onlooker at this reverence, one can well let it go by, without being inwardly touched by it: a fine ceremony which binds the individual to nothing. But one who goes up and takes part must pledge himself to the crucified God for life and death, must offer his longing to have part in Jesus' suffering, to have a share in the Passover, both here in ritual and in all the difficulty of daily life. If my act is to be no kiss of Judas it must say: 'Here is a pledge to you, Christ my Lord. Draw me into your holy Passover.' "[12] Here the liturgy has provoked not merely a pious comment, which the theologian could disregard. Rather, we are offered an affirmation about the life of discipleship as a participation in the redemptive suffering by which Jesus took what was negative in this world and transformed it into something positive through the power of the divine love.

Or again, the Exsultet, the solemn hymn in praise of the risen Christ sung by the deacon in the Roman Rite on the Vigil of Easter, is a major source for understanding the mystery of the resurrection as grasped by the Church's faith experience.[13] "Exsult, all creation around God's throne. Jesus Christ, our King, is risen! . . . Rejoice, O earth, in shining splendor, radiant in the brightness of your king! Christ has conquered! Glory fills you! Darkness vanishes for ever." What the Exsultet teaches the theologian is the universal, cosmic significance of the resurrection of Christ. This is not simply the resuscitation of a corpse: it is the point where the Creator God begins the re-creation of his world by transforming the corpse of Jesus into the nucleus of a new creation. Here the liturgy shows us theologically the universality of the call to salvation, the mission of the Church. At the same time, the resurrection cannot be irrelevant to biological nature either, for that nature will also receive a transfigured mode of existing in the age to come.

The liturgy is a necessary environment for the theologian. If he (or she) is cut off from these life-giving texts, his (or her) mind will soon cease to be the mind of the Church. It may remain, formally speak-

---

12. Ae. Lohr, *The Great Week* (English trans., London: 1958) 141.
13. For the origins and content of this hymn *see* G. Benoit-Castelli, "Le *Praeconium paschale*," *Ephemerides liturgicae* 67 (1953) 309–34.

ing, an orthodox mind, but it will not be a mind possessing that entire complex of attitudes which together reflect the Church's basic response to God: love, humility, gratitude for the redemption, and the rest. The liturgy expresses what we might call the "inside" of the act of faith: the interiority of the relationship with God which God's own saving plan, once entered into, set up. As the human expression of the covenant, the liturgy articulates the inside of the life of the household of faith, just as the conversation of husband and wife brings out what is implicit in their marital and family living. The theological student must learn how to interpret this language so as to find the voice of the Church, the Bride, calling on Christ, the Bridegroom.

We have to weigh the evidence the liturgy provides us with. We cannot simply seize on what may be an isolated text from a rather obscure liturgical use and build some vast theological edifice on top of it. Liturgical texts have varying degrees of evidential value for theology. The liturgies proper to individual monasteries, dioceses, or religious orders have the least evidential value, just because they are so highly particularized. Reflecting some local tradition or a particular spiritual family within the Church, they are not as important as the principal rites or liturgical families of which there are usually reckoned to be nineteen. Usually, these rites grew up by the participation of more and more local Churches from a given cultural milieu in a liturgy emanating from a see which had won general recognition because of the quality of its witness to the faith: a patriarchal see like Antioch or Alexandria or, at any rate, a primatial see like Seleucia in the eastern half of the Syriac-speaking world. But above all, it is where theologians can find a variety of different liturgies from various places and times, all converging in their testimony to some aspect of faith that they can draw from the liturgy with most confidence.[14]

To summarize: the liturgy is the continuation of the atoning work of Jesus Christ and, as such, is the Church's primary expression from within of the covenant relationship binding her life to God's. It is, therefore, rich in implicit theology. The texts of a wide variety of liturgies are all grist for the theologian's mill. However, the greater the agreement of these liturgies on a particular point, the stronger their evidential value for theology. If we think of the Christian liturgy as a sign system pointing to the truth of Tradition, it is where the signals flash most brightly that we can best follow them.

14. I. H. Dalmais, "La liturgie comme lieu théologique," *La Maison-Dieu* 78 (1964) 97–106.

But the Christian faith can be expressed not simply in verbal images: in words—metaphors, such as liturgical poetry uses—but also in visual images, in paintings, sculpture, and even entire buildings. Christian revelation has found expression in an artistic and architectural iconography as well as in the verbal sign system of the texts of the liturgy and the dramatic sign system of its gestures.[15] In fact, Christian art and architecture have always enjoyed intimate connections with the celebration of the liturgy, and so it is only right that we should mention them here alongside liturgy as monuments of Tradition.

To understand the significance of the emergence of Christian art, we need to look briefly at the Old Testament background. The Jewish religion, in the form it took from the time of Abraham onwards, was a religion of revelation. It insisted that its foundation was not something that people had discovered about God but something that God had freely chosen to disclose to people. Abraham is called, and the name of God, God's own reality, is revealed to him. The same happens at a higher level of intensity with Moses, and although after this point what can be called the basic identity of the God of Judaism is clear, nevertheless any advances in understanding the will and ways of this God are regarded as dependent on the divine initiative. So, for instance, the covenant with David and his heirs is presented as a divine disclosure through the prophet Nathan. And even the authors of the Wisdom books in their ruminations on the natural course of the world around them felt that their ideas could only lead to a knowledge of God if the spirit of Wisdom were sent them from the side of God. It is entirely consistent with this feature of the Old Testament that there should be in its religious practice no (visual) images of God.[16] Images of God are fashioned in paint and stone as a result of the creative use of the human imagination, which tries to find symbolic forms for expressing the Infinite. Because Judaism saw itself as God's gift and not as humanity's discovery, it could never accept that the artist has a special way into the presence of God. The difficulties of being both an Orthodox Jew and an artist have been portrayed in our own time in Chaim Potok's novel *My Name is Asher Lev*.

This state of affairs, however, cannot survive the incarnation. With the incarnation God makes himself visible in the life of Jesus, which is a human life in every sense and therefore a life capable of depiction

---

15. A. Nichols, *The Art of God Incarnate: Theology and Image in Christian Tradition* (London: 1980).

16. Cf. V. Lossky, "The Theology of the Image," *Sobornost* III. 22 (1956–58) 515.

in artistic terms. Not surprisingly, then, as soon as the Church ceased to be a persecuted sect and became a tolerated religion within the Roman Empire, Christian art begins to flourish in every place where the Church was established.[17] The fact of the incarnation makes the rise of Christian art virtually inevitable. That God had revealed himself definitively through a human being meant that henceforth true belief about the divine could be expressed in works of art. As St. John Damascene wrote in his defense of the use of images in worship during the iconoclast crisis of the eighth and ninth centuries: "Now that God has appeared in the flesh and lived among men, I make an image of the God who can be seen. I do not venerate matter, but I venerate the Creator of matter, who for my sake became material and deigned to dwell in matter, who through matter effected my salvation."[18] The dogmatic definition of the seventh ecumenical council, Nicaea II (787), in proclaiming the legitimacy of the making and venerating of holy images, settled decisively for the iconophiles against the iconophobes. The continuing history of Christian art as an attempt to re-express revelation in aesthetic terms is, therefore, one of the ways in which Tradition operates.

It follows that the more familiar we are with the art of the Church, the better a grasp we shall have of Tradition. What we are concerned with here is the meaning-content of art, its iconology, and not with the techniques artists have used, except insofar as such technical considerations subserve the iconographic expression of an iconology. The Christian artworks of every age have a contribution to make as monuments of Tradition. The German historian Leopold von Ranke once remarked that "all ages are open to God," meaning that no age is without its lessons for us about the ultimate pattern and purpose of life. So it is with art as an expression of Tradition. From time to time the attempt is made to privilege one period above all others in the story of Christian art, seeing it as a golden age in comparison with which other centuries are either immature or decadent. Thus in the Gothic revival of the nineteenth century, the English architect Augustus Welby Pugin regarded the Gothic style as the perfect architectural and iconographic expression of Catholic faith and spirituality, and attacked the classicizing style of his predecessors as virtually pagan.[19] They, no

17. F. Van der Meer, *Early Christian Art* (London: 1967); Charles Murray, "Art and the Early Church," *Journal of Theological Studies* 28 (1977) 303–45.

18. John Damascene, *On the Holy Images* I. 16.

19. A. W. N. Pugin, *An Apology for the Revival of Christian Architecture in England* (London: 1843).

doubt, could have answered that to turn any artistic style to the service of the Church is to transform its entire meaning and atmosphere. And indeed, in recent years, such a style as the baroque has been rediscovered as a theological art form.[20] Thus Owen Chadwick has written of Gianlorenzo Bernini and his contemporaries:

> Though they sought to portray emotional moments, their work was not emotional in the way of excess or sentimentality. This art was one of the strongest in the Christian centuries. The emotion which they sought to show was intelligent; an uplifting of the worshipping mind towards mysteries beyond the objects which the eye could see; to group or frame statues of church ornaments so that they pointed towards a reality not themselves. The bodies of statues grew more slender, the folds of their garments more abundant and tumultuous, the saints more agonized or more exalted, the touch of guardian angels more delicate and kindly, the flight of cherubim and seraphim more restless.[21]

The high baroque is a pneumatological art, in which the Holy Spirit communicates blessing and inspiration, falling through the space of light, as in the portrayal of Teresa of Avila in the Cornaro chapel at Santa Maria delle Vittorie at Rome. The late baroque and rococo are celebrations of light, intended to suggest glory, to introduce the worshipper to the space of paradise, and employing to this end a whole variety of means from silver rays, shiny surfaces, and mirrors to the use of stucco for Christ, Mary, and the saints, a material so light that by seeming to set the laws of gravity at nought, it could convey, symbolically, a sense of the nearness of heaven.[22]

Again, it has become fashionable today for people to regard the Byzantine Slav icon as the supreme form of Christian art, since its etiolated, numinous figures seem so obviously filled with grace, a transfiguration of the natural order.[23] Yet the Western Christian art of the Middle Ages and of the Renaissance has its own ways of intimating to us that it is depicting a history which includes God as agent: for example, in the golden backgrounds of gospel scenes in the paintings of Giotto.[24] As early as the Carolingian renaissance of the ninth century, Western artists found painterly means to express the entry of the divine energy into the created order through the economy of the Word

20. W. Purdy, *Seeing and Believing: Theology and Art* (Dublin: 1976) 90–97; cf. W. Weisbach, *Der Barock als Kunst der Gegenreformation* (Berlin: 1921).

21. O. Chadwick, *The Popes and European Revolution* (Oxford: 1981) 78–79.

22. N. Powell, *From Baroque to Rococo* (London: 1959) 84.

23. P. Evdokimov, *L'art de l'icône. Théologie de la beauté* (Paris: 1970).

24. C. Gnudi, *Giotto* (London: 1959).

incarnate. Thus in a gospel-book commissioned by the emperor Lothar and regarded as the high point of the school of Tours: "The divinity of Christ is expressed . . . by a linear incandescence, (while) galvanized by their inner inspiration the evangelists are like coiled-up balls of energy."[25] The Christian civilization which produced this art succumbed to its external enemies yet retained sufficient force to fire two later renaissances, those of Anglo-Saxon England and Ottonian Germany, themselves the precursors of the true Romanesque. In the best realizations of the latter, as at Vézelay in Burgundy: "The church building becomes a worldly representation in stone of a divine order. . . . The entire ensemble of church building, ornamentation, and furnishing is a complex fusion of medieval theological schemes with highly imaginative artistic abilities."[26] The juxtaposition of sacred motifs with evocations of daily life (the pruning of vines, haymaking, the chase) fused the empirical with the transcendent, the relatively known with the relatively unknown, producing an imaginatively credible cosmology. But the Romanesque was, in addition, an art concerned with mission: at Vézelay, Christ sends the apostles to preach the gospel throughout the world. Rays from his fingers touch their heads, while the statuettes on the lintel and around the arch depict the distant nations—Africans, Scythians, Indians—to whom the gospel will be carried.

The iconographic schemes worked out, in dependence on Scripture and earlier Tradition by the artists of the later Middle Ages and the Renaissance, deepen our understanding of the original gospel. Thus, in the Christological frescoes by Fra Angelico, which fill the priory of the Observantine Dominicans of St. Mark at Florence, the painting of the Redeemer on the cross, high and lifted up above an arid strip of land against a boundless sky, has been given a universal context by the figures placed in the semicircular cornice which frames it: nine prophets, a converted pagan (Denys the Areopagite), and a sibyl, whose writings, inscribed on fluttering pieces of parchment, refer to a coming bloody sacrifice which will restore freedom and peace to the entire creation.[27] Again, in Michelangelo's decoration of the Sistine Chapel, the nine historical paintings, based on stories from the Book of Genesis, span the distance between the divine creativity (at the altar end) and the degradation of man (in Noah's drunken stupor,

25. C. R. Dodwell, *Painting in Europe 800–1200* (Harmondsworth: 1971) 38.
26. R. Crozet, "Romanesque Art," NCE 12, 621.
27. V. Alce, *Homilies of Fra Angelico* (English trans., Bologna: n.d.) 33–34.

by the door). But they are intended to be seen in the opposite order, as a progression from the servitude of the body to the liberation and uplifting of the soul—an interpretation of Scripture in the light of the questions of Neoplatonic philosophy.[28]

But if the Romanesque, Renaissance, and baroque styles have their theological virtues, the two styles singled out by Western and Eastern Christians respectively as paradigmatic for a Christian art which would be a true monument of Tradition—the Gothic and the Byzantine Slav— certainly deserve their reputations. Though comparisons between the great Gothic churches and the "cathedral-like" proportions of a Scholastic *summa* can easily be overwrought,[29] high medieval art can rightly be described as the realization in imagistic form of the Thomist insight that grace, building on nature, does not destroy the latter but brings it to its fulfillment.[30] And just as Thomism, as a Christian wisdom, has its roots in the theological humanism of the twelfth century, so too with Gothic.[31] The stained glass windows of the Gothic style, replacing the mural decoration of Romanesque are "structurally and aesthetically not openings in the wall to admit light, but transparent walls. . . . The stained glass window seemingly denies the impenetrable nature of matter, receiving visual existence from an energy that transcends it."[32] The form of the Gothic cathedral owes much to the doctrine of creation: the world is a symphonic composition, made "in measure, number, and weight." Creation proper is, for the school of Chartres with its background in Platonic Augustinianism, the adorning of matter by the artful imposition of an architectural order. But because creation, the first of God's self-revelations, is linked by mystical correspondence to the second, the incarnation of the Word, the high medievals—for example, Peter Abelard—could regard a church building as symbol both of the cosmos and of the new Jerusalem ushered into being by the work of Christ.[33] Moreover, the luminosity of the sanctuaries of the twelfth and thirteenth centuries, singled out for praise by contemporaries, belongs with the light metaphysics whereby the sixth-century Syrian Doctor who worked under the name of Denys the

28. N. Wadley, *Michelangelo* (London: 1965) 17.

29. E. Panofsky, *Gothic Architecture and Scholasticism* (Latrobe, Penn.: 1951).

30. Cf. A. Emiliani, "Gothic Art," NCE 6, 642.

31. O. von Simson, *The Gothic Cathedral: The Origins of Gothic Architecture and the Mediaeval Concept of Order* (London: 1956) viii.

32. *Ibid.*, 4.

33. *Ibid.*, 27–39; cf. the representation of Christ as architect rebuilding Jerusalem, found under the figure of Ezekiel on the west façade of Amiens cathedral: L Lefrançois-Pillion, *Maîtres d'oeuvre et tailleurs de pierre des cathédrales* (Paris: 1949) 159.

Areopagite presented creation as an act of illumination, and, taking his cue from the Gospel of John, understood the divine Logos as the true light which shines in the darkness.[34] Both Hugh of St. Victor and Thomas will ascribe to the beautiful two main characteristics: consonance of parts, or proportion, and luminosity.[35]

Between the Gothic of, say, St. Denis or Chartres and the Byzantine tradition there is not necessarily a very great leap to be made. The column statues of the former are icons in stone, paralleled in such mosaic images as those of the Greek Fathers in the Palatine chapel at Palermo (for Norman Sicily was under strong Greek influence) or mid-Byzantine ivories such as the so-called Romanos group.[36] Noting the presence of Byzantine influence in the book illuminations of the early Cistercians, the historian of medieval art Otto von Simson speaks of the "spell" that the art of the Greek Church exerted on Latin Christendom in the age of Bernard[37]—even if the iconographic content (the focus of theological interest) could be a distinctively Western contribution, as in the Chartres tympanum where the Mother of God, portrayed as the Seat of Wisdom, is surrounded in the archivolts of the façade by personifications of the liberal arts, here standing for all secular knowledge, which reaches its fulfillment only by faith in the incarnation of her Son.[38]

In the developed *iconostasis*, or image screen, of the Byzantine Slav churches this wooden structure, covered with icons, at once divides the divine world from the human and unites them. Standing on the boundary line between the divine and the human, it reveals by images the way to their reconciliation. In its classical form (common in, for example, sixteenth-century Russia), upper storeys represent the patriarchs and prophets with, just below them, the story of the holy feasts, the principal moments in the action of divine Providence in the life of the incarnate Word (and his Mother) as history's center. Further down still comes the *deêsis* (in Slavonic, *tchin*), which represents the fulfillment of the New Testament: our standing in prayer before the Savior. The Mother of God supplicates from the right, the forerunner

34. Von Simson, *The Gothic Cathedral*, 50–55; E. de Bruyne, *Etudes d'esthétique médiévale* (Bruges: 1946), III. 1: "L'esthétique de la lumière."

35. Von Simson, *The Gothic Cathedral*, 50, with reference to Hugh, *Didascalicon* VII. 12, and Thomas, *Summa theologiae*, Ia., q. 39, a. 8, corpus.

36. O. Demus, *The Mosaics of Norman Sicily* (New York: 1950); Koehler, "Byzantine Art and the West," *Dumbarton Oaks Papers* I. (1941).

37. Von Simson, *The Gothic Cathedral*, 152.

38. E. Male, *L'Art religieux du XIIe siecle en France* (Paris: 1924) 104ff.

John from the left, and whole streams of saints and angels approach, drawing the spectator by their rhythmic movement into their own attitude. On the lowest storeys, a variety of images of more local interest testify to the history of grace in particular places and individuals. In the horizontal, as distinct from the vertical, center of the screen are placed the royal doors, which stand for the entrance into the kingdom, itself represented by the church sanctuary.

Surmounted by the annunciation and the figures who literally announced the Word in writing, the evangelists, the image immediately above the doors is that of Christ as high priest communicating the apostles at the Last Supper, while on the jambs where the hinges of the doors are leaved come the holy Fathers, portrayed in their vestments as liturgists. In the liturgy of St. John Chrysostom, the celebrant and deacon greet with incense both icons and congregation—thus uniting in one gesture the heavenly and the earthly Church.[39]

Such iconography remains normative in Churches of the Byzantine tradition until modern times. Its strength, as that of its Western medieval equivalents in the Gothic cathedrals, lies in its rendering of the whole pattern of the revealed history in images which known conventions could make accessible to all the faithful. The need for such a self-consciously doctrinal art (and its outstanding theological value) has been registered sporadically in the West of the postrevolutionary period, for instance by the Nazarene school in Germany and the Pre-Raphaelites in England. By and large, however, contemporary Christian iconography is more a matter of individual forays into the resources provided by the Church's faith.

As an example of contemporary iconography, we might do worse than cite the case of the Anglo-Welsh painter David Jones. In Jones' work, the central themes of Christian believing—the incarnation, the atonement—are treated in relation to the wider pattern of the human journey in its cosmic setting. In his early drawing "Tywysog Cariad" ("The Prince of Love," ca. 1929), he already relates the crucifixion to the Eucharist. As one of the poems which interpret his visual images puts it, Calvary is "where the stripped *mensa/* is set up/ where the long *lancea/* obliquely thrust/ must drain the cup/ for here/ is *immolatio oblata.*"[40] In illustrating Coleridge's *Rime of the Ancient Mariner*, the shooting of the albatross, the "immaculate" bird impaled on the crossbar

39. L. Ouspensky and V. Lossky, *The Meaning of Icons* (English trans., 1952; Crestwood, N.Y.: 1982) 59–68.

40. D. Jones, *The Sleeping Lord and Other Fragments* (London: 1974) 36.

of a ship's mast, is likened to Christ's sacrifice on the cross. As the barque of the Crucified, the Church is imaged in the timbers, in the keel and mast, of a ship.[41] Jones himself drew out the theological significance of such images in writing: "What is pleaded in the Mass is precisely the argosy or voyage of the Redeemer, his entire sufferings, death, resurrection and ascension. It is this that is offered on behalf of us argonauts and the whole argosy of mankind and indeed in some sense of all earthly creation, which, as Paul says, suffers a common travail."[42] And if Jones' iconographic evocation of the atonement is theologically instructive, so too is his account of its precondition, the incarnation, with, at its human heart, the role of Mary, the God-bearer. The Virgin's relation to the Crucified is depicted in the 1930 wood-engraving "The Bride," which shows her placing a votive candle at the feet of the crucifix. (In Jones' epic poem *The Anathemata*, Mary is called "both bride and mother of the cult-hero," and in a draft of the latter we find the words: "he her groom that was his mother/ he who cries/ as the stag *ad fontes*/ his desiderate cry."[43]) More characteristic, perhaps, is the late watercolor "Annunciation," set in the Welsh mountains, where Mary is surrounded by living creatures. As the art historian Kenneth Clark described this painting: "Dozens of birds fly round her, providing almost the only positive color in the picture. But the most brilliant of them is the goldfinch, the long-accepted symbol of Christian sacrifice; and when we turn to the angel, we see that he holds in his right hand a sword to which clings a broken strand of thorns."[44] Here the incarnation, represented in the moment of conception of the humanity assumed by the mother of the Word, is related both to the glory of the cosmic creation and to the redemptive death by which the incarnate Son showed forth the Father's ultimate splendor as love. In such a contemporary iconographer, the ordinary believer is confronted with symbols trickier to read than those of such classical iconological schemes as those of Byzantine or Gothic art. Yet what is, from the viewpoint of the construction of a parish church, a drawback in the contemporary situation, is for the theological student a possible advantage: since the more personally individualized artist of modern times may, by relating the great Christian motifs to a wider history and realm of being, draw out latent meanings of Tradition itself. And so Tradition never falls silent in any age of the Church.

41. P. Hills, "The Art of David Jones," in *David Jones*, ed. P. Hills (London: 1981) 46.
42. D. Jones, *The Dying Gaul and Other Writings*, ed. H. Grisewood (London: 1978) 90.
43. *David Jones*, ed. P. Hills, 177.
44. K. Clark, "Some Recent Paintings by David Jones," in *Agenda* 5. 1–3 (1967) 99.

There is, nonetheless, an especial importance to be attached to the art of the first Christian centuries. The art and archaeology of the earliest Christian period, palaeo- (from the Greek *palaios*, "ancient") Christian art, as it is often called, throws much light on what was believed and done by the first generations, the closest to the apostles. Italy, Syria, Egypt, and southern France are all important places to look for the evidence of early Christian art, but of all sites, while Ravenna is perhaps the most dramatic and certainly the best preserved, Rome has the richest variety of material to offer. The remains of this period are of course fragmentary, both because of the wanton destruction that beauty so often receives at history's hand and because of their over-laying by the work of later times. Here the simple symbolic forms of the catacombs, the narrative *historiae* in mosaic, and the portraits are all of theological importance.[45] So too are the buildings in which so many of these representations were housed: the basilicas and the memorial chapels built on the sites of events in the life of Christ, as over the places of martyrdom of the men and women who had become, by their deaths, the "seed of the Church." The basilica (whose plan formed the theme on which all subsequent types of church would be variations), by the interrelation of its constitutive elements—nave and apse, bishop's cathedra, reading desk, and altar, with the little building called the baptistery by its side—expresses in architectural form the priorities of patristic Christians in the doctrine of the Church. The Church, we infer from the evidence of architecture, is an assembly of the faithful who become initiates through baptism, an assembly taught by a bishop who expounds the Scriptures, and an assembly that as ministers and people celebrates the Eucharist as its central religious action.[46] No less theologically significant were the *memoriae* (in Greek, *martyria*), the memorial chapels raised over spots where events of crucial importance to the community had been enacted. In the Holy Land, memorials were erected on the places associated with the main events of the life of Jesus, especially his birth, death, and resurrection. Events of less central importance in the story of the Savior also had their *memoriae*: by the Sea of Galilee at the site of the multiplication of the loaves and fishes; at Cana where the Lord had changed water into wine; by Jacob's well at Sychar, the site of the meeting with the woman of Samaria in St. John's Gospel; in Bethany at the tomb of Lazarus,

45. F. van der Meer, *Early Christian Art* (English trans., London: 1967).
46. *Ibid.*, 53–69, 76–80.

and so forth.[47] This proliferation of buildings should convey to us a
vital point: the enormous theological importance of the historicity of
the gospel story. Jesus Christ is not an idea, a concept, an ideal, or
simply a symbol of what God is like: he was and is a living person,
with a biography like every other person's. The only difference is that
this biography is the biography of a man who was personally God,
and so every detail that we can find in it is precious to us and possibly
full of significance. We have already noted how New Testament scholars can regard some, many, or even most of the gospel stories as literary fictions: imaginative creations on the part of the original apostolic
community, which composed them so as to express its sense of the
identity of Jesus, its exalted Lord. The stories become spiritually true
if historically false. We can see, from the evidence of art and archaeology, that this view goes counter to the early Church's own instinct
to affirm the historicity of the gospel narratives by seeking out and
lovingly adorning the places the Lord had hallowed by his presence.
It is true that the Gospels are not biographies in the modern sense;
no book from the ancient world is. It is also true that the chief attention of the evangelists is the theological significance of the stories they
recount for us. But that these stories have no historical rooting presupposes that the first disciples suffered an almost total memory loss about
the life of Jesus virtually as soon as it had happened. On the contrary,
there is good reason to think that the role of memory in the early
Church was quite outstanding.[48]

The other type of site where *memoriae* were set up was, as I have
said, the places where the martyrs had made their final and greatest
sacrifice. These chapels are the points where the practice of the veneration of the saints really began. Originally the only sign of what had
transpired at a tomb of a martyr was the flat *mensa*, or table-like top
of the tomb itself, where pious people would gather to eat a com-
memorative meal on the anniversary of the martyr's death. This followed a universal practice of the ancient world, the eating of memorial
meals at the tombs of the beloved dead. The practice presupposes that
the Church is a family of which the martyrs are the most beloved de-
ceased members. But the table for the funeral meal of a martyr, a sort
of large memorial picnic, soon became the altar in honor of the martyr,
either directly, the altar being placed exactly over the tomb, or indi-

47. Ibid., 70–75.
48. B. Gerhardsson, *Memory and Manuscript: Oral Tradition and Written Transmission
in Rabbinic Judaism and Early Christianity* (2nd ed., Uppsala and Lund: 1964).

rectly, the altar being some little distance away with a shaft looking down on the tomb, as in the Basilica of St. Peter on the Vatican Hill today. Devout people would pray there, pour balm down on the slab of the tomb, or lower down little cloths to touch it as mementoes. In the Roman catacombs the tombs of the martyrs were so numerous that it proved impossible to set up a memorial church over each one of them. So either collective *memoriae* were constructed, like the one built by Pope Sylvester I in the cemetery of Priscilla for a number of martyrs together; or inscriptions were set up in fine script over their tombs, like those placed in the catacombs by Pope Damascus. Many fragments of these descriptions have been found; and others are known as a result of copies being made by pious pilgrims, especially Anglo-Saxons, who were particularly devoted to the Roman Church and its holy places, since they owed their own faith to the preachers sent to England by Pope Gregory the Great. Behind all of this pious activity we can discern a theological truth. In the martyr the crucified and risen Christ once again suffers and is victorious; the constancy of the martyr derives from the spirit of Christ who is still alive and active. As the martyr told the jailer who mocked her for her tears during her labor pains and asked what she should be doing on the morrow when thrown to the lions, "Today it is I who am suffering; tomorrow another will be suffering in me."[49] In the martyrs the presence of Christ is affirmed, and the hope is held out to all believers that Christ will take up their personality and transform it into the image of his own.

Commenting on the theological importance of Christian art, Canon William Purdy writes: "It is said that we are Christians not by inheritance but by commitment—but the antithesis is clearly fallacious; inheritance underlies and enhances the commitment of a man who possesses his past. . . . A monument links our hearts and minds with our origins. It makes us *remember.*"[50] An essential component in the definition of any theologian is, after all, that he or she is a "professional rememberer."[51] Though it is true that just to remember, simply to know what Jesus and the apostles said and did and what the Fathers and the Doctors thought about what they said and did, is inadequate; while we have, as theologians, to repossess the inheritance of the past in a distinctively modern way and to reorganize it on a basis that seems to us intellectually satisfying and pastorally helpful, we cannot do this

---

49. *Acts of SS. Perpetua and Felicity.*
50. Purdy, *Seeing and Believing: Theology and Art* (Cork: 1976) 124.
51. See ch. 1 of this book.

without a rich and detailed knowledge of the inheritance—the Tradition—which we are called by the rest of the Church to help pass on.

Christian art and architecture is very largely a lay monument of tradition. For while the occasional artist such as Fra Angelico may have been an ordained minister, the great majority of the Church's painters, sculptors, and craftspeople have been nothing of the kind. The liturgy itself is a largely anonymous product, though sanctioned officially by the Church's pastors. In this sense the liturgy lies halfway between the laicity of Christian art and those monuments of Tradition which depend on more highly particularized Spirit-given charisms and dominically founded ministerial offices in the Church. From an outgrowth of the faith instinct that runs through the whole body of believers, we must turn now to another set of vital phenomena for our grasp of tradition: the teaching work of Doctors in the patristic Church and the activity of the Church's pastors in the making of creeds and solemn definitions of the content of the faith.

15
Fathers, Councils, and Creeds

Fathers

The study of the Fathers of the Church has been regarded for centuries as a *sine qua non* in the formation of the Catholic theologian. The knowledge of the Fathers possessed by medieval theologians was very considerable. On the one hand, Augustine was incomparably the greatest nonbiblical influence on the Latin Church until the thirteenth century—arguably until as late as the nineteenth.[1] On the other hand, a heroic effort was made at various points in the Middle Ages to acquire adequate translations of all the Greek patristic texts that people could lay their hands on. On a celebrated occasion, Thomas Aquinas declared that he would exchange all of Paris for a certain commentary of the fourth-century archbishop of Constantinople, John Chrysostom (ca. 347–407), on St. Matthew's Gospel.[2] (Alas, it is now known to be the work of a semi-Arian Latin-speaking bishop from Illyria, the modern Yugoslavia!) Thomas himself left a *catena,* or patristic anthology, later called the *catena aurea* or "golden chain." Far more than just a hodgepodge of passages he had at hand, it shows a profound understanding of the thought of the Fathers at large.[3] The humanists of the

1. H. Marrou, *Saint Augustine and His Influence Through the Ages* (English trans., London: 1957) 147–79.

2. Evidence given by Bartholomew of Capua at Thomas' First Canonization Enquiry: see *The Life of St. Thomas Aquinas: Biographical Documents,* ed. K. Foster (London: 1959) 108–9.

3. For this *Glossa continua super evangelia,* see J. A. Weisheipl, *Friar Thomas d'Aquino: His Life, Thought and Words* (Oxford: 1974) 170–73. During the Tractarian Catholic Revival (the Oxford movement in the Church of England), one Oxford divine, Mark Pattison of Lincoln College, ascribed to it "a thorough acquaintance with the whole range of ecclesiastical antiquity, . . . a familiarity with the style of each writer, so as to compress into a few words the pith of a whole page, and a power of clear and orderly arrangement in this mass of knowledge . . . qualities which make this Catena perhaps nearly perfect as a conspectus of Patristic interpretation." Preface to *Commentary on the Four Gospels by S. Thomas Aquinas,* I. 1. (2nd ed., Oxford and London: 1864) iii–iv. For

early Renaissance, the founder of the Vatican Library, Pope Nicholas V (1397–1455) at their head, commissioned, in their enthusiasm for Christian antiquity, many new translations of the Fathers of the Greek-speaking East.[4] Again, one has only to look at the references in the speeches made at the Council of Trent to get an idea of the patristic culture of the sixteenth century.[5] In the succeeding century, interest in the Fathers became even more marked, partly because of historical and controversial concern with getting at the original texts, and partly because of a desire to go behind Scholasticism to what was seen as a warmer theology, more *praedicabile*, more easily turned into preaching and spirituality. In the nineteenth century, the Oxford movement in the Church of England was, in part, a movement of return to the Fathers, and some of its most influential converts to Catholicism, like John Henry Newman, spread the same patristic enthusiasm in their new communion. If the neo-Scholastic movement at the close of the nineteenth century could be said to have deflected Catholic studies from patristics by turning again to the golden age of the thirteenth century for its primary theological inspiration, many neo-Thomist writers such as Scheeben were nevertheless concerned to integrate into their writing, in explicit fashion, the teaching of those whom the Schoolmen had treated as such revered sources. In the first half of the twentieth century, a patristic revival, often known by its French title, *le mouvement de ressourcement*, "going back to the sources," reversed the pendulum once again, leaving behind it numerous editions and translations of the texts of the Fathers. Three of the fullest and most accessible of these are the French series *Sources Chrétiennes*, and two American collections, *The Fathers of the Church* and *Ancient Christian Writers*. It is, therefore, a matter of some concern that much Catholic theology in western Europe, North America, and elsewhere is now being written without overt reference to the Fathers—attempting to overleap the centuries, the patristic epoch included, by bringing together the Scriptures and present-day culture in direct confrontation, without the aid of intermediaries. We could call this Protestant rather than Catholic, save that to do so would be a grave injustice to many writers in the Reformed

Thomas' patristic explorations at large, *see* M. D. Chenu, *Towards Understanding Saint Thomas* (English trans., Chicago: 1964) 151–55.

4. C. Stinger, *Humanism and the Church Fathers: Ambrogio Traversari (1386–1439) and Christian Antiquity in the Italian Renaissance* (Albany: 1977).

5. For this, one would have to consult the indices of the *Concilium Tridentinum: Diariorum, actorum, epistularum, tractatuum, nova collectio,* ed. Görresgesellschaft (Freiburg: 1901ff.).

tradition from John Calvin to Karl Barth, and, in modern Britain, Barth's original disciple, T. F. Torrance.

What then was all the enthusiasm about? What is the significance of the Fathers for theology? Why have they been singled out as a *locus theologicus*, a monument of Tradition? We can distinguish three ways of arguing for their significance. The first way is by drawing attention to the importance of the historical epoch in which they lived.[6] Although there is no clear consensus as to when precisely the patristic period ended, many people would be happy to regard the age of the Fathers as the first seven centuries of the Christian era. These centuries are the centuries of the first seven ecumenical councils, the seven that were concerned with fundamental Christological and Trinitarian dogma. The question of the significance of the Fathers then becomes the question of the special importance to be attached to this patristic era for the formation of the Christian faith. And it can indeed be argued that these centuries were the time when the Christian religion became condensed into that basic format which is still recognizable today. Let us allow that the center of Christianity is the person of Christ: the life, teaching, saving passion, death, and resurrection of God made human. No matter how well prepared the ground was for the incarnation in the Jewish background, the coming of God in human flesh was a unique event of stupendous significance for humankind. In the New Testament writings, we see the first reaction of a group of contemporaries to that tremendous happening. Some of these reactions are rather simple, primitive, like St. Mark's in his Gospel or St. Paul's in his letters to the Thessalonians. Others are much more complex, like St. John's in the Fourth Gospel, or Paul's in the letters to Rome and Corinth. But notice that in the Church of the New Testament there is as yet no creed, no formulated statement of basic Christian beliefs. Neither is there as yet any liturgy, except of the most rudimentary kind, with a good deal left to the spontaneous effusions of individuals. Nor is there any clear pattern of Church order, of Church government. The Christian religion, in other words, is in the process of formation in the New Testament. It is still embryonic. It has not emerged in its classic lines. The consequences of the work of Christ are all there in nucleus, but they have not yet been worked out in anything like a systematic form. William Wordsworth once defined poetry as "emotion recollected in tranquility." The Church also needed a period of time to elapse before it could analyze and reflect more deeply on the mystery of Christ,

6. Congar, *Tradition and Traditions* 444–48.

his person, deeds, and words, so as to establish a pattern of believing, worshipping, and ordering its own communal life that would remain definitive forever afterwards.

And such is the essential achievement of the patristic age. The age of the Fathers sees the working out of the creed. It sees the creation of the liturgies, both Eastern and Western. It sees the manifest emergence of the Catholic Church as an episcopally ordered communion of local Churches centered on the local Church of the city of Rome, animated by a sacramental system presided over by a threefold ministry of bishops, presbyters, and deacons. The patristic period was, then, the crucial period in the crystallization of Christianity in its confessional, doxological, and governmental structure—as creed, worship, and Church order. Thus even theologians who think that the traditional creeds of the Church require reexpression, or that the liturgies need reconstruction, or that the governmental order of the Church's life should be radically reformed have to begin by paying attention to the patristic period as the age when the essential forms of all of these as we have them were first molded.

However, to say why the period of the Fathers is important is not in itself to show why their writings are important. Here we come to a second way of arguing for the importance of the Fathers, namely to concentrate attention not on their age but on the ethos of their theological work.[7] For it so happened that the age which witnessed the fundamental formation of the Christian religion was also an age providentially well endowed with theologians of a particular kind. There is a common ethos to the theological life of the patristic Church, even granted the great cultural differences that separate the highly sophisticated Churches of the Eastern Mediterranean with their wide learning in the Greek classics and Greek philosophy, from the rather more backward Latin-speaking Churches with their much poorer philosophical culture, and both from the quite different, Syriac-speaking and basically Semitic Churches of the non-Greek-speaking East, in areas that correspond roughly to Syria and Iraq today. Between a Greek like Gregory of Nyssa, a Latin like Augustine, and a Syrian like Ephraim, there are differences almost as great as the similarities, contemporaries though they were. Nevertheless, when compared with the theology of the epochs before and after they share a distinct family resemblance. Is it possible to say in what this common ethos of patristic theology consists?

7. *Ibid.*, 448–50.

Three characteristic features can be distinguished. First of all, patristic theology is, despite the occasional eccentricities of its biblical exegesis, a theology that concentrates on fundamentals. It focuses on the principal Christian dogmas of God, Christ, the Spirit, and the Church. We can contrast this with, say, the later development of Scholastic theology, where a great number of secondary or peripheral questions were treated so thoroughly that they threatened, at least in the hands of lesser writers, to dislodge the really essential doctrines from their central place. So for example, the Fathers in treating of the Eucharist will not consider it as an isolated issue, much less confine their attention to some peculiarly knotty problems within the totality of the sacrament, important as are motifs like the mode of Christ's presence there or the Eucharist's status as a sacrificial sacrament. Instead, when speaking of the Eucharist the Fathers will most likely deal with it in the context of Christian salvation as a whole, as does Augustine in Book X of the *City of God*. The Fathers were particularly good at sensing the "analogy of faith," the mutual conditioning of all doctrines. The unity of Christianity is like the unity of a face: change any one feature and every feature looks different. Because they reflect this sense of the faith as an interconnected whole, the Fathers are indeed effective witnesses of tradition. In its concentration on fundamentals, patristic theology has been described as theocentric, Christocentric, ecclesiocentric, and mysteriocentric. It is theocentric, presenting God as the primary reality. Everything else is seen in relation to him. The creature issues from God and moves back to God by tending through the Holy Spirit to the perfection God has willed for it. But this Spirit is the Spirit of Christ: hence Christocentricity. Furthermore, Christ gives the Spirit as head or source of the Church: hence ecclesiocentricity. The Church's life is, however, fully realized only through the celebration of her sacraments or mysteries: and so, finally, mysteriocentricity. The theology of the Fathers, because it is sustained in this way by continual reference to the primary theological realities, God in Christ, through the Church as a mystery of worship, has a unique claim on our attention.

A second feature of patristic thought relevant to the common ethos derives from the pastoral orientation of the Fathers. Most of the Fathers were pastors, often bishops, and they wrote in order to answer the need of the Church of their day. This accounts for many of the literary genres of patristic writing, such things as sermons, replies to enquiries, exhortations, manuals of instruction, refutations of the heresies that were *à la mode*. This makes the Fathers more time bound, perhaps, to the accidents of history. But it can be argued that it also corresponds well to the intrinsic finality or purpose of theology itself. Theology should not simply lay out Christian truth for its own sake, but aim to communicate the results of exploration into faith for the building up of God's people in wisdom and understanding.

Third, and connected with this, we find in patristic theology a union of what today might be thought of as purely theological with purely spiritual elements. The Fathers, a good number of whom were monks, committed Christian ascetics, did not regard the life of prayer—conscious striving for union with God in Christ and his Spirit—as irrelevant to the practice of theology. Theology and spirituality have not yet gone the separate ways. The writer regards it as vital to be in the process of becoming connatural with the subject. A lived familiarity with theological reality—God, Christ, the Church—at a deep level of receptivity has a refining effect on the theological judgment of the person concerned.

While a eulogy of the theology of the Fathers of the kind I have just offered under these three headings—concentration on fundamentals, pastoral fruitfulness, the symbiosis of theology and spirituality—is by no means unjustified, two caveats should be set against it. First of all, not all patristic writing is of this consistent high quality. Second, the features of the common ethos that I have extracted are not wholly restricted to authors of the patristic age. Awareness of this latter fact lies behind the insistence of some that the application of the concept of Church-fatherhood has no cutoff point in time. There are Fathers, that is, ecclesially fruitful theologians, in every age, including our own. But this approach, attractive as it is, is not really congruent with the notion of the Fathers which we find in Church documents. For instance, when the Council of Trent says that that interpretation of Scripture should be followed which reflects the *consensus patrum*, the "agreement of the Fathers," what is intended is obviously that we should consult in our use of the Bible a finite body of patristic writing from the past. It is not a completely open-ended appeal to all good theologians of past, present, and future.

This brings us to the third major way of presenting the significance of the Fathers, and this is in terms of their reception of biblical revelation. Cardinal Joseph Ratzinger has proposed that the Fathers have a constitutive role in Christian faith because their response to Scripture was a constitutive element in the happening of the Word of God in revelation.[8] Granted that revelation is always a process with two

---

8. J. Ratzinger, "Die Bedeutung der Väter im Aufbau des Glaubens," in Ratzinger, *Theologische Prinzipienlehre. Bausteine zur Fundamentaltheologie* (Munich: 1982) 139-58.

poles—God giving and people receiving—so that one cannot speak of revelation strictly so called unless one assumes that revelation has really been received, Ratzinger argues that the "moment" of the Fathers was an essential moment in the receiving of the Word of God by the Church. The formation of the canon of Scripture in the patristic period is the outward and visible sign of an inward and spiritual grace: namely, the grace of comprehending what it was that God was proposing to humanity through the Bible. It was through the agency of the Fathers that the biblical revelation was first understood. They have, therefore, an irreplaceable role in the Church as constituent receivers of scriptural revelation. According to Ratzinger, it is in this context that one must evaluate theologically the other considerations I have put forward: the role of the patristic age in the making of creed, liturgy, and Church order, and the qualities of the theological work of individual Fathers. Ratzinger's suggestion is a helpful way of considering the conventional estimate of the Fathers in Catholic theology, that they are both a *locus* and a criterion for all subsequent theological work.

Granted, then, that the Fathers have a unique role in the formation of Christian doctrine, and so in the provision of cues for theology, how may their work be consulted by the theological student today? Before the days of printing, of course, the transmisson of texts was a matter of the copying of manuscripts. The copying of manuscripts in the West was largely a monastic and clerical affair: indeed the English word "clerk," meaning "one who can write," is derived from *clericus,* "a cleric." The manuscripts of the Latin Fathers were handed down to their successors in the Latin Church, at first, in the age of late antiquity, by professional scribes, but then, during the centuries after the collapse of the Roman Empire of the West, by monks in their monastic scriptoria or by other clerics in the cathedral schools, university theology faculties, and religious study houses that blossomed in the High Middle Ages. In the Greek East, culture was much more broadly based because of the essential continuity of the Eastern Roman Empire from Constantine the Great, the first Christian emperor in the fourth century, to the final collapse of the Byzantine state in 1453. Throughout this millennium the eastern end of the Mediterranean possessed a literate and cultivated laity. There was for instance a lay bureaucracy at the court of Constantinople, and where bureaucrats were devout they would want perhaps a copy of some patristic tome. So the preservation and transmission of manuscripts in the Greek East took place via the general culture of the day, which was both clerical and lay at the same time. Further east again, in the non-Greek-speaking world, among the embattled Christian minorities of Syria and Persia and of Egypt, texts of the Oriental Fathers (those whose language was not Greek) were kept entirely by the monks. This remained the case until the nineteenth century when, Western travellers began to explore the more exotic corners of the decaying Ottoman Empire in search of literary and other treasures, sometimes finding them put to unusual uses, as when leaves of codices were used to preserve from flies the monks' pickled fruit. From more peripheral areas of the early Christian world, like the Caucasian kingdoms of Georgia and Armenia, and from Ethiopia, there often come valuable ancient translations which help scholars to reconstruct imperfectly preserved patristic writings, but these regions did not produce teachers of any great significance themselves.

It emerges from this brief overview that until recently we have been much better informed about the Latin and Greek Fathers than we have about the Orientals, who wrote in such difficult and obscure languages as Syriac and Coptic. With the invention of the printing press it became possible to collate manuscripts, to publish the best of them, and to gather up all the works of an individual Father or indeed of a number of Fathers in a single project. From the sixteenth century onwards the aim of collecting all known patristic texts into a single corpus or edition has fascinated scholars. If only this could be put together, they thought, the Church at its most crucial period in the formulation of faith would spring to life before our eyes. Already in the sixteenth century the Jesuit cardinal Robert Bellarmine (1542–1621) had made a start, although his interests were probably more a matter of controversy with Protestants about whose Church was better based patristically, and so less a matter of studying the Fathers for themselves. Preeminent among the collections of the ensuing two centuries was the work of the Benedictine scholars of the congregation of St. Maur, known as the Maurists. Two hundred Benedictines working in collaboration in six monasteries turned out a great variety of well-edited texts in the belief that the facts of history would themselves speak for the truth of the Catholic faith. As Leo XIII (1810–1903) would later say, ''The Catholic Church has nothing to fear from the truth of history.'' The Maurists were the first patristic scholars to use the full range of helps to scholarship practiced today: not only the original languages but also the study of script (palaeography), of seals (diplomatics), of dating (chronology), and of nonwritten materials (archaeology). Attacked more than once by the Jesuits, they were stoutly defended by Pope

Clement XI (1649–1721). They suffered dispersal or the guillotine during the French Revolution.[9]

But the most widely spread collection of the Latin and Greek Fathers in modern times has been that of the abbé Migne (1800–75).[10] Jacques-Paul Migne, born near Orléans in 1800, was one of the most extraordinary priests of the nineteenth century. A pamphlet supporting the 1830 revolution in France against the House of Bourbon led to disfavor with his bishop, and he left his diocese for Paris where he gave himself to ecclesiastical journalism. In 1836, after abandoning his fourth failed newspaper, he conceived the grandiose scheme of publishing a library of two thousand volumes, mainly for the education of the clergy, giving all the important texts and facts of Catholic history and theology from the beginnings until his own times. He founded his own publishing house and eventually employed a staff of three hundred people. By 1855 he had published 217 volumes of the Latin Fathers, taking the story up to the death of Pope Innocent III in 1216. By 1866 he had added 181 volumes of the Greek, going up to the Council of Florence—the council of attempted reunion of Catholics and Orthodox which met in 1439—virtually on the eve of the fall of the Greek Christian polity in 1453. In 1868 all Migne's presses and stocks were destroyed by fire. After a long legal case he got the insurance but was suspended by the archbishop of Paris for using Mass stipends to finance his continued work. He died almost blind, leaving behind him a unique reputation for energy and management. After Migne's death, Orientalists added to the two patrologiae a *Patrologia Syriaca*, the texts of the Syriac fathers, followed by a *Patrologia Orientalis*, containing texts in the other minor Eastern languages, both printed in Paris from 1894 onwards.

Today scholars are divided as to how to approach the Migne patrologiae. Some hold that Migne should remain the standard text. They point out that the texts used by Migne represent all the editing work of the Renaissance and the Maurists, which I mentioned. The manuscripts these men used were in large part destroyed by the French Revolution and so can no longer contribute directly to establishing the manuscript tradition. Pro-Migne patrologists believe that Migne should not be replaced but merely revised—for instance by correcting the series

9. For a brief overview, *see* O. Bardenhewer, "Histoire de la patrologie," in Bardenhewer, *Les Pères de l'Eglise: Leurs vies et leurs oeuvres* (2nd ed., Paris: 1905) 12–23.

10. For his life and work, *see* A. G. Hamman, *Jacques-Paul Migne: Le Retour aux Pères de l'Eglise* (Paris: 1975).

where its editors mistook the identity of an author, or by adding more recently discovered writings to those already included.[11] Since 1958 scholars of this viewpoint have been publishing a Migne supplement. Others think that this is not radical enough and that a new start must be made.

In the later nineteenth century some smaller collections rather more scientific than Migne had already come into existence. These are known by their places of origin as the Vienna Corpus—officially, *Corpus scriptorum Ecclesiasticorum Latinorum*—and the Berlin Corpus—originally, in fact, *Leipzig*, and known officially as *Die griechischen christlichen Schriftsteller der ersten drei Jahrhunderte*. At the turn of this century, an alternative edition of the non-Hellenic Fathers and ecclesiastical writers of the Christian East also came into existence. The *Corpus scriptorum Christianorum Orientalium* was originally published in Paris but has since been produced at Louvain (and Washington). Scholars out with the Migne succession have, more recently, been collaborating in the production of a massive series rivaling Migne's patristic output. This is *Corpus Christianorum*, existing in both a Greek and a Latin sequence, and offering, by way of addition, such valuable aids to scholarship as name lists and guides to specialized terms. It also boasts a *Continuatio mediaevalis*—a parallel to the Byzantine continuation of the Greek Fathers known as the Bonn Corpus—and a series of apocryphal writings. This monumental edition is being prepared at Steenbrugge in Flanders, and again, as in the seventeenth and eighteenth centuries, is under Benedictine management.[12]

Councils

Not the least significant monument of Tradition that crystallized in the patristic period was the institution of the Church council. Whenever in that period or after it there is serious dispute about the content of Tradition we find a council of the Church. Councils are a way of establishing what the *regula fidei* and the *institutio Christiana* are, the forms that orthodoxy and orthopraxy should take. As such, they are clearly of great importance for the theologian. Theologically considered, the least weighty result of a council is a canon, or practical rule, for the Church's life (later codified and supplemented as canon law). More

11. P. Glorieux, *Pour revaloriser Migne: Tables rectificatrices* (Lalli: 1952).

12. *Ibid.*, "Collections des Pères de l'Eglise," 24–31; this essay can be supplemented for the present century by reference to, for instance, P. J. Hamell, *Handbook of Patrology* (Staten Island, N.Y.: 1968) 14–17.

weighty is a doctrinal definition, since this concerns a point of believing principle and not simply a practical corollary of such a point. Most weighty of all is the formulation of a creed, or summary of divine revelation. Because of the paramount importance of creeds, I shall devote to them a section all their own.

The roots of the conciliar idea lie in the New Testament itself.[13] As we saw while looking at the concept of tradition, the Twelve were constituted by Jesus as vehicles of his teaching. A further nuance of this is that the Twelve did not become the vehicles of tradition as individuals but as members of the group of the Twelve. Although Peter is termed *ho prôtos*, the first, and acts as spokesman for the rest, the Gospels, the Acts, and the Pauline letters all imply that the Twelve had a corporate responsibility for passing on the truth. In later terminology, they formed a "college." We have seen that in the latest books of the New Testament, such as the Pastoral Letters, steps are being taken to preserve the activity and achievement of the Twelve in the future. Apostolic delegates like Timothy are charged with the selection of suitable overseers for local communities. In the subapostolic period, these overseers, or bishops, are said to succeed to the task of the apostles, either directly, in which case the apostles are thought of as the first bishops of the Church, or indirectly, in which case they are thought of rather as appointing the first leaders of the Churches, and it is to these apostolic appointees that the bishops succeed. As far as collegiality is concerned, the Acts of the Apostles portrays the Twelve as consulting together about a replacement for Judas Iscariot and taking a corporate decision to put Matthias in the vacant apostolic seat. Similarly, in the first major crisis to affect the primitive Church, the issue of the acceptance of Gentiles for baptism directly, that is, without first entering the Jewish covenant through circumcision, the author of Acts describes the problem as being resolved in a conciliar way, by a meeting of those of the Twelve still in Jerusalem with the representatives of the Church of Antioch, Barnabas and Paul. So the question arises, Did the men who succeeded the apostles as guardians of Tradition and heads of the local Churches believe that in order to establish the Church's Tradition in times of crisis they had a duty to reform the apostolic college by holding an episcopal council?

In point of fact, the earliest form that episcopal consultation took in the subapostolic period was not councils so much as journeys by

---

13. B. Botte, "La collégialité dans le Nouveau Testament et chez les Pères apostoliques," in Botte, *Le concile et les conciles* (Chevetogne-Paris: 1960).

individual bishops to other local Churches. Thus we find Polycarp of Smyrna travelling to Rome to expound and defend the tradition of the Asian Churches about the dating of Easter for the benefit of the Roman bishop. The earliest heresies, Marcionitism and Gnosticism, are not responded to by the calling of councils. Various explanations for this may be offered, such as the fact that the episcopate took time to realize the implications of its succession to the apostles; the practical problems of organizing a council in an age of periodic persecution; or again, the fact that movements like Marcionitism and (especially) Gnosticism were not so much Christian heresies as alternative religious systems which could be distinguished from the gospel tradition by a simple repetition of the rule of faith—which already existed in the form of baptismal creeds. Whatever the reason, the fact is that there were no councils until the end of the second century. Although the Montanist crisis around 170 is the occasion of the first known church council, a regional council of the Churches of Asia Minor, a more important move toward the idea of an ecumenical council was the series of simultaneous regional councils held around 190 in Italy, Asia Minor, Palestine, and Mesopotamia in order to resolve the paschal question, the problem of the dating of Easter. The same format was used by the episcopate for dealing with the issue of the *lapsi:* what to do about Christians who had apostatized temporarily under threat of persecution. But this time, in the 250s, there was a further development: official letters describing conciliar decisions and dubbed "synodal letters" were sent to any local Churches not represented at these councils, appealing for their adherence. The reception of synodal letters throughout the whole Church from councils representing parts of the Church was the next and the greatest step in the ante-Nicene period toward the concept of an ecumenical council. In fact we can say that by the 260s the idea of ecumenicity or universal decision-making theological authority had at last emerged. The reception by the universal episcopate of a council's teaching is seen as giving that teaching a definitive status as an expression of the Church's Tradition. A "monument of Tradition," which the theologian must take seriously as source and criterion, has arrived.[14]

Until the late sixteenth century, only eight or at most nine councils were regarded as ecumenical by the Catholic Church. These were the first seven, from Nicaea I in 325 to Nicaea II in 787, along with

14. H. Marot, "Conciles anténicéens et conciles oecuméniques," in Botte, *Le concile et les conciles.*

the Council of Florence of 1439, and sometimes the 869 council which condemned the Byzantine Patriarch Photius (ca. 810–95) for his Church policies, a council referred to by those who upheld its ecumenicity as Constantinople IV. The reason for the brevity of this list is that until the sixteenth century the Catholic Church accepted as criteria for ecumenicity (by and large) the tests generally agreed upon in the late patristic Church. According to these tests, it is not enough for a council to be attended or approved by the Roman pope in order to be ecumenical. It must also be attended or approved by the other apostolic patriarchs, the holders of the four great Eastern sees of Constantinople, Alexandria, Antioch, and Jerusalem, in whose persons the bishops of all the Churches of the East were seen as somehow present. Using this criterion, only the first seven universal councils plus Florence could be regarded as ecumenical, with the possible addition of the anti-Photian synod in the late ninth century. The status of the latter was odd, since its decisions were formally suppressed by the papacy itself some years after its meeting. It was only in the twelfth century that Western canonists began to maintain its ecumenicity because its provisions against laymen appointing the Byzantine patriarch became extremely relevant to the situation of the Latin Church during the Investiture Contest. In the late sixteenth century Bellarmine, then teaching at the Collegium Romanum, almost singlehandedly introduced the idea that the papally approved councils held in the Western Church (alone) since 1123 were also ecumenical. The most obvious reason for this innovation, which led to an immediate extension of the total number of councils to eighteen or nineteen, was the need to present the Council of Trent as a fully ecumenical council over against Protestant dissent. But the virtually instantaneous and universal acceptance of Bellarmine's list in the Latin Church testifies to the fact that whatever its immediate motivation, it corresponded to a deep and widespread theological instinct. However, it does not correspond to the criteria used in the patristic Church. Is there any way we can resolve this?

In writers of the century before Bellarmine, we occasionally find a distinction between two types of ecumenical council, and the distinction may be of use to theological students in their efforts to bring order into their theological authorities. To begin with, people spoke of an ecumenical council in its plenary form: universal not simply by virtue of approval by the pope as universal bishop, but also by virtue of its membership, with particular reference to the need for the participation of the Eastern patriarchs. But then in the second place, there can be an ecumenical council in a less than plenary form, where, despite the deficiencies of representation, sanction by the pope as head of the college of bishops confers sufficient authority on a council for it to be called ecumenical though not in the fullest possible sense.[15] Something like a return to this view of the councils seems implied in an important letter of Paul VI to Cardinal Jan Willebrands on the occasion of the seventh centenary of Lyons I in 1974. More widely, it may be suggested that the ecumenicity of the councils is an analogical, rather than a univocal, ecumenicity.[16] A council would only be ecumenical in the highest degree if Peter and the Twelve, the pope and the entire episcopal college, took part, and if the matter dealt with were a matter of fundamental Christian believing—and not simply, say, something for the disciplinary good order of the Church. Arguably, no one has ever supposed that all ecumenical councils were on the same level: that Lyons II or Trent has the same significance as Nicaea or Chalcedon. The most striking piece of evidence that might substantiate this assertion is the fact that no creed commissioned by a subsequent council has ever been made to substitute for the great liturgical creed, namely, the Nicene Creed, or as it is more correctly spoken of, the Creed of Nicaea-Constantinople. This remains the only creed used in the Eucharistic liturgy, the prayer of the Church at its most intimate and intense, even though it is less full, less developed than its successors. Given that, as we have found cause to believe, the liturgy is, after Scripture, the primary monument of the Church's Tradition, this fact must carry considerable theological weight. But to think more on this, we must turn explicitly, in a moment, to the subject of creeds.

Meanwhile, where can the theological student find information about the councils and their teaching? Still frequently cited in studies of the history of doctrine is a multivolume German work, translated early on into English: *Conciliengeschichte,* "The Story of the Councils." It was the brainchild of Carl Joseph von Hefele (1809–93), who in 1840 became professor of Church history, patristics, and Christian archaeology at the Catholic faculty of Tübingen in southwest West Germany.[17] Later bishop of Rottenburg, Hefele was, alas, one of those German bishops who opposed the definition of papal infallibility at the First

15. *See* V. Peri, *I concili e le chiese* (Rome: 1965).

16. B. de Margerie, "L'analogie dans l'oecumenicité des conciles: notion clef pour l'avenir de l'oecuménisme," *Revue Thomiste* 84. 3 (1984) 425–46.

17. For Hefele's life and work, *see* H. Tüchle, "Hefele, Karl Josef von," in *Lexikon für Theologie und Kirche 5,* cols 55–56. His *Conciliengeshichte,* 1–8, was published at Freiburg from 1855 to 1874.

Vatican Council. After the council, saddened by the defeat of the in-opportunists, he retired to his diocese and left another to finish his work. So after 1874, when volume 7 was published, there is a gap. Then in 1887, Joseph Hergenröther (1824–90), another professor of Church history but this time at Würzburg, took over the task. Hergenröther, who was the prefect of the Vatican Archive and made cardinal in 1879, published the final two volumes, 8 and 9, between 1887 and 1890.[18] In the period opened by the summoning of the Second Vatican Council, interest in the conciliar phenomenon has grown again among Church historians, and two notable new histories have emerged. These are the French *Histoire des conciles oecuméniques* edited by Père Gervais Dumeige, and the extremely ambitious German series, *Konziliengeschichte*, the project of Msgr. Walter Brandmüller of Augsburg: this monumental collection will document the entire outworking of the synodal element in the Church's life, including regional councils from Anglo-Saxon England to sixteenth-century Mexico.

The work of Hefele, Hergenröther, and their modern successors, great as it is, was itself made possible by an exhaustive compilation of the actual sources—the actual texts of the councils, not simply the doctrinal definitions and the canons but also the speeches and other writings generally relevant—by John Dominic Mansi, archbishop of Lucca (1692–1769). His work, usually cited simply as "Mansi," is entitled *Sacrorum Conciliorum nova et amplissima collectio*, "The New and Most Complete Collection of the Sacred Councils," and was compiled at Lucca in Tuscany where Mansi had founded an academy for the study of the history of the Church and especially the liturgy.[19] The usual edition in which Mansi is now consulted is the Parisian edition, which consists in an awe-inspiring fifty-three volumes, published at Paris between 1901 and 1927. More recently, an admirable edition of the decrees of the ecumenical councils, also created in Italy but this time at Bologna, has appeared under the editorship of Prof. J. Alberigo under the title *Conciliorum oecumenicorum decreta*, published at Freiburg in 1962, with a supplementary volume on the Second Vatican Council, which, in its most recently revised form, came out at Bologna in 1973.

18. A. Bigelmair, "Hergenröther, Joseph," in Tüchle, *Lexikon für Theologie und Kirche* cols 245–46. His continuation of Hefele was published likewise at Freiburg, from 1887 to 1890. Unlike the completed (and extended) French translation (principally edited by H. Leclerq, Paris: 1907–52), the English translation (by W. R. Clark, Edinburgh: 1883–96) only goes as far as 787.

19. For his life and labors, see H. Quentin, *Jean-Dominique Mansi et les grandes collections conciliaires* (Paris: 1900).

Creeds

A creed may be defined as an authoritative statement of basic Christian belief. The New Testament itself contains no creeds, a fact which bears eloquent witness to the claim that in the New Testament we find the Christian religion in the process of becoming rather than in the act of fully being. On the other hand, the New Testament does contain a large number of affirmations about God, Christ, the Church, grace, destiny, which are capable of being turned into credal form. Occasionally, there are references to what may have been credal tests administered to individuals in the apostolic period itself. An example would be the reply of the Ethiopian eunuch to the Apostle Philip in the Acts of the Apostles (a reply preserved only in the so-called Western Text of that book): "I believe that Jesus Christ is the Son of God."[20] Another example comes in Paul's Letter to the Romans: "If your lips confess that 'Jesus is Lord,' and if you believe in your heart that 'God raised him from the dead,' then you will be saved."[21] The earliest creeds are in fact baptismal creeds, little dialogues, question-and-answer sessions, used by the Church's minister in addressing the candidate awaiting entry into the Church.[22] A good example occurs in the *Apostolic Tradition* of Hippolytus of Rome, a Father writing in the early third century who thoughtfully provided specimen prayers for the sacraments in case there were bishops who had difficulty in making up their own.[23] Such dialogues are Trinitarian in form, thus corresponding to baptismal initiation itself. They crop up everywhere throughout the patristic Church. Thus, for example, Origen, in his commentary on the Gospel of John, speaks of those "articles of faith" that, in being believed, save the person who believes them, and cites specifically the confession that "there is one God, who created and framed all things. . . . We must also believe that Jesus Christ is Lord, and all the true teaching concerning both his Godhead and his manhood. And we must believe in the Holy Spirit and that, having free will, we are punished for our evil deeds and rewarded for our good."[24] On the other side of the Mediterranean, Firmilian of Caesarea (d. 268), in present-day Turkey, writing to Cyprian of Carthage in North Africa speaks of the "customary and established words of the interroga-

20. Acts 8:37.
21. Romans 10:9.
22. J. N. D. Kelly, *Early Christian Creeds* (London: 1950) 30–61.
23. Hippolytus, *Apostolic Tradition* 21.
24. Origen, *On the Gospel of John* 32:16 (by way of comment on John 13:19).

tion.''[25] We can safely conclude, then, that by the middle of the third century a formula of faith (with minor variations) had developed in all the main Churches based upon the Trinitarian formula cited in the words of Jesus about baptism at the end of St. Matthew's Gospel: ''Go into the whole world and preach the Gospel to every creature, baptizing them in the name of the Father and of the Son and of the Holy Spirit.''[26] From such interrogatory baptismal creeds, the Fathers evolved by a simple and obvious development what is known as the ''declaratory'' creed, a first-person statement: ''I believe'' or ''we believe,'' with the text following. Such a declaratory creed, though associated with one's baptism, could in principle be used at other times. Hence at the Council of Nicaea, Eusebius of Caesarea (ca. 260–340) prefaced a report of the belief of his Church with these words: ''As we have received from the bishops before us, both in our catechetical training, and when we received the baptismal bath, so we now believe and bring our faith forward to you.''[27] The best-known declaratory creed in the Western Church is the Apostles' Creed or, as it is more correctly known, the Old Roman Creed. By the fourth century, this creed had reached a final, standardized form, so much so in fact that Rufinus of Aquileia (ca. 345–410) in northern Italy reports that at its recitation in the baptismal ceremonies the faithful always listened very carefully to make sure that not a word had been changed. Rufinus was also responsible for a romantic account of the origins of the Apostles' Creed to the effect that each apostle contributed one verse to a common statement of faith just before separating to go off on their missionary journeys.[28] This legend, probably based on a misunderstanding of those ante-Nicene authors who describe their Churches as following the *regula fidei*, i.e., the traditional teaching handed down by the apostles, achieved a wide currency in the Latin Church. In later times in the Latin West, it was frequently illustrated in the glass of Gothic churches, each apostle holding out a scroll bearing the article he had contributed. The Latin bishops at the Council of Florence in 1439 were consequently scandalized on being told by their Byzantine counterparts that they had never even heard of the Apostles' Creed.[29]

25. Firmilian, *Epistola* 75, 10–11.

26. Matthew 28:19.

27. Cited by Athanasius of Alexandria in the appendix to his *De decretis Nicaenae synodi* (PG 20, 1535ff.).

28. Rufinus, *Commentarium in symbolum apostolorum* (PL 21, 335–86).

29. Kelly, *Early Christian Creeds* 1–6.

The one truly ecumenical form of the creed is the Creed of Nicaea-Constantinople, which was finalized in 381 and inserted into the Eucharistic liturgy by some local Churches as early as the decade afterwards.[30] In all likelihood, this Creed was arrived at by conciliar modification of short declaratory creeds like the Old Roman Creed, a clarification made in the light of the major heresies of the early centuries about the Trinity and the incarnation. Some of the great Fathers like Athanasius of Alexandria (ca. 296–373) and Basil of Caesarea (ca. 330–79) took a major hand in the shaping of the Creed we now say at the Mass of the Roman Rite on Sundays. Others, whose theology was eventually found to be in certain respects inadequte by the Church, contributed to the Creed negatively, so to speak: bits of it were put in to keep bits of *their* teaching out. The Creed of Nicaea-Constantinople was composed, as its name suggests, in two stages. In its purely Nicene form, the Creed was a response to the crisis in doctrine associated with the Alexandrian presbyter Arius (ca. 250–336).[31] In the early Church, the relationships between the Son, Jesus, and the Spirit, the Holy Spirit, to the Father, as attested in Scripture and celebrated in worship, were attended by no little confusion. Arianism tried to make a clean sweep of this confusion by a solution that was fundamentally unitarian, levelling out the triune form of Christian belief in God into a flat monotheism. Though in some ways conservative in its formulae, it understood inherited terms in a new philosophical conjunction which changed their inflection.[32] The divine Son, for Arius, was created by the Father as an instrument for the making and redeeming of the world. Not by nature divine, he received the dignity of divine sonship on account of his foreseen faithfulness to the Father's will. Athanasius records that at the Council of Nicaea, convoked to meet the emergency, many attempts were made to find a biblical term expressive of the antithesis of this position. As none was forthcoming, recourse was had to a nonbiblical term, *homoousios:* "of one substance with" the Father. During the next fifty years the Nicene Creed failed to obtain a general reception throughout the Church. The controversy over the divinity of Christ went on regardless, and to it was added

30. *Ibid.*, 96–331.

31. Kelly, however, takes the view that the Creed of Constantinople was not in a literary sense dependent on that of Nicaea, but rather attempted to express the Nicene faith in a way better suited to the needs (i.e., the heresies) of the hour: *Ibid.* 330–31.

32. The thesis of Prof. Rowan Williams' brilliant study: *Arius: Heresy and Tradition* (London: 1987).

the problem of the status of the Spirit. The Arian crisis is thus the principal moment in the "search for the Christian doctrine of God"[33] and, fittingly, therefore provides the crucial background for the adoption of the Creed in its present form (as used by Eastern Catholics, and by Westerners with the insertion of the term *Filioque*, a reference to the role of the Son in the procession of the Spirit) at the Council of Constantinople in 381. Elaborated out of the Nicene Creed, or at any rate formulated in conscious imitation thereof, this document probably also reflects the baptismal usage of the local Byzantine Church of Constantinople: the latter part of the Creed on such themes as the Church, baptism, the forgiveness of sins, the resurrection of the dead, and the life everlasting belong to the preparation of catechumens for Christian initiation rather than to the great controversies of the age. Reaffirmed at Chalcedon in 451, it became almost at once the standard Creed of the Eastern Churches. The unity of being of the Son with the Father, affirmed at Nicaea, became a touchstone for theological orthodoxy, as did the newly added assertions of the eternal character of the distinct personality of the Word (whose "kingdom shall have no end," a riposte to the notions of Marcellus of Ancyra, a Nicene over-enthusiast) and of the divinity of the Holy Spirit. In the West, however, there were a hundred years or so of silence on the topic of the Creed, perhaps because the Roman Church resented Constantinople's claim to be the second see, New Rome, a claim made at the very council where this Creed was approved. But in due course it made its way into the liturgical books of the Roman Christians as well and by the ninth century had been accepted into the order of the Mass throughout large areas of the Western Church.[34]

Judging (as we should) by liturgical practice, the Catholic Church regards this ecumenical Creed of Nicaea-Constantinople as the supreme instance of an infallible articulation of Christian revelation on the basis of Bible and Tradition. It is the primordial example of all those occasions when the Church in council has come to a definitive statement of her own grasp of revelation, and when the rest of the Church has definitively received that statement as the truth. All other creeds composed afterwards to meet specific emergencies are elaborations of this

33. R. P. C. Hanson, *The Search for the Christian Doctrine of God: The Arian Controversy, 318–381 A.D.* (Edinburgh: 1988).

34. J. A. Jungmann, *The Mass of the Roman Rite: Its Origins and Development* (London: 1949) 297–301.

fundamental Creed, derivatives from it, or footnotes to it.[35] Although there are postpatristic creeds dating from medieval and Counter-Reformation times, such creeds are not equally fundamental for theology. Corresponding to the inequality of councils, which we examined in the last section, there is also an inequality in the creeds produced by the councils.

The peculiar importance of the creeds, as distinct from other doctrinal definitions, for the theological student lies, of course, in the fact that a creed offers an overview of the entire Christian gospel. It sets an agenda for all theology. No theology which does not do justice to the entire creed is sufficient for the life of a Church community or an individual, no matter how accurate and well expressed the truths that such a theology does convey. Thus a creed is not "more true than" a noncredal statement of doctrine, but it is by its very structure more comprehensive. But since other solemn Church pronouncements on doctrine are no less true, they too will naturally form part of the theologian's sources or authorities. The student will note that such more-atomized determinations of the Church's faith can be either conciliar or papal in their organ of expression. This does not overthrow the principle that, despite Peter's prerogatives, the Twelve form essentially one corporate group. When occasion seems to render it needful or appropriate, the Roman pope may define doctrine just as a council does, but in so doing he acts as head of the episcopal college, bearing its moral persona within himself, something shown in his moral obligation to consult his fellow bishops prior to defining. The first among the successors of the apostles can act *for* all the rest, but never *against* them all.

Where may the theological student look for materials in the shape of the creeds and other dogmatic definitions, including the doctrinal determinations of the popes? The most important anthology of creeds and other doctrinal statements used by Catholic theologians is the *Enchiridion* of Denzinger, many times reedited, most recently by Karl Rahner. Heinrich Joseph Dominicus Denzinger was one of the greatest historical theologians of the Catholic Church in Germany.[36] Born in Liège in 1819 and educated at the German College in Rome, he became professor of dogmatic theology at Würzburg in Lower Bavaria

35. For the importance of this Creed for the ecumenical movement (in the modern, therefore, sense of "ecumenical"), *see* G. Voss, "Auf dem Weg zu einem gemeinsamen Ausdruck des apostolischen Glaubens heute: Ein Studieprojekt," *Una Sancta* 40 (1985) 2–14.

36. J. Hasenfuss, "Denzinger, Heinrich Joseph," *Lexikon für Theologie und Kirche* 3, cols. 233, 234.

in 1848, a position he held until his death in 1883. Denzinger was one of the foremost Catholic theologians in the nineteenth century who saw the need for positive or historical theology, that is, an exact investigation of the historical development of Christian teaching, rather than or at least as an essential supplement to philosophical speculation about that teaching. In 1854 he published his collection of the main historic documents of the Church's magisterium under the title *Enchiridion Symbolorum, definitionum et declarationum de rebus fidei et morum,* ''Handbook of the Creeds, Definitions and Declarations on Matters of Faith and Morals.'' The good use of Denzinger, as Père Congar has noted, involves awareness that Denzinger is inevitably a selection—and a selection based on what he and his successors considered important.[37] We will not know exhaustively what, for example, the Council of Trent thought about the sacrament of orders until we have gone behind Denzinger to the complete text itself. Yet, in practice, such selections are a necessity: a most useful recent volume, arranged in thematic rather than (as with Denzinger) chronological sequence, is *The Christian Faith in the Doctrinal Documents of the Catholic Church.*[38]

To sum up, the theological student is well advised to pay particular attention to the Fathers, for several reasons. First, their theology belongs to the age of Christianity's definitive formulation. Second, their age has high intrinsic qualities of its own. Third, it played an indispensable part in the Church's reception of the biblical faith. The early councils enshrine various central insights of patristic teaching as essential statements of the faith of the Church, but the conciliar principle does not cease to function with the close of the patristic age. Councils are a kind of continuing presence of the apostolic college in the later Church, though they are not for that reason of equivalent value. The peculiar status of the Creed of Nicaea-Constantinople witnesses to this fact: it is the theologian's universal *vade mecum,* the Church's summary of her own confession of God. Nevertheless, all dogmatic definitions, whether by council or by the pope as head of the college of bishops, are authoritative guides to the meaning of Christian revelation.

37. Y. Congar, ''Sur le bon usage de Denzinger,'' in Congar, *Situation et tâches présentes de la théologie,* (Paris: 1967).

38. *The Christian Faith in the Doctrinal Documents of the Catholic Church,* ed. J. Neuner and J. Dupuis (London: 1983).

16
The Sense of the Faithful

If the age of the Fathers saw the emergence of council and creed as monuments of Tradition, permanently valid summations of Christian faith, and modes of arriving at a discernment of the content of revelation which are with us still, it should not be assumed that only the *Ecclesia docens*, the "teaching Church," is of theological interest. On the contrary, the *sensus fidelium*, the "sense of the faithful" is also a monument or expression of Tradition. At this point, the *Ecclesia discens*, the "learning Church," is itself for theologians a *locus* of teaching authority.

A number of the Fathers made appeal in this way to the faith of the people, their spontaneous inward inclination. Thus the Cypriot student of the heresies, Epiphanius of Salamis, finds of extreme theological pertinence to the doctrine of Jesus' virginal conception the popular habit of adding, after the name of Mary, the words "the Virgin."[1] Still in the Greek East, the iconophile theologian Nicephorus of Constantinople draws attention to the religious care with which the faithful treated holy images.[2] And in the patristic West, Augustine appeals to what he called *dogma populare* on four issues especially—the necessity of grace as seen in the meaning given to prayer by the faithful, the needfulness—and efficacy—of baptism for salvation, the custom of not rebaptizing heretics, and the canonicity of such biblical books as Wisdom, listened to "with the veneration proper to divine authority."[3] The North African Doctor also provided a basis for under-

1. Epiphanius, *Adversus haereses Panarion, Haeresis* 78, c. 6; cited in W. M. Thompson, "Sensus Fidelium and Infallibility," *American Ecclesiastical Review* 167.7 (1973) 451.

2. For Nicephorus, *see* Y. Congar, *Lay People in the Church* (English trans., London: 1965) app. II: "The Sensus Fidelium in the Fathers," 466.

3. Augustine, *De praedestinatione sanctorum* 27. For the other Augustinian references, *see* Congar, *Lay People in the Church*, 466.

standing this paying of attention to the sense of the faithful: since all Christians are illuminated by Christ the internal teacher, they are enabled not just to receive the truth but "to make approval of that doctrine, to receive that doctrine as the truth."[4]

If the positive estimate of the *sensus fidelium* among the Fathers was rooted in their feeling for the Church as a mystery of solidarity with the Holy Trinity in Christ, and for the life of faith as a "salutary discipline" in which, as Gregory of Nyssa would put it, the development of a "spiritual sense" takes place in proportion to the mortifying of the carnal senses,[5] the interest of the medieval theologians was located firmly in the latter, or subjective, aspect: the grace of faith in the individual member of the faithful people.[6] What is at stake here is, fundamentally, the habit of faith, which we studied in the opening chapter of this book, as one of the two essential elements in the theological habit itself.

On some jaundiced views of the Catholic Reformation as a one-sided exaltation of the hierarchical Church over against the wider body of the faithful, it might be thought that this stream of thought would disappear into the sands of a dried-up Tridentinism. But not so: in a study published during the opening weeks of the Second Vatican Council, the Louvain theologian Gustave Thils demonstrated its continuing vigor in the Catholic schools of the sixteenth to nineteenth centuries.[7] The Counter-Reformation divines were, indeed, almost obliged to work out, over against Calvin in particular, an account of how the whole Church is unable to fall away from Christ—no matter to what degree individuals in the Church may err. Thus, for example, the founder of the notion of *loci theologici*, Melchior Cano, insists that the Church cannot fail in believing, as distinct from teaching, since, as she is in the pastors so is she also in the faithful.[8] Nor, by the time of the First Vatican Council, was it forgotten that Trent had described those who deny Christ's real presence in the Eucharist as "against the universal sense of the Church."[9] The draft document on the Church's infal-

---

4. E. Hughes, *The Participation of the Faithful in the Regal and Prophetic Mission of Christ According to Saint Augustine* (Washington: 1956) 50.

5. J. Daniélou, *Platonisme et théologie mystique: Doctrine spirituelle de Saint Grégorie de Nysse* (Paris: 1954) 235–41.

6. For a synoptic view of the high medieval Scholastics on this, *see* M. Koster, "Der Glaubenssinn der Hirten und Gläubigen," *Neue Ordnung* 3 (1949) 230.

7. G. Thils, *L'infaillibilité du peuple chrétien in credendo: Notes de théologie post-tridentine* (Paris: 1963).

8. *De locis theologicis* 121A, cited in Thompson, "Sensus Fidelium and Infallibility."

9. DS, 874.

libility at Trent's successor council of 1869–70, though never voted or promulgated, owing to the decision to proceed first with the infallibility attaching to the Petrine office bearer and the premature suspension of the council with the Italian invasion of Rome, spoke of the Church's incapacity to err as characterizing "as much the universality of the faithful as the universality of the bishops," since what all the faithful hold as of faith is necessarily true.[10]

Thils summed up the matter simply enough. Just as the magisterium of the Church cannot err in what it teaches, so the laity, the consensus of the faithful, cannot be deceived in what they believe. The gift of teaching Christian truth without deceiving is a useless gift unless it is matched by some sort of reciprocal gift of believing, some gift of infallibly receiving infallible teaching among the laity. However faithful pope and bishops may be to the apostolic deposit in carrying out their teaching office, their ministry remains inefficacious so long as it is not accepted by others. And moreover, if in the past the Christian people have been led to a grasp of the true faith through those commissioned to teach it, then unless they have forgotten everything overnight, they must surely constitute a resource for popes and bishops of the future to draw upon. Thus, according to Thils, infallibility, or a sure grasp on the gospel message, is a characteristic of the entire Church, laity and clergy together, though it is differentiated in various ways as between the episcopate on the one hand and the faithful on the other. The framers of *Lumen gentium*, the dogmatic constitution of the Second Vatican Council on the Church, thus circumstantially reminded of the traditional character of this doctrine, incorporated it into that conciliar document as a vital aspect of theological epistemology in Catholicism:

LG 12: The entire body of the faithful, anointed as they are by the Holy One, cannot err in matters of belief. They manifest this special property by means of the whole people's supernatural discernment in matters of faith when "from the bishops to the least of the lay faithful" they show universal agreement in matters of faith and morals. That discernment in matters of faith is aroused and sustained by the Spirit of truth. It is exercised under the guidance of the sacred teaching authority, in faithful and respectful obedience to which the people of God accepts what is not just the word of men but truly the Word of God. Through it, the people of God adheres unwaveringly to the faith given once and for all to the saints,

10. Mansi, 51, 579C.

penetrates it more deeply with right thinking, and applies it more fully in its life.[11]

The laity themselves are, then, not in isolation but in conjunction with those who bear magisterium, an instrument of Tradition, a means whereby the gospel comes to the Church, a place where Tradition becomes visible.

Historically, the fullest discussion of this idea took place in the mid-nineteenth century. That period as a whole was not one when the laity were taken with any great seriousness by Church leaders. Msgr. George Talbot, an adviser of Pope Pius IX, once expressed the view that the role of the laity should be confined to hunting, shooting, and fishing, the typical leisure-time pursuits of the English squirearchy.[12] As Talbot later went insane, we might be inclined to draw a charitable veil over this remark. However, Newman himself indicated that this dismissive judgment on the ecclesial significance of the laity was by no means an isolated case. He wrote to a friend, "So far as I can see, there are ecclesiastics all over Europe, whose policy it is to keep the laity at arms length, and hence the laity have become disgusted and become infidel, and only two parties exist, both ultras in opposite directions."[13] Newman had been thinking theologically about the contribution of the laity to the Church's preservation and unfolding of its faith for quite some while. His move within Anglicanism from a more Calvinist to a more Catholic school of thought had been motivated by the discovery that Christianity is not an individualistic creed with each soul related separately (not just personally) to God, but membership of a worshipping community that flows from the gospel. In a sermon of 1825 he had insisted that the most important Christian doctrines are only indirectly taught in the Scriptures because it is the Church which is the teacher that introduces people to the truths of biblical faith.[14] At exactly the same time he was stressing that the Church in this context is not just the clergy alone: "When then it is said, the Church is the mother of saints, the instructress and guardian of all Christians, by Church is meant not the clergy alone, but all who are concerned in the work of education with the clergy at this head—the

11. *Lumen gentium* 12, with an internal reference to John 2:21.
12. Cited by J. Coulson in *On Consulting the Faithful in Matters of Doctrine, by John Henry Newman*, ed. J. Coulson (London: 1961) 41.
13. W. Ward, *The Life of John Henry Cardinal Newman* (London: 1912) 2, 397-98.
14. "On the Use of the Visible Church" (December 4, 1825): *see* on this S. D. Femiano, *Infallibility of the Laity: The Legacy of Newman* (New York: 1967) 12–15.

clergy are not the only ministers—in one sense all parents and masters are ministers of the household of God.''[15]

By 1833 Newman's academic interests had settled on the Fathers, and it was while studying the Arian crisis that he came to realize that in that period the faith of the Church had been preserved, humanly speaking, by the laity rather than by the episcopate. In his 1837 treatise *The Prophetical Office of the Church*, an appeal to Anglicans to return to the faith and practice of antiquity, he suggested two ways in which the voice of the laity could be the voice of tradition. First, there was their role in what he termed "apostolic" or "episcopal" tradition, namely, the handing on of what is already defined in the Church's faith. Insofar as the laity have received the creeds and have believed them, they are capable of "traditioning" them. "The humblest and meanest among Christians may defend the faith against the whole Church, if need arise. He has as much right to it as bishop or archbishop, and has nothing to limit him in his protest but his intellectual capacity for making it."[16] Second, the laity have, Newman argued, a vital role in the transmission of the wider body of Christian truth he dubbed "prophetical," namely, the implicit understanding of tradition diffused through the Church in an inarticulate or semiarticulate way. However, it was becoming increasingly clear that Newman's thinking lay outside the mainstream of contemporary Anglicanism. The opposition he encountered did not seem to him merely an unfortunate political setback. He read it as the rejection by the Anglican laity as much as by the Anglican episcopate of the picture of the Church he was engaged in painting.[17] Thus one interpretation of Newman's conversion to Catholicism has it that it was this very principle of the consent of the faithful which in the end excluded him from the Anglican Church.

In defending the first of the works that he published as a Catholic—the *Essay on the Development of Christian Doctrine*—Newman took further the notion that there can be truths that are lodged in the mind yet not reflected on or become articulate. An obvious example would be the truth of one's own self-identity: I know that I am myself. This

---

15. Cited *ibid.*, 15, from "Instruction: A Duty of Members of the Church" (December 11, 1825).

16. As reprinted in *The Via Media of the Anglican Church* (London: 1877) 240.

17. In Newman's own words: "If there ever was a cause in which an individual teacher has been put aside, and virtually put away by a community, mine is one," cited in Femiano, *Infallibility of the Laity*, 272.

is the most certain knowledge that I possess. Yet I may well find it difficult to put the apprehension of my own identity into words, or to defend it against some philosophical puzzle with which I may be confronted. A truth can thus be possessed without its grounds becoming fully explicit in the mind of its possessor. In the "Newman-Perrone Paper" in which the future cardinal attempted to set forth the basis in a theological doctrine of knowledge for the interpretation of Church history he had given in the *Essay,* all for the benefit of the official theologians of the Roman Church of the time, Newman considers the Church as a person possessing the faith but not yet fully possessed of a total understanding of it. By this analogy, "the Word, insofar as it is subjective in the mind of the Catholic, has both the same condition and the same history in the Church as it has in the case of individuals, whether they be individual doctors, schools or [local] churches." It was as witnesses to the as yet unarticulated truth that Newman came to see the theological significance of the laity in the preservation of tradition. Their reaction to the preaching of the Church's ministers during the Arian crisis demonstrated their implicit grasp of doctrine and so not only saved that doctrine but also helped in the progressive articulation of the word of God.[18]

After the writing of the *Essay,* Newman was confirmed in his belief that his thinking was on the right lines by the events surrounding the proclamation of the dogma of the immaculate conception of the blessed Virgin Mary in 1853. Pius IX, in preparing this *ex cathedra* definition, had specifically asked the bishops to have regard to the faith of the laity about Mary's all-purity in reporting back to Rome before the final decision was made. Moreover, Newman's erstwhile correspondent, the Jesuit Giovanni Perrone, professor of dogma at the Collegio Romano, had produced a book on the topic of the definition in which he had said that the *sensus fidelium,* manifested in the devotion of the laity to Mary in her all-purity, was essential in determining whether the doctrine formed a genuine part of the Christian faith or not.[19] Newman was taken aback, therefore, at the outcry which met his own reiteration that the voice of the laity is an instrument of tradition in another essay, this time entitled "On Consulting the Faithful

---

18. While in *The Arians of the Fourth Century* the role of the laity was not Newman's main consideration (indeed, he merely stated the historical fact of its fidelity as he saw it), in an appendix to the third edition, published in 1871, he greatly expanded this.

19. G. Perrone, *De immaculato Beatae Virginis Mariae conceptu an dogmatico decreto definiri possit disquisitio theologica* (Milan: 1847).

in Matters of Doctrine," written in 1859. The occasion was a purely local one:[20] the English bishops had been attacking leading Catholic laity for putting forward a policy on Catholic schools which differed from the bishops' own. Newman had been questioned as to the theological basis of his support for the laity on the issue. In the end the bishop of Birmingham, William Bernard Ullathorne, went to see Newman and asked him to resign his editorship of the journal in which he had defended the laity. In a memo written the day afterwards Newman noted down the gist of their conversation: "He said something like, Who *are* the laity? I answered (not those *words*) that the Church would look foolish without them."[21] Thinking that Newman had asserted that pope and bishops must ask the laity's permission before proceeding to a definition of doctrine, another English bishop chose to bring the matter before the Roman authorities. However, Newman made it clear enough that in his view, the permission of the faithful was not sought, nor even their advice, but the factual state of their belief is and must be taken into account. As he wrote, "Doubtless their advice, their opinion, their judgment on the question of definition is not asked; but the matter of fact, viz. their belief *is* sought for, as a testimony to that apostolical tradition on which alone any doctrine whatsoever can be defined."[22] And Newman placed his remarks within the context of an account of tradition as a theological source:

> I think I am right in saying that the tradition of the apostles, committed to the whole Church, in its various constituents and functions *per modus unius*, manifests itself variously at various times: sometimes by the mouth of the episcopacy, sometimes by the doctors, sometimes by the people, sometimes by liturgies, rites, ceremonies and customs, by events, disputes, movements and all those other phenomena which are comprised under the name of history. It follows that none of these channels of tradition may be treated with disrespect; granting at the same time fully that the gift of discerning, discriminating, defining, promulgating and enforcing any portion of that tradition resides solely in the *ecclesia docens*.[23]

Newman goes on to give three reasons why he has come to lay such weight on the *sensus fidelium* in the finding out of what tradition says. First, in writers before the Council of Nicaea we find consider-

20. V. Blehl, "Newman: the Bishops and *The Rambler*," *Downside Review* 90, 29B (1972) 20–40.

21. Cited by Coulson, *On Consulting the Faithful*, 19.

22. *Ibid.*, 54–55.

23. *Ibid.*, 63.

able vagueness about such vital doctrinal topics as the Trinity and the nature of humanity's justification.[24] Here the sense of the faithful must be invoked as a compensation for the defects in patristic testimony to Catholic teaching. Second, on at least one occasion, the magisterium had appeared to define a point of faith by taking the *sensus fidelium* as the basis for its decision: this was the declaration by Pope Benedict XIII in 1336 that the saints enjoy the vision of God even before the final resurrection.[25] And third, the definition of the immaculate conception had thrown up a number of positive indications. Thus there had been Perrone's influential treatise in which he had spoken of the *sensus Ecclesiae,* the "sense of the Church" as that side of a question to which the Church has more inclined. To find out what this side is, one must follow up *indicia et manifestationes,* "signs and indicators," among which he cited *pastorum ac fidelium in unum conspiratio:* the convergence of pastors and faithful in a particular respect.[26] Then again, there was the language of Pius IX's own letter on the definition, and the bull which actually promulgated it.[27] And last, Newman was able to turn some words of Ullathorne against their author, citing the Benedictine bishop's own tract in defense of the 1853 definition. For there Ullathorne had written: "The more devout the faithful grew, the more devoted they showed themselves towards this mystery. And it is the devout who have the surest instinct in discerning the mysteries of which the Holy Spirit breathes the grace throughout the Church and who, with as sure a tact, reject what is alien from her teaching."[28]

On the basis of such references, then, Newman described the *consensus fidelium* in glowing phrases as a testimony to the fact of the apostolic teaching, an instinct for supernatural truth implanted in Christ's mystical body, a direction of the Holy Spirit, a divine response to the prayer of the Christian people for right faith, a jealousy of error, an instinctive repugnance toward heresy. And so he could conclude,

24. Cf. *Historical Sketches* 1 (2nd ed., London: 1894) 209–10—a passage somewhat curiously situated in an essay entitled "The Future of the Ottomans"; and *The Arians of the Fourth Century* (3rd ed., London: 1871), app. V: "The Orthodoxy of the Body of the Faithful During the Supremacy of Arianism."

25. In the bull *Benedictus Deus: see* on this D. Douie, "John XXII and the Beatific Vision," *Dominican Studies* 3 (1950) 154–74.

26. Perrone, *De immaculato Beatae Virginis Mariae,* 101. It is probable, however, that Perrone considered the case of the immaculate conception to be a uniquely difficult one to settle by appeal to the sources of revelation, and that he did not regard himself as putting forward a principle of general usefulness in Catholic divinity.

27. Pius IX, *Ineffabilis Deus* of 1854.

28. W. B. Ullathorne, *The Immaculate Conception of the Mother of God* (London: 1855) 172.

"Though the laity be but the reflection or echo of the clergy in matters of faith, yet there is something in the *pastorum ac fidelium congregatio* which is not in the pastors alone."[29] After this explanation, Newman was left in peace, though his name for orthodoxy was not fully cleared during what remained of the pontificate of Pius IX. However, it should be noted that the Pope, whom Newman could criticize severely in private correspondence,[30] had it in mind to invite him to the First Vatican Council as a consultor. According to Ullathorne, Newman demurred on the grounds of his health and inability to speak any language other than English.[31] Pius X felt obliged to write a public letter disassociating Newman posthumously from the Modernist theologians with whom his generous view of the making of Christian doctrine had caused him to be identified.[32] His teaching on the infallibility of the laity was, as we have seen, fully vindicated by the Second Vatican Council.

However, to state this teaching is one thing: to show what use it will have for the theological student is quite another. Clearly, taking the voice of the faithful into theological account does not mean that we can just run out to the street and ask any old lady with a rosary passing by for her views on Catholic Christianity. What is in question is the beliefs of the greater part, the *maior pars* of the faithful. But in that case, in an age of referenda, questionnaires, and opinion polls, should it not be possible to establish the beliefs of the *maior pars* of the faithful by such methods? Here again, we need to tread with circumspection. What is at stake is not the counting of heads so much as the weighing of testimonies. What we are concerned with is a *pars* which is *maior* because it is *sanior*, the better-judging and thus weightier part of the Christian people. But how is this *sanior pars* itself to be identified? The nineteenth-century English Catholic authors I have been discussing throw out two hints on this score.

First there is Ullathorne's comment that among the laity it is the devout who have theological primacy, since by their faith, hope, and love they will have penetrated the mysteries of faith more deeply than others. Deciding who are the devout is not itself easy, but clearly it cannot include people who practice their faith irregularly, or people

29. Coulson, *On Consulting the Faithful*, 103–04.

30. *See* I. Ker, "Newman and the Papacy," *Downside Review* 103. 351 (1985) 87–98.

31. C. Butler, *The Life and Times of Bishop Ullathorne* 2 (London: 1926) 46.

32. G. Lease, "Newman: The Roman View," in *Newman and the Modernists*, ed. M. J. Weaver (Lanham, Md. and London: 1985) 161–84.

not sharing the already defined faith of the Church, the already established sense or drift of tradition. Those leading manifestly holy lives, whose love of God is exhibited in efficacious love of neighbor, must be given a fuller hearing. This is why the lives of the saints play a considerable part in the obtaining of the *sensus fidelium*.

Second, Newman has left us a clue in his discussion of the role of the laity in the struggle for Nicene orthodoxy. Newman points out that where the witness borne by the laity entailed suffering, whether loss of property, limb, or life itself, there that witness should be taken the most seriously. It is those whose Christian discipleship is costing, yet who stick by what they believe through thick and thin, who should be most listened to by the theologian concerned to hear the authentic accents of Tradition. This enables us to appreciate the importance traditionally given to the confessions of the martyrs in registering the sense of the faithful. In most situations today, at least in the Western world, laypeople are unlikely to be physically persecuted for their beliefs about faith and morals, but they may undergo more subtle forms of harassment as a result of standing out against general trends in society.

Some would argue that since the Second Vatican Council, a too superficial notion of openness to the world has played havoc with the normal operation of the *sensus fidelium*. The specifically Catholic counterculture, sometimes termed, less flatteringly, a subculture, or, even more rudely, a ghetto, has declined in many places. Though that culture was in some respects too narrow in its human sympathies and even in its grasp of revelation itself, it did help the sense of the faithful to express itself in a relatively pure state. Today, it is difficult to know whether fluctuations in the *sensus fidelium* are the result of the activity of the Holy Spirit, leading the Church into all truth, or the effect of the corrosion of specifically Christian meanings, truths, and values by the spirit of the age—a spirit not unconnected with what the New Testament calls the "prince of this world." But candor about the ebbing fortunes of the Catholic community in a number of its ancient Western strongholds should not be allowed to breed a historical romanticism blind to the analogous difficulties the Church has faced from competing value systems and truth-claims in the past. Gauging the sense of the faithful has always needed human and Christian sensitivity. Nor is the theologian forbidden from attending to the voices of ordinary Christian experience echoing from the past, so as to supplement listening to those of the present.[33] And this is supremely so where

33. Cf. Y. Congar, "L'histoire de l'Eglise: 'Lieu théologique,' " *Concilium* 57 (1970) 75–83.

what we are listening to are the (statistically) extraordinary figures of the saints and martyrs. The theological testimony implicit in their utterances and *vitae* have the strongest evidential value where the sense of the faithful is concerned.[34] To see how such testimonies to experience might be integrated into the theologian's work, it will be useful to consider more expressly the concept of experience itself: for experience is, as I suggested in Chapter 2 of this book, the first of the aids to discernment which theologians have at hand.

34. For the dogmatic basis of such appeal, *see* G. Müller, *Gemeinschaft und Verehrung der Heiligen: Geschichtlich-systematische Grundlegung der Hagiologie* (Freiburg: 1986). Although the genre of hagiography, as shaped in the patristic period by such writers as Jerome, Athanasius, and Sulpicius Severus, was modelled on ancient rhetorical biography and eulogy, the hagiographer, nonetheless, "lived in an expanding Bible. . . . The writer of a saint's life felt that he was adding a new page to the Gospel story," B. Smalley, *The Historian in the Middle Ages* (London: 1974) 63.

Part Five

Aids to Discernment in Theology

17

Experience

Having considered the sources of theology, I now want to turn to aids or helps in the evaluation of these sources. Fundamentally, there are two such aids or helps. One is situated at the subjective pole of ecclesial life, and that is experience. The other belongs at the opposite objective pole, and that is magisterium, the daily teaching activity of bishops and pope. First, then, experience, and right at the outset, What is experience?

It is a strange thing that a concept which of all concepts should surely be the easiest to master, since it stands for what is closest to us, proves in point of fact extremely hard to define. We all talk about our experience, but what are we actually referring to thereby? Fr. Edward Schillebeeckx, O.P., in a discussion of the idea of experience from the theologian's perspective, has offered a reassuringly simple definition: experience is the "ability to assimilate perceptions."[1] The complexity emerges, however, when we ask what is involved in such an assimilation. Beginning from the other key term in the definition, perception, it is implied that in experience we are really confronted with something real and objective, existing independently of ourselves, our views, and attitudes. On the other hand, to speak of assimilating the object of perception implies that we never come at this independently existing reality neat, in a pure or raw form. We take in as much as we can manage of it within the preexisting framework we carry everywhere with us. For the restraints placed upon us by our mental constitution, our language and culture, our individual biographies and mind-sets, cannot simply be waved aside. Thus, experience is both objective and subjective at the same time. It is not wholly subjective, not

1. E. Schillebeeckx, "The Authority of New Experiences and the Authority of the New Testament," in *Christ: The Christian Experience in the Modern World* (English trans., London: 1980) 30–79, and here at 31.

fully determined from the side of the subject. We cannot simply make up our experience as we go along: something is given which we cannot altogether manipulate to suit our fancy. On the other hand, experience is not wholly objective either, not fully determined from the side of the object. We are given a taste of some other reality, but we never encounter it without the intermediary filter of preexisting concepts and language, already established patterns of belief and feeling. Nevertheless, the objective element remains the controlling factor, or what Schillebeeckx calls the "final criterion."[2] We can and do formulate hypotheses about what reality is like on the basis of the subjective-objective ambivalence we call experience, but if our hypotheses are wrong the reality itself will rear up and oppose us. From my experience of oceangoing liners I may come to the conclusion that I can sail my automobile on the North Atlantic. But reality will resist this interpretation in no uncertain fashion.

Thus there are two essential components of experience: on the one hand the interpretative element, what we bring to anything fresh and new, and on the other hand the refractory element, that which comes to us in its novelty, resistant of inappropriate ways in which we might wish to describe it.[3] It is through this refractory element that experience can be said to have its own authority, and so can guide us in our theological activity. If theology is about reality, then it must accept the authority of experience so defined. For to say that experience has authority is only another way of saying that it is a disclosure of reality, of being.[4] But just what should count as an appropriate instance of bowing before the authority of experience is not always obvious: the delicate dialectic of subject and object sees to that. Our first aid to discernment in theology itself requires discerning. Take, for instance, the twentieth-century campaign for the equality of women. Some would judge that in the movement to accord women equal rights with men the authority of reality is showing itself through a shift in the experience of certain women, and in response to them, in the experience of certain men as well. Others would argue that the movement for equal women's rights is yet another product of the ideological imagination, and that the reality of a differentiated human nature is perfectly well

2. *Ibid.*, 34.

3. M. Lefébure, "Schillebeeckx's Anatomy of Experience," *New Blackfriars* 64. 756 (1983) 270–86.

4. Thus a sound theory of experience requires not only a sound epistemology but also a sound metaphysics: *see* F. Alquié, *L'expérience* (Paris: 1957) 1–24.

expressed in the traditional structure of male and female roles. Thus on the one hand there is a claim that certain contemporary experiences are authoritative, and in their light the social mold must be broken and remade. On the other hand, there is a counterclaim that these experiences are not authority bearing but are the projections of conceptual misunderstandings or factual mistakes. The matter is also of theological concern, since a decision one way or the other would directly affect the Church's teaching on the nature of civil society, and indirectly affect, or at least be pertinent to, her teaching on the nature of ecclesial society with its many ministries, sacramental and otherwise. To the extent that the argument depends upon experience, it must appeal in the last analysis to some sort of discernment of spirits.

What forms of experience are relevant to theology? Schematically, we can identify four types or stages of experience which theology should take into account. First, there is the pre-Christian or secular human experience, which creates the need for the Christian religion in the first place. Our experience of the high and low points of human life constitutes most of what leads us to seek out or to persevere in a religious way of life. Were it not for joy and hope, pain and distress and the fear of death, mingled as they are in our daily lives, we might well not bother to find a religion to guide us in a confusing world. Secular experience thus prompts us to turn to religion for insight and illumination and for final redemption.[5] We expect our faith to, as we say, make sense of our experience. Second, there is the experience of conversion, or of the difference there is between what it is to be pre-Christian and what it is to be Christian. In conversion, the life, death, and resurrection of Jesus Christ are experienced as throwing light on my life. The Son of God's involvement in this world is used to interpret my own life and death, triumphs and failures, moral achievements, moral collapses, and recoveries from moral collapse. Here the Christian gospel intersects with my ordinary human experience. From this meeting, my past and present look different from what they did before.[6] Third, there is postconversion experience of life in the Church: an experience of life in faith, of sacramental life, of life within a spe-

5. Secular experience can be thought of as carrying signals of transcendence indicating that the phenomenon of religion will be the source of both healing and enlightenment for the human condition: *see* P. L. Berger, *A Rumour of Angels: Modern Society and the Rediscovery of the Supernatural* (Harmondsworth: 1971) 97–117.

6. For a series of vignettes of Christian conversions *see* A. J. Krailsheimer, *Conversion* (Oxford: 1972).

cific fellowship of persons. We can call this the experience of Christian existence, experience of a new quality of existence ushered in by conversion, which itself provides the Christian reinterpretation of pre-Christian experience.[7] Fourth, there is the mystical experience in which I begin to experience for myself the God who is the source of my faith. Participation in the life of the Church—that is, in the life of faith and of the sacraments of faith—brings within my grasp a direct if obscure contact with God himself, the ultimate reality.[8]

Theologically, we must distinguish here the first of these types or stages of experience from those that succeed it across the watershed of conversion. Notice, however, that although conversion is the beginning of Christian life and so qualifies in a special way all the experience that flows from it, pre-Christian experience despite its name cannot simply be said to stop with our conversion. We all continue to have secular experience even as Christian believers. Such experience, pre-Christian chronologically or logically, may be described as pre-theological yet still of great concern to theology. The reason for this is metaphysical and derives from the fact that God is in all things. Whether we think of our experience of one another, or our experience of nature, or of the events of history, or of such internal states as love, desire, pain, anxiety—in all of these we are engaged in a commerce with being, and so with the source of being, mediated through our experience.[9] By reflecting on our secular experience, either directly or with the help of novels, poetry, drama, film, the visual arts, and the like, or again through conversation with other people, we come to discern more fully the reality that is offering itself to us in our personal depths. And this reality, just because it is reality, must inevitably say something about the God who is "Creator of all things, visible and invisible." Such pre-Christian experience, or postconversion secular experience, is clearly not dependent on revelation as such. Rather, such experience possesses an autonomy of its own, comparable to the autonomy which must be accorded to philosophy. Just as a philosophy cannot be held to be false simply because it is non-Christian, that is, simply on the grounds that it started life outside the Church, so a claim

7. An evocation of ecclesial existence may be found in K. Adam, *The Spirit of Catholicism* (English trans., New York: 1929).

8. For an evaluation of mystical experience as part of the wider life of the Church *see* A. Stolz, *Theologie der Mystik* (Regensburg: 1936).

9. *See* A. Forest, *Consentement et création* (Paris: 1943) 27 for a comparison between metaphysical and mystical experience.

to theologically significant experience cannot be rejected simply on the grounds that the experience in question is extraecclesial in character.

Of course, this is not to say that all claims to theologically significant experience by anybody and everybody ought to be accepted at face value. Neither should any and every philosophy be accepted. There must be evaluation. Yet if God is the font and origin of all being, and if the human mind is open through experience, albeit in a glass darkly, to the being that expresses God, then it would be surprising if pre-Christian and secular experience produced no illumination about divine things. Thus theologians must be prepared to consider the voices of ordinary experience, extraecclesial experience, as among their helpers in the theological task.

But we must turn now to the other three types of experience I mentioned: the experience of conversion or coming to faith, the experience of the life of faith itself within the Church, and within that the deepest level of faith experience—mystical experience, or the experience of conscious communion with Father, Son, and Holy Spirit. Here we pass from a possible experience of God as the ground of the world, as the foundation of ordinary experience, to the experience of the self-revealing God made possible by faith. Schillebeeckx, in the book I cited earlier, speaks of the refractory element in human experience as itself leading us to formulate the concept of revelation. Since reality is given in experience, may it not be in fact a gift? And moreover, a gift from a source that we must think of in basically personal terms?[10] The well-known tendency of reality is sometimes to bring us meaning through our experiences and sometimes to deprive us of such meaning, once again, through our experiences. Meaning, the self-expression of being, comes and goes in such a way that we can never master it. Furthermore, when it does come within our reach, it often seems to address or call us.[11] Thus the experience of meaning tends to persuade us into the use of a personal model in which to construe reality. It is as though what we are doing in life is having a relationship with a personal being who is sometimes eloquent and sometimes silent, but is ever relating to us in our experiences of how reality is meaningful. But if reflection on experience—not on the content of experience so much as what it is to experience—invites us to see all experience as God's (general or natural) revelation, then when we come to speak of Christian revelation itself, God's special or supernatural revelation, the concept of ex-

10. Schillebeeckx, *Christ*, 47.
11. J. Mouroux, *L'expérience chrétienne: Introduction à une théologie* (Paris: 1952) 28.

perience will provide us with a basic framework for understanding what this intensified form of revelation is about. In Schillebeeckx's own words, "Revelation has a structure of experience."[12] Jesus Christ surely experienced his own relationship, one of essential sonship, with the Father, and through that experience came to an understanding of his own person and destiny. The apostles of Jesus Christ experienced their Lord and Master, living, teaching, dying, and rising again, and through that experience came to see what his role in human history was, and what theirs should be on the model of his. Although one might well not wish to follow Schillebeeckx in his somewhat minimalizing account of what the apostolic *memoria Jesu* contained on this experiential basis, the concept itself seems unexpectionable.[13]

For Catholic theology, after the apostles, more precisely with the death of the last apostle, revelation is closed. In terms of Scripture this means that the canon of the New Testament is completed in the moment when the apostolic Church understands herself as the Church of these Scriptures and no other. In terms of Tradition, it means that the *regula fidei* and *institutio christiana* of the Church are constituted in all essentials in the apostolic period, all else being crystallization and reformation, however enterprising. But does this mean that from that point on, experience can provide no elements of novelty to an understanding of specifically Christian revelation? Not at all, says Schillebeeckx. The New Testament literature has only laid down the basic story: there can still be legitimate transformations of this story in the personal experience of those subsequent to the apostles in whose lives Jesus Christ has in some way spoken.[14] Again, one might well not wish to follow Schillebeeckx in his somewhat exclusive stress on the role of story in Scripture—for this could mean to undervalue such factors as teaching, idea, symbol, and image, thus impoverishing an account of the revelation given us in Scripture, read in Tradition. For the Bible communicates revelation through these media also. But one can surely agree that the ancient experiences, registered definitively for us in Scripture and Tradition, do come to life again in the experience of grace in the later Church, being revived in transmuted ways as each generation and individual comes to faith. Thus Christian experience is found

12. Schillebeeckx, *Christ*, 63.

13. For a severe criticism of Schillebeeckx's handling of the relation between revelation and experience in his Christological writings, *see* L. Scheffczyk, "Christology in the Context of Experience: On the Interpretation of Christ by E. Schillebeeckx," *The Thomist* 48, 3 (July 1984) 383–408.

14. Schillebeeckx, "Jesus: The Story of a New Life-style," *Christ*, 19–25.

in an interaction between the time of Christ and his apostles on the one hand and, on the other, the here and now: what is new, different, perhaps unique in our own age and in each of our own lives. The Christian experience born in the tension between these two is an important aid to discernment, therefore, in theology.

Earlier this century, such remarks about the role of Christian experience within theology would have been found exceedingly daring.[15] One interpretation of the Modernist crisis, itself the most important piece of background to the strengths and weaknesses of Catholic theology today, holds that the eye of the storm was a concern for the theological rehabilitation of experience.[16] For such Modernists as Alfred Loisy and George Tyrrell, tradition and its distillation in dogma were precipitates of Christian experience, the original revelatory experience which lay at the origins of the Christian faith.[17] To go all the way with this view, however, is to finish by saying that the teaching of the Church is simply there to provide cues for Christian experience. Whether that teaching has changed heterogeneously, as severe critics of the history of doctrine allege, evolving into something formally incompatible with its original cast, does not matter one whit. The true unity of the history of dogma lies in the divine Spirit himself, impelling people through the ages to an ever-deeper experience of the divine. But since the experiences into which the Spirit draws believers are different—though somehow rooted in the ineffable experience of revelation itself—all that remains constant throughout is the fact of his leading. It was natural and proper that the Modernists should arouse a strong reaction against this excessive privileging of Christian experience over against the witness of Scripture and Tradition, and over against the Church's magisterium as their interpreter. But much of the anti-Modernist response went to an extreme. Revelation was thought of as purely and simply propositions (doubtless it contains some propositions and leads to more); dogma was held to be the defining of these propositions and their logical correlates so they might be held by all believers. Theology itself was deemed to consist in the proving of these defined propositions and the process of concluding to yet other

15. M.-D. Chenu, "Préface," to A. Gardeil, *Le Donné révélé et la théologie* (2nd ed., Paris: 1932) 8.

16. J. Lebreton, "L'encyclique et la théologie moderniste," *Etudes* 113 (1907) 497ff.; D. Dubarle, "Modernisme et expérience religieuse," in *Le Modernisme*, ed. D. Dubarle (Paris: 1980) 181–270.

17. *See* e.g. A. Loisy, *L'évangile et l'Église* (Paris: 1902) 173ff.; *Autour d'un petit livre* (Paris: 1903) 195ff.; G. Tyrrell, *Through Scylla and Charybdis* (London: 1907) 208, 306ff.

propositional candidates for definition.[18] And certainly such factors as theological logic and the desirability of public definition of truths of faith play a major part in the history of doctrine. But at no point in this entire scheme is Christian experience relevant; indeed, the very term could send the strict anti-Modernist spluttering across the room in search of a stiff Scotch.

Such a root-and-branch rejection of all theological appeal to Christian experience was based on three main points. First, if Christian experience means "religious feelings," these are surely secondary and derivative and could never embrace the Christian revelation as a whole.[19] Second, if by Christian experience is implied an assured grasp of the reality of salvation, then this is something explicitly condemned by the Council of Trent: there is no personal certainty of salvation (save perhaps by way of private revelation, an extraordinary act of God).[20] Third, if Christian experience should be understood as mystical experience, then this, though quite legitimate, only concerns a comparatively small number of people and so has nothing to say about Christianity as such.[21] These objections are weighty. The first major attempt to confront them was perhaps the study *L'expérience chrétienne* by Jean Mouroux, a work which, in the context of the French renaissance of Catholic theology before and after the Second World War, set out to vindicate appeal to the concept of experience in the Catholic tradition.[22]

18. For a stout defense of the term "intellectualist" as correctly describing the relation between Catholic dogma and revelation, *see* E. Dublanchy, "Dogme," DTC, IVb (1939) cols. 1574–1650. A rather more nuanced account of the subsidiary relation between such dogma and theology is found in Y. Congar, "Théologie: La conclusion théologique," *Ibid.* (1946) cols. 477–83.

19. One could hardly construct a Christian theology from the reports on Christian experience found in, for example, W. James, *The Varieties of Religious Experience* (New York: 1902).

20. Trent's articles on the nature of justification, together with the canons anathematizing where appropriate the positions of the Reformers are found at DS, 1520–83. On the whole issue, *see* A. Stakemaier, *Das Konzil von Trient über die Heilsgewissheit* (Heidelberg: 1947).

21. Highly relevant here is the controversy between Dominicans and Jesuits (with some outside contributors on either side) in the early years of this century about the universality or otherwise of the call to contemplation. *See* P. Murray, *The Mysticism Debate* (Chicago: 1974).

22. Mouroux, *L'expérience chrétienne,* and especially p. 5. Mouroux's study is notable for its circumspection: the Church has suffered many crises through an overvaluation of various kinds of experiential claim: Protestantism (justification); Jansenism (delectation); quietism (purity of spirit); traditionalism (experience versus reason); Modernism (heart versus brain). Mouroux comments: "Every time that man yields, there arise in the Christian life those crises which, by a redoubtable re-evaluation of feeling, end up

Mouroux argues that the concept of Christian experience is not simply the comparatively uninteresting one of religious feelings.[23] Such feelings play a part in a wider experience, which is one of contact, communion, or copresence with the reality of the triune God in the Church. Distinguishing between the purely empirical realm, that of uncritical experience, "halted or solidified" prematurely; the experimental realm, that of measurable, quantifiable experience; and the truly experiential, namely experience in its personal totality, Mouroux suggests that only the last provides the proper context for speaking of Christian faith experience, since this is a mediation of the infinite personal subject, God, and a series of finite subjects, ourselves. It was, evidently, this holistic sense of experience which the great Scholastics like Thomas and Bonaventure had in mind when they appealed to experiential considerations in their accounts of grace.[24]

Moreover, it is not true to say that the Council of Trent attacked the very notion of such experience. Rather, Trent attacked certain features of the Reformers' ideas about Christian experience. Specifically, what was in view in the Catholic response to Protestantism was the Lutheran *agnitio experimentalis*, the idea that a particular kind of experience of justifying grace is necessary before persons can believe themselves to be in the way of salvation,[25] and also the Calvinist notion that the elect are distinguishable by their grace-given certainty of individual salvation.[26] Against such pictures of faith, it was right and proper for the Church to insist that felt experience does not in itself constitute my subjective hold on the reality of revelation and salvation.[27] Personal Christian experience cannot be, by implication, a sufficient guide to Christian truth. Mouroux suggests that the council rejected a naive empirical (as distinct from fully experiential) doctrine of Christian experience.[28] Rejecting the view that the occurrence of one

by raising experience over against the goal, and oblige the Church to reject with vigor this disastrous 'experientialism'. . . . But this tireless resurgence of the selfsame claim witnesses clearly enough to the reality of a problem ceaselessly reborn and each time massacred."

23. *Ibid.*, 49–51.

24. On Luther, one might consult his *Freedom of the Christian Man* (1520), translated in *Martin Luther: Selections from His Writings,* ed. J. Dillenberger (New York: 1961) 42–85, and especially 66–67. Relevant here is J. Pelikan, *Spirit Versus Structure: Luther and the Institutions of the Church* (London: 1968).

25. On Calvin, *see* his *Christianae religionis institutio* I. 8. 1; III. 2; III. 13; III. 21 and 24.

26. Trent, *Decretum de justificatione* 9, DS, 1533.

27. Mouroux, *L'expérience chrétienne*, 46.

28. *Ibid.*, 46–47.

particular feeling forms the heart of that experience, Trent offered a much richer account of the proper structure of a supernaturalized life: a life lived under grace in faith, hope, and love, a more complex and subtle picture, then, of what Christian experience entails. Presenting the justification experience (though without the word *experimentia* or its cognates) in a more nuanced way than had the Reformers, it sees a relationship with two poles. One pole is that of an absolute confidence in the goodness and mercy of God, mediated to us through Christ via the sacraments of the Church. The other is a fearful recognition of our own weakness, the permanent possibility that we may reject this goodness and mercy. Thus the Catholic experience of justification would consist in an unconditional trust in the help of God, but within this trust, a genuine fear of separating oneself from God, leading to a conscious effort of union with God in prayer and penance.[29]

The theme of justification is central here because it was central to the controversies of the Reformation period. But Trent's approach can be generalized to other areas. Fundamentally, the council was affirming two things. First, the Catholic Christian as an experiencing subject is never separate from the life of the Church. He or she is nourished experientially by this life, which consists in a celebration of faith and of the sacraments of faith together with all those who coparticipate in such celebration. Second, the Christian, nourished in this way, is also directly open to the transcendent God. The Church mediates God by immediating him, by making him (through his own Word and grace) immediately present to each of her members.[30]

The final objection to the idea of a Christian experience which we should consider in Mouroux's company is that which would reduce it to the quantitatively insignificant terrain of the outstanding mystical experiences of the greatest contemplative saints.[31] But the special graces of union with God enjoyed by a John of the Cross or a Thérèse of Lisieux are a matter of especially intense or privileged moments in the development of a life of grace, which in itself is something common to all the baptized. The mystical experience, in its highest states or conditions, is not a radically different experience from the Chris-

---

29. *Ibid.*, 47.

30. The presupposition of such otherwise outstanding studies as A. Poulain, *Des Graces d'oraison* (Paris: 1901) introduction.

31. In just this way, however, giving mystical experience its dignity as a *locus theologicus* which brings to a climax the witness of Christian experience at large. *See* M. L. Gondel, ''La mystique est-elle un lieu théologique?'' *Nouvelle revue théologique* 108. 5 (1986) 666–84.

tian experience at large. Rather, it is a prolongation of that experience, which makes it purer, deeper, and more self-aware.[32] All Christian mysticism is founded in baptism, where our life begins again in the divine covenant and we participate in Christ's sonship, having God for our real Father and the Holy Spirit, the ultimate and plenary gift of God, as our own possession. Every believer, simply on the basis of the faith of his or her baptism, is, therefore, a primitive or inchoate mystic.

And so for all these reasons suggested by Mouroux, Christian revelation can be registered in subjective experience. Grace modifies the heart and mind, the imagination and the feelings, so that the believing person becomes to some extent a transcription of revelation itself. To the extent that I have faith, hope, and charity, the subjectivity engaged in what I call my experience is affected by revelation. As a result, when I come to reflect on my experience, I can find in it an aid to the discernment of revealed truth as found in revelation's sources, Scripture and Tradition. To this extent, my experience of the Christian reality provides me with a key to interpreting the Christian sources. And not just me, but anyone, who, by the grace of God, also believes in the Father's sending of his Son and his Holy Spirit to effect the redemption and transfiguration of the world. It may occur to me here that other people, whose experience is marked in some way by revelation, lead very different lives from mine. Thus it comes about that theology can be distinctive inasmuch as it is produced out of distinctive human situations. The leader of a Latin American *communidad de base* will naturally have his own aid to theological discernment in the Christian experience of the poor and marginalized in Central or South America; just as a Christian *sannyasi* in a Catholic monastic ashram in India will have his, and a friar teaching in a pontifical University his. And needless to say, a woman's experience of the Christian reality will not coincide with that of a man. However, we should not think of these humanly very different aids to discernment operating in splendid isolation from each other, and that for two reasons. First, although I can only have my experience and not your experience or the experience of some third party, nevertheless by sympathy, *Einfühlung*, I can have some understanding of another's experience and its significance as an aid to discernment. Here we encounter again a theme we touched on when considering the habit of theology at the outset of this book. There we saw how necessary historical or diachronic, ''across time,'' sym-

32. Mouroux, *L'expérience chrétienne*, 54–56.

pathy is for a student of a religion with a historical revelation. Here
we now see how necessary geographical or synchronic, "in the same
time," sympathy is for the student of a religion where a weird and
wonderful variety of experiencing subjects in a great diversity of human
situations are all practicing Catholic theology. This is why such things
as Latin American, Asian, and African theology are of value, and indeed, by the same token, Roman theology.[33] Second, this collection
of experiencing subjects is not just a random collection of people but
the Church: the people of God, the body of Christ, the communion
of the Holy Spirit, as an ordered or structured unity with its hierarchical organs founded, like the community they serve, by Jesus Christ.
What is the implication of this for the appeal to experience? Though
I am directly open to God by nature and by grace and so by the grace-
filled history in which nature is caught up in human living, nevertheless the reality of divine revelation and salvation does not come to me
explicitly except as a member of Christ's historic Church. I can never
appeal to Christian experience against that Church in order to deny
its common faith or disparage its common life. To appeal away from
the Church would be to cut off the branch on which I am sitting, to
cut myself off from the source of the experience I am claiming, to commit epistemological suicide. Experience is only an aid to discernment;
it is not itself the living source of enlightenment in Christian theology. Only Scripture and Tradition understood by the norms of the
Church herself can bring us to that source.

It is time to turn then to the second of our helps in considering
the fonts of revelation, namely, the magisterium of episcopate and
papacy. For of the two aids, the magisterium carries the greater responsibility. Whereas Jesus promised that he and his Spirit would dwell
among his disciples until the world's end, he also said that in the
apostolic college, among the Twelve and their successors, he and his
Spirit would not simply be present but be present as teachers of the
truth.[34] We must not, however, imagine that experience and magisterium are competing forces in theology—although this is how they are
often presented nowadays in the communications media. It is possible,

33. B. Chenu, *Théologies chrétiennes des tiers mondes* (Paris: 1987); P. Rosato, "Perché
studiare teologia a Roma?" in *Problemi e prospettive di teologia dogmatica*, ed. K. Neufeld
(Brescia: 1983) 495–520.

34. *See* on this J. Fitzmyer, "The Office of Teaching in the Christian Church According to the New Testament," in *Teaching Authority and Infallibility in the Church*, ed. P.
C. Empie, T. A. Murphy, and J. A. Burgess (Minneapolis: 1978).

as T. S. Eliot noted, to have the experience but miss the meaning.[35] The magisterium is there to ensure that, so far as possible, the Church and each person within it will not misconstrue their experience of divine salvation.

35. T. S. Eliot, "The Dry Salvages," *Four Quartets* (London: 1944, 1970) 39.

The Magisterium

In this chapter, then, we shall consider the second of these aids to discernment, the contemporary magisterium—an aid which is as public and objective as the first, experience, is personal and subjective. In Part 4 of this book, we have already seen how Tradition includes such monuments as councils and conciliar creeds and definitions. The apostolic deposit—the residue of the process of revelation up to the death of the last apostle—was, we found, both guarded and transmitted by "apostolic men," and passed thereafter, by general consent, into the care of the episcopate. Solemn declarations of the content of that apostolic deposit are, we noted, made by the episcopate in council or, more recently, through the pope as head of the episcopal college, and they come to us in the form of creeds and dogmatic definitions. Such creeds and definitions are not simply aids in the discernment of Tradition. They are Tradition, for they are monuments, that is, embodiments of Tradition. But, in addition to this special and relatively rare episcopal and papal activity of doctrinal defining, we must also come to terms with the fact that all the time, Sunday by Sunday and day by day, bishops and pope are teaching Christian doctrine. Although they may not be declaring solemnly in a high and festive manner what Tradition is and contains, they are nonetheless engaged in giving the faithful guidance as to the meaning of the Christian faith and the shape of the Christian life. Such everyday teaching is referred to in current parlance as the "activity of the ordinary magisterium."[1]

The bearers of this magisterium are the pastors of the Church who, because they succeed the apostles in overall responsibility for the Church, must of necessity have overall responsibility for the *faith* of

---

1. F. A. Sullivan, "The Non-definitive Exercise of Papal and Conciliar Teaching Authority," *Magisterium: Teaching Authority in the Catholic Church* (Dublin: 1983) 157–73. I am much indebted to this fine study, and to personal conversation with its author.

the Church. In times of crisis, or where a special pastoral solicitude urges, this responsibility for the apostolic faith is expressed in the making of solemn judgments about Christian truth. But at other times, which may still be filled with tension though not on the scale of, say, the Arian struggle or the revolt of the Protestant Reformers, the bishops and the pope continue to exercise their guardianship of faith and morals in other ways.

In the first place, there is that day-to-day teaching, which, despite its quotidian character, is intended to be held definitively by the whole Church, since no shadow of doubt falls across its luminous transparency. The objectivity of the redemption, the intrinsic evil of murder—these truths of faith and morals exemplify the assertion that most of the infallible teaching found in Catholicism is delivered by the ordinary magisterium on the foundation of the Creed and of the moral imperatives contained in Scripture and the traditions. But by no means does all the everyday teaching activity of pope and bishops fall into this category. There is also nondefinitive teaching, and we must now ask how the theologian stands in relation to this second form of episcopal and papal magisterium.[2]

Contemporary writers offer, broadly speaking, four ways of relating theologians to the ordinary magisterium (in this latter sense of nondefinitive teaching activity, which will be the sense presumed in what follows). The first presentation of that relationship regards theologians as characteristic *Christifideles*, typical members of Christ's faithful. The second sees them, rather, as servants of the magisterium. The third—in sharpest possible contrast to the second—considers them to be the unique possessors of the office of strictly doctrinal teaching within the Christian fold. The fourth, finally, locates the theologians' distinctive work within the context of those varied charisms that Church pastors are meant to channel and integrate, as well as respect and foster, for the good of Christ's ecclesial body at large. We must now review, and evaluate, each of these ways in turn.

The first way holds that theologians are related to the magisterium in just the same manner as are the faithful in general. And what manner might that be? According to the dogmatic constitution of the Sec-

---

2. *See* the useful document of the (pontifical) International Theological Commission, "Rationes magisterii cum theologia," available in *Enchiridion Vaticanum* 5 (10th ed., Bologna: 1979) 1310–25. An English translation is given in C. E. Curran and R. A. McCormick, *The Magisterium and Morality: Readings in Moral Theology* 3 (New York: 1982) 151–70, and a commentary in Sullivan, *Magisterium*, 174–218.

ond Vatican Council on the Church, the generality of the faithful should show to the bearers of the magisterium a "religious allegiance," *obsequium,* "of will and of mind." The same document, *Lumen gentium,* goes on to affirm that this is preeminently so in the case of the magisterium of the bishop of Rome. The judgments made by the pope are to be "sincerely adhered to, according to his manifest mind and will."[3] On the surface, these statements seem to say that the attitude of Catholic Christians should be identical with their attitude to that supremely authoritative expression of Tradition that we find in creeds and dogmatic definitions. And yet the teaching of the ordinary magisterium, whether offered by the pope or by the voices of the bishops *cum et sub Petro,* when these are not proposing some tenet as true in definitive fashion, cannot—by definition!—be called the very last word. Indeed, the Second Vatican Council itself considerably modified certain elements in the ordinary papal teaching (faithfully echoed by the wider episcopate) of the last hundred years. One might think here of Leo XIII's insistence on the duty of a Catholic state to deter Protestant evangelism—at any rate, without explicit qualification; or of Pius XI's root-and-branch condemnation of the ecumenical movement—at least as then existing; or of Pius XII's affirmation that the mystical body of Christ on earth is coterminous with the (Roman) Catholic Church—rather than, as preferred by the council, subsisting in that Church, that is, uniquely but not exhaustively identical with it.

Historically, therefore, the ordinary magisterium has been found in need of corrective supplement on certain points—though ultimately that supplement has been provided, we should note, by the selfsame episcopal college with the pope as its head. Yet if the magisterium has sometimes been found wanting in its claim to have sufficient certitude in teaching as to constitute for all the faithful a reliable guide in all aspects of faith and morals, how can it subsequently have the nerve to require from them, in such exigent language, religious allegiance to its judgments? (The translation "respect," sometimes met with, is much too weak as an Englishing of *obsequium,* though my own usage implicitly suggests that its chief rival, "submission," is correspondingly too strong.)[4] Surely the principle "once bitten, twice shy" should

---

3. *Lumen gentium* 25. On the interpretation of this passage *see* K. Rahner, "The Dispute About the Church's Teaching Office," *Theological Investigations* 14 (English trans., London: 1976) 85.

4. Sullivan, *Magisterium,* 172; R. Ombres, "The New Profession of Faith and Oath," *Priests and People* (1989) 341–42.

apply not only in individual experience but in Church-historical experience too.

The answer to this is that Catholic Christian faith in the guidance of the Church by the Holy Spirit justifies our confidence in the general reliability of the ordinary magisterium, even though we cannot deny *a priori* that some particular aspect of its teaching may eventually be perceived as needing mulching or pruning, cultivation or cutting back.[5] Furthermore, the teaching of the ordinary magisterium on this topic or that may well be, short of the parousia of the Lord, the closest we can come to a grasp of God's revelation in some one or more of its aspects.

From these considerations there derives the duty of Catholics to make a sincere, sustained effort to give *ex animo* assent to the teachings of the ordinary magisterium—teachings that are always more likely to be right than not. However, in a given case, they may find that, nonetheless, they are not convinced. Not only do they have difficulties with the teaching (the occurrence of difficulties would not in itself abrogate the duty of *obsequium*). More than this, they find themselves in a state of moral certitude on some point in a manner that could not leave the magisterial teaching intact. Such persons may not be "un-Churched." Having done all that they were capable of doing for the achieving of faithful assent, they have fulfilled their ecclesial obligation of obedience. The Church can ask no more of them in the internal forum.

This leaves as yet untouched, however, the issue of external or public dissent, whose legitimacy is a good deal more disputable. For public dissent from the ordinary magisterium involves values touching the common good of the Church, and not simply the conscience of the individual believer. Such dissent can undermine the welfare of the Church by polarizing the Church's members, diminishing charity among the faithful, and damaging or even destroying belief in the apostolic origin of episcopate and papacy. Yet one could hardly say that in the every case the risk of such consequences renders silence preferable to those truth-values that might emerge from the public criticism of bishops or pope in their nondefinitive teaching activity. Experience, and not least that of the postconciliar period in Catholicism, indicates nonetheless that where public dissent takes on an organized form, its effect on the common life of the Church is always deleterious

5. Sullivan, *Magisterium*, 201-2.

and embittering, which is why such theologians as Congar have felt
it incumbent on them to propose guidelines for the limitation of open
dissent in the assembly.[6] Moreover, it must be remembered that in such
disputed questions, what Church doctrine should be is something only
arrived at by a refinement of magisterial teaching, through a process
of development where continuity of underlying principle can be shown.

On this first approach to our problem, then, the theologian is, in
effect, lumped together with the rest of the faithful and required to
give religious allegiance to the teachings of the ordinary magisterium
just as the faithful are, and in exactly the same mode. While the possibility of internal, or even in some circumstances, external dissent from
such teaching cannot be ruled out, confidence in the Holy Spirit's gifts
to those who sit in the apostles' seats will (super) naturally predispose
the theologian to accept the general trustworthiness of the ordinary
magisterium and to be guided by it in interpretation of Scripture and
the traditions.

The trouble with this way of putting things is that it hardly does
justice to the distinctive place of the theologian among the faithful.
In Part 1 of this book, I described the theologian as carrying out a ministry in the Church, an ecclesial service directed to others and exercised
on their behalf. Indeed, one could speak of the theologian as possessed
of a vocational charism to the work which he or she has undertaken.
And surely, then, the pope and the bishops have a duty to recognize
this charism, as others, and not simply to reduce it to the lowest common denominator of Christian living among the people of God.[7] I will
return to this suggestion in connection with the fourth way, discussed
below. But meanwhile we must give some attention to a second view,
which would deny outright the premise on which it is based and de-
mote the theologian to the level of a (mere) servant or functionary of
the Church hierarchy.

For a second way of relating the theologian to the magisterium
would be to regard theological activity as a direct derivative from the
ordinary magisterium. On this view, the theologian would be even less
justified than the average *Christifidelis* in dissenting. During the pontificate of Pius XII, this seemed at times to be the officially sanctioned
view. Theologians, it was said, are mandated specifically and exclusively by the bishops and the pope, and, as servants of episcopate and
papacy, are wholly subordinate to their direction.

6. Y. M.-J. Congar, *Vraie et fausse réforme dans l'Eglise* (2nd ed., Paris: 1969).
7. *See* ch. 1 of this book.

Besides the legitimate successors of the apostles, namely the Roman pontiff for the universal Church and the bishops for the faithful entrusted to their care, there are no other teachers by divine right in the Church of Christ. However, the bishops, and in particular he who is the supreme teacher in the Church and the Vicar of Christ on earth, in fulfilling their task as teachers, can enlist other persons as helpers and advisors, to whom they confer authority to teach. . . . Those who are thus called to teach work as teachers in the Church not in their own name, nor by title of their theological scholarship, but by virtue of the mission which they have received from the legitimate magisterium.[8]

Clearly, what is involved here is not simply the theologians' confidence in the general reliability of the magisterium, leading to a presumption that it will usefully guide their survey of Scripture and Tradition. More than this, the theologian is described as essentially the delegate and official of that magisterium. Linked with this is the notion, especially dear to Pius XII—as in the previous century, to Pius IX—that the theologian's highest task lies in proving the present teachings of the magisterium from the evidence of the ancient sources.[9]

What are we to make of this second presentation of the relations between theologians and the teaching office of the pastors of the Church? First of all, let us note that its historical foundations are not of the securest.[10] In the New Testament Church there were, alongside the ministry of the apostles, other "teachers," or *didaskaloi*.[11] Admittedly, we know next to nothing about their activities, but it can reasonably be presumed that theirs was a service of teaching which went on *pari passu* with the authoritative preaching of the apostles and in agreement with it. While, to be sure, the later language of "divine right" is not used for the standing of these *didaskaloi*, Paul, in his First

8. Pius XII, "Si diligis," *Acta Apostolicae Sedis* 46 (1954) 314.

9. The so-called regressive method: *see* for Pius IX, "Inter gravissimas" (1862) *Acta Pii IX* (Rome: 1854–78), I. 5. 260; for Pius XII, *Humani generis* (1950) at DS, 3886. W. Kasper has traced the origins of the regressive method to the eighteenth century. In the 1771 *Theologia Wirceburgensis* (the work of the Jesuits of Würzburg), the Church's magisterium is already presented as the proximate norm of faith, rendering Scripture and Tradition simply remote norms. *See* his *Die Lehre von der Tradition in der römischen Schule* (Freiburg: 1962) 40–47. *See also* M. Seckler, "Die Theologie als kirchliche Wissenschaft nach Piux XII und Paul VI," *Theologische Quartal-Schrift* 149 (1969) 209–34.

10. On the history of the relation between theologians and the magisterium *see* M. Seckler, "Kirchliches Lehramt und theologische Wissenschaft," in *Die Theologie und das Lehramt*, ed. W. Kern (Freiburg: 1982) 17–62; and Y. Congar, "Pour une histoire sémantique du terme *magisterium*," *Revue des sciences philosophiques et théologiques* 60 (1976) 85–98, and "Bref histoire des formes du 'magistère' et ses relations avec les docteurs," 99–112.

11. *See* 1 Corinthians 12:28; cf. Romans 12:7; Ephesians 4:11; Acts 13:1.

Letter to the Corinthians, speaks about their ministry as a divinely given charism—a gift of the Spirit to the Church, and not, therefore, a derivation from the apostolate. In the patristic Church, we find theologians referred to, on occasion, as *didaskaloi*, for instance by Clement of Alexandria, thus suggesting that what those New Testament figures did in the apostolic age at any rate resembled what theologians were doing in the post-apostolic period.[12]

In the patristic Church, most theologians were bishops anyway. So for the first seven centuries of the Church's existence, the problem of the interrelation of bishops and theologians was hardly acute. In the medieval Church, where very few bishops were theologians (or even preachers—hence the rise of the Dominicans as an alternative *ordo praedicatorum*, a title earlier given to the episcopate), the problem did arise, but it was not handled along the lines proposed by Pius XII. In the thirteenth century, Thomas spoke of two kinds of authoritative teaching in the Church. These were, first, the "teaching of the pastoral chair," *magisterium cathedrae pastoralis*, exercised by the bishops, and, second, the "teaching of the masters' chair," *magisterium cathedrae magistralis*, carried out by masters or doctors—in other words, by theologians.[13] In Thomas' age, indeed, doctors of theology acquired consummate prestige, examining for heresy in something of the way the Holy Office of the Inquisition would do in later times. Intellectuals enjoyed an exalted position in medieval society, whose documents speak at times of three authorities: "empire," "episcopate," "studium."[14]

Between the fourteenth century and the Council of Trent it was, by and large, university theology faculties that censured works of the-

---

12. In the Greek Church, the title *didaskalos* was still in use as late as the reign of Alexius I Comnenus (1081–1118) for those commissioned to preach in place of the Byzantine patriarch: E. Herman, "The Secular Church," in *The Byzantine Empire, Part 2: Government, Church and Civilization*, ed. J. M. Hussey (Cambridge: 1967) 130.

13. For Thomas, *see Quodlibetales quaestiones* III. 9 ad iii; *Contra impugnatores religionis* 2 and 3; for his cognate distinction between the *officium praelationis* as preaching and the *officium magisterii*, the teaching in the schools, *see In Sent.* IV. d. 67, q, 2, a 2, sol, 2. Presumably a distinction of this kind underlies Thomas Becket's reference in the previous century to *episcopi et caeteri doctores ecclesiae*, Letter 179; PL, 190, 652A. We should note, however, that while teaching in the schools presupposed professional qualifications, the *licentia docendi* which sanctioned it conferred an authority. *See* G. Post, "Alexander III, the Licentia Docendi and the Rise of the Universities," in *Anniversary Essays in Mediaeval History for C. H. Haskins* (Boston: 1929) 255–78; and for the wider medieval context, R. Guelluy, "La place des théologiens dans l'Eglise et la société médiévale," *Miscellanea historica A. de Meyer* (Leuven: 1946) 571–89.

14. *See* H. Grundmann, "*Sacerdotium, Regnum, Studium.* Zur Wertung der Wissenschaft im 13 Jahrhundert," *Archiv für Kulturgeschichte* 34 (1951–52) 5–21.

ology or issued warnings about their less admirable features to the faithful. In the later Middle Ages, the university doctors could ride roughshod over the role of the bishops.[15] The Council of Constance, for instance, was dominated by the university faculties, while at the Council of Basle (papally recognized in its early sessions) three hundred doctors with voting rights confronted a miserable seven bishops.[16] At Trent itself, a more reasonable relationship between bishops and theologians was obtained. Before a question was put to the bishops, it was discussed in congregations of theologians, whose conclusions were then offered to the (real) conciliar Fathers for acceptance, rejection, or modification.[17]

Only in the years after the French Revolution and the Napoleonic Wars could the Pian picture of the theologian as the hired servant of the apostolic ministry become remotely credible. For the closure or destruction of so many Catholic faculties—the sites of the *cathedrae magistrales*—during that turbulent period in European history rendered episcopal and papal encroachment on the ecclesial space of theologians something of a cruel necessity. Predictably, then, we find that the idea of an episcopal and papal mandate, a "canonical mission," for the theologian is of nineteenth-century vintage. It was introduced by the German bishops after the 1815 Congress of Vienna as a way of maintaining the Catholic character of the revived theological faculties in the (sometimes Protestant, and always state-dominated) universities of the fledgling German Confederation. Adopted by the papacy, the concept of the canonical mission is found among the canons of the 1917 *Codex Iuris Canonici*, but in a purely negative sense: a theologian was presumed to possess it unless there was a declaration to the contrary. In the Latin Church's revived *Codex* of 1983, there is talk of a (cognate) ecclesial *mandatum* as something positively prerequisite. What this means is as yet not fully clear, but in all likelihood it will function in the same merely negative fashion as in the earlier code. The papacy's introduction of a profession of faith and an oath of fidelity for theologians teaching in specifically Catholic institutions in the spring of 1989

15. Even so radical a papalist as Agostino Trionfo thought that a heretical pope might be judged by a council to which masters and scholars would be convoked. *See* Y. Congar, *L'Eglise: De Saint Augustin à l'époque moderne* (Paris: 1970) 243.

16. Pierre d'Ailly, chancellor of the University of Paris from 1389 to 1395, took a high view of the Doctors of Constance: Mansi, 27, 561. But for his opportunism, *see* A. Emmen, "Peter of Ailly," NCE 11, p. 208.

17. H. Lennerz, "De congregationibus theologorum in Concilio Tridentino," *Gregorianum* 26 (1945) 7–21.

will doubtless also be treated in the same way. These instruments may be thought of as pointing up the theoretical implications of the structure of Catholic belief, and the practical consequences of life in a Church patterned as a communion, rather than as tools for the restoration of the Pian portrait of the relation between theologian and magisterium described above. Even the cursory account of the historical realization of that relationship offered here may show the point of a remark by Congar, who asks of Pius XII's version, "Is this consonant with what nineteen centuries of the Church's life tell us about the function of the *didaskalos* or doctor?" And he answers his own question with becoming modesty, "No, not exactly."[18]

And just as theologians have not been thought of, traditionally, as simply deriving their project from the magisterium, so their work, theology, has not usually been considered as aimed solely at the backing up of the magisterium's pronouncements. As Ratzinger pointed out in his commentary on *Dei verbum*, the dogmatic constitution of the Second Vatican Council on divine revelation, "To reduce the task of theology to the proof of the presence of the statements of the teaching office in the sources is to threaten the primacy of those sources, and were one to continue logically in this direction would ultimately destroy the serving character of the teaching office."[19] For that office is precisely to serve the word of God, and not to judge it, in the sense of exalting itself above it. It is reported that some bishops and curialists at that council wished to insert into the document Pius XII's notion that the norm of the theologians' activity, their "proximate and universal norm of faith," must be the ordinary magisterium. But the phrase occurs nowhere in the final text. Instead, in *Dei verbum* 23–24 we read, in accordance, I hope, with the approach of this book: "Sacred theology rests on the written Word of God, together with sacred Tradition, as its primary and perpetual foundation, and is carried out under the watchful eye of the magisterium, *sub vigilanti magisterii.*"[20] That final phrase replaced a much stronger draft alternative: *sub ductu magisterii,* "under the magisterium's guidance."

It is the nemesis of ecclesiastical extremism that it breeds its own counterimage in iconoclasm and revolt. And so it is here with the third

---

18. Congar, "Pour une histoire sémantique du terme 'magisterium,' " 109.

19. J. Ratzinger, "Dogmatic Constitution on Divine Revelation: Chapter II," in *Commentary on the Documents of Vatican II*, 3, ed. H. Vorgrimler (English trans., New York: 1969) 197.

20. *Dei verbum* 23–24.

way of relating the theologian to the magisterium which we should consider. Hans Küng has proposed that the episcopate's role in the Church should be conceived as simply that of pastoral direction together with preaching, but not as one of teaching in the strict doctrinal sense, at all.[21] The Church's teaching office, in his view, belongs exclusively to theologians. Küng's theory depends upon an inflated reading of the status of *didaskaloi* in the primitive Church, together with the assumption that the medieval magisterium of professors was regarded by contemporaries as genuinely determinative of doctrine.

But this is hardly so. In historical fact, the characteristic approach adopted by the medievals distinguished between, on the one hand, theological exposition—a matter for the scholars and doctors—and, on the other, the deciding of disputed points of doctrine which might arise from such theological exposition. For the latter, knowledge was, certainly, required, but even more necessary was jurisdiction—the Christ-given authority to determine what the faith of the Church is. What this involved may be seen from the writings of Gratian, the Camaldolese monk who figured centrally in the revival of legal studies in twelfth-century Bologna. Producing as he did a collection of all the known canons of his time, which he attempted to set forth in accordance with sound jurisprudential principles, Gratian was naturally obliged to confront the question of the relative weight to be given to his various authorities. In his *Concordance of the Discordant Canons*, distinction 20, he considers the comparative authority of the papal office vis-à-vis the learned people of past and present. Should the expositors of sacred Scripture—in modern terms, exegetes and theologians—be preferred to papal decretals—in modern terms, the Roman magisterium's articulation of Christian believing, in faith and morals, on behalf of the episcopal college as a whole? Gratian replies that apparently the theologians ought to be preferred, for the greater authority would seem to lie with those who have the most learning and the best arguments. But he goes on to point out that the deciding of cases, the resolving of disputed questions in Christian doctrine, is not the same thing as the expounding of the sacred page. In disagreements about the substance of Christian believing, decisive authority is located in the power of the keys, given to Peter by Christ the Lord himself.

The Church—or so we may gloss Gratian's text—can scarcely be said to have received the apostolic revelation if the apostolic ministry,

---

21. H. Küng, *Infallible? An Enquiry* (English trans., London: 1971).

summed up in the Petrine office of the Roman bishop, lacks the means
to establish what the apostolic faith is in some particular regard. In
wider historical perspective, the episcopate of the second century was
already well aware of its duties in this respect.[22] In the early decades
of the third century, the bishops took steps to protect the consistency
and continuity of Christian belief over against individual theological
figures deemed to have departed in some way from the *regula fidei* of
the Church: here the fate of Paul of Samosata may stand as emblematic.
The ecumenical councils, from First Nicaea to the First Vaticanum, also
took steps to arraign those theologians whom they regarded as devi-
ant, from Arius to Anton Günther, whether living or dead. The popes,
acting on their self-understanding as epitomes of the episcopate, followed their lead. In not all of these transactions was justice done—
much less seen to be done. One thinks with profound regret of the
treatment of Jan Hus at the Council of Constance, or of Galileo Galilei's
second trial, in 1638, before the Holy Office of his erstwhile friend Pope
Urban VIII. Yet, as Newman wrote in *The Arians of the Fourth Century*,
whether the duty of defining doctrine (and so of drawing the boundaries of orthodoxy and heresy) be done well, or be done badly, it is
the duty of the episcopate to do it, in fear and trembling.

No doubt Küng's views on the relations of theologians and
magisterium are psychologically explicable as his personal reaction to
the papacy of Pius XII, just as the latter's views and actions are perfectly intelligible as a response of the papal memory to the humiliations
of the popes of the Enlightenment and the Revolution at the hands
of temporal rulers aided and abetted by Gallican and Febronian
theologians—for example, conciliarism, an attempt to marginalize the
place of the Petrine officeholder in the life of the people of God.

But—and here we touch on the fourth and last view of this interrelationship to be discussed here, and the one I shall myself endorse—
one can maintain perfectly sturdily the independent origin of the theological vocation in the gifts scattered by the Holy Spirit through the
body of Christ, while also asserting that in the final analysis, appraisal
of how a particular theologian has used those gifts vis-à-vis the faith
of the Church rests with the bearers of the hierarchical magisterium.
The institutional charism of the hierarchy, bestowed with a view to
ensuring the continued mission of the Church as the sacramental organism of the divine covenant, necessarily takes priority over the voca-

22. H. J. Ryan, ''Considering Dissent from the Perspective of History,'' *New Oxford
Review* 54 (January–February 1989) 5–8.

tional charism of the theologian, which is received for the enrichment and upbuilding of that corporate reality. *Esse,* the basic being of the Church (inseparable from the integrity of the Church's faith, and hence her doctrine) is more fundamental than *bene esse,* attempts to construe how we should promote the Church's flourishing (not to be disconnected from the intellectual exploration of her fundamental beliefs). Put in another way: since the charism of the hierarchy is for the ordering of all other charisms in the common life of Christ's people, it must needs be superordinate when compared with the charism of the theologian, which is simply one among many. Yet, by the same token, the hierarchy must reverence the theological charism, since it can neither absorb that charism into itself nor substitute for it.

Although this ordering of charisms by bishops and pope is a matter of discipline, it has implications not only for the realm of the good but for that of the true also. As we have seen, in disputed questions a doctrinal debate is finally settled only by those who, through episcopal consecration, are rendered not simply guardians of the faith but its judges too. And this is not merely a matter of the pastoral or "regal" office of the bishops, an issue of Church discipline to be spoken of in the language of power. It is, further, an exercise of their teaching of prophetic office, and, as such, enters into the very texture of Catholic thinking as an intrinsic element in theological epistemology itself.

In a time of tension—amounting, on occasion, to open warfare—between theologians and the magisterium, it is easy to give the impression that competition, not collaboration, is the natural state of affairs. But supernaturally, this is not naturally so. Magisterium and theologians share a common service to Christian truth, bound as they are by the word of God in Scripture and Tradition.

More positively, then, how can magisterium and theologians help each other? The magisterium, by fulfilling its own functions, aids the theologian to identify the content of revelation—through the efforts of the bearers of magisterium to maintain the unitary consistency of Christian faith—and to preserve the historic continuity of the faith today with the faith of all preceding Catholic generations and, ultimately, of the apostles themselves. Similarly, theologians are called on to assist the magisterium, providing, in the words of Paul VI, "the help which the magisterium needs in order to fulfill its mission as light and norm for the Church." Theologians can give the magisterium deepened insight into Christian truth; they can also help it to communicate its message to the rest of the Church, and to the world.

Theologians need to remember that they are essentially *viri evan-gelici:* men and women of the Church, not monstrous hybrids, half ec-clesial, half mundane, occupying some limbo between the street (or, more likely, the university common room) and the sanctuary. Nor are they a profession or trade union within the Church. Nor, yet again, is it enough for them to define themselves by reference to some seg-ment of the Church rather than by the whole *Catholica*—which includes the faithful departed. Church officers, for their part, need to recall the not so distant sins, or at least blunders, of their predecessors, and to practice with graciousness and courtesy the tact, sensitivity, and con-sideration which that memory should inspire.

In this chapter, then, we have considered the issue of theology and the magisterium somewhat theoretically, outlining what ought to be their interrelationship in some abstraction from the actual theolo-gies that the magisterium is called upon to appreciate and, where neces-sary, to judge. In the final part of this book, I propose to offer an outline history of what, in the concrete, Catholic theology has been in its fas-cinating diversity and also, one hopes, in its ultimate unity.

Part Six
Plurality and Unity in Catholic Theology

19

Soundings in Theological History

In this chapter I aim to give a rough-and-ready account of the principal historical tendencies in Catholic theology so that in the next chapter, when we come to look at how plurality and unity fit together in theology, we shall have some idea at any rate of what it is, in the concrete, that we are talking about. And to begin with, a couple of preliminary notes of caution.

The first caveat concerns the fact that we are accustomed to a conventional idea of what a theologian is, based on our modern Western experience. The way of life of the theologian, we feel, consists in reading and writing books and articles on the basis of well-stocked libraries, and with the help of a formal training in the various theological disciplines that currently exist. Theologians work for sizeable institutions, generally universities, whether secular or Catholic. They give lectures, preside over seminars, and, in the more civilized reaches of the academic world, hold tutorials. They travel long distances to take part in international conferences—thinly disguised holidays where they meet other theologians identical in lifestyle to themselves. But of course all these presuppositions about what kind of animal the theologian is depend in fact on particular historical developments within theology. They depend on the conversion of theologians into academics, on the acceptance of specialization in theology, and on the adoption of a quasi-scientific model of what theology might be. However we assess the value of these developments (and to dismiss them would be as much of a sin against theological catholicity as to canonize them), the fact is that this picture of the theologian begins to evaporate as soon as we look back into the history of the subject. Very schematically, we can say that in the New Testament period, theology is the attempt of apostles and evangelists to express the difference Jesus Christ has made to the world, and especially to the Jewish world. In the patristic Church, theology is typically what a bishop says from his *cathedra* in his basilica. In the early medieval period, theology is what a monk writes in the foundation of his *lectio divina*. In the High Middle Ages it is what a Scholastic master propounds in giving a rationally coherent interpretation of Scripture and the Creed.

The second warning note has to do with the notion that the word "theology" has meant the same thing whenever it has cropped up on the written page. On this view, even if, *pace* our first caveat, the ambience, lifestyles, and practical aims of the practitioners of theology have differed, theology itself remains reassuringly a constant. When the word appears, we know we are back on home ground. Thus *theologia* would always mean the kind of thing that goes on in the St. Thomas University in Rome where I am writing these pages, or in the analogous institutions whose members may one day be reading them. But of course the word "theology" is not a Christian word, as we recognize when we so often qualify it: "Christian" or "Catholic (Christian)" theology. It took awhile for the word to be baptized, and even longer for it to acquire the denotation (reference) and connotations (associations) it has today.

The origins of the word *theologia* lie in the pre-Christian Hellenic world.[1] In Plato it means an ordered account of the word of the gods, and is used as such in the *Republic* during one of Plato's demythologizing attacks on the Greek poets.[2] For Aristotle, "theology" is the bit of philosophy which explains the cosmos in terms of an unmoved mover.[3] Neither of these uses of the word would necessarily have prejudiced early Christians against it, but harder to swallow was its role in describing the polytheistic civil cultus of the gods of Greece and Rome. The first known Christian use of the term comes in the second-century Alexandrian writer Clement, whose somewhat ambivalent attitude to his pagan *Umwelt* has been summed up by Prof. Henry Chadwick in the phrase "the liberal puritan."[4] For Clement, theology means primarily that knowledge of divine things possessed by pagan sages: such men as Orpheus, the legendary or at least semilegendary figure

---

1. F. Kattenbusch, *Die Entstehung einer christlichen Theologie. Zur Geschichte Ausdrücke "theologia," "theologein," "theologos"* (2nd ed., Darmstadt: 1962); Y. M.-J. Congar, "Théologie," DTC XVA, cols. 341–43; *A History of Theology* (English trans., New York: 1968) 26–28.

2. Plato, *Republic*, 379A.

3. Aristotle, *Metaphysics*, XI. 1. 1025 a. 19; 1026 a. 19–22.

4. H. Chadwick, *Early Christian Thought and the Classical Tradition: Studies in Justin, Clement and Origen* (London: 1966) 31–65.

behind the Orphic tradition in Greek religious thought, and the poets Homer and Hesiod.[5] Although Clement suspected that the ancient Greeks had pinched their knowledge of the divine from the Hebrew prophets and decked it out in the borrowed clothes of symbolism and allegory, it was nevertheless the pagan—or at any rate general—understanding of God which he termed "theology."[6] So as yet the idea of Christian theology has not emerged under that label: only the idea of (not wholly untrue) pagan or natural theology as entertained by a Christian—which is a rather different thing. With Origen, Clement's successor in the school of Alexandria, we find the beginnings of a specifically Christian use of the term. While Origen is willing to speak of Greek or Persian writers who dealt with the divine as "theologians,"[7] he possesses as well a properly Christian sense of the word. Thus *theologein,* to "theologize," is in particular to recognize and confess God in Jesus Christ.[8] Origen's career was at its height in the 230s, but it was another eighty years or thereabouts before we come across a writer who uses the word "theology" exclusively of an activity to do with Christian believing.

This writer was Eusebius of Caesarea, the counsellor of Constantine the Great, a disciple (at one remove) of Origen and the finest historian in the early Church. In the prologue of his Church *History,* Eusebius remarks that the history he is to describe is no ordinary history.[9] It transcends the humanly possible, since it records what God has done historically and thus what can be known of him by theology. Eusebius is the first Christian writer to accord the evangelist John the title *ho theologos* since his book is the place par excellence in which to find the true, that is the Christian, understanding of God.[10] Here the term has emerged from the baptismal waters of a linguistic conversion. From this time on, we can safely assume that it will always denote some aspect of the specifically Christian knowledge of God; some aspect, but authors were not agreed on which. Many of the Greek Fathers work with a distinction between *theologia* as the doctrine of God in himself, in his own inner Trinitarian life, what would now be called the doctrine of the immanent or absolute Trinity, and *oikonomia*

---

5. Clement, *Stromateis,* V. 8.
6. *Ibid.,* V. 4.
7. Origen, *Contra Celsum,* VI, 18.
8. Origen, *Commentarium in Joannem,* I. 24; II. 34.
9. Eusebius, *Historia ecclesiastica,* I. 1, 7.
10. Eusebius, *De ecclesiastica theologia,* I. 20; II. 12.

as the study of God's coming forth from his inner mystery in self-communication through the sending of the Son and the Holy Spirit.[11] The basic idea is that any theology worthy of the name should be about God in himself, not about God in relation to us. The economy is taken up with God's plan of salvation, seen as the happy design of the Master of history. God administers history to make sure that ultimately it tends to the happiness of humankind, just as the head of a household, an *oikonomos*, governs house and family with their temporal happiness in view. But the knowledge of God's happy design for history is not in itself the knowledge of God, though it leads to it. *Theologia* concerns God in himself—what in Scholasticism would be termed the treatises *De Deo uno* and *De Deo trino*—rather than the study of the mystery of Christ, the atonement or resurrection, the Church or grace even though it is only by way of these latter realities that in the *ordo cognoscendi*, as distinct from the *ordo essendi*, we rise up into union with the triune Lord. On the other hand, for more mystically inclined theologians in the Greek tradition, people like Evagrius of Pontus in the fourth century or Maximus the Confessor in the seventh, *theologia* is not, strictly speaking, a form of study at all.[12] Rather, it is the experiential knowledge of God arrived at when the Christian reaches the highest condition of prayer union that is possible in this world. So here "theology" means union with God made possible by Christian revelation rather than the study of that revelation.

This is a particularly maverick though not uninformative application of the word. But the diversity of use which we have seen among the Greeks is faithfully reflected if we now turn to the Latins. Whereas a number of the Latin Doctors—Cyprian, Ambrose, Gregory the Great—evince no interest in the word, Augustine necessarily confronts it because of his analysis in the *City of God* of the Roman civil cultus where the term was quite at home.[13] Augustine stresses the etymology of "theology," remarking that a true "discourse about God" would naturally lead people to Christianity. Accurate talk of God would prepare people to receive the faith of the Church.[14] What he has in mind, it seems, is a philosophy that can act as a propaedeutic to the recep-

---

11. F. Lakner, "Das zentrale Objekt der Theologie," *Zeitschrift für katholische Theologie* 62 (1938).

12. For Evagrius, *see* ps.-Basil, Ep. 8; for Maximus, PG, 90, cols. 1083 onwards. Cf. D. M. Rothenhäusler, "La doctrine de la *theologia* chez Diadoque de Photiké" *Irénikon* (1937) 536–53.

13. Augustine, *De civitate Dei*, VI. 8.

14. *Ibid.*, VIII 1–2.

tion of revelation: the kind of thing we looked at in Part 2 of this book. For Augustine, that propaedeutic theology can only be Platonism. It might be thought that Augustine's usage would have survived in the Scholastics since he was far and away the greatest single influence on medieval Western theology. But no: in the early Scholastics we discover the same distinction between a theology of God in himself and an account of the economy, the saving activity, as we noted among certain of the Greek Fathers and, classically, Athanasius.[15] Although the word *oikonomia* is replaced by a good Latin equivalent, such as Peter Abelard's *beneficia*, God's "good deeds,"[16] the early medievals knew enough of the Greek tradition to take their cue from it. Among the High Scholastics, and notably Thomas, "theology" appears to mean any linguistic transmission of the content of Christian revelation. This explains why in the opening question of the *Summa theologiae* Thomas uses what are to us very different expressions as though they were interchangeable: *theologia* itself; *sacra doctrina*, "the holy teaching"; *sacra Scriptura*, "Holy Scripture"; *sacra eruditio*, "sacred learning"; *sacra pagina*, "the sacred page."[17] All of these are arrangements of language through which we appropriate the First Truth by faith, and so tend to God as our last end.

So theology has meant, historically, a good many diverse things. Sometimes the word "theology" has stood for a reality quite distinct from what we would now call theology, as with Clement of Alexandria. At other times, what we would now call theology is going on under a different name (perhaps *gnosis*, or *sacra doctrina*), or maybe under no particular name at all. Again, the word "theology" can denote a wider range of reference than we would now be likely to accept, as with Thomas; or yet again, a narrower range than we would think helpful, as with Athanasius. But one might ask, what's in a name? A rose by any other name would smell as sweet. True, but the variety of linguistic usage does point, at least, to the variety that has existed historically in activity that is recognizably theology—however it was named. And this historical variety, or pluralism, of theology reflects the many different situations in which theology has been written in the history of the Church. What happens, then, to our original definition of theology as the "disciplined exploration of what is contained in revelation"? Should it not be abandoned as too self-consciously mod-

---

15. Cf. Eriugena, *Periphysicon* II. 30; *Homilies on the Prologue of the Gospel of John* 14.

16. Abelard, *Introductio in Theologiam*, PL, 178, 986D.

17. Cf. Lateran IV, *Constitutio* II: "to teach about the sacred page." And in general J. Ghellinck, *Le Mouvement théologique du XIVe siècle* (2nd ed., Paris: 1946) 92.

ern? Can it embrace writers as different as Paul, Augustine, Bernard, Thomas, Bellarmine, Newman, Rahner, von Balthasar? I still believe that the definition does identify successfully the central core of what we would call theology in every period, no matter what the period may itself have called it. As a definition it is sufficiently modestly equipped to be able to travel light, and so travel far across cultures. It is capable of exemplification in a vast variety of ways. Our job now is to look at some of these different ways in which theology so defined has been conducted in the principal epochs of the Church's life.

Theology in the New Testament Period

The first Christian theologians are the New Testament authors themselves.[18] Take, for example, the four evangelists. In the ancient Church there was some sense of the difference of the Fourth Gospel from the other three, the "spiritual Gospel," as Clement of Alexandria called it; but people had little awareness of the internal theological differentiation of Matthew, Mark, and Luke. More recently, with the massive development of New Testament research, we can speak with confidence about Matthaean, Marcan, and Lucan theology as well as about "John the Theologian." There are two basic ways of sensing the distinctiveness of the gospel writers. One, and this was always open to anybody, is in terms of the literary impression made by each Gospel, if we take a Gospel as a piece of literature, a finished text. What themes does it seem to convey, and how does it treat them? The other approach is the more difficult and complex one of full-scale historical-critical analysis. On this second approach, it is at the stage of redaction-criticism that we can identify the theological particularities of Matthew, Mark, Luke, and John. In other words, we can compare what they say with the tradition about Jesus Christ, first, as springing up from Jesus himself, his words and his deeds and, second, as found, in dependence on those words and deeds of Jesus, in a given community of the post-resurrection period where the apostolic faith had taken root. There are problems about the methodology of all this, some of which we noted in Part 3, but the results seem fairly satisfactory.

To the careful reader, each Gospel does put a different slant on Christ, and so on its entire presentation of the Christian mystery. It

18. E. Käsemann, "Die Anfänge urchristlicher Theologie," Zeitschrift für Theologie und Kirche (1960) 162–85.

is to express that slant that the new methods are set to work. In the case of the Gospel of John, analogous possibilities exist. Contemporary exegetes assure us that the gospel writer had some awareness of the Synoptic tradition, as well as access, doubtless via the Beloved Disciple himself, to a distinct stream of non-Synoptic material about the Lord. So here too we can ask, Why has the writer presented his materials in a given way? The answer we get confirms rather more scientifically our general impression of Johannine thought from reflecting on the literary themes of the Fourth Gospel.

Before commenting further on how the evangelists can really be called theologians, let me try to sum up the essential theology—the Christology—of each Gospel in a single sentence. This will not do justice to the Gospels, but it may keep us from floating off in total abstraction. In this way we can say:

> 1. The theology of Mark is that Jesus as the Son of Man, or the designated divine mediator, could only fulfill his destiny through suffering in which his disciples must expect to follow him.
> 2. The theology of Matthew is that Jesus as Messiah fulfills the Law by reexpressing it in the new code of his kingdom, which his disciples are to take to the ends of the earth.
> 3. The theology of Luke is that Jesus, as the king who was to come, enters by his ascension on his reign over human history; the saving efficacy of this reign is found in the foundation and miraculous spread of the Church in the (Lucan) Acts of the Apostles.
> 4. The theology of John is that Jesus as the preexistent Word entered human history in order to bring transcendent truth to those living in sin and error; rejected by his own, his exaltation on the cross was his return to the Father in which he promised his disciples would join him.

Now in what sense are these Matthaean, Marcan, Lucan, and Johannine approaches to Jesus theology? Certainly, they cannot be called theology if in fact they already formed part of the actual teaching of Jesus himself. If Jesus spoke about himself in exactly the way St. Mark spoke of Jesus (and this cannot be ruled out *a priori*), then St. Mark was not a theologian but rather a transcriber. Why may we not say that if St. Mark simply reflected the articulated self-awareness of Jesus, he expressed Jesus' *theology* (and so not his own)? It is unacceptable to call Jesus a theologian, since the human mind of Jesus is the actual site, or *locus*, of revelation. It is the unique point where God is immediately and intelligibly transparent to this world. The contents of the mind of Jesus and their expression should not be called theology because theology is the exploration of revelation, and not revelation itself. Only what is not already contained in the message and work of Jesus may be termed Christian theology. This may sound slightly paradoxical, but there is no way around it for those who share the faith of the Church in Jesus Christ as the God-man. It follows that it is insofar as as Matthew, Mark, Luke, and John put an interpretation on the words of Jesus and the events of his life, death, and resurrection, an interpretation not given immediately and explicitly in those words and events, that they can be called theologians.

Right at the start of the history of theology we are given an important insight into the deepest essence of what theology is. We might suppose that if theology is to bring us to the heart of Christianity, then it would seek to lay bare the originating events and language in which the revelation through Christ took place, stripping away all later accretions. If we regard the New Testament witness to Jesus as a painting which has been touched up and worked over at various junctures, the theologian's task would be to get down beneath the later overpaintings to the original image. This is how Hans Küng in the Christological section of his *On Being a Christian* treats the New Testament and, *a fortiori*, later Christian tradition. But we know from our study of Scripture and Tradition as sources for theology in Parts 3 and 4 of this book that this metaphor of the overpainted artwork is completely misleading. It is the finished biblical picture of Jesus that is the inspired and inerrant portrait: a portrait only to be appreciated fully within the context of Tradition, the life of the Church. So we are faced with the following dilemma: on the one hand, the theology of the evangelists is by definition what is not explicitly there in the life and teaching of Jesus Christ; on the other hand, only this theology, taken in its ensemble, is able to give us an authentic portrait of Jesus Christ in his divine and human significance. We can, however, resolve this dilemma by an appeal to what may be called the epistemological implications of the incarnation, throwing light as we do so on the value for us of the study of theological history.

The incarnation means that the infinite God entered the finite realm of history. The Creator, while not ceasing to be the Creator, became one of his own creatures. Part of what is meant by saying that God is infinite or that he transcends his creation is that his intrinsic significance, what his being means in itself, cannot be expressed by us in language drawn from this world. Part of what is meant by saying that we as creatures are finite, and so nontranscendent, is that in prin-

ciple our intrinsic significance can be expressed for each other's benefit. The perfect biography may not have been written, but it is not a
conceptual impossibility. In the incarnation, a finite reality, the man
Jesus, is assumed or taken up by the Logos, the divine person of the
Word, in such a way that this man Jesus *is* the Word incarnate living
in history. This means that an inexhaustible significance, namely that
of God himself, is to be expressed through what is normally only a
carrier of limited, exhaustible significance, namely, a human being.
Thus in this one case, a finite being contains and expresses an infinite
significance. There is a dimension to him that is inexhaustibly profound. It follows from this that Jesus could not have expressed himself in words or actions during his lifetime in a way that did full justice
to his own mystery as the Word incarnate, and as the divine-human
mediator, the Savior. The evangelists present us with four ways of reading the significance of Jesus, which bring out certain vital aspects of
that mystery. Jesus himself may well not have brought them out, but
they were there to be brought out. Thus, if we are to use analogies
drawn from aesthetics, we must say that revelation as given in Christ
is like a masterwork which cannot be taken in at a single glance by
one spectator or summed up in a single piece of art criticism. The only
hope of even beginning to do it justice lies in putting together the insights of many spectators or the art criticism of many sympathetic
critics. This is what is happening in the four Gospels.

Of course, any view of the New Testament which regards the theological creativity of the apostolic Church as weightier than the individual religious creativity of Jesus is incredible. We would have to ask,
What touched off this corporate outburst of creativity? And then at
once we are back with the personal creativity of Christ himself.[19] So
such a theory would defeat itself. But we can distinguish here between
two differing kinds of interpretation of Jesus within the New Testament corpus. First, there could be an interpretation whose expressive
elements were new though founded on genuine insight into Christ's
person and work; an example might be when John calls Jesus the
"Logos." Second, there might be a type of interpretation which consists in a selection and rearrangement of expressive elements that go
back to Jesus himself: for instance, when Mark has Jesus refer to himself as the Son of Man. But even here, we should note that a selective

19. H. Riesenfeld, *The Gospel Tradition and Its Beginnings: A Study in the Limits of "Formgeschichte"* (Oxford: 1957).

rearrangement is not the same as the original: it creates a new perspective in which some features are heightened and others fall back into shadow.

What I have been saying here about the Gospels may also be said, *mutatis mutandis*, about the rest of the New Testament. Essentially, the rest of the New Testament consists in three types of documents. To begin with, we have a theological reading of the early experience of the primitive Church: namely, the Acts of the Apostles. Then we have a series of letters from various hands, written to particular Churches or to the body of the Church at large and dealing with various problematic situations that have arisen. Finally, we have a theological interpretation of an aspect of the experience and problematic of the Church which most closely echoed that of Jesus himself: namely, martrydom. This we find in the closing book of the canon, the Apocalypse of John. In each of these texts there is an element which is purely given, and an element which is novel and theologically interpretative. The element given can take two forms. Either, if the text is basically didactic in character rather than descriptive, the given will be the apostolic *kerygma*, the fundamental confession of the early Church about God in Christ. Thus, the apostolic preaching is presupposed by Paul in the Letter to the Romans, and his creative theology in that letter consists in variations upon its themes, drawing out further implications, making fresh applications. Or, if the text is principally descriptive rather than didactic, the given will be providential events in the Church's story. So, for instance, the historical objectivity of certain happenings and their place in a divine scheme is presumed by the author of the Acts of the Apostles. His theological creativity consists in the way he presents those events, unpacking the meaning of their assumed providential quality. And once again, because the apostolic *kerygma* and the foundational experience of the apostolic Church are divinely given realities, they share in that same mystery and depth which attached to the being of Jesus himself. They require and impel a gradual theological unfolding through reflection and interpretation. Although, in the theology found within the canon, we believe this process of unfolding to be inspired, nevertheless, later theology within the Church, which is not inspired, retains a basic affinity to what is going on in the production of the New Testament corpus, both as to its materials and as to its aims.

Within the New Testament, then, we find the taking up of a variety of perspectives on what divine revelation or divine Providence has communicated.[20] The concrete totality of the New Testament message depends upon this succession of viewpoints, insightful looking from ever-different vantage points with widely differing aims, all ordered, however, to the penetration of the same realities. This discovery gives us our basic orientation for turning now to a consideration of the development of theology in the postapostolic Church.

Theology in the Patristic Period

We have seen so far that the earliest theology consists in interpretative reactions to the mystery of Jesus Christ, or interpretative applications of the apostolic preaching, or again, interpretative readings of experience, and especially experience of mission and martyrdom, in the apostolic Church. In moving into the patristic period, we sense at once a change of atmosphere in theology bringing with it new genres of theological writing. Basically, patristic theology tends toward a more doctrinal elaboration of Christian believing. In place of writing under the pressure of revelation itself, with the mystery of God in Christ flooding the Church through his Spirit as a reality directly before one, engaging one, theology now becomes—as Père Congar has put it—reflection on a world where these realities are central rather than a direct presentation of them in felt experience. It may be helpful to think of this in terms of two orders of reflection, one primary and the other secondary and dependent upon it.

Christian revelation is not in the first place a matter of propositions but of a new personal presence and relationship of God through Christ to humanity. New Testament theology aims at the communication of that presence and relationship, in their essence and their most immediate implications, for human salvation. In this sense New Testament theology deals in a primary order of reflection on the Christ event. We can compare it to one's immediate reactions to some overwhelming human event such as the outbreak of war, or of peace; a death, or a birth; or first love. In the patristic age, we are moving into a second order of reflection. Theology is reflecting on that primary or immediate reflection which is the New Testament. It is looking back, taking stock and asking itself what sort of a world this must be if its central realities are God, Christ, the Spirit, the Church, as the first fruits of the kingdom. Revelation is becoming doctrine. Theology may still

20. For a judicious statement of New Testament diversity, and its limits, *see* R. E. Brown, *The Churches the Apostles Left Behind* (London: 1984) 147–48.

be highly personal; an Ignatius of Antioch, an Augustine of Hippo, are as personally engaged in their writing as is John or Paul. But what they are engaged by is life in a world whose true structure is mediated by the faith of the Church. This tendency to the systematic elaboration of a belief structure (more marked, certainly, in some writers than others) is what gives patristic theology its main differentiating quality vis-à-vis the New Testament.

Two factors were especially important in this development. First, there was the need to come to terms with pagan culture and, in particular, with pagan philosophy. Although Judaism had attracted a certain number of converts in the Greco-Roman world, chiefly because of its ethical qualities, which appealed to high-minded people, it was not really a universal religion. According to Christ's mandate, however Christianity was, it had to be preached to all people in all cultures, from all intellectual backgrounds. For this reason it was obliged to come to terms with the claims of classical philosophy, dominant in the culture of its main area of missionary operation, to be an instrument of truth. Paul had told his Corinthian correspondents that the gospel of Christ crucified was folly to the Greeks, while the folly of God was wiser than the wisdom of people. This was a fine piece of rhetoric in the best Greek manner, but something more than this had to be said if the Church were to evaluate the assertions of Greek philosophy about such matters as God, the soul, the good life, immortality, the nature of the cosmos, and so forth. In such writers as Justin, Athenagoras, Clement of Alexandria, Origen, the Cappadocians, and Augustine, we find a serious encounter between the gospel on the one hand and classical culture and philosophy on the other. It is from the shock of their meeting that rational Christian theology takes its rise. By this is meant a theology which explicitly considers the relationship between Christian faith and the general patterns of human reason, at least as conceived in the ancient world.

Although Tertullian enquired what Athens had to do with Jerusalem, the same second-century African Christian could recognize in less combative moods that the Church simply had to work out a reasoned account of its faith in the God of Christian tradition. The first Latin Christian writer to attempt to do so on the grand scale was Marius Victorinus in the fourth century, whose very difficult writings left some mark on the young Augustine in his own working out of a synthesis between the gospel and Neoplatonism. But in the Greek East, this program for a rational theology to speak to the classical world was taken up much more quickly and with more conviction. Probably the reason why theology took off more rapidly at the Greek-speaking end of the Mediterranean Basin was that there the population was in general better educated, itself a consequence of its largely urban setting. While not every Hellenistic man or woman was a philosopher, philosophy was the principal academic subject of the period, and every cultivated person had some grounding in it. The kind of classical philosophy most often presupposed in Greek Christian theology is not the toughest academic philosophy of the time but a kind of commonplace mainstream philosophy which was an amalgam of Stoic ethics, Platonist metaphysics, and a smattering of Aristotelean logic. But this does not mean that the Christian theologians themselves were all second-rate minds. Some, such as Origen, could bring out intellectual weaponry at least the equal of their finest pagan counterparts. The Hellenistic or—since arguably Greek thought was the clearest discovery of reason to date—the rational interpretation of the gospel was being born.

The desire to interpret revelation in rationally accessible Hellenistic categories was so great in the patristic period that some unfriendly critics have spoken of a wholesale Hellenization of the gospel in these authors. By this they do not simply mean that the Fathers theologized revelation in terms drawn from Greek thought, but that in so doing they betrayed the very gospel they set out to serve. The most massively erudite statement of this point of view is found in the German Lutheran historian of early Christianity, Adolf von Harnack.[21] According to Harnack, the original teaching of Jesus on the merciful love of the Father for every soul, and the consequent love commandment laid on humanity, was lost to view in the metaphysical speculations of patristic thought. In the 1960s this assessment enjoyed a certain modest revival among some Catholic writers, notably the Canadian Leslie Dewart.[22] However, three points may appropriately be made by way of reply. First, unless we are going to say that only biblical categories may be used for the expression of biblical truth, then the patristic program is justified. When an essentially Semitic gospel encountered the Hellenistic world, it had to express itself in categories that could be understood by those who belonged to that world. Patristic theology was the first major exercise in indigenization and *aggiornamento* of the

---

21. A. von Harnack, *Das Wesen des Christentums* (Berlin: 1900); English trans.: *The Essence of Christianity* (London: 1901).

22. L. Dewart, *The Future of Belief* (New York: 1966).

kind desiderated by Pope John XXIII at the Second Vatican Council and summed up in the crucial notion that while the substance of the primitive doctrine must remain unchanged, its formulation may differ widely from place to place and age to age. Second, the picture of the original gospel or of original revelation as found in antipatristic writers can itself be shown to be tributary to certain aspects of a nineteenth- or twentieth-century world-view: for instance, in Harnack, the presupposition that ethics and personal relationships of an ethical brand are the most important part of religion. Third, patristic theology is not an outright capitulation to Hellenism but a dialectic or conversation with Hellenism in which some things are accepted as a vehicle for Christian truth and others are not. Thus, for instance, in Justin Martyr we find a theologian who can speak in classical accents of Jesus as a philosopher who taught the way to happiness by embodying right reason in his own person; yet the same Justin also affirms that Christ as the "power of the Father" spoke with the authority of God himself, thus transcending the order of the naturally knowable, sealing his testimony with miracles, with the amazing fulfillment of ancient prophecy, with his resurrection, and with the rapid extension of the gospel around the world. On the basis of these signs, Justin insists, we can rightly believe what would otherwise be wildly improbable, namely that a crucified man is Son of the supreme God and Judge of all humankind. As the Russian Orthodox historian of theology John Meyendorff has written, with particular reference to the world of the Greek fathers: "Greek patristic thought remained open to Greek philosophical problematics, but avoided being imprisoned in Hellenic philosophical systems. From Gregory of Nazianzus in the fourth century to Gregory Palamas in the fourteenth, the representatives of the Orthodox tradition all express their conviction that heresies are based upon the uncritical absorption of pagan Greek philosophy into Christian thought."[23] And while admitting that some major figures of early Christian literature, namely Origen, Nemesius of Emesa, and the Pseudo-Denys, present systems of thought which could be defined as Christian versions of Greek philosophy, Meyendorff points out that for others, equally systematic, such as Gregory of Nyssa and Maximus the Confessor, their philosophical mentality was so opposed to pagan Hellenism on such issues as creation and freedom that charges of excessive or distorting Hellenization of the gospel at their hands can-

23. J. Meyendorff, *Byzantine Theology* (New York and London: 1974) 24–25.

not possibly be sustained. Nevertheless, from the encounter of the gospel with classical reason there emerged two major theological genres, which were novel when compared with the work of the New Testament writers. These were the apologia and the dialogue—the dialogue, that is, with pagan philosophy.

So much for philosophy as a spur to theology in the patristic age. But there was a second major factor underlying the development of theology in this period, and that was the ideal of the gnostic, the man who knows. Roughly speaking, the gnostic was someone who did not simply believe on the authority of others but turned his belief into conscious understanding and direct experience. One of the great problems that faced the early Church was Gnosticism, which must be carefully distinguished from the idea of gnosis although it is connected with it as well. As early as Paul's letters to Corinth we hear of people who say that they know it all and so have no need of the apostle's teaching. Such people claimed not only intellectual comprehension of revelation but also what would now be termed "mystical experience" of such a kind that they were in a different bracket from the ordinary Christian believer, the person in the first-century pew.[24] In the course of the next two centuries, a fully fledged Gnostic religion, rather than simply Christian heresy, grew out of such groups. To sum it up, it taught that certain human souls have a divine spark; that this divine spark derives from the fact that God himself has undergone some kind of internal dissolution in a struggle with evil; that the Savior, Christ, has come into the world to recall these special souls to the unity of the Godhead.

To sensitive souls in the early Church, those who felt they were not like the common herd, Gnosticism, or radicalized gnosis, did two things. First, it provided a systematic theory to explain the human sense of alienation from the world and of nostalgia for another world. Second, it held out the hope of a conscious identification with the Godhead through spiritual exercises and study of the elaborate Gnostic teaching, half science, half mythology. The Gnostics worked with a threefold division of mankind into *pneumatikoi*, "the spiritual ones," i.e., themselves; *psychikoi*, "the ensouled ones," whom they identified with the great mass of ordinary believers in the Christian Church, and finally *sômatikoi*, those who thought only, like Papageno in *The Magic Flute*, of satisfying their natural appetites. While Gnosticism was

24. J. Dupont, *La connaissance religieuse dans les épîtres de saint Paul* (Louvain: 1949).

attacked both by the Fathers and by certain pagan philosophers like Plotinus, the Church accepted that at one level the Gnostics had a point.[25] They were surely right in saying that the simple acceptance of the gospel by faith was only a beginning. People should go on to understand their faith from inside, to develop themselves intellectually and spiritually as believers. They should expect to experience the reality which the gospel conveys. In other words, the Church's response to the Gnostics was to repudiate Gnosticism but to accept the ideal of the Christian gnostic, the person who develops his or her faith intellectually and spiritually. And quite clearly, the acceptance of gnosis as an ideal meant a commitment to theology because without theology, gnosis, knowledge, understanding, is impossible.

Thus, in a figure like Clement of Alexandria, we can observe a patristic theologian who does not simply wish to rebut paganism where it differs from the gospel, as Justin did. Rather, we have someone who wants to grow via theology into greater union with God. Mature and thoughtful Christians, says Clement, will seek for deeper understanding than that contained in the elementary outlines of the catechetical instruction. They will penetrate beyond the letter of Scripture to its inward spiritual meaning. This is the way of the true gnostic, on a ladder ascending from faith through understanding to the vision of God, which awaits us after this life. For Clement, the Father himself is beyond our understanding, and we can only say of him what he is not: here the so-called *via negativa* makes one of its first appearances in Christian thought. But the Father is revealed in his Son, who is the alpha and omega of the Christian knowledge of God, and we ourselves can come to know the Son by an intellectual and contemplative reappropriation of the revelation found in the Church's rule of faith.[26] Owing, in part, to the widespread Gnostic concern with experience, then, the Fathers evolved three further new theological genres: the treatise on prayer, the exposition or commentary on Scripture, and the catechetical exposition or commentary on the Church's rule of faith.

A third general feature of the late antique world which affected the development of patristic theology was rhetoric. If the philosophers were concerned with sheer intellectuality, and the Gnostics with religious sensibility, the focus of the rhetoricians was culture, and, above all, culture's highest instrument, language. The orator had succeeded

25. L. Bouyer, "Gnosis: Le sens orthodoxe de l'expression jusqu'aux pères alexandrins," *Journal of Theological Studies* 4 (1953) 188–206.

26. W. Völker, *Der wahre Gnostiker nach Clemens von Alexandrien* (Berlin: 1952).

the poet and rhapsode as sustainer of the virtues of the polis, but with the disappearance of the Greek city-state, such oratory, highly developed in its forms and figures, was increasingly ordered to the preservation of a cultural rather than political tradition. Although rhetoric could degenerate into the mere manipulation of stylistic tricks, it could also be the vehicle of a rich, humane culture, of which a training in the rhetorical schools was the crown. Though Church leaders frequently affected to despise pagan letters, they soon found themselves obliged to present Christianity as not only a higher philosophy but a higher eloquence as well. Otherwise, they would have condemned the Church to permanent exclusion from the high culture of the time. And so a Christian rhetoric emerges as the vehicle of theological persuasion in doctrine and discipline. Its two most common genres were the oration and the letter.

The fourth century is the high point in the appearance of such theological forms: Gregory Nazianzen's *Theological Orations* is perhaps our best example of the first of these rhetorical genres, while his letters were "carefully polished to be little gems of language."[27] In his oration on his friend Basil, Gregory implicitly defends his use of these vehicles for theology by attacking Christians who are anticulture and make boorishness a virtue. But this was not just a matter of staying inside the cultural elite. For Gregory, *logos*, the use of language, is the most fitting offering there can be to a God who is himself Logos, the Word. As he put it in his festal oration on Pentecost, though different people have different ways of keeping a festival, "to the worshipper of the Word, a discourse seems best."[28] Christian rhetoric was an offering of sacred eloquence, and by teaching others about doctrine and morals, it honored God and served him.

In the light of all this activity, it is not surprising to find that the patristic age produced, alongside rational apologias for Christianity and dialogues with philosophically minded interlocutors, besides treatises on prayer and expositions of biblical or catechetical themes, some early general statements of what theology is. Of these the two principal examples are Origen's *Peri archôn*, "On First Principles," sometimes referred to as the first piece of systematic theology ever written, and Augustine's *De doctrina Christiana*, "On Christian Teaching," a guidebook to the interpretation of Scripture. These two texts represent very

---

27. R. R. Ruether, *Gregory of Nazianzus: Rhetor and Philosopher* (Oxford: 1969) 124.
28. Gregory Nazianzen, *Orations*, 41, 1; PG, 36, 428A–29A.

different literary genres. Origen's book is definitely for philosophers, whereas Augustine's is essentially for educators. In Origen's case the title gives him away: *archai archika,* "foundational principles" of all reality, were the goal sought by Middle Platonist philosophers. Origen identifies these principles with the faith of the Church and thus transforms what would be a philosophical treatise into a work of theology. For Origen, the role of theology as stated here is threefold.[29] First, theology must investigate the grounds or the credibility of the Church's faith. Second, it should consider questions left open in that faith, questions like the nature of the original act of creation, or what kind of state the end of the world will be. Third, theology seeks to discover the deeper meanings of the Bible, above all the mystical or anagogical meanings, those which help us to grow in the contemplation of our last end.[30] Origen's book is more of a "Theological Investigations" than a *Summa theologiae:* he distinguishes carefully between what he is saying on the basis of the Church's faith and what he puts forward tentatively as a personal theologian.[31] The later condemnation of some of Origen's bolder hypotheses at Justinian's council of 553, Constantinople III, cast a blight on his memory, a poor reward for his elaboration of this vital distinction. Yet his basic picture of theology remained influential in the East and West.[32]

Augustine's *De doctrina Christiana,* by contrast, is concerned with the more down-to-earth aim of providing well-formed teachers and preachers of Christian doctrine. Although it puts forward a general program for theological formation, the nature of this program is virtually antisystematic.[33] Augustine's main concern is with the Bible and the ways in which secular knowledge of various kinds can help clarify its meaning. *Scientia,* science, can help *sapientia,* wisdom, the religious knowledge to be derived from Scripture. The primary stress is on getting together bits and pieces of biblically relevant scientific information so as to become a kind of walking *Pears Encyclopaedia* on Scripture. But over and above this, Augustine thinks that the Christian teacher

---

29. Origen, *Peri Archôn,* prologue.

30. Scripture for Origen speaks to the simple person by its body, to the person making progress in Christian *gnosis* by its soul, and to the perfected believer by its spirit; *Peri Archôn* IV. 2. 4.

31. J. Bonneefoy, "Origène, théoricien de la méthode théologique," *Mélanges F. Cavallera* (Toulouse: 1949) 87–145.

32. J. Beumer, *Die theologische methode* (Freiburg: 1972) 33.

33. For the later use of the *De doctrina Christiana* as a program for theology, *see* R. W. Southern, *The Making of the Middle Ages* (London: 1953, 1959) 177–79.

should also possess some general theoretical equipment to help interpret the Bible and to dismantle the erroneous interpretations of others. For instance, a knowledge of grammar will show us the exact role a word is playing in a particular biblical sentence; an acquaintance with dialectics will teach us the art of defining key terms as well as give us an ability to identify and expose bad arguments. Augustine's book is really a treatise on scriptural hermeneutics. Scripture and its words, for him, are signs pointing to spiritual reality, and in the last analysis, the rules that are to govern the interpretation of these signs must take this into account. Thus, in disputes over the meaning of Scripture, the Catholic exegete should follow that reading which better serves not only soundness of doctrine but also purity of life—not only knowledge of God and our neighbor but love of them. Indeed, Augustine goes so far as to say that the person whose life is rooted in faith, hope, and (above all) love has no further need of the biblical sign, save for the purposes of instructing others.[34] In two very different forms, then, in Origen and Augustine, we get a sixth theological genre—the programmatic statement of the task of Christian theology, an attempt of some kind to provide an overview of what Christian understanding might be.

In the later patristic period, all of these six genres which I have mentioned develop further and diversify. Thus the genre of apologia lives on in a work like Augustine's *De civitate Dei*; the genre of dialogue with philosophical paganism in Gregory of Nyssa's *On the Soul and Resurrection* (a Christian version of Plato's *Phaedo*); the genre of the treatise on prayer in the blossoming of ascetical and mystical theology, represented in, say, Evagrius of Pontus' *Chapters on Prayer*; the genre of biblical exposition in Cyril of Alexandria's commentaries on John and Luke; the genre of catechetical exposition in the sermons of Leo the Great; finally, the genre of programmatic statement of theology is reflected in a systematic work like John Damascene's *On the Orthodox Faith*.

Unfortunately, the attempt to reexpress Christian revelation in these various literary forms uncovered various divergences, whether of basic conviction, that is, doctrine, or about the way in which to express that conviction, namely, theology. This led to an enormous surge of controversial theological literature within the Church. It is this literature, represented by, say, Cyril of Alexandria's *Quod unus sit Christus*

---

34. Augustine, *De doctrina Christiana* III. 14; i. 43; cf. H. J. Loewen, "The Use of Scripture in Augustine's Theology," *Scottish Journal of Theology* 34 (1981) 201-24.

(in Christology) or Augustine's *De predestinatione sanctorum* (in the theology of grace) which the phrase "patristic theology" now most clearly brings to mind. Here then we find the origin of a seventh genre, doctrinal polemic. But it would be to misconceive the achievement of the patristic period in theology if we were to restrict that achievement to the great set battles over disputed points of Christian doctrine. The picture is wider and richer than that. So much so, indeed, that the patristic age shows a complex variety of theologies, taking further the variety we have already found in the canon itself. Thus, patristic scholars speak of an Asia Minor theology, an Alexandrian theology, a Syro-Palestinian theology, and an African theology—in each of which philosophy, Scripture, Tradition, experience, and episcopal teaching are mingled in characteristic ways.

The *mélange* of genres which the patristic age produced in synthesizing, for its own purposes, these essential elements of all Catholic theology should serve to remind us that in the ancient Church there were almost no theological academies dedicated to the systematic study of the subject. Neither the patterns of early and secondary education nor the more advanced rhetorical or philosophical schools of late antiquity have any but the rarest close analogues in the first centuries of the Church's life. Thus, as one student of the Fathers of Roman North Africa has written, "If we are to understand how doctrine was taught and learned in the early Church, we must look to less clearly defined and less obviously educational factors in the life of patristic Christianity."

And speaking generally of the "more subtle processes" whereby a culture is transmitted, a tradition given shape, W. S. Babcock draws attention in particular to the "immediacy of interaction" between patristic author and his audience in an age when both reading and writing stood close to oral discourse.[35]

Theology in the Early Middle Ages

Between the patristic age and the High Middle Ages there were six or seven hundred years of Christian history which were by no means theologically barren. Concentrating on our Western Christian tradition, we can distinguish three elements in the theological achievement of

35. W. S. Babcock, "Christian Culture and Christian Tradition in Roman North Africa," in *Schools of Thought in the Christian Tradition*, ed. P. Henry (Philadelphia: 1984) 31–48 and here at 33, 35.

this in-between age, which was postpatristic but pre-Scholastic. First of all, a great effort was made in socially and politically disadvantageous conditions to conserve the heritage of patristic thought.[36] When communications between Western and Eastern Europe permitted, the Latins were in the process of incorporating new elements of the Greek patristic tradition into their own. Second, in the monasteries, a fresh theology was being written which concentrates on the sanctification of the individual and of the group. Third, toward the end of the period, the same Christian humanism which gave the monastic theologians a fuller confidence about humanity also brought a fuller confidence about human reason. And so we come to the age of *Vorscholastik*, the immediate pre-Scholastic period. Here some of the methods and concerns of the High Scholastic theologians were already visible.

We will consider each of these elements—which are also approximately equivalent to chronological periods—in turn. In the postpatristic age, a great effort was made to conserve the texts and the thought processes of the Fathers. The main characteristic of the period from, say, 600 to 1000 was a thoroughgoing, some would say excessive, devotion to the Fathers of the Church. Thus Alcuin (ca. 735–864), Charlemagne's librarian and the chief intellectual animator of the Carolingian renaissance wrote to a correspondent, "I wish to follow the footsteps of the holy Fathers, neither adding to nor subtracting from their most sacred writings."[37] The testimony of the Fathers was described as the "royal road," the "public highway of apostolic doctrine."[38] The principal component in theological method for Alcuin, and those who thought like him, was the compiling of anthologies of citations from the Fathers on selected themes.[39]

Such compilation could take at least five forms.[40] First, there were the homilaries, collections of patristic readings for the liturgy, of which the oldest, those of St. Peter's Basilica in Rome and of Verona, date from the sixth century. The most widespread, that of Paul the Deacon, would serve as the common basis for such access to the Fathers

---

36. Gregory of Tours, *History of the Franks*, prologue: "The study of letters is dying, and no one is capable of preserving in writing the doings of the present."

37. Alcuin, *Epistle to Beatus of Liébana*, cited by W. Levison, *England and the Continent in the Eighth Century* (Oxford: 1946) 322; cf. A. J. Kleinclausz, *Alcuin* (Paris: 1948) 312.

38. Alcuin, *Against Felix*, prologue.

39. J. Pelikan, *The Christian Tradition, 3: The Growth of Mediaeval Theology* (Chicago and London, 1978) 9–11, 15–17.

40. A. G. Hamman, *Jacques-Paul Migne: Le Retour aux Pères de l'Eglise* (Paris: 1975) 22–30.

in the medieval West.[41] Second, there were the *florilegia*, literally "bouquets of flowers," an ancient literary form now turned to Christian use.[42] Christians produced *florilegia* of biblical testimonies, like that by Cyprian,[43] but also of patristic extracts, such as the pieces of Origen gathered together by Basil and Gregory Nazianzen. Dogmatic *florilegia* grew up in the course of the theological controversies of the patristic age, for instance, at the hands of Cyril of Alexandria, Theodoret, and John of Damascus. Third, there were the *catenae*, "chains" of patristic commentary on the Bible, a form initiated apparently by Procopius of Gaza in his *Eclogues* on the first eight books of Scripture and brought to a fine art with John of Damascus' *Sacra parallela*. Not easily distinguished from such *catenae* was the gloss, or *glossa*, originally a marginal or interlinear note on a text used by lawyers. Its Christian use, for the commenting of Scripture, began in the fifth century. The most famous gloss is the *Glossa ordinaria* ascribed to the ninth-century German monk Walafrid Strabo and preserved and recopied well into the Middle Ages, sometimes mixed in with its runner-up in popularity, the *Glossa interlinearis* of Anselm of Laon. (The *glossa* would reach its acme in the *Postilla* of the Franciscan scholar Nicholas of Lyra [ca. 1270-1340], described as the "best-equipped biblical scholar of the Middle Ages."[44]) Fourth, there come *sententiae*, "sentences," lists of patristic citations which developed from the simple, sometimes alphabetical *florilegia* of the Carolingian age and took on a much more systematic form in the Middle Ages.[45] Finally, we have the canonical collections in which chunks of the patristic corpus relevant to Christian living and Church discipline were handed down. An important channel of patristic texts, this genre would disappear in the twelfth century with the creation of Gratian's *Concordantia*, described as "no longer a compilation of texts and decretals but a treatise on ecclesiastical law, a veritable canonical *summa* which makes the law throughout the Middle Ages."[46] Such zeal for the patristic heritage led to a drive to locate more and more of the patristic corpus and, especially, to trans-

41. R. Grégoire, *Les Homéliaires du moyen-age* (Rome: 1966).

42. H. Chadwick, "Florilegium," *Reallexikon für Antike und Christentum* 8, cols. 1131–60.

43. *Testimonia, ad Quirinum*: PL, 4, 675–780.

44. *The Oxford Dictionary of the Christian Church*, ed. F. L. Cross (London: 1958), "Nicholas of Lyra," sub. loc.

45. M. Grabmann, *Die Geschichte der scholastischen Methode* 1 (Freiburg: 1909) 185–88.

46. Hamman, *Jacques Paul Migne*, 26; cf. S. Kuttner, *Gratian and the Schools of Law, 1140–1234* (London: 1984).

late the Greek Fathers into Latin. Very few Westerners knew Greek in this period, and communications between the Byzantines and the barbarian successor states to the Roman Empire of the West were haphazard. So the task took time and patience. Its most impressive representative is John Scotus Eriugena, the "man of Erin" (ca. 810–877), a scholar at the court of Charlemagne's grandson, Charles the Bald. Eriugena succeeded in putting into Latin a good deal of Origen, Gregory of Nyssa, and the sixth-century Syrian author who wrote under the pseudonym of Denys the Areopagite and whom most people believed to be identical, therefore, with the Athenian disciple of Paul mentioned in the Acts of the Apostles.[47] Since these three figures were probably the most gifted speculative minds of the patristic Church in the East, their translation into Latin markedly increased the intellectual resources of the Western theological tradition.

The Carolingian renaissance, which formed the setting for this burst of Christian literary activity, has attracted the interest of Church historians since the term was first coined in the 1830s.[48] Though recent scholars have suggested that it was a development, albeit a brilliant one, of the cultural growth of the immediately preceding centuries, there remains a considerable nugget of truth in the Carolingians' own contention that they had revived the culture of antiquity. It was a *Wiedergeburt Studien*,[49] an intellectual regeneration seen as a necessary prelude to the reform of the clergy. Its ultimate aim was a rebirth of the whole Frankish people, modeled on the individual renaissance of the Christian as a new creature, transformed at baptism by the infusion of divine grace.[50] Its pioneers deliberately adopted a theological program, whose proposals for the instruction of both clergy and laity were outlined in royal and ecclesiastical decrees of the eight and ninth centuries.

Unfortunately, not all of the patristic translations stimulated by that renaissance were widely disseminated in the somewhat chaotic conditions which followed the breakup of the Carolingian Empire; they

47. On the vital figure of Denys, see J. Vanneste, *Le mystère de Dieu. Essai sur la structure rationelle de la doctrine mystique du Ps.Denys l'Aréopagite* (Louvain: 1959); S. Gersh, *From Iamblichus to Eriugena: An Investigation of the Prehistory and Evolution of the Pseudo-Dionys and Tradition* (Leiden: 1978).

48. R. McKitterick, *The Frankish Church and the Carolingian Reform 789–865* (London: 1977) xvi–xvii.

49. P. Lehmann, "Das Problem der karolingischen Renaissance," *Settimane* 1 (Spoleto: 1954) 310–57.

50. W. Ullmann, *The Carolingian Renaissance and the Idea of Kingship* (London: 1967) 6–7.

lay gathering dust for several centuries in French and Burgundian libraries. But in the twelfth century, a new interest in the East stimulated by the monastic search for the roots of the ascetic movement in the Eastern Mediterranean, *lux orientalis*, led to their rediscovery and amplification. It has been calculated on the basis of the monastic library of Clairvaux (now at Trier) that in the time of Bernard, monastic theologians in the area would have had access to some twenty of the works of the Greek Fathers. This was of no small importance if Henri de Lubac is correct when he contends: "Each time, in this West of ours, that a Christian renewal has flourished, in the order of thought as in that of life (and the two orders are always linked), it has flourished under the sign of the Fathers. All the centuries witness to this—the history can be retraced, and the law it exemplifies verified still in our own day."[51] The Western Church owes an enormous debt of gratitude in this respect to its monks. If Cassiodorus made it the duty of the members of his *Vivarium* to translate, transcribe, or ponder the texts—both Christian and pagan—that would help them understand Scripture, it was, more widely, the monastic practice of *lectio divina* which made monastic concern with texts so urgent and widespread: if one had nothing to copy, one had nothing on which to meditate either.[52] Later in the Middle Ages, the torch would pass to the secular clergy as in the remarkably ambitious translating program of Robert Grosseteste, chancellor of Oxford University and later bishop of Lincoln.[53]

The concern for the Fathers ensured the survival of various features of patristic theological culture right through the intervening period into Scholasticism itself. One such feature was the centrality of biblical exposition. Theology is a commentary on the Bible carried out in the company of the Fathers, and so *theologia* can be used interchangeably with *sacra Scriptura* or *sacra pagina*. Thus at the end of this period, the early Scholastic Peter Abelard can still begin his theological synthesis, the *Sic et non* by admonishing the reader, "Please read the sacred Scriptures frequently, and relate your other reading to them." Along with a stress on the central importance of the Bible went

51. H. de Lubac, *Les Chemins vers Dieu* (Paris: 1967) 7.

52. *See* L. Gougaud, "Les scribes moines au travail," *Revue d'histoire ecclésiastique* 27 (1931). The most important texts are Cassiodorus, *Institutiones* 1, 30; *Regula Benedicti* 48, 28–31; Columbanus, *Regula Coeonbialis* 3, PL, 80, 211; Benedict of Aniane, *Codex Regularum*, Interrogatio 8; PL, 103, 521.

53. J. de Ghellinck, *Patristique au moyen-âge* (Brussels-Paris: 1947).

the hermeneutical scheme inherited from patristic exegesis; thus in the glossed Bibles of the early Middle Ages, the biblical text is placed in the middle of the pages and the various "senses" identified by the Fathers arranged in a constellation around it. Another continuing element in theological culture was interest in the utilization of secular knowledge in biblical interpretation, along the lines of Augustine's *De doctrina Christiana*. The desire to salvage elements of secular knowledge as adjuncts to the study of Scripture is well expressed in such encyclopedic works as Isidore of Seville's *Etymologies*,[54] and the program itself is fully set out in the *Institutiones* of Cassiodorus, a kind of blueprint for a dark-age ecclesiastical university.[55] Rather later, in the Carolingian period, Alcuin founded a series of schools for theological students where the liberal arts were taught as preparatory courses before theology itself was tackled. Divided into the *trivium*, grammar, dialectics, and rhetoric, and the *quadrivium*, arithmetic, geometry, music, and astronomy, such arts represented the universe of learning of the time. In such ways the postpatristic period contributed to the later flowering of high medieval theology both a positive approach to secular knowledge and the conviction that theology is the "queen of sciences," a form of human understanding which crowns or completes everything we know by other means.

Finally, veneration of the Fathers also meant an openness to their own use of Greek philosophy. The main philosophical influence on the content of postpatristic theology was Platonic, but methodologically it was Aristotle who was increasingly important. Aristotle made three decisive appearances on the stage of Christian thought, two of them within this period. First, there was the Aristotle of the "old logic," the *logica vetus*. Aristotle's book *Categories*, an analysis and classification of terms, or different types of words, had been translated by the sixth-century Latin Christian author Boethius, along with the *Peri hermeneias*, "On Interpretation," an analysis of propositions. These two treatises would now be called essays in the philosophy of language,[56]

---

54. B. Smalley, *The Historian in the Middle Ages*, 22. Much of Isidore's information derived from textbooks and reference works which disappeared during the Arab invasions. F. Ogara called it, "an immense farrago of the ancient world," "Tipología biblical según S. Isidoro," *Miscellanea Isidoriana* (Rome: 1936) 141.

55. On Cassiodorus, *see* J. J. O'Donnell, *Cassiodorus* (Berkeley and Los Angeles: 1979) especially, for the Vivarium, 177–222.

56. For the *logica vetus* as *Sprachlogik*, a "critical analysis of thought on the basic of linguistic expression," *see* F. Ueberweg, *Grundriss der Geschichte der Philosophie II: Die patristische und scholastische Philosophie*, ed. B. Geyer (Berlin: 1928) 216.

but in the postpatristic age they were thought of as studies in grammar: how to do things with words. They provided theologians with the technical means wherewith to analyze the statements made in biblical or patristic writings. For those strongly influenced by the *logica vetus*, theology was an understanding of the Bible based on grammar, linguistic philosophy.[57] Aristotle's next appearance was between 1120 and 1160, when the rest of his logical writings were put into Latin.[58] The *Prior* and *Posterior Analytics*, the *Topics*, and the *Sophistici elenchi* together make up the *logica nova*, the "new logic" and stick less closely to language: they are, rather, essays on reasoning in general—how to do things with arguments. These are the places in which to look to find the traditional formal logic—such things as the syllogism—which held the field in logic until the rise of mathematically based symbolic logic in the nineteenth century.

And so out of this encounter, we get the emergence of a theology which expresses itself most characteristically in problems or questions. The reasoning mind of the Christian consults the text of Scripture. It then analyzes this text by applying to it Aristotelean linguistic analysis, the grammar of the old logic. And from there it goes on to raise some general speculative questions through appeal to the new logic. But the "ideas content" brought into play through the new logic was, in the twelfth century, fundamentally that of Christian Platonism, just as in Augustine or Denys. Finally, around 1200 the rest of Aristotle's metaphysical and ethical writings are translated, and the result of this is a theological revolution. For the first time in the postantique world, Christians are faced by what appeared to many the option of either the religious world-view of Scripture or the naturalism of Aristotle on people and the world around them. High Scholasticism will be the attempt to integrate a more adequate account of the natural order—the created order as Christians would say—into a supernatural vision of the world and especially of human destiny. But here we are anticipating the next section of this chapter and running ahead of the story.

---

57. On the *logica vetus*, see A. van de Fyver, "Les étapes du développement philosophique du haut moyen-âge," *Revue belge de philosophie et historie* 7 (1929) 425–52. In fact, dialectics in this early period relied mainly on the *De nuptiis Mercurii* of Martianus Capelli, Cassiodorus' *Institutes*, and Alcuin's *Dialectic*. The old logic was not widely known. See J. Isaac, *Le "Peri Hermeneias" en Occident de Boèce à St. Thomas* (Paris: 1953) 38–42.

58. See *The Cambridge History of Later Mediaeval Philosophy: From the Rediscovery of Aristotle to the Disintegration of Scholasticism, 1100-1600*, ed. N. Kretzmann, A. Kenny, and J. Pinborg (Cambridge: 1982) II. "Aristotle in the Middle Ages," 43–98.

So much for the patristic absorption of the period from 600 to 1000 in particular, and the fruits it bore in the years from 1000 to 1200 in keeping theological culture at least relatively open to wider things. It is time to turn to the second chief element in the theology of the post-patristic period as a whole, an element especially influential in the eleventh and early twelfth centuries, namely monastic theology. The principal setting of theology in this age was the monastery. The collapse of educational institutions with the barbarian invasions had not been total, but it was far reaching.[59] For limited periods and over restricted areas what we would now call the "state" protected study and teaching, as with Alcuin and Eriugena in the brave Carolingian renaissance.[60] But on the whole, at least until the eleventh century, theology retreated to the monasteries, which were islands of literacy and culture in the sea of an uncertain world. The monks shared the general enthusiasm for the Fathers, but they played down the philosophical element in the patristic inheritance, putting in its place a concern with experience: the experience of the monk in his community before God, a personal and corporate experience of the God of Christian revelation, gradually converting the person from sin to grace and so preparing him for the life of glory, the vision of God.

The language of monastic theology is quite distinctive. There is a conscious attempt to limit theological utterance to image and symbol out of respect for the mystery of God, for the limits that God's ineffability naturally creates. At the same time, the images selected in monastic theology are the ones closest to primary human feelings: negatively there is anxiety, fear, the sense of transience, humiliation, sickness; positively there is love, hope, joy, confidence, friendship, affection, gratitude. The aim of monastic theology was to bring the person closer to God. St. Benedict, the author of the main monastic Rule, had called a monastery a "school of the Lord's service," and while he did not have theology in mind this was how monastic theologians understood him. By reflection and by learning, one could progress in the search for God, but only on condition that this seeking was the actual driving force behind the theological enterprise. The opposition of the

59. M. L. W. Laistner, *Thought and Letters in Western Europe A.D. 500–900* (New York: 1966) 136.

60. Though even there the Capitularies at some periods restrict educational resources to boys proposing to become monks. More generally, however, the aim was to provide clerics capable of passing on doctrinal and moral instruction to the community of the faithful, teaching the teachers. *See* McKitterick, *The Frankish Church and the Carolingian Reform, 789–865*, 8, 16.

monastic theologians to the invasion of theology by Aristotelean logic was chiefly a fear that the subject would grow so complex and so fascinating as a purely intellectual exercise that the God-dimension would become secondary or even peripheral. They spoke disparagingly of the *nemus Aristotelicum,* the Aristotelean "forest" or jungle where one might, spiritually, become hopelessly lost. Avoiding what they saw as unnecessary subtleties of argument and religiously useless questions, they proposed that the subject of theology is the Christian man or woman in love with God.

There are, in effect, only two themes in monastic theology as we see that in the eleventh and twelfth centuries: the divine economy, the manifestation of God's love for us, and the Christian life, seen as our appropriation of this same love. The monk's mind in studying these two themes is nourished by the Bible, by the liturgy, and by the corporate life of the community; the spiritual insight he acquires through the words or actions of his abbot and his fellow monks. The essential notion in theological method here is that of sympathetic knowledge. Through a way of life in which prayer is central, one moves into union with the divine Object of theology. The result is an attempt to communicate theologically, and particularly with those who themselves are seriously engaged on the same quest. As Bernard puts it: "It is not disputation, it is holiness which comprehends if the Incomprehensible One can in a certain way be understood at all. And what is this way? If you are a saint, you have already understood, you know. If you are not, become one, and you will learn through your own experience."[61] It might be thought that with such attitudes, monastic theology would simply be a rehearsal of already established theological themes. Yet in practice it could achieve some remarkable breakthroughs. For instance, the first Western theologian to propose the notion of Mary's original righteousness or "immaculate conception," was Eadmer of Canterbury (ca. 1060–1128), a black monk of the sixth-century Benedictine foundation there.[62] Using the Scriptures, the liturgy, and his own connatural instinct for what might be fitting, *conveniens,* to divine salvation, Eadmer came up with a piece of theology that would gradually establish itself as not simply a *theologoumenon,* theological opinion, but as an expression of the faith of the Church.

---

61. Cf. Bernard, *De erroribus Abaelardi,* 1.

62. Eadmer, *Tractatus de Conceptione S. Mariae,* PL, 159, 301–18; G. Geenen, "Le premier théologien de l'Immaculée Conception," in *Virgo Immaculata* 5. (Rome: 1955) 90–136.

Again, the ontological argument found in Anselm's *Proslogion* is known to have first occurred to its author during monastic Office and was expressed by him in a treatise which is little more than a tissue of scriptural and liturgical quotation.[63] But once again, we are running ahead of the story. Mention of Anselm brings us to the third major element in the postpatristic period, the twelfth-century renaissance of Christian humanism and the full recovery of confidence in reason which it brought. Here we are in what German scholars call *die Vorscholastik*, and the High Middle Ages are around the corner.

The twelfth century saw theology moving out of the monastery into the cathedral school and eventually into the university faculty of theology. The new stability of European society gave people a fresh access of confidence in human powers, and while the great monastic theologians reflect this at the level of sensibility, a sense of the potentialities of human love and the life of feeling, the increasing tendency was to register it rather at the level of intellect and reasoning.[64] By coincidence, a revival of dialectic akin to the early Scholasticism of the West was taking place about the same time in the Byzantine Church—still (just) in union with Rome. Although the greater part of Byzantine theological literature is either exegetical or polemical, with the Christian faith assumed as a given reality and no attempt made to give it "exhaustive formulation,"[65] such figures as Michael Psellos (d. 1018) and John Italos (d. 1082) show remarkable resemblances to the first of the Scholastic divines of Latin Christendom.[66] In that Latin world, Carolingian theology in the early postpatristic period had, as we have seen, managed to combine logical interests with a reverential stance toward Scripture and the Fathers, but this was partly because its philosophical equipment was so rudimentary. A monastic writer like Anselm could incorporate significant elements of logic and philosophy, but the whole mental atmosphere of monastic living was conducive to a spiritual rather than to a speculative grasp of Christian truth. As the new logic came into increasing vogue, we find a virtual state of war between theologians favoring the use of philosophical method almost to the exclusion of any other factors, and theologians who, on the contrary,

---

63. Anselm's *Proslogion* may be consulted conveniently in English translation in *The Prayers and Meditations of St. Anselm*, trans. B. Ward (Harmondsworth: 1973) 238–67; cf. her introduction: "Background to the 'Prayers and Meditations,'" especially 27–56.

64. R. W. Southern, *Mediaeval Humanism* (Oxford: 1970).

65. J. Meyendorff, *Byzantine Theology* (London: 1974) 4–5.

66. J. M. Hussey, *Church and Learning in the Byzantine Empire 867–1183* (London: 1937).

wished theology to remain within the monastic mold. The extreme monastic party, represented by, say, Peter Damian (1007–72), had held that reason has no authority in Christianity. Any encroachment of dialectics on the text of Scripture is sacrilege. Christian revelation has been given us not to be made into a science but so that we can lead good and holy lives in purity of heart. The extreme dialectical party, represented at the dawn of *Vorscholastik* by, for instance, Berengar of Tours, held that reason is higher even than authority in theology, for it is by reason, they said, that humanity is in the image of God. Around the turn of the twelfth century, something of a compromise position was worked out. Anselm tried to hold together the monastic theology, which regarded faith as epistemologically self-sufficient, with the speculative tendency, which saw the effort of rational enquiry as essential to the theological project. This is the background of the Anselmian definition of theology as *fides quarens intellectum:* "No Christian should openly call into question why the Catholic Church . . . believes and . . . confesses a certain doctrine to be true. However, while believing it and living it with all his heart, he may patiently look for its rational basis. If he succeeds in understanding it, let him give thanks to God. If not, it is stupid to protest. Let him bow his head in submission."[67] Anselm's view is that reason only finds its own fullness, what he calls its *rectitudo,* "rightness," within the life of faith. God himself is the ultimate source of rationality. Because created reason has a connaturality with the God of reason, it can only be assisted, not impaired, by Christian faith, which is the gift of this same God. The theologian presupposes faith, and not just any faith but the ardent loving faith typical of monastic devotion. But, presupposing just this kind of faith, the theologian uses all the rational means at his or her disposal to penetrate the content of faith and to find in that way a glimpse of the reality to which faith adheres. This is why Anselm can say that the aim of theology is to bring us *gaudium,* "joy": insofar as loving faith can by understanding discern the object of faith, it has a foretaste of the everlasting joy of the City of God.

Unfortunately, Anselm's admirably balanced position did not hold, and in the mid-twelfth century we find the argument renewed once

---

67. Anselm, *De fide Trinitatis et de incarnatione Verbi,* 2; PL, 158, 263; on Anselm's concept of theology, *see* J. Bainvel, "La théologie de saint Anselme: esprit, méthode et procédés, points de doctrine," in *Revue de philosophie* (1090) 724–46; for the wider context, G. R. Evans, *Anselm and a New Generation* (Oxford: 1980).

again, albeit in a form which ensured a high level of debate.[68] So far as personalities were concerned, this was a battle of wits between Peter Abelard, a brilliant young thinker trained in the cathedral school of Laon in northern France, and Bernard of Clairvaux, the great Cistercian abbot living somewhat to the south in Burgundy. Abelard, who was well trained in the *artes liberales*, set forth a program of biblical study in which the authoritative text would be interpreted not in terms of the traditional hermeneutic found in the glosses, but by sheer intellectual ingenuity. In his autobiography, *The History of My Calamities*, he explains his fundamental position: "It happened then that I applied myself to discourse on the foundations of our faith using the help of comparisons furnished by human reason, and that I composed a theological treatise on God's unity and trinity for the use of my disciples. They, in point of fact, positively demanded human and philosophical reasons, intelligible explanations rather than mere affirmations. They said it is useless to talk unless one communicates understanding of what one says, that they cannot believe if they do not comprehend, and that it is ridiculous to teach others something of which neither those nor those who teach have an understanding."[69] Thus Abelard did not hold that theology can survive without revelation, but believed rather that theology consists essentially in a critical investigation into the intelligibility of the assertions of Christian doctrine found in Scripture.[70] Nevertheless, the reaction from the monastic side to even this moderate theological rationalism was severe.[71] Bernard insisted that the only proper theological disposition before God is *admiratio*, "wonder." There is no place for *scrutinium*, "scrutiny."[72] And yet at least

68. Opposition to Scholastic thought in the twelfth century was not, however, only monastic in inspiration. It could also be literary, or natural scientific: *see* R. W. Southern, *Robert Grosseteste: The Growth of an English Mind in Mediaeval Europe* (Oxford: 1986) 84–85.

69. Abelard, *Historia calamitatum mearum*, prologue; PL, 178, 1444a.

70. *See* R. E. Weingart, "Theologia: The Dialectic of Faith and Reason," in Weingart, *The Logic of Divine Love: A Critical Analysis of the Soteriology of Peter Abailard* (Oxford: 1970) 1–31. Weingart concludes that, for Abelard, "authority establishes the truth of the dogma and gives the authentic formulas of the faith, dialectic enters in its constructive role to explain the sense of the formulae by logical processes," 27.

71. Note, however, Abelard's own invective against the anti-dialecticians whom he characterizes as "blind leaders of the blind, who damn what they do not know and curse what they cannot understand," *Epistola* 13; PL, 178, 353a. Note too his conviction that it is by reason that human beings are in God's image, and his claim that the Logos in becoming incarnate proposed to make his disciples "supreme logicians in disputations": *Ibid.*, 355 BC; *Expositio in Epistolam ad Romanos* III. 7; PL, 178; 896C.

72. Bernard, *Sermo* 36, 3; PL, 183, 967.

one major Abelardian principle survived into the future: this was the recognition that, in Abelard's own words, "one can often solve a controversy by showing that the same words are used in different senses by different authors."[73]

The upshot of the Abelard-Bernard conflict was the occupation of the middle ground by the succeeding major figures of early Scholasticism. In the school of St. Victor in Paris, Abelard's use of dialectic was accepted but was modified by contextualization in a fervent conventual and mystical milieu where any Abelardian excesses are corrected. Hugh of St. Victor pointed out in his *De Scripturis* that the ability to respond theologically to Scripture depends not only on the meaning of words. It is also a matter of acquaintance with the meaning of *res*, "realities."

Hugh proposes that the purpose of all human pursuits, including, then, the arts and sciences, is in the last analysis the restoration of human nature in its integrity. Their aim, though they themselves do not know it, is spiritual and salvific. All artistic and scientific disciplines, when undertaken by someone undergoing transformation by grace, can lead to an awareness of things as expressive of the Creator. But this entails that those who practice such secular disciplines must learn the right dispositions from divine revelation before they can make full use of them. Once these dispositions are acquired, then the secular knowledge of the Christian student can also be a means of union with the uncreated wisdom of God.[74]

Parallel to this Victorine humanism was the school of Chartres, which also offered to students a rich Christian humanism—literary as well as theological, with a deep feeling for ancient culture—notable in its chief representatives Bernard of Chartres, William of Conches, and John of Salisbury.[75] As you may have noticed, the center of theological life throughout the early Scholastic period is northern France. In that part of Europe, there came together the monastic and cathedral schools inherited from the Carolingian renaissance; others which owed their being to more recent movements of ecclesiastical and educational reform or to the patronage of the Capetian kings; and the intellectual

73. Abelard, *Sic et non*, prologue; PL, 178, 1344D. Cf. J. de Ghellinck, *Le Mouvement théologique du XIIe siècle* (Paris: 1927) 65.

74. On Hugh, *see* R. Baron, *Science et sagesse chez Hugues de Saint-Victor* (Paris: 1957); on the Victorines at large, F. Bonnard, *Histoire de l'Abbaye royale et de l'Ordre St.-Victor de Paris* (Paris: 1904–8); the Victorine library constitutes a significant section of the French Bibliothèque Nationale.

75. A. Cheval, *Les écoles de Chartres au moyen âge* (Paris: 1895).

excitement generated by individuals like Abelard, who had no particular institutional connections in what has been called an age of "theological entrepreneurs." Such theologians did not only apply the insights and methodologies of the liberal arts to their own discipline; they also contributed to the *artes* themselves. Thus, Marcia Corish, in a study of the theological world of medieval France, has suggested that "antagonists such as Abelard and Bernard of Clairvaux with their respective attachments to logic and rhetoric are equally incomprehensible apart from the current educational revival. Bernard's use of antithesis as a structural device in his *De consideratione*, posing extremes and mediating between them rhetorically, can be seen as a parallel, from his preferred disciplines, of the logical sifting, criticism and synthesis of contrasting authorities typified by Abelard's *Sic et Non*, and by the genre of Sentence commentaries represented most canonically by Peter Lombard."[76]

No account of the emergence of Christian Scholasticism would be complete, indeed, without a mention of Peter Lombard (ca. 1100-60), the "Master of the Sentences." Incorporating much of Abelard's critical and systematizing spirit, Peter Lombard worked with a much clearer acceptance of the tradition, thus managing to carry others with him as is demonstrated by his election, though an Italian, as bishop of Paris. The *Sentences*, his last and greatest book, dealing in ordered fashion with the Trinity, the creation and sin, the incarnation and the virtues, and finally the sacraments and the four last things, is at once a storehouse of scriptural and patristic texts and a bold attempt to adjudicate between witnesses when they seem to disagree. The comprehensiveness and balance of the *Sentences* made it the acknowledged king of textbooks in the Middle Ages. All the great Scholastics commented on it in studies which were the literary precipitate of their day-to-day oral teaching to students in the schools. Not till the end of the Middle Ages did the *Summa theologiae* of Thomas come to oust the *Sentences* from their preeminence, and that only in certain circles. Even in the early seventeenth century, commentaries on Peter Lombard were still being produced in Catholic Europe.[77]

76. M. L. Corish, "Teaching and Learning Theology in Mediaeval Paris," *Schools of Thought in the Christian Tradition*, ed. P. Henry (Philadelphia: 1984) 108.

77. P. Delhaye, *Pierre Lombard: Sa vie, ses oeuvres, sa morale* (Paris: 1961); I. C. Brady, "Peter Lombard," NCE 11, 221-22. When in 1604 Vincent de Paul graduated in theology, what he became was *baccalaureus sententiarus*—that is, he acquired the right to comment on the text of the Master of the Sentences. *See* L. Cognet, *Saint Vincent de Paul* (Paris: 1959) 34.

Theology in the High Medieval Period

Theology in the High Middle Ages was for the first time on any large scale theology in a university setting. Universities there were in the ancient world, but they were never Christianized. The University of Athens, for example, remained a stronghold of pagan thought until the reign of the emperor Justinian in the sixth century, and was closed down by him for that very reason. The people who got nearest to the idea of a Christian university in the patristic period were the Nestorians. After they had been chased over the imperial border they regrouped their resources in the Persian city of Nisibis and founded there what was in, effect, a university.[78] But this example had almost no influence on the great Church to the West, and itself collapsed in the political turmoils that engulfed the region with the arrival of first the Arabs and then the Tartars. So far as the Christian West is concerned, universities are a product of the twelfth century, a product of urbanization, of improved communications in a comparatively peaceful epoch, of a more numerous bourgeoisie whose sons had time to spare.[79] The task of medieval lecturers in theology was primarily to teach university undergraduates, "bachelors" as they were called, either by commenting on a text or by moderating formal disputations in which some knotty theological problem, or *quaestio*, was at stake. The writings left by the Scholastic Doctors of the High Middle Ages show every sign of originating, for the most part, in these ways, although in many cases they were written down by scribes, or amanuenses, rather than by the teachers themselves.

Thus in the case of Thomas, we have his commentaries on a number of scriptural books as well as on Aristotle, on the Pseudo-Denys, and on the *Sentences* of Peter Lombard. We also have sets of resolved *quaestiones*, like the *Quaestiones disputatae*, or the *Quaestiones de veritate*. Then there are the two great compendia of Christian doctrine, the *Summa contra Gentiles* and the *Summa theologiae*. These are neither commentaries nor simply collections of disputed questions, but attempts to place a great deal of *quaestio* material within a single structure, highly

78. For a brief characterization, *see* G. Every, *Understanding Eastern Christianity* (London: 1980) 77–79.

79. H. Rashdall, *Universities of Europe in the Middle Ages*, ed. M. Powicke and A. B. Emden (London: 1936); R. W. Southern, *Western Society and the Church in the Middle Ages* (Harmondsworth: 1970) 277–79, where the development of the universities, along with the freedom of the towns, is presented as a *condition sine qua non* for the emergence of the friars, and so of Mendicant theology.

wrought in form. Finally, it should be added that Thomas' *oeuvre* includes as well a variety of minor works, occasional treatises, little commentaries on the Creed or the *Ave Maria*, and so forth. Such *opuscula* do not represent any major breakthrough in theological method or in the concept of theology. But they are a necessary part of the whole for anyone wanting to form a complete picture of the work of a medieval Doctor like Thomas.[80] The same pattern would emerge again, as can be seen by a glance at Thomas' fellow Dominican Albert the Great (ca. 1200–80) who both taught him and outlived him, leaving expositions of Scripture, commentaries on Aristotle, and the (Neoplatonic) *Liber de causis* on Denys and Lombard as well as an early *Summa de creaturis* (ca. 1244) and a mature *Summa theologiae* (after 1274) together with a quantity of devotional writing.[81]

The most important methodological advance in high medieval theology is the emergence of the *quaestio*. As early as Augustine we come across theological treatises with the word *quaestio* in the title. Normally in the patristic period, such *quaestiones* arise from the study of a text, generally that of Scripture. At some point the text is hard to master, and the "question" arises: What exactly does the author mean, then, at this point? Somewhat less often in that earlier period, an answer to the textual question suggests some wider question to the author: Given that this is what the original writer means, what sense are we to make of it? Here the *quaestio* represents the difference between textual exegesis and a wider hermeneutics. But in the High Middle Ages we encounter a dramatic development in the life of the *quaestio*. It is not just that sometimes texts generate questions. Rather, questioning becomes the heart of the entire theological enterprise. As Peter Abelard had already put it, "To doubt concerning anything is not useless: by questioning we perceive the truth, according to what the Truth himself said, 'Ask and you shall find; knock, and it shall be opened to you.' "[82] The early Scholastics, we have seen, had noticed that two theological authorities may present us with conflicting theses in which each has some of the arguments on his side. In the *Summa theologiae* of Thomas Aquinas, the procedures of Abelard's *Sic et non* are brought to a fine art. Although the didactic and argumentative resources of the

---

80. M. D. Chenu, *Toward Understanding Saint Thomas* (English trans., Chicago: 1964) 203–348, for an account of Thomas' works organized in terms of genre.

81. For a detailed account of Albert's corpus, *see* J. A. Weisheipl, "Albert the Great (Albertus Magnus) St.," in NCE 1, 254–58.

82. Abelard, *Sic et non*, prologue; PL, 178, 1359b.

theological tradition are displayed with a new mastery, the homelier background of the *Sic et non* can still be detected. Many of the arguments against the position Thomas would defend are those of nameable individuals. And every position defended belongs to some historical figure, whether a philosopher, a biblical author, a Church Father, or a pope writing a decretal.

We can assume, in fact, that the composition of theology for a writer like Thomas has four stages. First of all, there is the exposition by a master in theology of some authoritative text, either (supremely)[83] a biblical text or the *Sentences* of Peter Lombard seen as an encapsulation of patristic thought. This is the *lectio*, "the reading" from which we take our word "lecturer" (or, in some ecclesiastical study houses, "lector"). Second, there is the putting of *quaestiones* to the text or, stimulated by the text, to other authorities. Third, if the arguments for or against some eventual thesis seem evenly weighted, the *quaestio* will become the subject of a formal discussion, a *disputatio*. Finally, the results of the discussion will be summarized and written up either as a *quaestio disputata* or as part of some more-comprehensive study of Christian teaching, a *Summa theologiae*.

So much for the literary form of the High Scholastic achievement. But this is chiefly a matter of presentation. What of the deeper method, and above all, the content? Here the most striking thing is the radicalization of the influence of Aristotle, referred to by Thomas simply as *Philosophus*, "the Philosopher." Aristotle's influence can be analyzed in two ways. To begin with, there is the contribution of explanatory concepts drawn from him for the rational elaboration of doctrine. Thus the Aristotelean notion of a virtue as a disposition to act in a certain way was pressed into service to highlight the nature of supernatural regeneration. So for instance, in order to throw light on the transformation by grace which takes place at infant baptism, the theologian could propose that at the moment when sanctifying grace takes possession of the soul of the baptized infant, the supernatural virtues of faith, hope, and charity are implanted thereby in the psyche: though really present, they are not manifestly so until the growing child learns how to express them. In such ways, theologians came to grasp more clearly how the processes of revelation and salvation might actually

---

83. Hence the high medieval identification of *sacra doctrina* with *sacra pagina*. *See* J. de Ghellinck, *"Pagina* et *sacra pagina:* Histoire d'un mot et transformation de l'objet primitivément désigné," in *Mélanges Auguste Pelzer* (Louvain: 1947) 23–59.

work.[84] The assumption made in high medieval reflection was that a profound structural similarity exists between nature and grace. Thus the description of what is involved in natural processes in people can provide a model for understanding what is involved in supernatural. This assumption is not of course itself Aristotelean, because Aristotle had no notion of a supernatural elevation of humanity by the grace of Christ. It is possible to argue that it is biblical, but perhaps it is better thought of as a fundamental option in the understanding of biblical revelation, an option which emerged at a certain point in the theological history of Catholic doctrine and which, when it had emerged, the Catholic tradition would embrace in a decisive way.[85]

Second, theological students became more aware through Aristotle's influence of the need to work out an epistemology for theological statements. There was and is a need to show just what kind of understanding theology represents: how it differs from both reason and faith, yet is sustained by both. Pioneering attempts at writing a theological methodology had been ventured by two writers of the later twelfth century: Gilbert de la Porrée and Alan of Lille. Gilbert, in his commentary on Boethius' *De Trinitate*, had come up with the idea that every discipline should have resource to the critical rules proper to it and congruent with its own object. The point was taken up by Alan in his *Regulae de sacra theologia*. Disappointingly, while Gilbert made a potpourri of general observations, articles of faith, first principles of reasoning, and the common opinions of theologians, with almost no attempt to discriminate between them as to status and value, Alan's "rules" are more philosophical than theological—oddly, since in his companion work, the *Distinctiones dictionum theologicalium* (the first-ever theological dictionary), he showed himself to be a largely biblical theologian, his face close up to the sacred page.[86]

The crucial breakthrough here was perhaps that of William of Auxerre, archdeacon of Beauvais and professor at Paris, who died in 1231. Williams' *Summa aurea* opens with the epoch-making comparison of theology with an Aristotelean science.[87] "Science" for Aristotle was not at all what we take it to be today, in current English usage

---

84. On the theological epistemology of the high medieval Scholastics, *see* A. Lang, *Die theologische Prinzipienlehre der mittelalterlichen Scholastik* (Munich: 1925).

85. Congar, "Théologie," cols. 375–76.

86. *Ibid.*, cols. 389–90.

87. R. W. Martineau, "Le plan de la *Summa aurea* de Guillaume d'Auxerre," *Etudes et recherches d'Ottawa* 1 (1937) 79–114.

at least. Most people would now say that science is an examination of the natural world in which data are collected and quantified (mathematically measured, so far as is possible) and a hypothesis is presented to account for their being as they are. The hypothesis implies statements about how the data will behave in the future: if these predictions are met then it is verified and if not, not. But this view of science is post-seventeenth century and derives from the privileging of physics in the period from about 1650 onwards. Aristotle's picture of science is markedly different. For Aristotle any body of knowledge may be called a science if it can be rationally organized in terms of principles which are either self-evident or are drawn from some higher science whose own principles are self-evident. William of Auxerre was the first person to suggest that the role played, directly or indirectly, by self-evident principles in secular science was played in theology by the principal revealed truths—the articles of the Creed or the doctrine of the Church. Such principles, drawn as they are from God's own knowledge of himself, possess that transparency which *principia per se nota* carry in the rest of scientific understanding. Similarly, the light of faith, the supernatural elevation of our judgment whereby we come to grasp the real by faith, is comparable to the natural light of reason, which accompanies our acceptance of self-evident principles as foundations of the knowledge of things.

This analogy is used by St. Thomas to convey his own idea of the relation between revelation and theology. The divine truth remains transcendent, not only in its origin but frequently in its content as well, being in many cases beyond the power of human reason to grasp. Yet it lodges in the human mind in such a way that it can be expressed in a coherent and orderly fashion. St. Thomas' theology is poised between, on the one hand, a pedagogical, evangelical, pastoral concept of what theology should be and, on the other, a systematic, reflective approach. He insists that in itself the revelation we have received from apostles and prophets is both entirely intelligible and also complete. The theologian uses philosophy not because of any inherent defects in the "holy teaching" which need to be made good, but because of the subjective limitations of the *incipientes*, those who are beginning to reflect about the Christian religion. In this sense, Thomas' concept of *sacra doctrina* reflects St. Dominic's original *sancta praedicatio*, the "holy preaching," which takes people as they are and where they are, adapting the expression of the gospel to the needs of an Albigensian innkeeper. This idea of theology as pedagogy is embodied in St.

Thomas' *Summa de veritate Catholica contra errores Gentium*, usually known as the *Summa contra Gentiles*. In that work, in order to show that the Catholic faith is true, Thomas appeals to whatever authority a hearer of the Gospel might accept: for Jews arguments from the Old Testament; for Manichaeans, arguments from the New Testament; for Christian heretics, arguments from both Old and New Testaments; for the Greeks, arguments from the common Doctors of East and West; for Muslims and pagans, arguments from natural reason.[88] On the other hand, as St. Thomas explains in the fourth *Quodlibetal Question*, a master in theology should show not only that, *an*, the Catholic faith is true, but how, *quomodo*, it is so.[89] His fullest attempt to fulfill this second task is the *Summa theologiae*. Disappointed, as he tells us in his prologue, by the rambling, bitty, or downright useless quality of a lot of Scholastic writing, he proposes to set forth the *veritas Catholica* in terms of an *ordo disciplinae*, a pattern or structure suitable for learning how the truth is as it is. Not all the commentators are agreed, however, on what the inner structure of the *Summa theologiae* actually is. Most construe it as an *exitus-reditus* scheme, an account of the coming forth of creatures from God and their return to him. In the case of humanity, this return takes the form of a life of virtue, enabled and supernaturalized by the grace of Christ, in which human potentialities are fulfilled both in earthly society and in the beatific vision. However, others suggest that the *Summa theologiae* is constructed in terms of a threefold modality of the divine presence to humans: through nature, through grace, and through the hypostatic union.[90] The argumentation employed by Thomas in the *Summa theologiae* is by no means as deductive as his statement about the status of theology as a science might lead us to expect. It takes the form of proposals about the meanings of texts; arguments from *convenientia*, or what is fitting to either the divine or the human, and considerations of what the coherent use of various concepts demands—the last being related to the interest in deducing new theological propositions or consequences which would characterize much Scholasticism in the early Modern and Modern periods.[91]

88. Q. Turiel, ''La intencion de Santo Tomas en la Summa contra Gentiles,'' *Studium* 14 (1974) 371–401.

89. Thomas Aquinas, *Quaestiones quodlibetales* IV. q, 9, a. 3.

90. G. Lafont, *Structures et méthode dans la ''Somme théologique'' de S. Thomas d'-Aquin* (Bruges: 1961).

91. *See* additionally on Thomas' concept of theology: P. E. Persson, *Sacra Doctrina: Reason and Revelation in Aquinas* (English trans., Oxford: 1970); A. Patfoort, *Thomas d'-*

It would be wrong to give the impression that medieval theology simply leads to Thomas, or that all of Thomas' theological notions commanded instantaneous and total assent. In some ways, medieval theology resembled modern theology in the degree of its explicit, and not just implicit, pluralism. Among the schools of thought which flourished in the high medieval period, those of the neo-Augustinians and the Scotists deserve special mention. How did their conception of theology differ from that of the Thomists? neo-Augustinians characteristically maintained that reason, while competent to deal with earthly and temporal matters, had no strict rights in what was spiritual and eternal. They sought to distinguish between two levels of thinking, two manners of thinking, and two sources of the ability to think, depending on whether one was dealing with *temporalia* or *eternalia*. In effect, they distinguished between reason on the one hand and metaphysical or spiritual intuition on the other, a distinction which is constantly surfacing in the philosophy of religion under a variety of names.[92] Only intuition serves to order the revelation of eternal reality, as the English Franciscan Alexander of Hales (ca. 1186–1245) wrote in the introduction to his *Summa theologiae*, here paraphrased in the words of Père Congar: "Theology is not a rational or demonstrative science, but one which is affective, moral, experiential and religious. . . . Its certitude does not stem from rational inferences derived from self-evident principles but from the light of the Holy Spirit which the spiritual man experiences inwardly."[93] Theology is inspired by the Spirit and belongs to the order of love rather than to that of rational enquiry. Although it is genuine knowledge, its knowledge is orientated to God as the good or lovable, rather than to God as the truth.

A second major manifestation of the difference between Thomists and medieval Augustinians has to do with the role of appeal to the

Aquin: Les clés d'une théologie (Paris: 1983) 13–70; V. White, *Holy Teaching: The Idea of Theology According to St. Thomas Aquinas* (London: 1958). Among modern works broadly faithful to the Thomist conception of the theological task, *see* G. van Ackeren, *Sacra Doctrina* (Rome: 1952); V. Preller, *Divine Science and the Science of God: A Reformulation of Thomas Aquinas* (Princeton, N.J.: 1967).

92. For Kant, this spiritual intuition would correspond to *Verstand*, "understanding" whereby we grasp concrete objects of perception in their wholeness. In Coleridge, it would be the "imagination" which enables us to discern God in nature or in the "living oracles" of the Scriptures. The Thomist distinction between *ratio* and *intellectus* is really more of a distinction between getting to know something by reasoning about it from without (*ratio*) and by union with it in a knowing which is more intimate, sympathetic, and even feminine (*intellectus*).

93. Congar, "Théologie," cols. 393–94.

creaturely realm in their respective systems. For Thomas a philosophical understanding of the creaturely realm is presupposed before we begin to write Christian theology, which it both underpins and illuminates. For an Augustinian writer like Bonaventure (ca. 1217–74), Franciscan minister-general and cardinal, nature's "book of creatures" only provides us with images and mirrors of the divine after the Bible has revealed to us the symbolic value of the creation as an expression of its Creator.[94] Theologians like Bonaventure and Alexander of Hales were contemporaries of Thomas, and their thought was in a certain degree of conflict with his from the start. This debate within Catholic divinity was not just a battle between the different Orders, each with its intellectual *amour-propre*, though it is often presented as such. Some of Thomas' severest critics were fellow Dominicans like Robert Kilwardby (d. 1279), the only preaching friar to be archbishop of Canterbury. The principal issue at stake was the degree to which philosophical reason could be utilized by the theologian proper. Thus we find Pope Gregory IX writing in 1231 to the masters of theology at the Sorbonne: "Nor shall they (theologians) present themselves as philosophers. . . . Rather, in their classes they will discuss only those questions which they can solve with the help of divine books and the treatises of the holy Fathers."[95] And in 1277 Bishop Stephen Tempier of Paris condemned certain theses of Thomas and his mentor Albert the Great (ca. 1200–80) in a document which began with the words, "Some students of the arts at Paris, exceeding the proper limits of their faculty. . . ."[96] The canonization of Thomas in 1323 was a recognition by the Church's highest authority of the legitimacy of his way of doing theology, even though this did not have to be the only way of doing theology there was. Indeed, Bonaventure, in particular, provided something, which in Thomas, if not absent, was only rudimentarily present: a theology of history.[97] History was not a subject on which the Philosopher, Aristotle, had offered much guidance. As Beryl Smalley wrote: "His many works contain historical allusions in plenty and he used a historical approach to problems that interested him but he did not write any history. . . . Thirteenth century schoolmen put their creative effort into

---

94. Bonaventure, *Breviloquium* II. 12; *Commentary on the Hexaemeron* XIII. 12.
95. *Cartularia Universitatis Parisiensis* I. 79, 138; cited Congar, "Théologie," cols. 392–93.
96. *Ibid.*, I. 473, 543; cited Congar, "Théologie," col. 393.
97. J. Ratzinger, *The Theology of History in St. Bonaventure* (English trans., Chicago: 1971).

the discussion of problems concerning man *as he is.*"[98] Though the history of salvation formed the backdrop to their work and they exploited history for practical purposes, like the furnishing of illustrations for preaching or precedents in disputes over privilege, they made no attempt to continue the genre of universal history writing, which runs from Eusebius in the fourth century to Otto of Freising in the twelfth. What caused Bonaventure to rediscover the theology of history thus abandoned with Otto's *History of the Two Cities* (1143–45) was the dangerous influence in his Order of the heretical theology of history originated by the Calabrian abbot Joachim of Fiore, with its threefold periodization: an age of the Father in the Old Testament, an age of the Son in the New Testament and the Church, and a coming age of the Holy Spirit in which hierarchical authority would be swept away and a millennium, presided over by contemplative monks, would come on earth.[99]

Well established by the date of Thomas' canonization was the third major school within the medieval pluralism, that of John Duns Scotus (ca. 1265–1308). Scotus, born in the Scottish border country, teaching at Cambridge, Oxford, and Paris, dying in Cologne, had taught that the proper subject of metaphysics is not so much God as being—seen univocally as the bare fact that something exists. Philosophy can speak of God very briefly by describing him as the author of being, but theology alone offers a direct discourse about him. But even here there is a caution. A knowledge of God *ut hic*, he is in his own *haecoeitas*, "individuality," is only possible through the divine essence. So far as theology in the strict sense is concerned, therefore, only God can be a theologian. Human theology is dependent on revelation, which gives it a knowledge not of God "as he is," but of God as self-revealing. Even if to some extent these two sorts of knowledge coincide, for what God reveals in revealing himself cannot surely be different from what God is in himself, nevertheless, theology, like revelation, is totally dependent in this on the will of God. It depends on what may be called God's own "selection" of what to reveal. So Scotus strongly underlines the dependence of theology on Scripture and Tradition. However, he is also keen on the idea that theology should try to discover the intrinsic rationality of the mysteries of faith. It should seek out the *rationes necessariae*, a phrase borrowed from Anselm, which explain

98. B. Smalley, *The Historian and the Middle Ages* (London: 1974) 180–81. Emphasis added.

99. M. Reeves, *The Influence of Prophecy in the Later Middle Ages: A Study of Joachimism* (London 1969).

why, for instance, God is the Trinity or why the incarnation happened. In fact, theology for Scotus will never be able to reestablish successfully the rational necessity of these mysteries, but it must still make this its theoretical aim, approaching it asymptotically, in such a way as to get ever closer while never coinciding with its goal.[100] Because the goal of theology, so defined, can never be attained, theology cannot be a science. God is not *scibilis*, knowable, in this life, but he is *operabilis*, attainable in the practice of a life of faith. Thus in ways perhaps anticipatory of the liberation theology of the later twentieth century, Scotism proposes that in loving God in our concrete service of him in this world we are united with him and so attain in practice that grasp of God which eludes us in theory.[101] Thus the Scotist concept of theology is at once less philosophical and more philosophical than that of Aquinas. Less philosophical because, like the Augustinian, it is more sceptical of the ability of rational metaphysics to speak about God. More philosophical in that, like some early Scholastic rationalists, its conceptual target is an understanding of God so thorough that even the revealed mysteries of God's inner life become rationally self-evident.

The later Middle Ages saw the continued development of each of these three schools: Thomism in a figure like Hervé of Nedellec (d. 1323), Augustinian in Gregory of Rimini (d. 1358), Scotism in Francis of Meyronne (d. ca.1328). But the most celebrated theological movement of the time was that of nominalism. The nominalist theologians were so called from their basic philosophical option.[102] They held that human concepts are not generated by a real union between our minds and the nature of things but are merely names, *nomina*, by which we label the world around us for our convenience. Nominalism was a curious combination of scepticism and profound religiosity,[103] as we can see from its greatest exponent, the English Franciscan William of Ockham. Ockham was born in Surrey around 1285 and died in 1347 in

---

100. J. Finzenkeller, *Offenbarung und Theologie nach der Lehre des Johannes Duns Scotus* (Münster: 1961).

101. N. Lobkowicz, *Theory and Practice: History of a Concept from Aristotle to Marx* (Notre Dame, Ind.: 1965) 71–74.

102. M. D. Chenu spoke in this connection of the strange interweaving of "an excessive Augustinianism" and "an unconscious Pelagianism" in the late medieval nominalism, adding: "This was the first of a series of experiences—at once spiritual and theological—where the Church felt the price of the balance of the Thomist theology of nature and grace," *Une Ecole de théologie: Le Saulchoir* (Paris: 1937, 1985) 107.

103. R. Guelluy, *Philosophie et théologie chez Guillaume d'Ockham* (Paris: 1947).

Germany, where he had been under the protection of the emperor Louis of Bavaria to whom he had fled for protection against the Pope.[104] Ockham and the nominalists at large defined God as omnipotent creativity. Because God is omnipotent he can do anything; because he is creative he is likely to do anything. Because he is both of these things together, his own inner nature cannot be described nor can his behavior be predicted. One thinks of the words of Yahweh to the prophet in Isaiah:

> My ways are not your ways,
> nor my thoughts your thoughts.[105]

It so happened, however, that this God has communicated some of his thoughts to us in the form of revelation. What is contained in revelation we are obliged to believe as the word of the living God. But the connection of the revealed word of God with God as he is in himself, and with the world as it is in itself, is quite obscure.[106] This is nowhere more patent than in the nominalist view of the moral law. For nominalists, goodness is simply a quality attaching to whatever God commands, whereas for Thomists, for instance, God necessarily commands what is good, since his own being prevents him from doing otherwise.[107] Although the abyssal, and indeed appalling sense of the divine sovereignty in such a theology has its own religious appeal to certain tempers, many late medievals failed to find theological nourishment in a diet of this sort. Thus there emerged by way of reaction a theological and in some ways antitheological tendency to concentrate on a mysticism of inner experience, best summed up in the *devotio moderna*.

The literature of Christian mysticism in the later Middle Ages possessed a diversity reflecting that of the Scholastic schools. Only perhaps the Brethren of the Common Life, growing up around Jan van Ruysbroeck's (1293–1381) disciple Geert de Groote (1340–84), a mystically inclined lay preacher in the Diocese of Utrecht, and their monastic offshoot, the Canons of Windesheim, most famous of whom was Groote's biographer, Thomas Hemerken (à Kempis, ca. 1380–1471),[108]

104. On Ockham's career, *see* G. Gál, "William of Ockham," in NCE 14, 932–35.
105. Isaiah 55:9.
106. Cf. K. Michalski, *Les sources du criticisme et du scepticisme dans la philosophie du XIVe siècle* (Cracow: 1926).
107. G. Leff, *William of Ockham: The Metamorphosis of Scholastic Discourse* (Manchester: 1975) 480.
108. A. Kempis wrote Groote's life; for his significance, *see* E. F. Jacob, "Gerard

could be accused of a flight into pure spirituality: that is, an unreflective account of mystical practice. The Carthusian school, associated with Ludolf of Saxony (ca. 1300–78) and Denys van Leuuwen (1402–71), were of a different mettle: the former enriched his *Vita Christi* with doctrinal expositions and extensive patristic citations, while the latter left learned commentaries on Scripture as well as on the works of Boethius, on the Byzantine ascetical writer John Climacus (ca. 570–649), and on Peter Lombard, as also on his namesake, Denys the Pseudo-Areopagite.[109] The German Dominican mystics were even more Dionysian in their conceptual scheme and, as did the work of the French secular priest Jean Gerson, chancellor of the University of Paris and a noted figure on the conciliarist movement (1363–1429), offered both a theory and a practice of the *experimentalis Dei perceptio*, the experiential knowledge of God.[110] In the German Dominican school, whose fountainhead was Meister Eckhart (ca. 1260–1328), Scholasticism of a Christian Platonist kind was used to enthuse its hearers for union with God.[111] While Eckhart's vernacular works contain his most accessible spiritual teaching, his Latin writings represent his professional output, which comes to its climax in the magnificent torso of the *Opus tripartitum*. This was meant to comprise a "Work of Propositions," some thousand or so philosophical theses; a "Work of Questions," the fruits of Eckhart's preparation in the debates of the schools; and a "Work of Commentaries," his exposition of select books of Scripture, together with an anthology of Latin homilies. While Eckhart does not deny that Scripture embodies a revelation which human reason by itself cannot attain, his more characteristic emphasis is on the truths of philosophy contained in the Bible when interpreted subtly, after the manner of a series of parables. Eckhart's attempts to startle his hearers into spiritual wakefulness led to the condemnation of a number of his more daring statements about the relation of God to the world, the Word to the soul, at the end of his life. This fate no doubt played its part in encouraging his followers, Henry Suso (ca. 1295–1366) and John Tauler (ca. 1300–61), to return to the more sober religious metaphysic of Thomism, although, interwoven in his devotional and mystical writings, Suso has his own doctrine of Wisdom, the mediating link between God and the world in the Old Testament, identified by Paul with Christ himself.

Groote and the Beginnings of the 'New Devotion' in the Low Countries," *Journal of Ecclesiastical History* 3 (1952) 40–57.

109. P. Teuuwen, *Dionysius de Kerthuizer en de philosophisch-theologische Stroomingen aan de Keulsche Universiteit* (Brussels: 1938).

110. J. L. Connolly, *John Gerson: Reformer and Mystic* (Louvain: 1928).

The most systematic attempt to combine a mystical and a metaphysical reading of the faith was that of Cardinal Nicholas of Cusa (1401–64), whose theological contribution was combined with an increasingly necessary enthusiasm for Church reform. Nicholas attempted to balance once more the claims of reason and of faith—weighting the scales to the side of reason, yet, by way of compensation, pointing out the limitations of rational method in a "learned ignorance." Influenced by the Padua mathematicians with whom he had studied, as by the ancient example of Eriugena, he explored the relationship of the infinite and the finite in quasi-mathematical terms, while at the same time seeking the union of created humanity with the creating Father by the mediation of the Son's humanity—*Verbum Patris abbreviatum super terram*—and the "harmonizing" activity of the Holy Spirit.[112]

The eve of the Reformation found Catholic theology in a state of some division, but division is not in itself disarray. Whatever one may think of the foundational framework of nominalism, in particular areas of Christian thought the work of Gabriel Biel (ca. 1420–95) was no mean achievement.[113] The Thomist school was undergoing a revival, stimulated by the simple pedagogical innovation of substituting Thomas' *Summa theologiae* for Peter Lombard's *Sentences* as the basic textbook. The varieties of late medieval mystical theology offered penetrating Christian insights which influenced both Reformers and Counter-Reformers. Moreover, the principal intellectual force of the age, humanism, was already being turned to the service of the Church in, for example, the work of Lorenzo Valla (1407–57), who initiated the textual criticism of the New Testament, collating the best manuscripts that came to hand,[114] and the efforts of Giovanni Pico della Mirandola, who sought echoes of Catholic truth in the *prisca theologia*, the "pristine theology," or as he sometimes called it, the *pia quaedam theologia*, the "pious theology, sort of," found among the sages of the ancient world, barbarian as well as Greek, and in the masters of the Jewish *kabbalah*.[115]

111. F. Tobin, *Meister Eckhart: Thought and Language* (Philadelphia: 1986) 19.

112. E. F. Jacob, "Cusanus the Theologian," *Bulletin of the John Rylands Library* 21 (1937) 406–24. More fully, J. Koch, *Nikolaus von Cues und seine Umwelt* (Heidelberg: 1948).

113. H. A. Oberman, *The Harvest of Mediaeval Theology: Gabriel Biel and Late Mediaeval Nominalism* (Cambridge, Mass.: 1963).

114. R. Montano, "Valla, Lorenzo," NCE 14, 523.

115. H. de Lubac, *Pic de la Mirandole: Etudes et discussions* (Paris: 1974) ch. 5: "Prophétisme païen." For Pico's use of the *kabbalah*, see F. Secret, *Les kabbalistes chrétiens de la Renaissance* (Paris: 1964).

Valla's career amounted to a declaration of distaste for the achievement of medieval theology, carrying with it a threat of rupture. In the words of the historian of the Catholic Reformation, A. G. Dickens, "The humanists did not demolish but merely abandoned the cathedral of medieval Christian thought; their sheer lack of wonder at its lofty vaults—as well as their revulsion from its gargoyles—would henceforth set special problems to any Catholic reconstruction."[116] The passage from medieval to Renaissance sensibility, a shift remarkably resistant to sharp definition, was, among other things, the development of a cultural and educational ideal based on classical models as the proper preparation for the reading of Scripture—over against its main competitor, the Scholastic construction of Christian doctrine, and despite the fact that the Scholasticism of the Middle Ages had taken into itself numerous features of the classical inheritance. What was new was not knowledge of the ancients but the kind of use made of it. As the French medievalist Régine Pernoud has written, "Instead of seeing classical antiquity as before as a treasury to be exploited, a treasury of wisdom, knowledge, and artistic and literary procedures, on which one might draw indefinitely, people took the view that ancient works should be regarded as models to be imitated."[117] The clearer perspective in which the humanists discovered "the past *as* past"[118] could thus substitute an extrinsic, mimetic relationship for one that was more intrinsic and sapiential—but it could and did also lead to fuller appreciation of the distinctive achievement of the world from which the classical texts had emerged. The classics (at their best) might then be approached as a preparatory school for a deeper appreciation of the dignity of people: training the mind in the appreciation of the good, the true, and the beautiful; inclining people to righteous living; integrating, as texts, the literal with the allegorical, and in all these ways serving as a prelude to the highest study of which the human mind is capable, the study of Scripture. Stressing the role of the pagan ancients—with everything of value about them, in Erasmus' words, "applied and referred to Christ"—in preparing the Christian for life in the world, these sixteenth-century authors gave birth to a classicizing Christian humanism still vigorous three centuries later in John Henry Newman's *Idea of a University*.[119] At a price, it provided service-

116. A. G. Dickens, *The Counter-Reformation* (London: 1968) 12.
117. R. Pernoud, *Pour en finir avec le moyen-âge* (Paris: 1977) 17–18.
118. Smalley, *The Historian in the Middle Ages*, 193.
119. "The grace stored in Jerusalem, and the gifts which radiate from Athens, are

able tools for that "Catholic reconstruction": "Their world was that of the grammarian, the philologist, the rhetorician; it contained methods of communication and propaganda superior to those of the Middle Ages. Time was to show that these multi-purpose techniques could be employed as readily by Catholic traditionalists as by critics of the Church."[120]

Catholic Theology from 1500 to 1700

The period from the end of the Middle Ages until the end of the seventeenth century is perhaps comparable, where Catholic theology is concerned, with the period between the age of the great Fathers and the rise of Scholasticism. A great deal is going on, yet there is little to show for it in terms of masterworks: nothing comparable to Origen's *On First Principles*, or Thomas' *Summa theologiae*. Nevertheless, some highly significant new tendencies emerge. At the beginning of the early Modern period, in the age of Renaissance and Reformation, four such general trends can be noted.

First, there is a desire to have a theology that is warmer, more overtly religious. This began with the Christian humanism of the fifteenth century, whose rhetorical theology dwelt on the redemptive incarnation as the chief among God's wonderful deeds, understanding it as conveying a message of love that moves the person to enjoyment and delight, to imitation of what is loved, since seen as beautiful and beneficent, and to praise of God for it in the liturgy.[121] This tendency reaches its climax in the mystical-Christological theocentrism of Pierre de Bérulle (1575–1629) with its insistence that the hypostatic union between the divine Word and Jesus' humanity is the exemplar and prototype of all union with God.[122] There is a brave effort to put theology and spirituality back together again after the parting of the ways between nominalism and the *devotio moderna*. Most commonly, this was attempted through the adoption of some theological principles, of order

made over and concentrated in Rome. To separate these distinct teachings, human and divine, that meet in Rome is to retrograde," J. H. Newman, *The Idea of a University* (reprinted, New York: 1960) 201.

120. Dickens, *The Counter-Reformation*, 12. Cf. P. Burke, *The Renaissance Sense of the Past* (London: 1903); D. R. Kelley, *Foundations of Modern Historical Scholarship: Language, Law and History in the French Renaissance* (New York and London: 1970); Smalley, *The Historian in the Middle Ages*, 193.

121. J. W. O'Malley, *Praise and Blame in Renaissance Rome: Rhetoric, Doctrine and Reform in the Sacred Orators of the Papal Court, c.1450–1521* (Durham, N.C.: 1979) 70-71.

122. *Oeuvres complètes*, ed. J. P. Migne (Paris: 1858); J. Orcibal, *Le Cardinal de Bérulle: Evolution d'une spiritualité* (Paris: 1965).

of an explicitly evangelical kind such as the love of God or the mercy of God, even though the period would end with theology and spirituality yet more self-consciously separate than before.

Second, the humanist movement fostered a new interest in the reconstruction of ancient texts and the mentality of those who had produced them. Although most people think of the Renaissance in terms of a new enthusiasm for the classics of Greece and Rome, the texts of the Bible and the Fathers were of equal or greater concern to such figures as John Colet, dean of St. Paul's (1446?-1519) or Erasmus of Rotterdam (1446?-1536). Such men were concerned to read a book as a whole rather than to pass on a few isolated proof texts. Erasmus' *In Praise of Folly*, a bitter attack on contemporary Scholastic theologians whom he pilloried as intellectual monsters, criticizes the Schoolmen for borrowing the odd text from Scripture here and there and accommodating it to their doctrine without bothering to look up the meaning of the words in context.

Third, there is a heightened awareness of humanity as subject, as center and source of thought and action. Schematically, we can say that ancient thought was cosmos centered, medieval thought was God centered, and modern thought is human centered. Though endless exceptions and qualifications would be required before taking such a statement *au pied de la lettre*, it carries, nevertheless, more than a grain of truth. The subjective or anthropocentric turn, as historians of culture describe it, is the most characteristic feature of the early Modern age, and it led philosophy to ponder more deeply what it is in people that enables them to be religious. The impulse worked itself out in very different ways, but its classical expression is perhaps that of Pascal in the *Pensées* with its attempt to present an entire apologetics in terms of the internal exigencies of the human spirit.

Finally, the advent of Catholic reform, then Protestant Reformation, and ultimately Catholic Counter-Reformation, brought with it a whole harvest of controversial literature. The work of such men as John Fisher (1469-1535), Peter Canisius (1521-97), and Robert Bellarmine (1542-1621) stressed positive rather than speculative theology.[123] The

123. On this *see* M. Grabmann, *Geschichte der katholischen Theologie* (Freiburg: 1933) 148–51, 158–61. For Fisher: R. Rex, "The Polemical Theologian," in *Humanism, Reform and the Reformation: The Career of Bishop John Fisher* ed. B. Bradshaw and E. Duffy (Cambridge: 1989) 109–30; for Canisius, B. Schneider, "Canisius, Peter, St.," in NCE 3, 24–26, with particular reference to the catechisms, which went through two hundred editions in his lifetime; for Bellarmine, J. de la Servière, *La théologie de Bellarmin* (2nd ed., Paris: 1928).

need to find proofs of specifically Catholic doctrinal tenets from Scripture and Church tradition left little time or energy for the making of speculative systems. But while these four tendencies—attempted reintegration of spirituality into theology, critical interest in Bible and Fathers, concern with the human subject as a religious animal, confessional controversy—provide a key to the broad tendencies of the period, there were also, as we shall see, theologians who remained consciously aloof, preferring to build on the secure results of the best theology of the past.

Let us look somewhat more closely at some of the milieux of schools within this period as a whole, and first at Catholic humanism.[124] By and large, the Catholic humanists welcomed radical reform of the Church "in head and members" but ended by breaking with the (Protestant) Reformers as people who were leading the Church and Europe into schism and violence. In theology, humanism was marked by a deliberate rejection of the Scholastic method, shunned for giving nothing to humanity save useless and oversubtle distinctions. Instead, the humanists argued, theology should speak of Christ and lead to Christ. Thus their most favored description of theology is *philosophia Christi*, a philosophy coming from Christ and centered upon him. While such Christocentrism was very welcome, the humanist reaction against speculative theology proved excessive. For Erasmus, say, theology was the intensive study of texts, partly patristic but chiefly biblical, preferably in their original languages, with a view to letting these texts inspire my moral living, and that of others.[125] I read the words of the gospel, above all, the narratives of the passion, and am encouraged by what I find to become a better person, a better neighbor. Thus the Christian helps to transform the world by renewing or restoring the original creation, a theme Erasmus borrowed from the Greek Fathers: "The true theologian is somebody who teaches what doings are to be avoided, not by syllogisms artificially twisted, but by love, by the radiance of his own face and eyes, through his life itself."[126] Finely said

124. For the wider background of Renaissance humanism, *see* P. O. Kristeller, *Renaissance Thought: The Classic, Scholastic and Humanist Strains* (New York: 1969).

125. Erasmus' most important study of what theology is, the *Ratio verae theologicae*, was first issued by itself in 1518, but subsequently published as a preface to the second edition of his New Testament. M. O'Rourke Boyle in her *Erasmus on Language and Method in Theology* (Toronto: 1977) argues that implicitly fundamental to this text is the notion of Christ as Logos (understood as the discourse of God): "the paradigm for his renaissance of true theology in imitation of God's own eloquent oration," 127.

126. Cited from Erasmus' *Paraclesis* of 1516, the "trumpet blast" of his theological renaissance, *Ibid.*, 59.

though this is, there is little room here for an intellectual exploration of Christian revelation in response to the demands of reason. Indeed, the sense of Christian teaching as a unitary body of truth has virtually disappeared. Instead, the Church's doctrines become, almost exclusively, aids to piety.[127] Despite their sincere attachment to the Church, humanists of the Erasmian mold, by their faulty concept of theology, played a part in the emergence of the modern Western idea of a religion without dogmas—a notion which became a major force in the eighteenth century and is alive and flourishing today. Nevertheless, justice must be done to the fact that for Erasmus himself, the doctrine of the redemption (understood as beginning with the incarnation of the Word) remained central as giving the whole world a Christocentric orientation: the goal of all living is the harmony of all things, and especially of all human beings, with God, a harmony realized, in principle, in Christ.[128]

Moreover, the humanist concern with texts, supplemented by Trent's teaching on canonicity and inspiration and its call for renewed Scripture study, led to a massive revival of Catholic exegesis. The Munich historian of theology Martin Grabmann regarded over twenty names as deserving of memory in what he termed the "blossom time" of a theological spring whose biblical endeavors were sometimes *riesenhaft:* "on a giant scale." The supreme monument to this activity was perhaps the work of the industrious Fleming Cornelius a Lapide, who, at his death in 1637, left erudite commentaries on all the biblical books save Job and the Psalter.[129]

Second, while this book is an introduction to Catholic theology and so does not claim to do justice to that of Protestants (or of the Orthodox), a word must be said about the eventual influence on the mainstream of Catholic thinking that derived from the theological approach of the Reformers. Admittedly, Calvin's theology remained in form and spirit within the Scholastic mold, the theses of medieval orthodoxy being replaced by those of a divergent dogmatic vision. In terms of theological method, that is, Calvin's theology had little influence on Catholics precisely because it was so like the Catholic theology that

127. J. P. Dolan, "The Theology of Erasmus and Christocentric Piety," in *Erasmus, The Handbook of the Militant Christian,* trans. J. P. Dolan (Notre Dame, Ind.: 1962) 23.

128. *See* J. W. O'Malley, "Erasmus and Luther. Continuity and Discontinuity as Key to Their Conflict," in O'Malley, *Rome and the Renaissance: Studies in Culture and Religion* (London: 1981) 47–65, and here at 55.

129. Grabmann, *Geschichte der katholischen Theologie seit dem Ausgang der Väterzeit,* 155–58.

had preceded it. Thus in a classic study of Calvin's achievement, Fançois Wendel describes the final version of Calvin's *Institutes of the Christian Religion* as "truly a theological *summa* of Reformed Protestantism." With his considerable knowledge of such medieval authors as Peter Lombard, Anselm, and Thomas, as well as Scotist and Occamist works, Calvin tried to bring into harmony various biblical concepts by what Wendel called "some sort of application of the formal method taught in the schools: that is, by expounding the opposed conceptions one after another and showing that they are joined together in a higher principle,"[130] in other words, for all the world like Abelard's *Sic et non* or one of Thomas' *quaestiones.* Later Lutheran orthodoxy, from Melanchthon's *loci communes* of 1559 to Buddeus' *Institutiones theologiae dogmaticae* of 1724, would return to Scholasticism in many ways—but much influenced by the distinctive confessional texts of Lutherans from the *Confessio Augustana* to the *Formula Christianae concordiae.*

The case of Luther himself, however, was very different. Luther's theology was original in style, method, and resources as well as in content. At first, Luther's concept of theology influenced Catholic theology only negatively. People set out to defend what he was attacking, and a new set of theological treatises, regularly treated topics, began to proliferate. Thus, in reaction to Luther, Catholic writers addressed themselves more thoroughly to such matters as the Church as the presupposition of Christian believing, the role of reason as a preamble to faith, tradition as a theological authority, the magisterium as the final court of appeal in disputed questions. In other words, this is a period when many of the ideas already set forth in this book on such topics as philosophy, Scripture, Tradition, and magisterium as crucial elements in theology began to be clarified and made systematic. But eventually some of Luther's more positive notions about theology also found a hearing within Catholicism, though not until the Modern period. Which were they? In the first place, there was Luther's idea that theology is not a speculative wisdom but is, above all, an account of salvation. Theology finds its rationale only in the salvation experienced by the Christian on the basis of the work of Jesus Christ. "Christ has two natures: how does that concern me? If he bears the magnificent and consoling name of Christ, that is because of the ministry and task he has undertaken. It is that which gives him his name. Be he by nature man and God that is his affair. But that he has . . . poured out

---

130. F. Wendel, *Calvin: The Origins and Development of His Religious Thought* (English trans., London: 1963) 358.

his love to become my salvation and my redeemer, it is in this that I find my consolation and my good."[131] The rejection of a metaphysical theology here is alien to the Catholic doctrinal tradition which is in character robustly realist: concerned to affirm what is really there for its own sake. But the stress on salvation as the principal theological concern and on subjective experience as the manner in which that salvation is appropriated could and did find a home in Catholic thought. Thus, in the comparatively conservative modern Christology of Bishop Walter Kasper, the starting point of Christology is held to be the human need for salvation as fulfilled in Christ, while metaphysical Christology is seen as simply an exploration of the ultimate presuppositions of Christ's saving power in our regard. And again, as we have already noticed in Part 5, Schillebeeckx's Christology in accepting this same soteriological emphasis goes on to present the Christian experience of grace as our chief clue in the decipherment of Christ's salvation. Lutheran theology has had an effect here, even though its own roots sink deep into the medieval and patristic past. A second element in Luther's picture of theology which ultimately achieved reintegration with the Catholic tradition is the concept of *theologia crucis*, the "theology of the cross." Luther opposed a theological principle of order based on Calvary to a philosophical principle of order in theology drawn from the natural, rational order.[132] The cross is the seat of the wisdom of God, a wisdom which in its foolishness is wiser than the wisdom of people. Nature and rationality must make their submission to the God revealed on Calvary. There the normal meanings of such concepts as happiness, dignity, divinity, are overthrown before the mystery of a God who humbles himself unto death. In a *theologia crucis* one accepts the moment of the cross as the moment of supreme theological illumination, the point from which our sense of what God and man are like must be reformed.[133] In the Modern period, these themes have entered Catholic theology mediated by their revival in the work of the great neo-orthodox Evangelical theologian Karl Barth.[134] For Barth, there is a Luther-like radical contradiction between the world and God, but there is also the statement that Christ

131. Cited by Congar, "Théologie," col. 416.
132. Luther did, however, recognize a positive role for reason *after* faith: *Tischreden* 5, 5245, cited in Beumer, *Die theologische Methode*, 99.
133. W. von Loewenich, *Luthers Theologia crucis* (4th ed., Munich: 1956).
134. H. U. von Balthasar, *Karl Barth: Darstellung und Deutung seiner Theologie* (Cologne: 1962) 32, stresses that Barth's theology is a return to Luther (and Calvin) suitably "purified" and "radicalized."

and his Spirit can reconcile things that are by nature poles apart. In the writing of the contemporary Swiss theologian Hans Urs von Balthasar, the notion that all theology must be in some sense a *theologia crucis* has been Catholicized. For von Balthasar, everything that is said about God and man in Christianity must be profoundly affected by the knowledge that God the Word emptied for humankind, to the final point of death and descent into hell.

Returning to the main story line, a third theological school worth noting in the early Modern period is that of postmedieval Scholasticism. Not all theology in this age was dramatically affected by the change of intellectual and religious temper through Renaissance and Reformation. In the Iberian Peninsula, above all, this was an age of Thomist revival, the *Summa theologiae* taking pride of place among pedagogues as the theological textbook par excellence.[135] Some of those who represented the unbroken chain of Scholastic thought were first-class minds: one thinks especially of Thomas de Vio Cardinal Cajetan (d. 1535), a major theologian at Trent, whose commentary on Thomas' *Summa theologiae* would, at the end of the nineteenth century, accompany the official edition of Aquinas' text at the personal wish of Leo XIII himself.[136] Again, there was Domingo Bañez, the confessor of St. Teresa, whom we have encountered before in the context of the theology of biblical inspiration; and yet again the *Salmanticenses*, Carmelite theologians of the College of St. Elias at Salamanca.[137] Their *Cursus theologicus* (1631–1712) and *Cursus theologiae moralis* (1665–1724) are the earliest examples of large-scale theological collaboration. In general, the Spanish contribution was especially notable, assisted as it was by the propitious political, economic, and social conditions of Spain's *siglo d'oro* as well as the absence of nominalism in the Iberian Peninsula. Spaniards were not only active at Trent: Soto, Vega, but taught widely abroad: Maldonatus at Paris, Francisco de Toleto (Toledus) in Italy, Gregory of Valencia in Germany.

135. Introduced at, for instance, Salamanca in the 1520s by Francisco de Vitoria, the effective founder of the Dominican school of San Esteban. *See* L. G. A. Getino, *El Maestro Fray Francisco de Vitoria y el renacimento teológico del siglo XVI* (Madrid: 1930). On Vitoria, M. Grabmann, no mean judge, praises his combination of theological depth, humanistic elegance, and knowledge of the positive sources of theology in Scripture, councils, and Fathers: *Geschichte der katholischen Theologie*, 151–52.

136. Rome 1888–1906; for Cajetan's work, *see* J. A. Weisheipl, "Cajetan (Tommaso de Vio)," in NCE 2, 1053–54. For Cajetan's (and other) commentaries on the *Summa theologiae* of Thomas, *see* A. Michelitsch, *Kommentatoren zur Summa Theologiae des hl. Thomas von Aquin* (Graz-Vienna: 1924).

137. Enrique del Sagrado Corazón, *Los Salmaticenses: Su vida y Su obra* (Madrid: 1955).

Such theologians were essentially commentators on St. Thomas, but commentators of a creative kind who often clarified things left obscure by Thomas himself. Yet one cannot overlook a certain tendency to narrow and rationalize the theologial enterprise, found especially in the increasing concentration on the "theological conclusion." While for Thomas himself the highest office of theology consists in relating in illuminating ways the various aspects of revealed truth, showing how particular aspects are united in more architectonically revealed principles, the baroque Scholastics saw the heart of theology as lying not so much in the articles of faith themselves as in the conclusions that can be drawn from them. Theology is then in danger of ceasing to have any contemplative relationship with its subject matter, becoming simply a logical deduction from it. The queer thing is that a number of these writers were personally contemplatives of no mean stature.

But the Thomist school comprised more than just this. It also produced people who wanted to retain what was valuable in Scholasticism but to integrate with it the gains of the humanist movement—the new sense of history, the concern with texts, and accurate texts at that. Thus Melchior Cano (1509-60), a Spaniard like most of the baroque Thomists, reacted strongly against a rationalizing view of theological method. The prime concern of theology for Cano is the appreciation of the primary data of revelation, not the conclusions that may be drawn from those data which are precisely derivative, secondary. Cano wanted theologians to devote most of their time to the sources that bring us the revealed datum and permit us to see it in its beauty.[138] He was the first Catholic theologian to write explicitly about the sources or *loci* of theology in something of the way represented by the discussion of the monuments of Tradition in Part 4 of this book.[139] His *De locis theologicis* was published at Salamanca in 1536 and enjoyed a wide diffusion, even among theologians who, though Scholastics, were not Thomists—such as the survivors of the Scotist school and eclectics like the Jesuit cardinal Francisco de Suarez (1548-1617). For Cano, strictly theological fonts of knowledge—the *loci theologici proprii*—fall into two groups: those which are constitutive of revealed understanding, namely Scripture and Tradition, and those which interpret that understand-

---

138. *De locis theologicis* I. 3. But Cano was weak on the role of speculation and on the organic unity of the *Fundorte*, as pointed out by M. J. Scheeben, *Handbuch der Katholischen Dogmatik* (Freiburg: 1873, 1882) no. 213.

139. *See* A. Lang, *Die "Loci theologici" des Melchior Cano und die Methode des dogmatischen Beweises. Ein Beitrag zur theologischen Methodologie und ihrer Geschichte* (Munich: 1925) 155.

ing. The latter, five in all, are the Catholic Church, that is, the faith awareness of the universal Church; the ecumenical councils; the *ecclesia Romana* (the pope); the Fathers; the Scholastic divines. In addition, Cano identifies another set of fonts which theology borrows from elsewhere—the *loci theologici alieni*. And these, three in number, are human reason, or human knowing as born of natural experience; the authority of the philosophers; and *historia humana*, world history.

All in all, perhaps the most lasting result of the period from 1500 to 1700 was the rise of theological specialization. People began to write not just theology *tout court*, but dogmatic theology or moral theology or mystical theology. They thought of themselves as experts in one or another of these fields, and got on with digging their own gardens without worrying too much about what others were doing with theirs. It is hard to say exactly why this came about. It may be that in a period of rapidly expanding factual knowledge—knowledge of the ancient world, knowledge of the contemporary world beyond Europe through voyages of discovery and overland exploration, knowledge of the physical world through early modern science—the habit of specialization was simply picked up from secular culture.[140]

Whatever the causes, the facts are clear enough. Take for instance moral theology. In the late sixteenth century we find for the first time distinct treatises on moral theology, mostly written by Jesuits. These books outline principles of Christian ethics and give examples of how to apply them to practical decisions. Their main readership is evidently intended to be priests with the job of helping people to evaluate their actions in confession, and in this they are indebted to an older genre, the confessors' handbooks of the Middle Ages. While the detailed ethical analyses in the new treatises is often useful, they suffer from being cut off from an account of the main Christian dogmas. Inevitably, they treat the moral life of Christians in abstraction from their concrete relation to God by grace. They describe what Christians ought to do, but give little idea of the resources available to help them do it. Thus there is a marked contrast with an integrated theology of the sort found in Thomas' *Summa theologiae*. There, morals and grace are dealt with together, occupying the central section of the work, the *secunda pars*. As a result, the portrait of ethical activity which emerges from high

---

140. But Grabmann believed that the best writing of this period showed a remarkable integration of elements, *Geschichte der katholischen Theologie*, 155: "alle Seiten der Theologie in innigster Gemeinschaft und Wechselswirkung gepflegt wurden." This is, presumably, relatively speaking.

medieval theology is more fully evangelical than that found among the later moralists. After all, according to the New Testament, we love God because he first loved us. Therefore doctrine comes before morals: the gospel is the grace of God before it is the demand of God.

Also newly hatched in this period is a separate treatise on ascetical and mystical theology, something represented in the modern Church by books on spirituality. Toward the end of the sixteenth century we are suddenly deluged with a flood of spiritual classics, of which the best known are perhaps the *Spiritual Exercises* of Ignatius of Loyola (1491 or 1495-1556)[141] and the writings of the two Carmelite reformers Teresa of Avila (1515-82)[142] and John of the Cross (1542-91),[143] although in fact these endlessly republished works are the merest tip of an iceberg. For these writers the chief center of interest is the experience of the human soul in relation to grace, to Christ, to God, taking the individual person as their subject in a way that would have seemed strange in an earlier period. Although these writers are at one level traditional, indebted as they are to the Victorines, Bonaventure and Thomas as well as to the Rhenish and Flemish ascetical and mystical literature of the late Middle Ages, in another sense they are quite novel. As one student of St. Teresa has written: "The grand theme of Christian life culminating in the *unión mistica* is given a peculiarly private and internal treatment. Her seven major works and numerous lesser ones all form one immense autobiography."[144] Ascetical and mystical theology represents an effort to consolidate, arrange, and systematize the spiritual teaching of such works. Yet the attempt to introduce scheme and perspective into such autobiographical accounts of felt experience could not avoid the danger of sealing off spirituality in a hermetic compartment of its own.[145] It is interesting to see that the drawbacks of such an approach were recognized within the limits of the period itself. Studies like Guillaume Vincent de Contenson's (1641-74) *Theologia*

---

141. H. Rahner, *The Spirituality of St. Ignatius Loyola* (English trans., Weston, Md.: 1953).

142. E. A. Peers, *A Handbook to the Life and Times of St. Teresa* (London: 1954); A. Mager, *Mystik als seelische Wirklichkeit* (Graz: 1947).

143. E. W. T. Dicken, *The Crucible of Love* (New York: 1963).

144. R. T. Petersson, *The Art of Ecstasy: St. Teresa, Bernini and Crashaw* (London: 1970) 4.

145. Noted already by J. E. Kuhn, *Katholische Dogmatik* I (2nd ed., Tübingen: 1859) 438-89. *See further* F. Vandenbroucke, "La divorce entre théologie et mystique. Ses origines," *Nouvelle revue théologique* 72 (1950) 373-90.

mentis et cordis were aimed at recovering a lost unity of mind and heart, as the very title shows.[146]

But the most portentous of these various differentiations of specialties within theology was not that between moral and dogmatic nor that between dogmatic and spiritual, but an increasing parting of the ways between systematic and positive theology. Positive or historical theology is, as we saw in Part 1 of this book, the study of facts—facts relevant to the Christian religion whether they be to do with the Bible or with any succeeding period in the life of the Church. Systematic theology, on the other hand, is an intellectual structure built from, on, and with such facts. Thus Louis Carbonia, in his *Introductio ad sacram theologiam*, published in Venice in 1589, informs us that "Christian theology is usually divided into scholastic and positive theology": the term "usually" qualifying a period of perhaps some forty years.[147] The principal stimulus to the making of works of positive theology was the challenge brought by Protestantism to the Catholic Church. Protestants claimed to represent the mind of the apostles and the ancient Church as well as, or a good deal better than, did Catholicism. Catholic theologians were therefore obliged to evolve a discipline where theology might be blended in with history. The greatest early master was the Jesuit Denis Petau, "Petavius," whose *De theologicis dogmatibus* is the first full-scale positive study of Catholic doctrine. It appeared between 1644 and 1650 and is still consulted and cited.

It seems clear that just because of the enormous volume of data which historical theologians must, or at any rate, might incorporate, few people if any could combine the tasks of positive and systematic theology on any large scale. Had Thomas lived after Petavius he could hardly have written a *Summa theologiae* which was both as systematically constructed as the one he did write and at the same time included Petavius' historical approach with his degree of completeness. But on the other hand, it is also clear that when systematic theology begins to distance itself from positive theology, or vice versa, there will be trouble. A systematic theologian who is largely ignorant of the actual genesis of the ideas found in Catholic teaching will hardly be taken seriously by those who know a thing or two about history. Similarly,

146. On Contenson, *see* C. Lozier, "Contenson, Guillaume Vincent de," in NCE 4, 24. The *Theologia mentis et cordis* was published in 1681, in nine volumes.
147. Congar, "Théologie," col. 426, citing the *Introductio in sacram theologiam* I. 8. The same distinction is found at the end of Ignatius of Loyola's *Exercises* (rule 11) among the rules for orthodoxy.

a historical theologian who cannot connect the facts together in any way that makes either rational or religious sense will hardly be taken seriously as a theologian, no matter what his or her qualities as a pure historian. Moreover, such writers may well deprive themselves of the insight into their own subject matter brought by the faith of the Church. We shall see how in the later modern period the fears of Churchmen about historical studies led to an increasing gap between positive and systematic theology: one of the causes of the battle between Modernism and anti-Modernism which is still with us.[148]

Catholic Theology from 1700 Onwards

The eighteenth century is perhaps the least creative of the modern centuries for Catholic theology.[149] The lack of creativity is betrayed by the choice of literary forms for theology in the period: above all, the manual and the encyclopedia. Around 1680, commentaries on Thomas' *Summa theologiae*, hitherto the most common textbook for the student, were replaced by manuals.[150] The manual, combining positive, Scholastic, and controversial theology, was the normal means of seminary training until the Second Vatican Council. Essentially, it developed out of an attempt to apply Melchior Cano's *loci theologici* in a condensed form suitable for immediate ingestion. The order in which the manualists dealt with theological questions, once arrived at, stayed very much the same. First there was the thesis, that is, the doctrinal statement with which the manual was concerned at some given point. Next came the *status quaestionis*, an account of various opinions about the issue which Catholic authors had held. Then the thesis was proved by reference to authoritative sources, Scripture and Tradition, but also in terms of theological reason, showing that what the thesis affirmed was necessarily or any any rate coherently bound together with other

---

148. Cf. L. de Grandmaison, "Théologiens scolastiques et théologiens critiques," *Etudes* 74 (1898) 26–43. Note also the apologetic need to defend Scholasticism against Protestant attack, since it was the conceptual form of much Catholic doctrine: M. Cano, *De locis theologicis* VIII. 1: "Contempt for Scholasticism and the plague of heresy are truly connected with one another. They always have been, ever since the Scholastic discipline took shape."

149. And one of the least explored: *see* W. Kasper, *The Methods of Dogmatic Theology* (English trans., Shannon: 1969) 8.

150. On this method, *see* B. Durst, "Zur theologischen Methode," *Theologische Revue* 26 (Münster: 1927) 297–313, 361–72. It has didactic and mnemonic advantages, but does not represent an integrated formal methodology giving unity to dogmatic investigation: so Kasper, *The Methods of Dogmatic Theology*, 11–12.

things already proven. Fourth, objections or difficulties were raised and solved. Last, the manualist suggested some implications or corollaries of the thesis, especially for life and devotion. Manuals doubtless appealed to many theological teachers and students: they offered all one needed to know about any major issue in instant form. Useful pedagogically, their strict format, which excluded any broad understanding of either historical or speculative matters, rendered them somewhat sterile as an expression of the Church's faith.

The other preferred form of the eighteenth century was the theological encyclopedia. The people who produced these encyclopedias were aware that theology had fallen apart in the age prior to theirs, the sixteenth and seventeenth centuries, and wished to put the pieces together again. Part of what this involved was the gathering up of the fragments within a literary unity. At the most obvious level, this was what the encyclopedias offered: a report on the various disciplines now existing within theology as a result of the emergence of theological specializations. This is, in fact, a genre of theology which is still with us, but as one commentator has remarked, "It is evident . . . that a collective volume cannot cure the problem but is itself a symptom of it, demanding more of theological students than is expected of their teachers."[151] The theological encyclopedists, however, went beyond the "material encyclopedia" with its basic information about the state of individual disciplines. They also tried to produce "formal encyclopedias," which would establish the unity of the disciplines as parts of a single whole. We can get an idea of their project from perhaps its last and greatest representative, F. A. Staudenmaier's *Enzyklopädie der theologischen Wissenschaften als System der gesamten Theologie*.[152] Such attempts were partially inspired by the model of system-building encyclopedias in the secular world, for instance the *Encyclopédie* of the French Enlightenment philosophers edited by Denis Diderot, or rather later, G. W. F. Hegel's *Encyclopaedie der philosophischen Wissenschaften im Grundrisse*. But the Catholic encyclopedists lacked the genius required for creative system building on the grand scale, and their attempts to produce an architectonic account of theology, while worthy, were pedestrian. Moreover, at the same time as they were trying to overcome some of the more baleful effects of specialization by

151. B. A. Garish, "Encyclopaedia, Theological," in *A New Dictionary of Christian Theology*, ed. A. Richardson and J. Bowden (London: 1983) 178–79.

152. Mainz 1834; for a brief account of this figure, *see* P. Hünermann, "Staudenmaier, Franz Anton," in *Lexikon für Theologie und Kirche* 9, col. 1024.

resystematization, the process of specialization itself was gaining further momentum. Thus, homilectics and catechetics began to emerge; there arrived on the scene a new subdivision of theology, pastoral theology, and Church history acquired greater independence of theology as a scientific discipline in its own right.

However, one should not paint too black a picture. The eighteenth century also saw the achievement of Alphonsus Liguori in moral theology, the herculean labors of John Dominic Mansi and Louis Anthony Muratori (1672–1750)[153] in collecting historic Christian texts, conciliar and liturgical respectively, as well as the continuing activity of Thomists and Scotists, especially within the two mendicant Orders, the Dominicans and Franciscans, most closely identified with those schools of thought.

A major new phase, with more promise for the future, opened in France and Germany around 1800. The theology of the period from 1800 to 1850 may be called "Romantic theology." The first Catholic Romantic theologians were laymen: representative of them are Françios René de Chateaubriand (1768–1848) and Karl Wilhelm Friedrich von Schlegel (1771–1829). Both men were writing in the 1800s amidst the upheaval in both society and Church caused by the French Revolution and its aftermath. In the second generation, from, say, 1820 to 1850, the dominant figures are the priest-theologians of the Tübingen school. Overall, the fullest statement of Romantic theology is found in the Protestant Friedrich Daniel Ernst Schleiermacher (1768–1834), whose influence, incalculable in German Protestant thought, was considerable in the Catholic Tübingen school also. For Schleiermacher, religion is based on intuition and feeling, its highest experience a sensation of union with the infinite.[154]

What is meant by the term "Romantic" as applied to theology in this context? The answer is best approached by situating Romantic theology within the context of that general movement of the human spirit, Romanticism itself. In terms of the history of the arts, Romanticism

---

153. S. Bertelli, *Erudizione e storia in Ludovico Antonio Muratori* (Naples: 1960).

154. Especially clear in the first two editions of his *Über die Religion: Reden an die Gebildeten unter ihren Verächtern* (Berlin: 1799, 1806). English trans.: *On Religion: Speeches to Its Cultured Despisers* (London: 1893, New York: 1958). The term "intuition," *Anschauung*, was suppressed in subsequent editions. Although Schleiermacher's exaltation of human experience tends to usurp, by a human norm, the primacy of revelation, his thought can be seen more positively: as God is the active source or ground of our responses, it is he who reveals himself through historical events or processes: *see* W. E. Wiest, "Schleiermacher, Friedrich, Daniel Ernst," in NCE 12, 1136–37.

involves an attempt to fuse the finite and the infinite, matter and spirit, real and ideal. Romantic theologians would regard literature and the arts as directly relevant to the philosophy of religion for this very reason. A Romantic artwork strikes us by its emotional and imaginative power through which it tries to press beyond the boundaries of the finite to suggest or evoke that which is strictly ineffable. It prefers what is particular and distinctive in reality, and is itself strongly personal and subjective. Rather than conforming to an inherited pattern imposed from without, it appears as the organic outgrowth of the artist's inward consciousness. It is willing to sacrifice architectonic wholeness to the full and rich elaboration of a part. It deems conceptual language to be very secondary in comparison with truth conveyed through symbolic images that have their operation on various levels in the human mind. Although such Romanticism entailed a higher estimate of religion than the rationalizing classicism of the Enlightenment, it also posed a threat to Christianity because of its tendency to anthropolatry, the worship of human creativity.[155]

Romantic philosophy was the attempt to conceptualize this Romantic intuition of man and his relation to being. Romanticism views man as pure vital activity, generating his own selfhood and the world as a significant environment. It sees him as a finite principle disclosing an infinite principle. This infinite principle shows itself as an inexhaustible life force, manifested through an endless multiplicity of expressive forms. Over against the rationalism and intellectualism of the Enlightenment, the Romantics emphasized the positive role of the imagination in our understanding of reality. Over against a mechanistic view of nature, they saw spontaneity and vital purpose in the cosmos as well as in humans. In regard to man, they awakened a new interest in history, understood as the "place" of human freedom and creativity.[156] The harbinger of Romantic philosophizing was Giovanni Battista Vico (1668-1744), professor of rhetoric at Naples University, who argued in his *Scienza nova* that history and literature should be the main object of human enquiry. Since God made the natural world, he alone comprehends it, whereas the "world of nations" was made by humans and so can be fully grasped in a human fashion. Vico proposed that

155. See L. Abercrombie, *Romanticism* (London: 1926); J. Barzun, *Classic, Romantic and Modern* (2nd ed., Boston: 1961).

156. G. Boas, *French Philosophies of the Romantic Period* (Baltimore: 1925); R. Haym, *Die romantische Schule* (5th ed., Berlin: 1928); W. Schulz, *Die Vollendung des deutschen Idealismus in der Spätphilosophie Schellings* (Stuttgart: 1955).

the keys to the understanding of human history are language, especially poetry, and ritual and myth. Poetry and myth are what express the deepest convictions of our ancestors. Further, those convictions may contain deep truths, for in every age an "ideal and eternal" history—a fundamental relationship between God and humans—has entered into each particular history, each segment of human experience.[157]

Vico's attempt to overcome the dualism between time and eternity was mirrored in the efforts of a number of post-Kantian thinkers in Germany to close the alarming gap between appearance and reality, phenomenon and noumenon, which Kant's philosophical revolution had opened up. Such writers as Johann Gottfried Herder (1744–1803) and Johann Georg Hamann (1730–88) censured Kant for his fragmentation of human understanding into three unrelated varieties in his three *Critiques*. They proposed instead that "sensibility" or sensation gradually transforms itself into "ideality" or intelligibility. Finally, taking up the clues offered by Kant's critics, the Romantic-idealist philosophers from Fichte to Hegel elaborate a system of reason that is simultaneously a phenomenology of spirit or mind. They see reality as a living process that embraces both the self and the world and aims at the self's total penetration of itself through its self-expression in the world. Here the search for systematic unity indicates that the Romantic movement proper is being left behind.

It is nevertheless within this general cultural and intellectual climate that we should see the work of such lay theologians as Chateaubriand and Schlegel. In his four-volume apologetics, *Génie du christianisme ou beautés de la religion chrétienne*, Chateaubriand considers Christianity as a human phenomenon.[158] He sets out to prove that of all religions Christianity is the most truly humane, the most favorable to human culture and development, and therefore the most divine. He aimed to show not that Christianity must be excellent since it comes from God, but that it must come from God since it is so excellent. It has renovated the moral basis of culture by giving man a higher idea of nature, of himself, and of the divine. Christian art and literature witness to the Church's incomparable civilizing potential. Such a perfect effect cannot arise from ourselves, an imperfect source. Chateaubriand's apologetics contain a very limited amount of rational argumen-

157. A. R. Caponigri, *Time and Idea: The Theory of History in Giambattista Vico* (London: 1953).

158. V. Girard, *Le Christianisme de Chateaubriand* (Paris: 1928).

tation, being rather an appeal to imagination and sensibility. They confront us with the inspirational force of the gospel in the Church and invite us to find there the divine Spirit himself. As he wrote, *"Ma conviction est sortie du coeur."*

Schlegel was raised as a Pietist but became a Catholic in Cologne in 1809. Deeply read as he was in the Greco-Roman classics, in Indian and Persian literature, and in the writings of the Latin Middle Ages, the bulk of Schlegel's work consists of a fragmentary history of human culture in terms of aesthetics. Schlegel held that all reality is a symbol, or allegorical expression, of what he termed the "ideal infinite": his root metaphysical concept for God. He analyzed human literature in terms of what has been called a "transcendental aesthetics," arguing that literature bears testimony to the human situation as a situation suspended between sin and grace. Thus, for example, the genre of satire manifests the absolute diversity of the real and the ideal. Elegy has the task of awakening in us the felt need for their reunion. The idyll form evokes the satisfaction which such a reconciliation of the real with the ideal would bring. Irony is the crucial literary means of distancing ourselves from the present order so as to situate it within a wider whole. In theological terms, literature discloses, therefore, that an original harmony between people, nature, and God has been tragically spoiled. Revelation shows us the way to recover this harmony: through the spread of the reign of charity, which is the kingdom of God. The extension of this reign gives history its meaning. Schlegel's last years were devoted to an unfinished trilogy which would locate humanity's existence, history, and language within a Christian worldview.[159]

Some of the emphases of these Romantic lay theologians carried over into the work of the more conventional priest-theologians of the Catholic Tübingen school.[160] The influence of Romanticism on that school can be seen in its emphasis on human subjectivity as the point within creation where grace is principally active. It can also be detected in the ecclesiology of the Tübingen men, for they stressed the historical becoming of the Church rather than its enduring being. The story of the Catholic Tübingen school opens in southern Germany soon after 1800. The origins of the school were somewhat fortuitous. In the territorial restructuring of Germany which followed the Revolutionary

---

159. J. J. Anstett, *La Pensée religieuse de Friedrich von Schlegel* (Lyons: 1941).

160. J. R. Geiselmann, *Die katholische Tübinger Schule: Ihre theologische Eigenart* (Freiburg: 1964).

and Napoleonic Wars, a large part of Catholic Swabia was handed over to the Protestant duke of Württemberg. This prince, anxious to demonstrate his liberality to his newly acquired Catholic subjects, founded a school of Catholic theology which eventually settled at Tübingen in the Black Forest. The Tübingen school was characterized from its inception by two main features. First, it was marked by devotion to the Catholic tradition in a wide sense: to the liturgy, the Fathers, and the thought and literature of the Church through the ages. Second, it was remarkably open to the stimulating if at times slightly oddball philosophical culture of early nineteenth-century Germany: the various strains of Romantic and idealist thinking associated with such names as Schiller, Schleiermacher, Schelling, and Hegel. Furthermore, as biblical criticism was entering into its first phase of maturity in (mainly) Protestant circles at about this time, the Catholic Tübingen school also tried to integrate this element, along with the commitment to Catholic history and contemporary philosophy.

The two principal concerns of the Tübingen theologians were fundamental theology and ecclesiology. In the former they confronted head on the critique of revealed religion found in the German Enlightenment, and especially in Lessing and Kant. They argued that reason finds its absolute foundation not in its own intellectual quality but in its acceptance of a revelation mediated in a salvation history where human nature is brought to its transcendent fulfillment. In ecclesiology, the most characteristic idea of the Tübingen school was that of the Church as a supernatural organism. Johann Adam Möhler spoke of the Church as an organism whose basis is the supernatural life given by Christ. Since Christianity is a divine reality, it transcends any particular statement of its content. But as time goes on and the Church develops, we can glimpse different aspects of this revelation, which the various phases of its carrier organism show us as they unfold.[161] Möhler's ideas had an affinity with those of John Henry Newman, a largely self-taught theologian, who, after his conversion from Anglicanism to the Catholic Church, worked very much on his own.[162] Just as the more philosophical side of the Tübingen theologians aroused anxiety in less adventurous Catholic circles, so the ideas of Möhler and

---

161. R. H. Nienaltowski, *Johann Adam Möhler's Theory of Doctrinal Development* (Washington: 1959).

162. I. Ker, *John Henry Newman: A Biography* (Oxford: 1988), with excellent summaries of Newman's main works.

Newman on the Church and doctrinal development were later suspected of too hasty a surrender to the historicist spirit of the age.[163]

The fear that Catholic intellectual life would dissolve into chaos under the impact of the myriad philosophical movements of the nineteenth century underlies the meteoric rise of neo-Scholasticism in the middle to late decades of the century. neo-Scholasticism, as its name suggests, was an attempt to revive the methods and conclusions of the medieval Schoolmen, and notably of St. Thomas, in a new age. After the Reformation, Thomism had made little impact on a European scale outside the Dominican Order. By the nineteenth century, not only were the *studia generalia* of that Order closed to the Church public at large, but the Order itself was in considerable disarray. It was not until the Chapter of 1838 that the Dominicans took steps to reestablish the study pattern of the pre-Revolutionary period. This move led to the creation of the Parma edition of Thomas' works, the revival of the teaching of Thomas at the Roman College of the Minerva, and by the 1870s, the emergence of a new light: Tommaso Zigliara, who would come to command the intellectual respect of Leo XIII.[164] At the same time, Ceferino Gonzales, O.P., later bishop of Málaga, founded the first explicitly Thomist journal, *La Ciencia tomista*. Parallel to the Dominican revival of Thomism, interest in his thought was blossoming elsewhere. As early as 1810, the Collegio Alberoni in Piacenza had become a cradle of neo-Thomism, using Thomas-inspired manuals.[165] In 1824, the newly restored Society of Jesus made what may be called a "closet Thomist" director of its Roman college, soon to become the Gregorian University. Luigi Taparelli d'Azeglio was obliged, however, to organize his Thomist study group in secret, owing to the hostility of his fellow Jesuits, since the official theologian of the Society was not Thomas but the baroque Scholastic Suarez. The group included among its members Gioacchino Pecci, the future Leo XIII, who in 1846, on becoming bishop of Perugia, determined on the introduction of Thomist philosophy and theology into his seminary and, in 1878, on becoming Pope, into the wider Church.[166]

163. Note also the important faculty of Munich, home of von Baader, Görres, Döllinger, and, after 1835, Möhler. For a brief characterization *see* A. Nichols, *The Theology of Joseph Ratzinger: An Introductory Study* (Edinburgh: 1988) 19–24.

164. A. Walz, "Il tomismo dal 1800 al 1879," *Angelicum* 20 (1943) 300–26.

165. G. F. Rossi, *La filosofia nel Collegio Alberoni e il neo-tomismo* (Paicenza: 1961).

166. L. Boyle, "A Remembrance of Pope Leo XIII: The encyclical *Aeterni Patris*," in *One Hundred Years of Thomism. "Aeterni Patris" and Afterwards: A Symposium*, ed. V. B. Brezik (Houston: 1981).

To say that neo-Thomism was papally approved would be an irresponsible understatement. The subtitle of Leo XIII's encyclical *Aeterni Patris* sets forth an entire program: "The establishment of Christian philosophy in the tradition of St. Thomas Aquinas, the Angelic Doctor, in our Catholic Schools." What was the rationale of this program? Neo-Thomists held that an epistemology of intuitive reason, the claiming of an *a priori* grasp of God, was the philosophical source of the ills of nineteenth-century theology. More specifically it lay, they said, at the root of two seemingly opposed evils, rationalism and traditionalism.[167] Theological rationalism, summed up in the work of the Viennese theologian Anton Günther (1783–1863), reduced theology to philosophy by claiming that the mysteries of divine revelation, once communicated, are amenable to rational demonstration.[168] Theological traditionalism, conveniently represented in the thought of L. E. M. Bautain (1786–1867) and widely held at Louvain where Pecci had visited as papal nuncio in Belgium, reduced philosophy to theology by claiming in effect that the first principles of human understanding could only be justified by a grasp of the divine Being on the basis of a primordial revelation mediated in all successive human culture.[169] This denied to human reason the power of attaining by itself to any truths, especially those of natural theology. It considered that an act of faith in a revealed tradition, deriving originally from a primordial revelation to Adam and found in fragments in all cultures, was the true origin of all knowledge. Here rational and revealed truths were once again set on the same level, and in such a way that trust in tradition, whether the tradition of humanity at large or the tradition of the Church, could easily turn into scepticism, since by definition it had no rational foundation. Neither of these systems could preserve a proper balance between faith and reason nor distinguish adequately the supernatural from the natural knowledge of God. The neo-Thomists concluded, therefore, that in the interests of orthodoxy, Catholic theology must abandon the subjective starting points of post-Cartesian philosophical systems and return to the metaphysics of St. Thomas, grounded

167. G. A. McCool, *Catholic Theology in the Nineteenth Century: The Quest for a Unitary Method*, 29.

168. E. Winter, *Die geistliche Entwicklung Anton Günthers und seiner Schule* (Paderborn: 1931).

169. L. Foucher, *La philosophie en France au XIXe siècle avant la renaissance thomise et dans son rapport avec elle, 1800–1880* (Paris: 1955): concerns also L. G. A. de Bonald, F. R. de la Mennais, A. Bonnetty. On Bautain, *see* P. Poupard, *Un Essaie de philosophie chrétienne au XIXe siècle: L'Abbé Louis Bautain* (Paris: 1962).

as this was on a grasp of finite being, attained through the cooperation of the lowly human senses and the agent, or abstractive intellect,
of the Aristotelean theory of knowledge.

Furthermore, the neo-Thomists held that, just as the natural and
supernatural orders might be successfully distinguished at the level
of a theory of knowledge with the help of St. Thomas, so the same
was true at the level of an account of being. For, drawing on the
Aristotelean metaphysics of substance and accident, Thomas had
presented the order of grace as a supernatural supervention (accident)
through whose causality the order of human nature was raised up into
a realm beyond itself. Sanctifying grace modified the essence of the
soul, while the theological virtues of faith, hope, and charity transformed the soul's faculties, mind and will. It was not surprising, neo-
Thomists, argued, that Catholic theologians who had abandoned
Thomas' metaphysics were no more able to describe satisfactorily the
relation between nature and grace than they were that between reason and faith.

Although the centenaries of the births or deaths of other great medieval theologians were opportunities for the papacy to commend the
historical movement of which they formed part—as with Bonaventure
in 1904 and Anselm in 1909—this was not really meant to underwrite
Scholastic pluralism. Pius X made it clear in 1914 that if the doctrine
of "some other author" has been specially recommended, this is done
only to the extent that his teaching agrees with the principles of St.
Thomas. The *Codex Iuris Canonici* promulgated by Benedict XV in 1917
obliged professors of philosophy and theology teaching in Catholic institutions to follow "the reasoning, the doctrine, and the principles
of the Angelic Doctor." Such an imposition of a single theological
method was a quite unprecedented action on the part of the Roman
See, and although it was in many places widely evaded, it accounts
for the groans with which many people greet the name of Thomas
today.

In spirit, neo-Scholasticism, at least in the hands of many of its
practitioners, was not especially close to the original or historical St.
Thomas. To begin with, the sheer volume of the Thomistic tradition
proved something of an obstacle to a historically accurate reading of
the texts of Thomas himself—though around the years of the Great
War with the arrival of the medievalist Pierre Mandonnet at the French
Dominican study house, Le Saulchoir, and given the concern of its re-
gent, Ambroise Gardeil, for the historical dimension of doctrine, the

application of historical method to the study of Thomas became a characteristic trait of that school.[170] Second, the apologetic or defensive nature of the impulse behind neo-Scholasticism led to an overemphasis on the rational aspect of Thomism at the expense of its contemplative or mystical aspect. Even neo-Thomists deeply convinced of the need to renew the contemplative life of the Church, like the Roman Dominican Réginald Garrigou-Lagrange, seemed, in the area of systematics proper, to think it an advance to show how one's theological ideas might be reduced to their origins in the smallest number of basic concepts possible.

However, the dislike of neo-Scholasticism in many quarters did not derive mainly from its imposition from above, nor from its concern with apologetics and deductive logic, but from its apparent indifference to historical context.[171] Although in the years after 1880 Catholics were producing historical studies of enormous distinction, whether in the Bible, the Fathers, or the medievals, positive or historical theology seemed increasingly sealed off in a compartment of its own. But if speculative theology were to become simply a rearrangement in ever more rigorous form of the theses and theological conclusions of neo-Scholasticism, then a kind of schizophrenia would overtake Catholic consciousness. The formal grasp of faith as a meaning and the historical genesis of that meaning would become two utterly unrelated things, and ne'er the twain would meet. To some who feared the implications of historical studies for traditional faith, this thought was a solace rather than a threat. The struggle within Leo XIII's curia over whether to open the Vatican Archives to independent scholars showed how deep such anxieties could go.[172] However, to more farseeing Catholics, the increasing distance between the ''official theology'' (since, in effect, that was what neo-Scholasticism was) and the work of historians and historical theologians gave rise to grave disquiet, and the more prophetic spirits foresaw that a reckoning must come.

The crisis broke with the Modernist movement. Modernism is an extremely complex phenomenon whose definitive history and theo-

170. For the growing historical mentality at Le Saulchoir, *see* M. D. Chenu, *Une école de théologie, Le Saulchoir* (Paris: 1937, 1985) 113.

171. ''This rigorously unhistorically understood Scholasticism,'' as Friedrich von Hügel called it in a letter of June 6, 1899, to Wilfrid Ward; cited in M. de la Bedoyére, *The Life of Baron von Hügel* (London: 1951) 113.

172. O. Chadwick, *Catholicism and History: The Opening of the Vatican Archives* (Cambridge: n.d.).

logical evaluation remains to be written. Nevertheless, certain key elements can be identified, both in its sources and in what it did with
them. First, there was the massive advance of historical studies as such,
and in particular the long-suppressed attempts of positive theology
to gain a hearing for history within theology proper.[173] Second, there
was the idea of the development of doctrine, found in Newman as at
Tübingen.[174] Third, there was the new apologetics of Maurice Blondel
with its "method of immanence," which sought the intellectual justification of Christianity in the felt needs of the human spirit.[175]

However, Modernism was not simply the sum total of various
legitimate movements in Catholic theology, just as anti-Modernism was
not simply the counterreaction of neo-Scholasticism and its supporters. Lines of reflection in earlier and unimpeachably orthodox writers
were projected and taken to conclusions their original authors would
not have recognized, and in Blondel's case, did refuse to recognize.
First, in the matter of history, the Modernists tried to use historical
science to determine the theological meaning of biblical and other texts
rather than accepting a role for Tradition in the hermeneutical process. Instead of saying that there is an important place for historical
study within theology, history becomes everything. Second, on dogma,
the Modernists gave the impression that doctrine was simply a vehicle
for the response of a given age to the divine. Thus a doctrine well suited
to one age might be quite ill suited to another. Instead of saying that
there is a historical dimension to the explicitation of doctrine, evolution becomes everything.[176] And third, on revelation, the Modernists
appeared to be saying that the orientation of the human spirit to transcendence was the entire explanation of the Christian religion. Scriptures, sacraments, dogmas, Church institutions, became so many

173. For example, Louis Duchesne (1843–1922), on whom see F. Cabrot, "Mgr. Louis
Duchesne: son oeuvre historique," Journal of Theological Studies 24 (1922–23) 253–81. On
those ecclesiastics who saw historical studies as a threat to the received faith, see B. Welte,
"Zur Strukturwandel der katholischen Theologie im 19. Jahrhundert," in Welte, Auf
der Spur des Ewigen (Freiburg: 1965) 380–409. For a Modernist view of the revolutionary
nature of the nineteenth-century discovery of radical historicity, see G. Tyrrell, Through
Scylla and Charybdis (London: 1907) 109. On the whole issue, C. Théobald, "L'entrée
de l'histoire dans l'univers religieux et théologique au moment de la 'crise moderniste,'"
in De la crise contemporaine du Modernisme à la crise des herméneutiques (Paris: 1973) 7–85.

174. O. Chadwick, From Bossuet to Newman: The Idea of Doctrinal Development (Cambridge: 1957, 1987).

175. See ch. 6 of this book.

176. See A. Nichols, From Newman to Congar: The Idea of Doctrinal Development from
the Victorians to the Second Vatican Council (Edinburgh: 1990).

symbolic forms thrown up by the movement of the human spirit toward God in history. Instead of saying that the immanent orientation of man to God was a necessary complement to the external signs and teachings of divine revelation, interiority becomes everything—not unassisted by Kantian subjectivism and Schleiermacher's sentimentalism.

It is important to note that not all those accused of Modernism taught all of these things, and others taught a more limited version of them which, in a more tolerant ecclesial world, might have been regarded as compatible with Catholic truth. The intolerance was bred of fear, for perfect fear casteth out love. In reality, the Modernists were a tiny group of people scattered between France, England, and Italy. Like many people after the improvement of mail services in the later nineteenth century but before the invention of the telephone, they were tremendous letter writers. Although they did indeed hope to bring about a revolution in theological studies, and so in the culture from which doctrine and preaching were shaped, it would be a mistake to regard their correspondence as evidence of a conspiracy. Moreover, the decree *Lamentabili* of the Holy Office, in concocting for the purposes of condemnation a potpourri of citations or paraphrases of the Modernists' works, managed to lump together innocuous sounding statements genuinely destructive of Catholic faith with more startling ones that admit of an orthodox interpretation.[177] As with the roughly contemporary pronouncements of the early Pontifical Biblical Commission, the overly narrow drawing of the boundaries of theological discourse meant that the work of a sane evaluative response would have to be done over again. At the same time, the crudity of the Holy Office's intervention reduced the credibility of subsequent (and perhaps much more intelligent as well as more just) interventions in a way whose effects are still felt in the later 1980s. Such strictures cannot be made against Pius X's encyclical *Pascendi*. Surely the most intellectually heavyweight papal encyclical ever, it was a brilliant attempt to identify the logical direction of Modernist movement, summed up in the catchwords "agnosticism," "immanentism," and "historicism."[178]

The problem with the anti-Modernist reaction, which was purely penal in nature, was that many of the questions raised by Modernism were extremely sensible and even urgent questions. What is the relation of religious experience to revelation? What is the relation of reve-

177. DS, 3401–65.
178. *Ibid.*, 3475–3500.

lation to dogma? What is the relation of dogma to the history of dogma? Such questions would not go away simply because the pope said they must, as one of the most sensitive neo-Thomists of the period, Ambroise Gardeil, O.P., realized, when in his own answer to Modernism he proposed not to refute them so much as to replace them.[179] For while an ecclesiastical condemnation gives theology more time in which to pay an intellectual debt, in itself it does not remit it. The negative effect of anti-Modernism was that few theologians were willing to run the risk of being dubbed Modernists by investigating further the questions that the Modernists had asked.[180]

Here the fact that the German episcopate managed to secure the exemption of its theology faculties from the operation of the rigorist oath appended to *Lamentabili* and *Pascendi* must surely be accounted among the reasons why Catholic theology in its early and mid-twentieth century renaissance owes so much to those of German speech in its liberation from a frequently stale and repetitive neo-Scholasticism.[181] The German Catholic theology of this century has five notable characteristics: it is liturgical, ecclesial, historically minded, missionary, and philosophically alert. Something must now be said by way of defense of each of these keynotes, which, as we shall see, surface in the other principle theological culture of contemporary Catholicism, France. At the Second Vatican Council, ''the Rhine'' (which washes both France and Germany) ''flowed into the Tiber'': the council's teaching can be seen as a precipitate of the theological activity of the finest German- and French-speaking theology of the interwar period. As the postconciliar period finds Catholic theology in a state of considerable disarray, it is no bad thing to have a clear grasp of the successes of an earlier generation as a yardstick for what ought to be a continuing achievement.

179. A. Gardeil, *Le Donné révélé et la théologie* (2nd ed., Paris: 1932) xxxv.

180. The only possible defense, or at any rate extenuation, is that offered by Lagrange, when he wrote of Pius X's policy: ''This great Pope acted in certain cases like those leaders who proclaim a state of siege or martial law in circumstances where a pressing period demands exceptional measures. There was a peril, and the Pope knew it. It was up to him to reestablish general security, though this cost dear to some individuals,'' *Le Père Lagrange: au service de la Bible. Souvenirs personnels* (Paris: 1985) 170.

181. Note also Döllinger's statement that Germany must be the land of the theological future since no other people ''cherished both eyes of theology, philosophy and history, with the same care, love and thoroughness,'' *Kleinere Schrifte*, ed. F. H. Reusch (Stuttgart: 1890) 184.

First of all, then, we are dealing with a theological culture which drew inspiration from the liturgy.[182] The liturgical dimension in theology is associated in particular with the Benedictine school of Maria Laach in the Rhineland, and above all with its quondam abbot, Odo Casel (1886–1948).[183] Casel's idea was that the liturgy is the Church's deepest response to revelation: it should, therefore, be the principal stimulus to theological reflection. Moreover, once we consider the pattern of the liturgy and the liturgical year as a guide to the Christian religion, we discover that the center of it all is Christ in his death and resurrection: the *pascha Domini*, the Lord's passing over from death to new life, celebrated in every Mass, on every "first day of the week," and at the climax of the year, Easter itself. Basing himself on the Letter to the Hebrews and the Apocalypse of John, Casel argued that the paschal mystery is in some sense outside of time. Until the end of time, the crucified and glorified Christ stands before his Father as mediator between God and the world. But the point where this permanent paschal mystery of mediation touches our world is precisely the liturgy itself. For the liturgy is the real presence of Christ's passover, and his continuing prayer before the Father, as given under the signs of human ritual. Therefore, the liturgy is not only the principal stimulus to theology but in a sense its principal subject matter. Everything that is crucial about Christ has passed over, to adapt a phrase of Leo the Great, into the liturgical sacramentality of the Church. Casel's approach is clearly discernible in the document of the Second Vatican Council on the liturgy, while in theology itself it can be seen in the account of the mysteries of Christ's life offered in Karl Rahner's *The Eternal Year*.[184]

Second, German Catholic theology was ecclesial. It saw revelation as mediated through the common Tradition of the Church, regarded as a corporate life together with a shared religious vision and shared spiritual values. This ecclesial or communitarian dimension is associated with such writers as Romano Guardini (1885–1968),[185] an Italian brought

182. For the context, the liturgical movement itself, *see* O. Rousseau, *Histoire du mouvement liturgique* (Paris: 1945); and with greater emphasis on the German-speaking world, A. Heitz, "Dernières étapes du renouveau liturgique allemand," *La Maison-Dieu* 7 (1946) 51–73.

183. For Casel, *see* T. Filthaut, *Die Kontroverse über die Mysterienlehre* (Darendorf: 1947).

184. K. Raher, *The Eternal Year: Meditations on the Mysteries of Faith Expressed in the Liturgical Cycle* (English trans., London: 1964).

185. *See* H. Kuhn, *Romano Guardini: Der Mensch und das Werk* (Munich: 1961); J. Laubach, "Romano Guardini" in L. Reinisch, *Theologians of Our Time* (Notre Dame: 1964) 92–108.

up in Germany who became the first professor of Catholic philosophy in the Prussian capital, Berlin, and Karl Adam (1876–1966),[186] who carried high the flag of the Tübingen school in a period still dominated by a somewhat wooden Scholasticism. The idea that theology is not simply a matter of deducing conclusions from revealed propositions (though it may also be that) but is the transcribing of the life and faith of the Church community released Catholic thought from much of its fear of the concept of experience. A book like Adam's *The Spirit of Catholicism* offers a concrete, intuitive account of the faith of the Church, drawing on the experience of the common people of God as well as on that of great mystics and saints.[187] The idea that the Church is itself a sacrament of the presence of God in Christ, and not simply an authorized teacher speaking in Christ's visible absence, had a reinvigorating effect on ecclesiology and is well to the fore in the dogmatic constitution of the Second Vatican Council on the Church, *Lumen gentium*.

Third, this theology was also historically minded. Men like Guardini and Adam did not simply make it all up as they went along in an impressionistic kind of way. They made a conscious effort to integrate into dogmatic theology the historical studies which had revealed in their original colors some of the great figures of the theological past: Augustine and Cyril of Alexandria, Bernard and Bonaventure. Adam's Christology, *The Christ of Faith*, exhibits a wide knowledge of theologians of the past, each with their characteristic insights.[188] This reintegration of historical theology brought with it a recognition that theology has taken different forms and used different methods in the history of the Church, and that a modern theology which fails to listen to the voices of the past will be thin and impoverished as a result. We can note, too, that the research into the history of Scholasticism carried out by such men as C. Baümker and M. Grabmann enabled theologians to refer back gratefully to the past tradition of early Scholasticism, and helped to bring about a reconciliation between those working within and without the Scholastic tradition.[189]

Fourth, the theological reflections of German and Austrian Catholicism at their best were decidedly missionary or "kerygmatic" in orien-

186. A. Auer, "Karl Adam 1876–1966," in *Theologische Quartalschrift* 150 (1970) 130–43.
187. K. Adam, *The Spirit of Catholicism* (English trans., London: 1929, 1934).
188. K. Adam, *The Christ of Faith* (English trans., New York: 1957).
189. Such research into early Scholasticism made possible the overcoming of the perplexities of neo-Scholasticism: *See* W. Kasper, *The Methods of Dogmatic Theology* (English trans., Shannon: 1969) 20–21. And Kasper, a Tübingen man, predicted that such research, once absorbed, would render anti-Scholasticism unnecessary.

tation. People looked for a truly evangelical theology which would identify the central core of the gospel, God in Christ with his good news, and relate all else to that. At Innsbruck a school of kerygmatic theology arose concerned to produce an articulation of the original proclamation in compelling language.[190] But the deficiencies of their program, if taken as a universal agenda for the future, soon became apparent. For the kergymatics implied and even at times explicitly stated that the rest of theology could be happily left to Scholastic academics, since it was largely irrelevant to the Church's fundamental message as well as to fundamental human needs. The bluntness of this proposal acted as a goad to the more sensitive practitioners of neo-Scholasticism. They realized that their own tradition had become cut off from what was most creative in the life of the Church: her liturgy, her community sense, her memory of the past, and the exigencies of her mission. The result was a kind of conversion within (largely German) neo-Scholasticism such that, without throwing overboard the philosophical rigor characteristic of Scholastic thought in all its phases, nevertheless they would integrate into their writing as much as possible of the new concerns.

The attempt to infuse a new breadth of vision into Scholastic theology found an expositor of genius in Karl Rahner (1905–84).[191] For Rahner it was not sufficient to inject dosages of the repristinated liturgical, ecclesial, historical, and missionary sense into the existing body of Scholastic thought. A more intimate transformation was required. In effect, what would remain would be the deep springs of Christian Scholasticism in its Thomist form: the theological epistemology that saw the knowing subject as open to the divine mystery, the dynamic and mutually supportive relationship of nature and grace. Rahner's new conceptuality draws on the philosophical enterprises of Kant, Hegel, and Heidegger in order to transform traditional Scholasticism into a theological anthropology that remains, however, oriented toward the mystery of God. All human life was to be seen as permeated by the offer of God's grace. Since the offer of grace was universal, Rahner deemed it an "existential," a constituent feature of human existence; but since grace was thus present only as offer, Rahner qualified this existential as "supernatural," not given in and with humanity as such, but God's free gift to those who stand before his saving mys-

190. L. de Cominck, "La théologie kérgymatique," *Lumen vitae* 3 (1948) 103–15.
191. D. Gelpi, *Light and Life: A Guide to the Theology of Karl Rahner* (New York: 1966); L. Roberts, *The Achievement of Karl Rahner* (New York: 1967).

tery. Rahner thereby became one of the founders of transcendental Thomism, a Thomism which accepts the post-Kantian stress on man's creative contribution to knowledge but which finds latent in his drive toward knowledge an implicit self-direction toward God.[192]

Rahner was not, however, the only father of this contemporary offspring of the Thomist tradition. To trace its genealogy more fully we must turn now to the theological culture of French-speaking Europe in this same period, from the Great War to the Second Vatican Council. The French Catholic renaissance was originally literary and social in character. The achievement of Charles Péguy (1873–1914) and Paul Claudel (1868–1955) was to evoke through their poetry and prose a new vision of Christian society. Turning to the Latin Middle Ages for inspiration, they hoped for a rebirth of specifically Christian philosophy and social values, expressed in a Christian architecture and a Christian music (these were years of the recovery of the Latin Church's classical voice, Gregorian chant) and even a renaissance of Christian chivalry, *le scoutisme*. In Belgium, on the other hand, the apologists of the *Jeunesse ouvrière chrétienne*, the Young Christian Workers, began from the opposite conviction: that they were living in a largely dechristianized society and must reimplant the Church and theology at a quite elementary level. As M. Etienne Fouilloux has written of the impact of *Jeunesse ouvrière chrétienne* on Le Saulchoir: "With them, it was no longer the historical method but History with a capital "H" which penetrated powerfully into Le Saulchoir."[193] Here the watchwords were those of engagement, incarnation, and presence in the world. These differing inspirations form the background of much Francophone theology in the Modern period, and from the two groups of partisans that correspond to them—integral Catholics and theological humanists, sometimes known confusingly as integral humanists—the considerable internal tensions of French Catholicism today largely derive. The integralists have in their favor the fact that a rich and complex religion aiming of its nature at the transformation of the whole of life cannot exist without creating a culture to sustain it. The theological humanists have on their side the fact that the secular world in its very secularity contains elements of truth and goodness, and with that secular world the history of the Church as of theology shows a constant give-and-take. Over against both of these tendencies, however, and less con-

---

192. W. J. Hill, "Transcendental Thomism," NCE 16, cols. 449–54.
193. E. Fouilloux, "Le Saulchoir en procès 1937–1942," in M. D. Chenu, *Une école de théologie: le Saulchoir* (Paris: 1985) 44.

nected with the stratagems of cultural politics, stood a third party, whose watchword was "eschatological theology." Men like Jean Daniélou, S.J., and Louis Bouyer, an Oratorian and formerly a minister of the Reformed Church, set themselves resolutely against any confounding of the kingdom of God with human achievement. There is a duty to transform *les réalités terrestres* insofar as it is in our power, but to speak of such transformation as, in a phrase beloved by some theological humanists, the "flower" which becomes the "fruit" of the kingdom, makes of that kingdom no more than the result of human progress.[194] The controversy between eschatological theologians on the one hand and theological humanists and integralists on the other foreshadows the debate over a theology of secularization and liberation theology in the years after the Second Vatican Council.

Belgium, and more precisely Louvain, was the home during this period of the Jesuit Joseph Maréchal, a metaphysician of Catholic mysticism who, more than any other, has the right to be called the founder of transcendental Thomism. His post-Kantian interpretation of St. Thomas stressed that one can accept the insistence of modern philosophies of subjectivity that the mind makes a large contribution to its account of reality, so long as one also emphasizes the dynamic tendency of the human spirit toward the real, in a continuous dissatisfaction with its own conceptions.[195] The question as to whether transcendental Thomism does justice to the by now traditional realism of Catholicism in matters of philosophical theology remains a lively issue today, as the critical studies of P. Cornelio Fabro of the University of Perugia amply show.[196] However, the most celebrated figures in Francophone theology in the interwar years were not Belgian but French. Apart from Daniélou and Bouyer, already mentioned, these were the Jesuit Henri de Lubac (b. 1896), now a cardinal, and the Dominicans Marie-Dominique Chenu (b. 1894) and Yves Congar (b. 1909). De Lubac's name was at the center of the crisis in the 1950s over the so-called new theology, *la nouvelle théologie*.[197]

194. For this debate, *see* B. Besret, *Incarnation ou eschatologie? Contribution à l'histoire du vocabulaire religieuse contemporaine, 1935–1955* (Paris: 1964).
195. J. Maréchal, *Le Thomisme devant la philosophie critique* (2nd ed., Louvain: 1949); A. Hayen, "Le père Joseph Maréchal, 1878–1944," in *Mélanges Joseph Maréchal: Oeuvres et hommage* (Brussels: 1950) 1, 3–21.
196. C. Fabro, *La svolta antropologica di Karl Rahner* (Milan: 1974).
197. On this, *see* J. Daniélou, "Les orientations présentes de la pensée religieuse," *Etudes* 249 (1946) 5–21.

The principal objection of the papacy to the "new theology" appears to have been its patristic enthusiasm, seen at Rome as the symptom of a desire for a less developed theology, which might by that very token be more acceptable to non-Catholic Christians who had either not shared (Orthodox) or repudiated (Protestants) the medieval inheritance of the Latin Church. In fact, de Lubac's work as a historical theologian was directed just as much to medieval as to patristic theology, especially in the history of biblical interpretation.[198] His single most important contribution to Catholic theology lay in his recovery of the notion, vital not least for Rahner's work, that there is only one history of grace, which embraces every individual in this world. Argued on the basis of texts of Augustine and Thomas, read hitherto through the tinted spectacles of baroque commentators, this thesis was of outstanding significance for the debates about the world, the Church, and the kingdom. A vote for supernature as embracing nature was a vote for the theological humanist position that there is no reality wholly untouched by God's grace. There is only one story of sin and grace, in which all people are actors, and so the themes of engagement, incarnation, and presence in a secular world are vindicated. At the same time, de Lubac's insistence that the orders of nature and grace remain in principle distinct justified the anxieties of the eschatological school about incarnational immanentism, and even, to a degree, the desire of the Integralists for a distinctive Catholic culture which would set out to express the transformation of nature wrought through grace.

The two directions in which de Lubac looked, back to tradition and forward to the social and cultural future, turned out to be the central features of the French theological revival. Certainly, they characterize the work of the two Dominican masters, Chenu and Congar. Chenu's theological method consisted in looking to the Church in the world of today in order to find important questions to put to the past, and then looking to the past to find constructive answers to the questions of the present. More than this, he also suggested a total perspective in which to see historical theology, the kind of perspective that had been so seriously lacking since the later sixteenth century.[199] The object of theology for Chenu may be said to be the mystery of Christ,

---

198. H. U. von Balthasar, *Henri de Lubac: Sein organisches Lebenswerk* (Einsiedeln: 1976), ch. 4b.

199. Chenu spoke of the great promise, and positive aspect, of historical study in relation to faith as "faith, and, in faith, theological science, taking possession of new rational instruments," Chenu, *Une Ecole de théologie, le Saulchoir,* 117.

his life, death, and resurrection expressed diversely through the different ages in which the Church has lived. We approach this object, the mystery of Christ in its multiple theological incarnations, not as antiquarians but in such a way that we can hear Christ speaking to the world of today. It was this attempt to introduce a historical dimension into the very heart of systematic theology which aroused the concern of theological conservatives.[200] Chenu's program for the Dominican studium of the province of France, seen by its supporters as a workshop for theology in the wider Church, was placed on the Index, and Chenu himself was obliged to leave the faculty in 1942. A similar complaint, that historical relativism and epistemological subjectivism would end up destroying systematic theology in the Catholic tradition, was issued some years later by the Dominican Michel Labourdette, this time against the Jesuit theologate of Lyons, the home of de Lubac and Daniélou. Looking back from the vantage point of the later 1980s, it is difficult not to feel some sympathy with Père Labourdette's view, though the greater awareness of historical context is in itself a major gain.[201]

Congar's picture of theology was similar to that of Chenu, except that for Congar, ecumenism, of which he has been the most notable Catholic theorist, should be a dimension of all theology. Above all, Congar's genius lies in his profound and detailed grasp of the history of Catholic theology. It was this depth of acquaintance which led him to wish to integrate into the theological life of today whatever was best about that life in the past.[202]

The various theological developments I have been charting came together at the Second Vatican Council. The best of the interwar theology in French and German provided many of the distinctive emphases and insights of that council. These are contextualized in documents offering overviews of the whole Christian economy reminiscent of patristic theology at its best and exhibiting, at least at times, the concern for careful conceptualization typical of Christian Scholasticism. While addressing itself to almost every major aspect of Church life, the council had surpisingly little to say about the place of theologians in the Church—as two of its Dominican members, Cardinal

---

200. *See* R. Garrigou-Lagrange, "La nouvelle théologie, ou va-t-elle? Vérité et immutabilité du dogme," *Angelicum* 23 (1946) 126–45; 24 (1947) 124–39.

201. M. Labourdette, "La théologie et ses sources: fermes propos," *Revue Thomiste* 46 (1946) 353–71; 47 (1947) 5–19. *See also* M. Labourdette, J. Nicolas, R.-L. Bruckberger, *Dialogue théologique* (St. Maximin: 1947).

202. A. Nichols, *Yves Congar* (London: 1989).

Michael Browne and Fr. Anicetus Fernandez, the master of the Order of Preachers, lamented. Its concept of theology, if clearest in *Optatam totius*, an account of priestly formation, must be pieced together from here and there in its documents.

The council emphasized the importance of the role of philosophy within theology: both "that philosophical patrimony which is forever valid" (an obvious reference to Thomism and related approaches as a *philosophia perennis*); and also "modern philosophical studies," notably those influential in the student's own region. That this is not merely a matter of "know your enemies" but of concern that no fragment of truth should be lost seems clear from the council Fathers' recommendation that "the history of philosophy should be taught in such a manner that students may grasp the fundamental principles of the various sytems, retaining those elements which are proved to be true, while being able to detect and refute those which are false."[203] Students must be helped to see the connection between such philosophical argumentation and the mysteries of salvation, as contemplated by theology "in the higher light of faith."

The council's account of the sources of theology gives priority, properly enough, to Scripture. It cites Leo XIII's description of the Bible as the "soul of theology" and proposes that students be trained in both literal and spiritual interpretation. This is, at any rate, my understanding of the statement that "after a suitable introductory course, they should receive an accurate initiation in exegetical method. They should study closely the principal themes of divine revelation and should find inspiration and nourishment in daily reading and meditation upon the sacred books."[204] After Scripture, the council unhesitatingly places next the Fathers of the Church. The theological student is to learn "what the Fathers of the Church, both of the East and West, have contributed towards the faithful transmission and elucidation of each of the revealed truths."[205] With this solid biblical and patristic basis, the student may then go on to investigate the subsequent history of dogma, finishing with a more speculative exploration of the mysteries of salvation, "with St. Thomas as teacher." This last requirement is meant to underline the uniquely exemplary fashion in which Thomas is a Doctor, with particular reference to the comprehensive-

---

203. *Optatam totius*, 15.
204. *Ibid.*, 16.
205. *Ibid.*

ness of his account of revelation and his sense of the interconnection of all its parts.

This investigation of the sources of theology does not take place, however, without some reference to what I have called "aids to discernment." If a reference to experience in *Optatam totius* is somewhat guarded (students should "learn to seek the solution of human problems in the light of revelation"), a more generous account is offered in *Gaudium et spes*: "With the help of the Holy Spirit, it is the task of the whole people of God, particularly of its pastors and theologians, to listen to and distinguish the many voices of our times and to interpret them in the light of the divine Word, in order that the revealed truth may be more deeply penetrated, better understood, and more suitably presented."[206] But the results of such interpretative activity remain within the general rubric which governs the council's entire account of the theological enterprise: "Theological subjects should be taught in the light of faith, under the guidance of the magisterium of the Church."[207]

Theology Since the Second Vatican Council

What theologies are, then, on offer since the council? We can divide them into two groups. First, there are individual authors who have continued the work of some of the earlier schools we have already met with in the last two or three sections. For instance, the Canadian Jesuit Bernard Lonergan took further the transcendental Thomism associated with Joseph Maréchal and Karl Rahner, and provided in its service the fullest account of method in theology since the work of Melchior Cano in the 1650s.[208] Jean-Hervé Nicolas, O.P., produced a new dogmatic synthesis based on the mainstream Thomist tradition flowing as that does from the medieval disciples of Thomas through the baroque Scholastics to the neo-Thomism of the nineteenth and early twentieth centuries.[209] The Tübingen theologian Kasper worked consciously in the tradition of the Catholic Tübingen school, being deeply rooted in the sources of Catholic theology yet taking as his preferred philosopher Lutheran F. W. J. von Schelling and his so-called transcendental

---

206. *Gaudium et spes*, 44; implicitly related to this is the concept of the signs of the times: *see* M. D. Chenu, "Les signes du temps," *Nouvelle revue théologique* (1965) 29–39.
207. *Optatam totius*, 16.
208. B. Lonergan, *Method in Theology* (London: 1972).
209. J.-H. Nicolas, *Synthèse dogmatique: De la Trinité à la Trinité* (Paris: 1985).

idealism.[210] Even the Romantic theology of the early nineteenth century can be said to have enjoyed a revival in the work of the American David Tracy, whose aim is to present the Christ of Catholicism as what he calls a cultural "classic," that is, a figure with the power to transform culture and so bring human existence to a new level of meaning.[211] De Lubac's ransacking of patristic and medieval sources in the service of new total vision of Catholicism is continued in the amazingly learned and original theology of Hans Urs von Balthasar (d. 1988), a trilogy consisting of a theological aesthetics—a study of the beauty or glory of God; a theological dramatics—a study of the saving action of God in the theater of the world; and a theological logic—a study of the truth of God, which comes to light in those first two.[212]

Second, there are whole schools of theology which constitute a relatively new start compared with anything in the past. Thus we find, for instance, the school of liberation theology, beginning in South America in the wake of the Medellín congress of 1968 but now remarkably widespread in the world beyond. Liberation theology aims to unite sociology with theology in such a way that Christian redemption is redefined, at least in part, in the categories of social, political, and economic emancipation.[213] Again, there is the school of narrative theology, originating in North America but now exported to Western Euope. Here a new theological method takes as its starting point the fact that so much of Scripture, and some, at any rate, of the monuments of Tradition consist of narratives or stories. Thus, for instance, the Gospels are stories, the central act of the Eucharist is a re-enacted narrative, and the lives of the saints, too, have a story line. Narrative theology concerns itself with stories seen as literary constructions aimed at disclosing a meaning and truth which goes beyond that of purely historical reporting.[214] Finally, there is the school of hermeneutical theology,

---

210. *See* A. Nichols, "Walter Kasper and His Theological Programme," *New Blackfriars* 67. 787 (January 1986).

211. D. Tracy, *The Analogical Imagination* (London: 1981).

212. *Herrlichkeit. Eine theologische Ästhetik* (Einsiedeln: 1961–69); English trans.: *The Glory of the Lord* (Edinburgh: 1982 onwards); *Theodramatik* (Einsiedeln: 1973–80); *Theologik, I. Wahrheit der Welt; II. Wahrheit Gottes* (Einsiedeln: 1985). On Balthasar's work, the fullest account is A. Moda, *Hans Urs von Balthasar* (Bari: 1976).

213. The pioneering work is G. Gutierrez, *A Theology of Liberation* (English trans., Maryknoll: 1974); for the controversy aroused by the success of this school, *see* R. Gibellini, *Il debattito sulla teologia di liberazione* (Brescia: 1986). The fullest methodological self-reflection of the school is C. Boff, *Teologia e pràtica: Teologia do politico e saus mediaçoes* (Petropolis: 1978).

214. *See*, for example, T. W. Tilley, *Story Theology* (Wilmington, Del.: 1985).

which originated in Western Europe and spread to North America. This takes its starting point from the fact that Christianity is a tradition, something passed on, handed down. It concerns itself with the proc- ess whereby a tradition is constantly reinterpreted in new cultural situ- ations. Hermeneutical theology has been made the basis of the five-volume French *Initiation à la pratique de la théologie*, now translated into several other languages, and meant as the successor to the best of the neo-Thomist manuals, the *Initiation théologique* published by the French Dominicans in the 1950s.[215]

In any sketch, however rough, of the present state of Catholic the- ology, it should be acknowledged that a great deal of admirable work is being produced quietly and consistently in historical theology as well as in the study of particular aspects of Catholic doctrine. What gives rise to alarm in various quarters is not the quality of historical mono- graphs, nor the level of presentation of this or that particularized fea- ture of Christian revelation. Anxieties focus rather on the state of theology in its highest sense: namely, as an articulation of the Chris- tian mystery as a whole.[216] Even though all theological visions or sys- tems remain ineluctably particular in the sense that they approach the totality of revelation from a single vantage point, their right to be termed a vision or system depends on their ability to present revela- tion in its entirety, albeit from a single, determinate starting point. The weakness of present systematic or speculative theology has serious repercussions for the wider Church. It both reflects and reinforces the difficulty many Catholic Christians have in grasping their faith as a unitary vision of the world, a total way of understanding things, as well as an invitation to activity or, in the current vogue word *praxis*, adequate to the human enterprise today.

In the language favored by this book, the weakness of much con- temporary theology derives from the peculiar inadequacies of its prin- ciples of order—especially philosophically, but to some degree also

---

215. *Initiation à la pratique de la théologie*, ed. B. Lauret and F. Refoulé (Paris: 1982–84).
216. Y. Floucat, "La Crise contemporaine de la vérité et l'unité de la sagesse chré- tienne," *Revue Thomiste* 84. 1 (1984). Also: V. Messori (in colloquio con Joseph Ratzinger), *Rapporto sulla fede* (Milan: 1985) 71–77. With this may be compared the concern of the (Yale) "postliberal"; school of Protestant thought, that the teaching of the Christian faith should be freed from a functionalism in which revealed religion loses its own consis- tency, and is instrumentalized in the service of other human agendas (for instance of psychological self-fulfillment, or of some political vision of global society). *See* W. C. Placher, "Postliberal Theology," in *The Modern Theologians* 2, ed. D. Ford (Oxford: 1988) 115–28.

theologically. Among the philosophical principles of order most favored in Catholic theology today, three raise peculiar difficulties. These are, first, the use of sociology, whether Marxist or not, as a philosophical principle of order in liberation theology; the use of the concept of narrative found in current literary theory in narrative theology; and the use of the interpretation theory of hermeneutical philosophy in hermeneutical theology.

The lack of what may be termed "metaphysical authority" in these undergirding philosophical principles of order makes them ill equipped to render the theological totality of Catholic Christianity, which needs to speak about being as well as meaning and about eternity as well as time. There is a marked contrast here to the continued flourishing of the Scholastic metaphysics of being in Nicolas, of Schelling's metaphysic of infinite, and of finite freedom in Kasper. And yet, as our survey of the history of Catholic theology should serve to remind us, it is not necessary that every theology carry out all possible theological functions which the faith and life of the Church require. Liberation theology, narrative theology, and hermeneutical theology have their own particular tasks to fulfill, tasks related to the nature of the human being as a political animal, as a creature that expresses the meaning of existence by the telling of stories, and as someone stretched between past and present, scanning by interpretation the texts and other artifacts that come down to it in tradition. What is vital, however, is that such theologies do not set themselves up as the universal theology calculated to meet all the Church's needs, albeit on a local or regional scale. They must find ways of making space for other kinds of theological discourse, and above all, for those which, in their cherishing of ontology, enable the expression of Catholic doctrine as a description of reality—in its two poles, finite and infinite, and the relation between them. At the same time, such other kinds of theology, of which Thomism may stand as the paradigm by presenting human intelligence as above all the capacity for intake of the real, highlight in an irreplaceable fashion the Church's fundamental intuition about truth: namely, that it is not first and foremost an action to be done (cf. liberation theology) or a story to be told (cf. narrative theology) or a text to be interpreted (cf. hermeneutical theology), though it may indeed also be all of these. Primordially, truth is an encounter with what is not humanity's work: the deed of God in creation and salvation.

Père Nicolas' work, by preserving the formal structure of St. Thomas' *Summa theologiae* with its *exitus-reditus* pattern, is also exceptional in this. For the theological principle of order in almost all would-be speculative theology today is firmly soteriological: taking its point of departure from the New Testament as a proclamation of salvation. Not only is this fully traditional, any theology which failed to relate divine revelation to human needs and human destiny could hardly be termed Christian at all. Nevertheless, the preference for a theological principle of order drawn from the doctrine of salvation may leave in the shadow other aspects of the Christian mystery which a different theological ordering principle might bring into relief. Thus, in von Balthasar's work, the theological principle of order is the eternal self-giving love of the Trinitarian persons, a theme of objective revelation if ever there was one, yet with a power to move and satisfy curiously deeper than alternative theologies concerned in a more straightforward *ex professo* way with human flourishing. This is not to say, however that the soteriological principle of theological ordering found in, say, Kasper's theology is any less valuable for the Church's contemporary exploration of her own faith. Those members of the Church, whether lay or ordained, whose concern is her mission in the world, need all the theological help they can find in their pursuit of the transformation of human beings, individually and in society. Yet it is worrying when contemplatives, who embody a different aspect of the Church's total mystery, report how meager is the diet they receive from much modern theology. For the contemplative life is, in a sense, the fundamental form of Christian discipleship: it is the one that most anticipates what we shall all be doing, please God, in heaven. Here again, there is a pointer to the need for an integrated variety of theologies.

The reference here to the desirability of a number of theologies within the single *Catholica*, each with, one hopes, its own distinctive contribution to make to the overall richness of theological culture and perception, brings me to the last chapter of this book. Our last task is to look more closely at the theological principle of ordering in Catholic theology or—what amounts to much the same thing—at that theology's simultaneous possession of both unity and plurality. The potted history of theology offered in these pages should have convinced the reader that a certain pluralism has always characterized theology in the Catholic tradition. And while I have not even tried to draw up a comprehensive balance sheet of today's theology, its diversity will be obvious from even this cursory *tour d'horizon*. Where the unity lies may not be so obvious, though it can be said at once that all the writers

I have mentioned shared the same ecclesial communion and abided by, at least implicitly, the same rule of faith. Today, while theological pluralism is taken for granted by some, the need for unity in theological culture is not so widely recognized. Yet, if it is clear that the variety of cultures in which the Church is incarnated will mean a corresponding variety of theologies, it is equally clear that all theological articulations of Christian revelation, if they are to be truly Catholic, must share certain features. Otherwise, ''Catholic theology'' will mean no more than ''theology practiced by Catholics'' and so have no more inner unity than ''Catholic astronomy'' or ''Catholic horticulture'': for there is nothing to prevent our adopting such catchphrases for astronomers or dahlia growers if they happen to belong to the same Church and occasionally stand side by side at her worship. There may be some who will be content with this analogy and its lesson that Catholic theology may be simply theology practiced by those who happen to be Catholics, but the present author is not among them.

20

The Theological Principle of Order

The historical pluralism of Catholic theology is not just *de facto*, a brute fact. It is a reality acknowledged as *de jure*, right and proper, by the Church's magisterium itself. So Leo XIII, at the end of the nineteenth century, was happy to cite in this regard some words of Thomas: *In his quae de necessitate fidei non sunt, licuit sanctis diversimode opinari, sicut et nobis.*[1] (In matters not imposed upon us by faith's authority, the saints are allowed to differ, just as we are ourselves.) The earliest papal acceptance of theological pluralism was, however, a good deal earlier than this. Some of the sharpest *odium theologicum* in the Western Church has been vented on controversies about grace, and it is with reference to various theologies of grace that we find seventeenth- and eighteenth-century popes explicitly affirming the possibility of different ways of reading theology's sources in the light of reason and experience. Thus we find Pope Paul V affirming theological pluralism in 1607, when he brought to a close the special commission on the relation of free will and grace set up ten years earlier. Pope Clement XII set out the case more fully in his bull *Apostolica* in 1733, while Pope Benedict XIV was forced to write a letter on the subject to the Grand Inquisitor of Spain in 1748 chiding him for his failure to respect such an elementary principle.[2]

But that principle was not confined to one comparatively specialized area of theological reflection. In the pontificate of Pius XII its scope was recognized as taking in the very Bible itself, the supreme monument of the Church's faith and highest norm of her grasp of her own tradition. As the Pope wrote in his encyclical on biblical studies, ''There . . . remain many matters, and important matters, in the exposition and explanation of which the sagacity and ingenuity of Catholic inter-

1. In *libros sententiarum* II, d. 2, q. 1, a. 3.
2. *See* for references, Y. Congar, *La Foi et la théologie* (Tournai: 1962) 198.

349

preters can and ought to be freely exercised, so that each in the measure of his powers may contribute to the utility of all, to the constant advancement of sacred learning, and to the defense and honor of the Church."[3] Even more remarkably, Pius XI, in his enthusiasm to restore to Eastern Catholics their full Oriental heritage, had insisted that the training centers of their clergy boast a proper course of Eastern theology. While Eastern theology would surely be something of a pantomime horse, for the Eastern tradition is as internally diverse as the Western, the Pope's laudable intention was to draw to our notice the existence of a different way of approaching *all* theological subject matter in the Churches of the East. The implications of this would be spelled out more clearly by the Second Vatican Council: "The heritage handed down by the apostles was received differently and in different ways, so that from the very beginnings of the Church its development varied from region to region and also because of different mentalities and ways of life. . . . What has already been said about legitimate variety we are pleased to apply to differences in theological expressions of doctrine. In the study of revealed truth East and West have used different methods and approaches in understanding and confessing divine things."[4] And indeed, John XXIII on the eve of the council had reminded his hearers: *In necessariis unitas, in dubiis libertas, in omnibus caritas;* "In what we have to affirm, unity; in what is open to question, liberty; and in everything charity."[5]

This is all very well, but where are we to draw the line between *necessaria* and *dubia*? And even when we are agreed on the content of such *necessaria*, surely there are different ways of presenting those necessary affirmations of Catholic Christian faith, different contexts and conceptualities in which to understand and communicate them. But in that case how can a single and unitary revelation be homogeneously expressed in a plurality of ways? It would not be so bad if we could suppose revelation to be simply a divine spur to human creativity, some kind of ineffable experience which stimulated both thought and action in ever new and different ways. That is how such Modernists as George Tyrrell saw things, why they regarded the Church's attempts to control theology as pointless, why they accepted the notion of a plurality of systems of Christian thought as self-evident and detested Scholasticism for its claim to be a *theologia communis*. Non-

3. DS, 3831.
4. *Unitatis redintegratio* 14, 17.
5. In his encyclical *Ad Petri Cathedram* of June 29, 1959.

Modernist writers like Ambroise Gardeil were certainly right to insist against the Modernists that for Catholicism theology must be in the last resort homogeneous, not heterogeneous, with revelation. It must be a refraction of revelation, which presents a part at least of revelation's own content in a new medium of thought. We can see this when we consider the nature of the Church's dogmas. Dogmas are, as we have seen, solemn proclamations of the content of revelation in some particular respect. Yet dogmas cannot be framed without the assistance of theologians. They are, in fact, theological hypotheses elevated to a new dignity by the common mind of the Church, which recognizes in them the adequate, though not exhaustive, expression of her own faith. Were Catholic theology not homogeneous with revelation, then Catholic dogma would be impossible.

In Part 2 of this book we have seen already that at one level the diversity of theologies follows from a diversity in their philosophical underpinning, in the operation within them of a philosophical principle of order. People come to theology with certain patterns of rationally ordered perception about meaning and truth. These lead them to put some questions to revelation and not others, and to articulate the answers they receive (or think they receive) in a particular conceptual idiom. And there are, after all, many philosophies which are formally compatible with revelation, though some may be more inclined to accept baptism than others. Again, even among the philosophies which are formally incompatible with revelation such as Marxism, the questions these philosophies raise may still be of theological interest. Thus, while one might agree that to use Marxist analysis in theology will inevitably import into the domain of faith, a Marxist vision of meaning and truth, and hence a Marxist prescription for the future, it is not so clear that theology would be damaged by considering Marxism as a series of questions, what may be called an interrogative resource. But be this as it may, the selection of a philosophical principle of order cannot in itself be determinative of a theology. Assuming that we are dealing with genuine theology and not simply with philosophy masquerading as theology, it will always be possible to extract the theological component from a theological system, leaving the philosophical element behind. So, for instance, Chalcedon's consensual theology of the union of human and divine in Christ can be separated from its philosophical underpinning in Greek ontology and reexpressed in a new, Schellengian philosophical idiom in Kasper's *Jesus the Christ.*

The deepest source of theological plurality does not lie, then, in the selection of a philosophical principle of order. Where, therefore, does it lie? I suggest that it should be located in the choice of a perspective on revelation from among the many such choices revelation suggests. The richness and complexity of the internal structure of Christian revelation is able to suggest an infinite number of theological approaches to revelation's content. The themes, motifs, models, metaphors, found in the New Testament can and do suggest entire perspectives on the Christian mystery as a whole. They can be taken up and developed systematically, or at any rate extensively, in such a way that they offer a view of the Christian revelation in its entirety. Thus, for instance, the New Testament motif of the cross as the foundation for a wisdom wiser than the wisdom of this world suggested to Justin Martyr a picture of theology in which revelation is presented as fulfilling and going beyond the insights of pagan sages. The theme of the upbuilding of the Church into the plenary humanity of Christ, as found in the Pauline letters, lies behind Clement of Alexandria's presentation of theology as exploring the gospel's power to bring us human and spiritual maturity. The Johannine motif of the gospel as judgment on this world may be related to the understanding of theology found in Martin Luther and the early Karl Barth; while the pervasive metaphor of the divine glory in the Fourth Gospel inspired von Balthasar to offer a theology whose axis is the entry into this world through Christ of a beauty, *Herrlichkeit*, beyond all description. Again, the implicit model found in the narrative structure of the canon as a whole, from Genesis to Apocalypse, may be said to have been brought out in St. Thomas' patterning of theology around the "going forth," *exitus*, of creatures from God and their *reditus*, "return," to him redeemed by grace. And perhaps the New Testament image of Jesus as an exorcist or deliverer from evil, most prominent in the Gospel of Mark, could be described as the original vantage point for the perspective taken up by liberation theology. These are only samples of the theological principle of order in action, and I am sure that many more, and perhaps better ones, could be found. The most important question we can put about any figure in the history of theology would thus become, What overall perspective on Christian faith did revelation suggest to this person? The search for an implicit or explicit theological principle of order will be the most illuminating aspect of any research into a theology of the past or present.

Revelation's ability to suggest a multitude of approaches to itself is echoed in the human mind's capacity under grace to take up the various hints that revelation throws out. In the story of theology, we find out this irreducible plurality for ourselves. However, the variety of theology is not simply a matter of the variety of theological perspectives, the use made of particular themes, motifs, models, or images drawn from revelation as the theologian's starting point. For many theologies come to a self-conscious grasp of what it is they are about: they formulate their aims in terms of a particular kind of project in faith. Thus theology can think of itself as a mystical exploration (Denys), as the construction of a Christian wisdom (Augustine), as a science (Thomas), or again, in the more complex case of von Balthasar, as a divine aesthetics forming the foundation for a "dramatics," a study of God's action, and finally a logic, an account of the divine-human mode in which we understand the beauty communicated in that action. Here it is not simply the perspectival starting point which distinguishes one theology from another, but the way a theology comes to look at itself and at its role in the Church. Fundamental perspective *and* self-definition together give us what is most characteristic of each major theology in the tradition. This means, I believe, that strictly speaking, no theology can be called in any absolute sense better than any other—provided that each meets the minimum definition of an authentically Catholic theology, something I shall be looking at in a moment. But if a theology is genuinely Catholic (and surely those of Denys, Augustine, Thomas, and von Balthasar are so), then it is hard to see how one theology could be deemed superior to another in any unconditional sense. For it is difficult to think of a definition of theological excellence which would wholly prescind from fundamental perspective and self-definition; and yet all concrete statements of these would derive from particular Catholic theologies, whether of past, present, or future. What, then, is one to make of the warm commendation of St. Thomas' theology, which the Church has gone in for in recent centuries? I have already said that I believe the attempt to canonize Thomism as the Church's official theology to have been a blunder. Divine revelation cannot be squeezed into a single human-made system of thought, even when that system is as wonderful as is St. Thomas'. Nevertheless, one can well regard the fundamental perspective and self-definition of a theology as fitting it for some purpose high on the agenda of the Church's mission. Thus, in the case of Thomism, the rational setting forth of the intelligibility of revelation within the framework of a metaphysics of being (theology as science) is or should be in the forefront of the Church's mission, since this is something which enables us to say that Catholic Christianity is true, not just imaginatively satisfying or morally good for people.

So much for plurality, but we have still to look into unity. From what has been said, it should be clear that the Church's various theologies are not in the main conflicting answers to the same questions. They are presentations of the same content, divine revelation, from various angles and with differing ends dependent on their self-understanding. But we need to know, first, What are the conditions for acknowledging a theology as authentically Catholic? And second, Is there a duty to bring together their various contributions, or is it enough simply to say, let a thousand flowers bloom? At the deepest level of faith impulse, any theology worthy of the Catholic name should manifest a fascination with the mystery of Jesus Christ, as revealer of the Father and bearer of the Holy Spirit. But at a level more easily susceptible of critical appraisal, every Catholic theology should incorporate the five features I have proposed in this book as the five basic constituents of the theological task. Thus, a Catholic theology will incorporate rationality into itself; it will take Scripture and Tradition as its life-giving authorities; it will discern their message in the light of Christian experience and the magisterium of the Church. Conversely, no theology uninformed by reason, Scripture, Tradition, Christian experience, and the Church's authoritative day-to-day teaching by the voice of her pastors can claim to be Catholic.

Once these criteria are met, however, a theology has its right to a place in the sun in the life of the Church. But this does not mean that we can rest content with a *de facto* pluralism of legitimate theologies. Our soundings in theological history have shown again and again how anxious theologians have been not to let any fragment of theological wisdom be lost. They have sought to draw into their own work the best of their predecessors, whether these predecessors were near-contemporaries like the *novi theologi* for the great Scholastics; or the masters of a few generations back, the *magistri*; or again, ancient sources of insight, the *Patres*.[6] At the present time we have in the Church a great number of very diverse theologies existing side by side, working with different philosophical and theological principles of order, and so highlighting different aspects both of human experience and of divine revelation. This is, in principle, as it should be. Yet such pluralism can make it particularly hard for one theologian to draw into his

6. *See* on this P. de Vooght, *Les Sources de la doctrine chrétienne d'après les théologiens du XIIIe siècle* (Paris: 1954).

or her work even some of the materials and insights of others. And of course, this is compounded by the difficulties of language (in various senses of that word) and of cross-cultural communication, as well as by the sheer volume of theological output in modern Catholicism. As we move into the twenty-first century, it seems that we stand in need of a theologian who can synthesize the best elements from a number of theological traditions, thus producing a work that will be classical in something of the same sense as is the work of St. Thomas for the preceding and contemporary Latin tradition of his time. Such a classic would itself remain bound by its particular perspective (freely drawn from the totality of revelation in its richness) and its self-adopted role (the unification of theological culture). Yet it would also tend to transcend particularity by throwing light on how the Church's various theologies are not sheer cacophony but an orchestra of instruments playing in celebration of a single faith in a single spiritual city. As the medieval hymn sang of the heavenly city, which is sacramentally imaged in the Church's communion, "In hac urbe lux solennis,/Ver aeternum, pax perennis/Et aeterna gaudia." Granted, a *pax perennis* cannot be created by sentimental souls who cry "Peace, peace!" where there is no peace. There are issues of meaning and truth at stake which must be confronted and resolved. Not all problems in the contemporary Church will yield to a generous dose of reconciliation all round. Nevertheless, the intention of a theologian may point to what is true even when his or her ideas and judgments are at sea.[7] Much unnecessary conflict is created when different yet complementary insights are turned into false opposites. Is it too much to hope that theologians, who are responsible for a share of the ugly cycle of contestation, dissatisfaction, and recrimination in the Church today will, in years to come, take the lead in the making of true and lasting peace? This is eminently desirable, not simply so that those who are and wish to remain members of the Church may lead a quiet life—though a large degree of serenity and stability in the possession and living of the faith is a perfectly reasonable and evangelical desire. It is also a matter of the mission of the Church, which cannot be prosecuted with either vigor or fervor unless the energies of Catholics are mobilized positively, for the salvation of the world, and not simply negatively, in continuous criticism of each other.[8]

7. Y. Congar, "St. Thomas and the Spirit of Ecumenism," *New Blackfriars* 55, 644 (1974) 206-7.

8. As early as 1974, Paul VI spoke in his "Apostolic Exhortation on Reconciliation" of the danger threatening the unity of the universal Church from "the creation of opposing factions fixed in irreconcilable positions," cited from *Origins* 4 (1975) 454.

Appendix on Encyclopedias and Bibliographical Aids

The student may find it useful to know of the existence, in various modern languages, of some compendious alphabetically ordered summaries helpful in theological study, as well as of guides to searching out relevant reading.

Encyclopedias

Beinert, W., ed. *Lexikon der katholischen Dogmatik*. Freiburg: 1987.

Catholic Encyclopedia: An International Work of Reference on the Constitution, Doctrine, Discipline of the Catholic Church. New York: 1907–14, with supplementary vols. 1 (1922) and 2 (1950).

Cross, F. L., and Livingstone, E. A. eds. *Oxford Dictionary of the Christian Church*. Second edition. London: 1974. A third edition is to appear shortly.

D'Alès, A., ed. *Dictionnaire apologétique de la foi catholique contenant tous les preuves de la vérité de la religion*. (Paris: 1911–31).

Davis, H. F., ed. *A Catholic Dictionary of Theology*. London: 1962ff., incomplete.

De Meyer, A., and others, eds. *Dictionnaire d'histoire et de géographie ecclésiastiques*. Paris: 1912 ff., incomplete.

Enciclopedia cattolica. Vatican City: 1949–54.

Enciclopedia de la religión catolica. Barcelona: 1950–56.

Fries, H., ed. *Handbuch theologischer Grundbegriffe*. Munich: 1962–63. Not precisely encyclopedic, but important.

Galling, K., ed. *Die Religion in Geschichte und Gegenwart. Handwörterbuch für Theologie und Religionswissenschaft*. Third edition. Tübingen: 1957–65. Especially useful for Protestantism.

Gryglewicz, F., and others, eds. *Enzyklopedia katolicka*. Lublin: 1973 ff., incomplete.

Hastings, J., ed. *Encyclopaedia of Religion and Ethics*. Edinburgh and New York: 1908–26.

Höfer, J., and Rahner, K., eds. *Lexikon für Theologie und Kirche.* Freiburg: 1957–68.

Jacquemet, G., ed. *Catholicisme, Hier, aujourd; hui, demain.* Paris: 1947 ff., incomplete.

Klauser, Th., ed. *Reallexikon für Antike und Christentum. Sachwörterbuch zur Auseinanderstezung des Christentums mit der antiken Welt.* Stuttgart: 1950 ff., incomplete.

Krause, G., and Müller, G., eds. *Theologische Realenzyklopädie.* Berlin: 1976 ff., incomplete.

Komonchak, J. A., and others, eds. *The New Dictionary of Theology.* Dublin: 1987.

Lopuchin, A. P., and Globukovskii, N., eds. *Pravoslavnaya bogoslavnaya enciklopediya.* Moscow: 1900–11, incomplete. Especially good on Orthodoxy.

New Catholic Encyclopedia. New York: 1967.

Rahner, K., and Darlap, A., eds. *Sacramentum Mundi. Theologisches Lexikon für die Praxis.* Freiburg: 1967–69. English trans. New York and London: 1968–70.

Rahner, K., and Vorgrimler, H., eds. *Kleines Theologishes Wörterbuch.* Freiburg: 1961; English trans. London: 1965.

Rayez, A., and others, eds. *Dictionnaire de spiritualité ascétique et mystique. Doctrine et histoire.* Paris: 1937 ff., incomplete.

Thrêskeutikê kai êthikê enkyklopaideia. Athens: 1962–68.

Vacant, A., and others, eds. *Dictionnaire de théologie catholique.* Paris: 1903–50.

Wetzer und Welte's Kirchenlexikon, oder Encyclopädie der katholischen Theologie und ihrer Hilfswissenschaft. Second edition. Freiburg: 1882–1903.

Biographical Information

Bautz, F. W., ed. *Biographisch bibliographisches Kirchenlexikon.* Hamm: 1970ff.

Delaney, J. J., and Tobin, J. B., eds. *Dictionary of Catholic Biography.* London: 1962.

Hurcer, H. *Nomenclator literarius theologiae catholicae.* Third edition. Innsbrück: 1903–13.

Tusculum Lexikon griechischer und lateinischer Autoren des Altertums und des Mittelalters. Second edition. Munich: 1963.

Bibliographical Information

Barrow, J. G. *A Bibliography of Bibliographies in Religion.* Ann Arbor, Mich.: 1955.

Schwinge, G. *Bibliographische Nachschlagwerke zur Theologie und ihren Grenzgebieten.* Munich: 1975.

Select Bibliographies

Chapter 1

Bilz, J. *Einführung in die Theologie.* Freiburg: 1935.
Latourelle, R. *Theology: Science of Salvation* (Staten Island, New York: 1967).
Leclerq, J. *Theology and Prayer.* St. Meinrad, Ind.: 1963.
Rocchetta, C., and others. *La teologia tra rivelazione e storia.* Bologna: 1985.
Sertillanges, A. D. *La Vie intellectuelle.* Paris: 1921.
Soiron, Th. *La condition du théologien.* Paris: 1953.
Von Balthasar, H. U. "Théologie et sainteté," *Dieu vivant* 12 (1948) 17–32.

Why not read some biographies of great theologians? E.g.:

Brown, P. *Augustine of Hippo: A Biography.* London: 1967.
Busch, E. *Karl Barth.* English trans., London: 1976.
Chadwick, H. *Augustine.* Oxford: 1986.
Chesterton, G. K. *St. Thomas Aquinas.* London: 1943.
Dessain, C. S. *John Henry Newman.* London: 1966.
Trigg, J. W. *Origen.* London: 1983.
Vorgrimler, H. *Understanding Karl Rahner.* English trans., London: 1986.

Chapter 2

Beumer, J. *Die theologische Methode.* Freiburg: 1977.
Chenu, M. D. *Is Theology a Science?* English trans., London: 1959.
Colombo, C. *Il compito della teologia.* Milan: 1982.
Journet, C. *Introduction a la théologie.* Paris: 1947; English trans., Westminster: 1952.
Latourelle, R. *Theology: Science of Salvation.* English trans., New York: 1969.
Muniz, F. P. *The Work of Theology.* Washington: 1953.
Rahner, K. "Theology," *Sacramentum mundi* 6.
Rocchetta, C., Fisichella, R., and Pozzo, G. *La teologia tra rivelazione e storia.* Bologna: 1985.

Sauter, G., and Stock, A. *Arbeitsweisen Systematischer Theologie. Eine Anleitung.* Munich/Mainz: 1976.
Thornhill, J. "Methodology (Theological)," *New Catholic Encyclopedia* 9.
Van Ackeren, G. "Theology," *New Catholic Encyclopedia* 14.
Wohlmuth, J., and Koch, H. G. *Leitfaden Theologie. Eine Einführung in Arbeitstechniken, Methoden und Probleme der Theologie.* Einsiedeln: 1975.

Chapter 3

Charlesworth, M. J. *Philosophy of Religion: The Historical Approaches.* London: 1972.
Davies, B. *An Introduction to the Philosophy of Religion.* Oxford: 1982.
Gilson, E. *Philosophy and Theology.* New York: 1962.
Léonard, A. *Pensées des hommes et foi en Jésus-Christ. Pour un discernement chrétien intellectuel.* Paris: 1980.
Muzio, G. "Pluralismo filosofico e teologico nell'ambita di una filosofia cristiana," *Sapienza* 19 (1966) 227–33.
Nédoncelle, M. *Is There a Christian Philosophy?* New York: 1960.
Tresmontant, C. *La Metaphysique du christianisme et la naissance de la philosophie chrétienne.* Paris: 1961.

Chapter 4

Davies, B. *Thinking About God.* London: 1985.
Küng, H. *Does God Exist?* London: 1980.
Swinburne, R. *The Existence of God.* Oxford: 1979.
Ward, K. *The Concept of God.* London: 1980.

Chapter 5

Farrer, A. *Love Almighty and Ills Unlimited.* London: 1962.
Hick, J. *Evil and the God of Love.* Second edition. San Francisco: 1978.
Sertillanges, A.-D. *Le problème du mal.* Paris: 1948–51.
Werner, C. *Le problème du mal dans la Pensée humaine.* Lausanne: 1946.

Chapter 6

Blondel, M. "The Letter on Apologetics," in *Maurice Blondel. The Letter on Apologetics and History and Dogma,* ed. A. Dru and I Trethowan. London: 1964.
Dulles, A. *A History of Apologetics.* London: 1971.
Falcon, J. *La crédibilité du dogme Catholique.* Paris–Lyons: 1933.
Fisichella, R. *La rivelazione: evento e credibilità.* Bologna: 1985.
Gallie, W. H. *Philosophy and the Historical Understanding.* London: 1964.
Rahner, K. *Hearers of the Word.* London: 1966.
Richardson, A. *Christian Apologetics.* London: 1947.

Chapter 7

Baron, E. *Science et sagesse chez Hugues de St-Victor.* Paris: 1957.

Gilson, E. *The Christian Philosophy of Saint Augustine.* English trans., New York: 1960.

_____. *The Christian Philosophy of Saint Thomas Aquinas.* English trans., New York: 1956.

_____. *La philosophie de saint Bonaventure.* Second edition. Paris: 1943.

Guardini, R. *Systembildende Elemente in der Theologie Bonaventuras* Leiden: 1964.

Rahner, K. "Philosophy and Theology," *Theological Investigations* 6 (1969) 71–81.

Söhngen, G. "Die Theologie im Streit der Fakultäten," in *Die Einheit in der Theologie.* Munich: 1952.

_____. "Philosophie und Theologie," *Handbuch theologischer Grundbegriffe,* ed. H. Fries. Munich (1963) 322.

Vass, G. *Understanding Karl Rahner: A Theologian in Search of a Philosophy.* London: 1985.

Wippel, J. F. *Peter Abelard, Philosophy and Christianity in the Middle Ages.* London: 1970.

N.B. When reading these or analogous books, one should ask oneself: What did X's philosophy contribute to the overall pattern or organization of his theology?

Chapter 8

Barr, J. *Holy Scripture: Canon, Authority, Criticism.* Oxford: 1983.

Gnuse, R. *The Authority of the Bible: Theories of Inspiration, Revelation and the Canon of Scripture.* New York: 1985.

Sand, A. *Kanon. Von den Anfängen bis zum Fragmentum Muratorianum.* Freiburg: 1974.

Turro, J. C., and Brown, R. E. "Canonicity," *The Jerome Biblical Commentary* (1970) 515–34.

Chapter 9

Alonso-Schoekel, L. *La Parole inspirée.* Paris: 1971.

Beumer, J. *Die Inspiration der heiligen Schrift.* Freiburg: 1968.

Burtchaell, J. T. *Catholic Theories of Biblical Inspiration Since 1810: A Review and Critique.* Cambridge: 1969.

Grelot, P. "Dix propositions sur l'inspiration scripturaire," *Esprit et Vie* 96. 8 (1986) 97–105.

Rahner, K. *Inspiration in the Bible.* English trans. New York: 1964.

Smith, R. F. "Inspiration and Inerrancy," *The Jerome Biblical Commentary* (1970) 499–514.

Vawter, B. *Biblical Inspiration.* London: 1972.

Chapter 10

Most accounts of biblical inspiration also treat of inerrancy as a consequence of inspiration. Additionally:

Forestell, J. "The Limitations of Inerrancy," *Catholic Biblical Quarterly* 20 (1958) 9-18.
Lohfink, N. "The Inerrancy of Scripture," *The Christian Meaning of the Old Testament* 1968.

Chapter 11

Barthes, R. *Structural Analysis and Biblical Exegesis.* English trans., Pittsburgh: 1974.
Barton, J. *Reading the Old Testament: Method in Biblical Study.* London: 1984.
Brown, R. E. "Hermeneutics," *The Jerome Biblical Commentary* (1970) 605-23.
Charlier, C. *The Christian Approach to the Bible.* English trans., Westminster: 1958.
Gandolfo, E. *Lettera e Spirito. Lettura della bibbia dalle origine cristiane ai nostri giorni.* Rome: 1972.
Jeanrond, W. G. *Hermeneutics: An Introduction.* London: 1988.
Marshall, I. H., ed. *New Testament Interpretation: Essays on Principles and Methods.* Grand Rapids, Mich.: 1977.
Patte, D. *What Is Structural Exegesis?* Philadelphia: 1976.
Sanders, J. *Torah and Canon.* Philadelphia: 1972.
Steinmann, J. *Biblical Criticism.* New York: 1958.
Tuckett, C. M. *Reading the New Testament.* London: 1986.

Chapter 12

Brown, R. W. *The Sensus Plenior of Sacred Scripture.* Baltimore: 1955.
Daniélou, J. *From Shadow to Reality.* English trans., Westminster: 1960.
Kelsey, D. H. *The Uses of Scripture in Recent Theology.* Philadelphia: 1975.
Robinson, J. M. and Cobb, J. B. *The New Hermeneutic.* New York: 1964.
Toinet, P. *Pour une théologie de l'exégèse.* Paris: 1983.

Chapter 13

Beumer, J. *Die mündliche Überlieferung als Glaubensquelle.* Freiburg: 1962.
Congar, Y. *Tradition and Traditions.* English trans., London: 1966.
Geiselmann, J. R. *The Meaning of Tradition.* English trans., New York: 1966.
Pieper, J. *Überlieferung. Begriff und Anspruch.* Munich: 1970.
Tavard, G. *Holy Writ or Holy Church?* London: 1959.

Chapter 14

Brehier, L. *L'art chrétien. Son développement iconographique des origines à nos jours.* Second edition. Paris: 1928.
Cabrol, F., and others, eds., *Dictionnaire d'archéologie chrétienne et de liturgie.* Paris: 1907-53.

Farioli, *Elementi d'iconografia cristiana*. Bologna: 1964.

Federer, K. *Liturgie und Glanbe. Eine theologiegeshichtliche Untersuchung*. Freiburg in der Schweiz: 1950.

Martimort, A. G., ed. *The Church at Prayer: Introduction to the Liturgy*. English trans., New York: 1968.

Nichols, A. *The Art of God Incarnate: Theology and Image in Christian Tradition*. London: 1980.

Ouspensky, L., and Lossky, V. *The Meaning of Icons*. English trans., London: 1952.

Purdy, W. *Seeing and Believing: Theology and Art*. Cork: 1980.

Schiller, G. *Die Ikonographie der christlichen Kunst*. Gütersloh: 1966–76.

Vagaggini, C. *Theological Dimensions of the Liturgy*. English trans., Collegeville: 1976.

Chapter 15

Altaner, B., *Patrology*. English trans., London: 1960.

Congar, Y. "Les saints Pères: Organes privilégiés de la tradition," *Irénikon* 35 (1962) 479–98.

Dvornik, F. *The Ecumenical Councils*. New York: 1961.

Kelly, J. N. D. *Early Christian Creeds*. London: 1950.

Peri, V. *I Concili e le chiese*. Rome: 1965.

Quasten J. *Patrology*. English trans., second edition, Westminster, Md.: 1980–83.

Ramsey, B. *Beginning to Read the Fathers*. London: 1986.

Ratzinger, J. "Die Bedeutung der Väter im Aufbau des Glaubens," *Theologische prinzipienlehre* (Munich: 1982) 139–58.

Wiles, M. *The Christian Fathers*. London: 1966.

_____. *The Making of Christian Doctrine*. Cambridge: 1967.

Chapter 16

Coulson, J., ed. *John Henry Newman: On Consulting the Faithful in Matters of Doctrine*. London: 1961.

Femiano, S. D. *Infallibility of the Laity: The Legacy of Newman*. New York: 1967.

Thils, G. *L'infaillibilité du peuple chrétien in credendo*. Louvain: 1963.

Chapter 17

Dupuy, M. "Expérience spirituelle et théologie comme science," *Nouvelle revue théologique* 88 (1964) 1137–62.

Jossua, J. P. "Théologie et expérience chrétienne," *Le Service théologique dans l'Eglise, Melanges offerts au Père Yves Congar*. Paris: 1974.

Léonard, A. "L'expérience spirituelle," *Dictionnaire de spiritualité* IV. 2, (Paris: 1961) cols. 2004–66.

Mouroux, J. *The Christian Experience*. English trans., London: 1955.

Schillebeeckx, E. *Christ: The Christian Experience in the Modern World*. English trans., London: 1980.

Chapter 18

Alfaro, J. "Theology and the Magisterium," in *Problems and Perspectives of Fundamental Theology*. ed. R. Latourelle and G. O'Collins. New York, 1982.

Chantraine, G. *Vraie et fausse liberté du théologien. Un Essai*. Paris-Bruges: 1969.

Daniélou, J. "Vescovi e teologi" in *La Collegialità episcopale per il futuro della Chiesa*. ed. V. Fagiolo and G. Concetii. Florence: 1969. 201-7.

Derrick, C. *Church Authority and Intellectual Freedom*. San Francisco: 1983.

Kern, W., ed. *Die Theologie und das Lehramt*. Freiburg: 1981.

Lehmann, K. "Zum Verhältnis zwischen kirchliches Amt und Theologie," in *Begegnung. Festschrift für H. Fries*, ed. M. Seckler. Graz: 1972. 415-30.

Olsen, G. "The Theologian and the Magisterium: The Ancient and Mediaeval Background of a Contemporary Controversy," *Communio* 7 (1980) 292-319.

Sullivan, F. *Magisterium: Teaching Authority in the Catholic Church*. New York: 1983.

Chapter 19

Aubert, R. *La théologie catholique au milieu du XXe siècle*. Tournai: 1953.

Beumer, J. *Die theologische Methode*. Freiburg: 1972.

Cayré, F. *Manuel de Patrologie et histoire de théologie*. Paris: 1936-40.

Congar, Y. *A History of Theology*. English trans., New York: 1968.

De Letter, P. "Theology, History of," *New Catholic Encyclopedia* 14, 49-58.

Ford, D., ed. *The Modern Theologians*. Oxford: 1989.

Grabmann, M. *Die Geschichte der katholischen Theologie seit dem Ausgang der Väterzeit*. Freiburg: 1933.

Hocedez, E. *Histoire de la théologie au dix-neuvième siècle*. Brussels-Paris: 1947-52.

Morgan, R. *The Nature of New Testament Theology*. London: 1973.

Neill, S. *Jesus Through Many Eyes: An Introduction to the Theology of the New Testament*. Lutterworth: 1976.

Pelikan, J. *The Christian Tradition*. Chicago: 1971-

Schlier, H. "The Meaning and Function of a Theology of the New Testament," in *The Relevance of the New Testament*. English trans., London: 1968. 1-25.

Schoof, M. *A Survey of Catholic Theology 1800-1970*. New York: 1970.

Seckler, M. *Tendenzen der Theologie im XX. Jahrhundert*. Stuttgart and Olten: 1966.

Sperna Weiland, J. *New Ways in Theology*. Dublin: 1968.

Van der Gucht, R., and Vorgrimler, H., eds. *Bilan de la théologie du XXe siècle*. Tournai: 1970.

Chapter 20

Daniélou, J. "Unité et pluralité de la Pensée chrétienne," *Etudes* 312 (1962).

Fritzsche, H.-G. *Die Strukturtypen der Theologie.* Göttingen: 1961.

Labourdette, M. M., and Nicolas, M. J. "L'analogie de la vérité et l'unité de la science théologique," *Revue thomiste* 47 (1947) 417–66.

Nichols, A. "Unity and Plurality in Theology: Lonergan's *Method* and the Counter-claims of a Theory of Paradigms," *Angelicum* 62 (1985) 30–52.

Rahner, K. "Pluralism in Theology and the Unity of the Creed in the Church," *Theological Investigations* 11. 1974.

Ratzinger, J. "Le pluralisme: Problème posé à l'Eglise et à la théologie," *Studia moralia* 24 (1986) 298–318.

Seibel, W. "Der eine Glaube und die Vielfalt der Dogmen," *Stimmen der Zeit* 169 (1961–62) 264–77.

Index of Names

Abelard, *see* Peter Abelard
Abraham, 84, 188
Adam, K., 336
Alan of Lille, 299
A Lapide, C., 313
Alberigo, G., 214
Albert the Great, 48, 297, 303
Alcuin, 283, 287, 289
Alexander of Hales, 302, 303
al-Hallaj, 59
Ambrose, 266
Anselm of Canterbury, 19, 291,
    292, 304, 314, 330
Anselm of Laon, 284
Aristotle, 49, 131, 264, 287-88,
    296, 297-300
Arius, 217, 258
Arhauld, A., 31
Athanasius, 217, 267
Athenagoras, 274
Augustine, 21, 68, 71, 94, 134,
    136, 143, 203, 204, 221, 267,
    268, 274, 279-81, 282, 286, 288,
    297, 336, 340, 353

Babcock, W. S., 282
Balthasar, H. U. von, 26, 32, 95,
    269, 315-16, 344, 347, 352, 353
Bañez, D., 118, 316
Barnabas, apostle, 210
Barth, K., 43, 202, 315, 352
Barthes, R., 152
Barton, J., 145
Basil, 217, 279, 284
Bäumker, C., 336
Bautain, L. E. M., 329
Bellarmine, R., 132, 207, 212, 268,
    311

Benedict, 289
Benedict XIII, 228
Benedict XIV, 349
Benedict XV, 135, 330
Benoit, P., 126, 127, 129
Berengar, 292
Bernard of Clairvaux, 193, 268,
    286, 290, 293-94, 295, 336
Bernard of Chartres, 294
Bernini, G., 190
Bérulle, P. de, 310
Biel, G., 308
Blondel, M., 74, 77-78, 332
Boethius, 289, 299
Bonaventure, 48, 65, 172, 303,
    330, 336
Bouyer, L., 339
Brandmüller, W., 214
Browne, M., 342
Bultmann, R., 85-86, 159

Cajetan, 103, 316
Calvin, J., 43, 175, 202,
    313-14
Canisius, P., 311
Cano, M., 222, 317-18, 321
Carbonia, L., 320
Casel, O., 335
Cassian, John, 155
Cassiodorus, 286, 287
Chadwick, H., 264
Chadwick, O., 190
Charlemagne, 283
Charles the Bald, 285
Chateaubriand, F. R. de, 323,
    325-26
Chenu, M. D., 339, 340-41
Chesterton, G. K., 56

366

Index of Subjects